THE
SOPHISTICATED
TRAVELLER

Also in **The Sophisticated Traveller** Series

Beloved Cities: Europe

Great Tours and Detours

Enchanting Places and How to Find Them

· THE SOPHISTICATED TRAVELLER ·

· WINTER ·

LOVE IT OR LEAVE IT

EDITED BY

A. M. ROSENTHAL & ARTHUR GELB

IN ASSOCIATION WITH

MICHAEL J. LEAHY, NORA KERR

AND THE TRAVEL STAFF OF

THE NEW YORK TIMES

EBURY PRESS   LONDON

Published in 1986 by Ebury Press
Division of The National Magazine Company Ltd
Colquhoun House 27-37 Broadwick Street
London W1V 1FR

ISBN 0 85223 518 5 (hardback)
0 85223 558 5 (paperback)

Illustrations by Tom Lulevitch
Cover illustration by Nancy Stahl

Computerset in Great Britain by ECM Ltd, London

Printed and bound in Great Britain
by Butler & Tanner Ltd, Frome

CONTENTS

INTRODUCTION
A. M. Rosenthal and Arthur Gelb
11

BENEDICTION
Joyce Carol Oates
14

ISLAND SUN
John Updike
15

WINTER: LOVE IT

—— **The City In Winter** ——

WARMTH IN CHILLY LONDON
Hortense Calisher
19

VENICE IN AUTUMN AND WINTER
Muriel Spark
26

EUROPE'S HIGH NOTES
Harold C. Schonberg
31

ON THE ROAD FROM NAZARETH TO BETHLEHEM
Malachi Martin
36

FROM SPIRE TO SPIRE IN YULETIDE LONDON
R. W. Apple, Jr.
42

'BUON NATALE, ROMA'
Maureen Howard
52

THE JOIE DE VIVRE OF MONTREAL
Margaret Atwood
58

COSMOPOLITAN CITY OF SMALL WORLDS
David Harris
63

QUEBEC CITY'S PRIME TIME
Mordecai Richler
70

—— **The Outdoor Life** ——

CLASSIC TYROL
James Salter
79

NOUVELLE VAIL
Peter Benchley
85

SKIING IN NEW ENGLAND'S NORTH COUNTRY
David Shribman
90

IN SEARCH OF WINTER'S ESSENCE
Adam Nicolson
95

SKIING PEAK TO PEAK IN UTAH
Clifford D. May
100

TAOS: A SKIER'S MARTINI
Donal Henahan
105

CROSS-COUNTRY: THE POETRY OF SILENCE
Nelson Bryant
110

YELLOWSTONE: FIRE AND ICE
William E. Schmidt
113

WINTER IN ITS PLACE
Peter Viertel
118

THE QUESTION: TO SKI OR APRÈS-SKI?
Enid Nemy
124

WINTER: LEAVE IT

—— **Southern Routes** ——

FLORIDIANA
Alison Lurie, Budd Schulberg, Elie Wiesel, Frank Conroy,
Roger Tory Peterson, Mark J. Sosin, Charlotte Curtis, José Yglesias,
Eugene C. Patterson, James Rosenquist, John Noble Wilford, Harry Crews
133

DREAMING OF SAVANNAH
V. S. Pritchett
149

DOWN HOME IN ACADIA
Roy Reed
154

THREE DAYS ALONG EL CAMINO REAL
Robert Lindsey
161

GRAND HOTELS, L.A. STYLE
Aljean Harmetz
169

HOLLYWOOD: THIS WAY IN
Aljean Harmetz
177

ONE-DAY DRIVES INTO HISTORY
Marlise Simons
186

LEGACY OF THE CONQUISTADORS
Gordon Mott
191

THE CAPITAL'S MANY MOODS
Alan Riding
198

MEXICO: A WORLD OF DIFFERENCES
John Canaday
203

THE RIO BEAT
Warren Hoge
208

THE SORCERY OF THE AMAZON
Edwin McDowell
215

THE ALGARVE: PORTUGAL'S PLACE APART
Enid Nemy
223

COMING OF AGE IN KENYA
Peter Maas
228

VAST, STILL, TIMELESS, AWESOME
Colleen McCullough
235

—— **By The Sea** ——

AN INN ON THE PACIFIC'S EDGE
Herbert Gold
243

CARMEL
Robert Lindsey
247

SAMPLING THE VARIED WORLDS OF JAMAICA
Barbara Crossette
252

SLOWING THE PACE IN BARBADOS
Flora Lewis
259

DOWN-TO-EARTH CREOLE COOKING
Craig Claiborne
263

IN MARTINIQUE: CREOLE CUISINE WITH FLAIR
Craig Claiborne
267

TWO ISLANDS À LA CARTE
Craig Claiborne
270

ISLAND HIDEAWAYS: A SAMPLER
Paul Grimes
275

A BOAT OF ONE'S OWN
William F. Buckley, Jr.
279

THE RUMS OF THE ISLANDS
Frank J. Prial
285

COPING WITH LUXURY
Charlotte Curtis
289

A REDISCOVERY OF ISLANDS
Derek Walcott
295

AROUND THE CARIBBEAN: THIRTY-FOUR ISLANDS
Stanley Carr
300

THE MAGICAL REEF ABOVE AND BELOW
Robert Reinhold
333

NOTES ON THE CONTRIBUTORS 338   INDEX 342

PUBLISHER'S NOTE

The Sophisticated Traveller Series was originally written, edited and compiled for an American audience and in view of the fact that it is the outstanding quality of the writing that readers will most appreciate, factual information (including prices) remains as in the original American edition. When prices are given they should be taken as a general guide, since inflation and fluctuations in the exchange rates can have a significant effect on costs.

INTRODUCTION

In one of the articles in this book, the fourth volume of *The Sophisticated Traveller* series, the novelist James Salter writes that when the bad weather came, Hemingway would leave Paris with his wife and small son and go to a place where the rain would become snow, coming down through the pines and creaking beneath their feet as they walked home at night in the cold. The Hemingways would go to the Tyrol in Austria and ski in Schruns, and the Silvretta, at Kitzbühel and across the Swiss border in the Engadine.

Of course, the very idea of the Tyrol and places with names like the Silvretta were dreams for most of us growing up when Hemingway was writing, for people like the editors of this book.

Skiing the Engadine – how lovely the name! – was for others – the famous, the rich. Wintering in Kenya? Taking the sun in the Caribbean at Christmastime, or exploring the wintry Rockies? Realities for others, perhaps, a very few others, but dreams, dreams for most of us.

This book, therefore, really is not so much about how to spend the winter doing things rather more enjoyable than shivering, but about dreams that have come true.

The travel revolution, created quite unwittingly at Kitty Hawk by the brothers Wright, has done a great deal more than move large numbers of people from one place to another.

It has created a whole new world of freedom, including that particularly luxurious freedom, so recently the property and very hallmark of the rich, the freedom of choice of place and pleasure.

We are now even free, almost all of us, to choose our seasons. If summer in winter is our fantasy, our fantasy can become reality in Caribbean Decembers and Key West Januaries.

We can move away from winter or move toward it eagerly. Somehow, the realization that we can leave winter if we wish has made many of us love it more. The ability to choose has made winter a time of openness and movement instead of huddled greyness.

So here is winter – love it or leave it, or both, your choice. This book, like its predecessor and the volumes to follow, are expansions of *The*

Sophisticated Traveller, a semi-annual magazine published by *The New York Times*.

The articles are by correspondents of *The Times* and by writers of renown, all writing for a most sophisticated kind of traveller – people quite like themselves. They write with affection and knowledge and with the special exhilaration that comes from knowing that almost all dreams of travel have become realities of life, that everywhere is within reach, anytime.

When the first man was about to land on the moon, the editors of *The Times* were so seized with a sense of the glory of the moment arriving that the only way they could think to express it was to ask a poet, Archibald MacLeish, to write a poem for the occasion. He did, and it became the first and only poem ever printed on the first page of the paper.

When the time came to create the issue of *The Sophisticated Traveller* from which this book grew, the editors decided again that the way the mind travels best is with poetry. And so this book, dedicated to the gift of choice, opens with the gift of poetry.

A.M.R. & A.G.

BENEDICTION

Joyce Carol Oates

This hawk in silhouette
   gliding weightless
      sheerly black
         light as a scrap of paper,
            forked to sail –
               the black-feathered muscles
                     scarcely moving
                         the eye
                            unerring –
                 January winds
            like waves washing
         through the tallest trees –

           We are crossing the snow-stubbled field
      in awe of
        that singular motion,
    flawless, seemingly
idle –
    and the Sunday sky a hard ceramic blue

                    Splendid bird! –
                     in black-on-white motion
               Japanese in grace,
         execution –
       a razor's edge
     in silhouette
       now slowly banking,
         circling
            and again soaring
       as if such winter beauty
     were a mere whim of the air –
               as if such winter benediction
                 were deserved,
                     or merely ours –

ISLAND SUN

John Updike

When the albums of this century's intermingling
are assembled, I hope a page will show
two sunburned young honeymooners from Woonsocket,
Rhode Island, or an aged duo from Short Hills,
New Jersey (he in green pants, she in pink pleats)
gazing into the teeth of a black steel band
beating away and pealing in full flight
while the tropical moon leans lopsided overhead–

lopsided because its face is tilted differently
at these holiday latitudes, just as the air
yields different constellations, and summer
is not a season to be earned but always there:
outside the louvered door, the vertical sunlight,
like a face of childhood, too good to be true.
The steel band wears mismatching tank tops
and speaks an English too liquid to understand.

Ghosts, we flit through a phantasmal summer
we have earned with dollar-shaped months of living
under clouds, in cold cities that are clouds.
We burn. Our noses have been painted red!
For the white transparent fish that flutter
away from our glass masks, the turquoise water
is paradise; but what of the mahogany man
entranced in his shack by the sea-grape tree?

His irises are like licked Lifesavers, so thin.
He smiles to see us rob him of the sun,
the golden pain he has anaesthetized with rum.
Let's play that he's invisible. Six days
of sand like sugar, salt baths, and soft nights, and
we have learned to love our bodies again:
as brown as a stranger beheld in a mirror
whose back is gilded each time the planet turns.

WINTER: LOVE IT
THE CITY IN WINTER

WARMTH IN CHILLY LONDON

Hortense Calisher

London in the 1950s. Winter. Men and women in the grave 'utility clothing' left over from the war. Home fires foul with a compressed coal dust called 'nutty slack.' Bus conductors walking ahead of their vehicles like elephant handlers, in what was to be one of the last of the great fogs. My first season ever outside my own country, on a scholarship won me by stories I would have been compelled to tell anyway. Though I have come by boat, it half seems as if I am really there by magic carpet.

Yet when we Americans of any age or era arrive there we still bring our magic with us: language. England is as foreign a country as any in Europe. Yet it is also the one where, in spite of the patois grumbles on both sides, we know the language best – and, indeed, very well. With a little effort we can listen to these strange people in utter intimacy, whether they know it or not, and whether they seem aborigine or aristocrat. We may even come to recognize British chaff for what it is – a good-humoured attempt to set the world to rights by temporarily inverting it. That year, though on a limited stipend, I came to see how language is sometimes the real money.

Personal introductions? I had a cherished few. In Paris, such formalities can seem like an exchange of crystallized violets, with no future in them. In London, where the mere man in the street, asked for directions, may take your arm and lead you near, because he is house-proud and the city is his house, even the 'contact' with whom you strike no bond may feel some obligation. Americans are said to make friends in jig time. But whereas at home we tend to jig on, make a friend over there and you have one for life. What I discovered was that London in winter can be a very warm place.

But even the invaluably found live native must get on with his or her life. Then it is time to remember that places are people. Soon or late in this demi-grey North Europe season (Paris can be as grey, though with flashes of aluminium, and Berlin as dark as cinders) a place is sure to greet you like a lost acquaintance, and at any moment the live folk, map-addicted all of them, and each at the very least a minor character, may reappear. As one did to me, from behind a bush in some bomb rubble in the vicinity of the Old Lady of Threadneedle Street, crying the name of a rare wildflower, not indigenous. From which I learned the affecting fact that many such had been blown thither by the winds of blitz – and that when London repairs, it first sends botanists.

In a London winter, the very climate will everywhere accompany you, importantly as a guide. 'Periods of rain,' the news will understate, though this alone won't bring out the umbrellas or make London girls conceal their shoes in rubber. Hard rain does bring on a doughtiness that can irritate the alien. Now and then Britain has an enormous Worst Winter Since – when the lambs freeze e'en in the fold. (It is also said to have a summer, when at 50 degrees Fahrenheit those same girls bare legs and shoulders, and male academics run to sandals, though protected from pernicious doctrine by woolly socks.)

But the secret of London weather is simple. Expect a constant alternation, of continuous duration. With winter somewhere between an autumn less brisk than ours and a damply wan brink of spring, the city, like many near the sea, is ever water-inflected. For any but the thin-blooded traveller, a fur coat is a mistake. The British may have invented 'layering,' as our ancestors did bundling. The smartest thing to do is to buy some of their underwear. (While they now have some central heating, they seem rarely either to abuse or use it, so, though they run to flamboyant colds, the sinuses otherwise remain clear, in a way all except country or desert Americans have forgotten.)

What they really prefer is rawbone chill that will somewhere conduct them to a hearth, electric though it may be, and to a teatime coziness (from a cuppa almost anywhere, on up to the ethereal chestnut meringues in the Buttery at Fortnum's), and on to the jocundity that after work lights up secretaries and civil servants in pub after pub, in an amiable cheer that our nervous energy cannot imitate.

Meanwhile, in the 'periods of dry' that slip into almost any day, watch for the extraordinary skies of winter London, brief North Sea illuminations of violet-blue crossed with antiphonal blushes, clouds piling up expressions of winds not felt, a whole baroque school of *'lumière'* at the end of some dull street you mightn't give a penny for – except, of course, under the eerie shivers of literature. For if you have come to London in winter without other business, it may be that for you, as for me, it is part storyland.

I am always lucky there. My first day, England presented me with a story so eccentrically true to type that I have never been able to write it. My landlord-to-be, friend of a friend at home, met me at the train. A director of the Arts Theatre Club, he was off for Paris, leaving the ground floor of a house behind the Royal Hospital in Chelsea to me. There were halberds and armour in the front hall. I assumed they were real, like the three kinds of heat in the cavernous sitting room: coal, electric, and, next to the desk where I would huddle, gas.

Everything but the armour would turn out to be authentic – of a sort. Two housekeepers, sisters, the head one so smarmy I took to her at once. Besides, she did my smalls, over my insistence that we Americans did our own, saying with lilting bluntness: 'Miss C. You may be a very good writer, but you're not a very good washer.' Really she was determined to keep me the lady her sociospiritual status had to have. Otherwise the two were caretakers for the whole house, owned by the old lady above me, a former client when the sisters had been dressmakers.

Meanwhile, the story grew, or more exactly was revised. In a Thames-side gloaming, with the lamps not lit and the throat already locked in that certain feeling, there came a creaking at my draughty double doors. I parted them warily. The old women came down the stairs, arms stretched as if in séance, crying a name not unspeakable – 'Olga-ah. Ol-lga-ah' – but belonging to nobody in the house.

'It's what she calls me,' the housekeeper later said. 'I don't know why. She knows my name as well as well. And that rumbling you kept hearing over your desk. It's the piano. She likes to push it about. We tried to shift her on to moving the big chest in her bedroom instead, but she'll have none of it. It's who she is, d'ya see. Who? You may well ask.' A posed photo was brought, of a not-so-young beauty, tricorned and plumed, on a horse.

She was a Mrs. Delarno, friend or more of the art dealer Duveen. His habit had been to keep her house stocked with paintings, bringing clients to be dined, and to view. The two sisters were clearly her keepers. 'Coronation Day, she put on her furs, went out on the front balcony and took bows.' They got her back inside by co-operating. 'Three cheers for Mrs. Delarno!' they cried. But, oh, she was the devil to watch, taking a hate as she had to some of the paintings still upstairs. I yearned to hear what was there, but they were vague, with one exception. 'Last week she put her foot through a Sir John Lavery,' they pridefully said.

In London, the facts are often even better than the dizzily romantic preconception. But even in London, winter is a time when one does well to bring along one's own life – work, interests, idées fixes, or vanities – and live as a city does out of the silly season. Even shopping in Bond Street and the Burlington Arcade is more home centred, allowing one to ask at Noble Jones whether they are out of those pink suspenders with angels on them, or to take back the Prickett pepper grinder, which in the warm United States only jams. 'Ivory swells,' the man says sternly, as if one should have known. And all down the line, the sales ladies chime with the winter intonation they love – 'Ow naow, nothing like that, moddom.' During the June sales that most choice department store, Liberty's, which keeps art nouveau ever fresher, will look like an overturned laundry bin, but not now, with all the boys and girls from Oxbridge going Pre-Raphaelitely out and in. In the high boutiques of South Molton Street or Beauchamp Place you may see the cool wives of diplomats or the smart beauties on their way to being them. Pass then to the hoyden shops of the King's Road, where side streets of houses with poets' plaques on them may atone for frivol. In Savile Row I have been privileged to wait out of the rain in an anteroom, so overhearing how a military of the old sort chats with his tailor – still a coup for my gender, and I am hoarding it.

Otherwise, as with us, gender is either fashionably not what it was or becoming more so. Some of us are more welcome in Clubland than formerly, but you need not see the great marble-pillared upstairs of the Athenaeum, or the crony group around its downstairs hearth, to glimpse the nineteenth century again, or hear its parliamentarian echo. You need only observe how its polar-white façade clarifies the air immediate to it.

Yes, Pall Mall is instructive, one of those rigorously handsome avenues that lead straight to a country's institutions. But at the Garrick Club, if you are on your way to a play, a doorman more used to theatre folk may let you mount the steps for a question or two, or even a peep within. You are now on the edge of Soho, as well as near some of London's most sexually explicit streets and most durable restaurants. The winter town is now a beggar's opera of punks, and many of the high-styled ones, hair sprouting like the vegetable fantasies of the sixteenth century painter Arcimbaldo, are here. After the play, if you have enough cash for the 1920s, hare off to the Strand, to the Savoy.

Up a few streets are the law courts, but that's for morning. Walk then, through Middle Temple Lane to the Victorian Embankment, venturing into doorways or up the narrow stairs to see how a barrister sports his oak, or his bowler – noting how the creamy black-inscripted doors, once all double-barrelled Anglo names, show many more Indian and African, and some women, too. Take shelter in the Old Bailey, or in Sir John Soane's Museum near Lincoln's Inn. Then take the Underground (Temple Station); one can't stay with the nobs forever, or even the petty thieves.

One of the Underground's virtues, the Circle Line especially, is that you can go round and round, thinking how to slow your social descent. Will you have Islington first – trendy, arty, antiquey, with some good Greek bootmakers? Or pop into Cheapside – Guildhall and Stock Exchange. Or Liverpool and Euston stations. Those great railway arcades, still echoing of steam engines and shouting newsboys – what is a mere mall to them? Yet Covent Garden has such a pretty new one, in the espresso-table style – but where there is also Suttons, that gentle but formidably arrayed seed shop, in which even the cynic non-gardener, fingering a packet for A Child's Garden, may wonder if Pippa has just passed.

Or will you backtrack up Ludgate Hill, with the voice of Mrs. Dalloway leading you to St. Paul's? Or to St. Mary-le-Bow (Bow bells) or the Brompton Oratory, resoundingly Catholic, nasally Kensington, and in the middle of Young Matronland? Or one of the small outlying park museums: Kenwood, after Sunday elevenses at a Hampstead pub, or Richmond's Ham House. Ask an ordinary Londoner along if you know one; in these winter byways they bloom.

And we still have not got where I know you must go –if you are to see winter London plain. The slums – I shall not humble them by naming them. Under socialism, which has changed the starkly starving to the inured poor, the name may no longer apply. But as with any metropolis, these are some of its most evocative, vital parts. Vocal, too, with that sullen fun and bloodiness which the English spirit can imprint equally on a first-generation West Indian kid and Norman-descended carrot top.

Apologize to Dickens, if you feel you must refuse. Settle at least for some of London's miles and miles of subfusc grey drear. After all, they do. Arnold Bennett, and the young Tom Eliot – who got a poem out of it – will be at your side.

Then treat yourselves to oysters and music, in my mind more than seasonally connected. The London-served mollusc is no gross diva, with maybe a brooch of ice in her bosom, nor yet quite that briny sea lace from Brittany. It's a neat bit of sea history, swallowed. One is not seeking the pearl but finding it. And how they are nurtured. I sometimes think they have nannies for them.

In the same way, London breeds musical performance with less of our dependence on the star. And when these come along they have a pure, comforting musicianship, along the line, say, from Kathleen Ferrier and Peter Pears to Janet Baker and the newly arrived Henry Hereford, whom you may have the luck to hear enunciating our own Ives. As for their rock stars, they are now England's sociologists, and on occasion its Shakespeareans – an old story there. Civil complaint in the form of entertainment, and coarseness with class.

In the concert season, what I like to listen to also is their halls. Not the Albert, of whose power of reprise Sir Thomas Beecham said that you could hear the music twice for the same money. I have heard some score the newer halls as naked-sounding or lacking in blend – and do recall a Berlioz *Birth of Christ* in which the chorused esses seemed at one's earlobe. But generally London's acoustical trouble is that one can hear everything, often in halls where wood has been made much of, or stone churches where the music rises as if from the composer's own brook.

It will be the same at the play, in old theatres that have been well kept, with no idea that they have been nullified by the new. After seeing what hasn't yet got to New York, I look for what won't. Drama in London has less heavy obligation to be a masterpiece each time. It can be just a bit of fun, or very peculiar without half trying – and no guilt or pomp alongside. Go to a music hall; you may be wooed to join in. At Yuletide, take in one of the pantomimes, which may be part charade, Miltonic revel, and medieval peep show, and are alleged to be for children.

Which brings us to Christmas Day and perfidious Albion. Goose and flaming mince? Cracknels and ruby port? Glorious song at St. Martin-in-the-Fields, home of English chamber music? Not 'alf likely.

I knew a young woman once caught unawares in the old Dukes Hotel, which then ran only to whisky in one's room. A book, she thought, and a nice table for one. Maybe Bentley's in Swallow Street – oysters from their own beds, lobster salad, Stilton, and the house Médoc, the weekday bar lunch of many excellent-appearing gentlemen. But I'll dine upstairs, like the lady I am.

Bentley's was closed, but she was still ignorant of how much else was. Round and round she went, Piccadilly to Regent Street – the high tart's trottoir on any day but this, and she the only girl going. 'Are you busy?' a lone moustachio said. She was, but not an hour later, in front of Simpson's-in-the-Strand – closed down, too, those silver meat trolleys – he caught up with her. 'Still busy?' Offered a sure meal, she might have said no. She ended up at Charing Cross Station, eating railway soup made of deathless brown essence and sow's dug.

On Christmas Day, even *The Times* does not publish. Hotels may feed their own guests, though hollowly. Get thee into somebody's home or country weekend until this rictus of enclosure is over. Otherwise, well before, hie to Harrod's Food Hall, one of the great Lucullan sights anyway. Or if less flush, to Marks and Sparks (rhyming slang for Marks and Spencers) for an electric kettle, tea, coffee – the next day, Boxing Day, you may still be in trouble – and some goodly cheese and fruit. Romary's Tunbridge Wells biscuits, England's best and so the world's (though made in Glasgow), are unprocurable now that Rowntree's, I'm told, has bought them under – for which may all that company's future mergers fail. (I have one copyable tin of same, in case they see this, and have a change of heart.) Fortt's Bath Olivers, a more national symbol, were saved, by an outcry in Parliament.

Buy at least one bottle of double cream (the fresh, not the long-lasting) and plunge in. When you consider that they will deliver this to your door, you may never return home. Milk, too, still comes in bottles, which among other conveniences means that when a sufficient row of them is seen on a doorstep, one may tell the axe-murderer's been.

Finally, forget not the vintner's (watch the hours here, too), or the chocs. And so to your bedsitter or hostel, with Tiny Tim outrun? God bless us everyone – you may do even better.

Should the weather not be too vile (it can be mild), you may take your viands out of doors. Why not, they have gone in and left you all London. I recommend only the nonpicnic places. On foot, perhaps, to the place where in softer weather you might have boarded the boat to Greenwich Observatory – at the base of Westminster Bridge. The ever frailer Abbey will rise for you, age-spotted as an old relative. The House of Commons and New Scotland Yard will flank. (Can even the old Scotland Yard be Gone for the Day? Possibly just along the Embankment, into Henry VIII's wine cellar, with the door firmly closed.)

Or go on, by Underground to Putney, to that bit of tenderer river by the boat clubs. Just beyond is the Duke's Head pub, one of the last in London to have a skittle alley. The ninepins are the same shape as for bowling but heavier, and you do not have a ball, but something called a 'cheese,' which you do not roll but throw, a distance of about thirty feet. A clean sweep, called a 'scorer,' is rare. First time you do it, everybody buys you drinks. You may never wish to see this, much less do it, but it's nice to know.

Or if you have motorcycle or car, then what choice is yours – remembering that the garages, too, have their eyes screwed closed. If your own Christian vision has gone dark, then for you the blackly sympathetic South Circular Road, on whose thundering limbo, though this day truckless, you might even feel at home. Otherwise, slip through dockside walled road to the Isle of Dogs, passing the Tower, a dream from the Middle Ages, on the way. Not a soul may greet you but in the newly cleansed waters of the vast estuary before you – sunrise on the left, sunset on the right – the fish are back. Thames-side is always generous. A minor character may be excused for lunching there, in situ, with found friends. Return to base erratically, by one or other of the embankments, at the cold hour when all the bridges star.

So – will you have outwitted these odd Londoners? No, my dears. Just for the day, you have become one.

Three cheers!

VENICE IN AUTUMN AND WINTER

Muriel Spark

Most people who write about Venice do not tell you what they think of it but how they feel. Venice is a city not to inspire thought but sensations. I think it is something to do with the compound of air, water, architecture, and the acoustics. Like the effect of these elements on the ear, there are acoustics of the heart. One can think in Venice, but not about Venice. One absorbs the marvellous place, often while thinking about something else.

I have never been to Venice in summertime, or in festival time, nor at the time of any of the cinema and great art shows. My Venice belongs to late autumn and winter, the Venice of meagre tourism, the Venetians' everyday city.

I have never known Venice to be crowded or hurried. Perhaps for this reason, when I published a novel set in autumnal Venice, someone was puzzled by the facility with which some of my characters encountered each other in the street. It transpired he had only been in Venice during the crowded and stifling tourist seasons, when you could not very likely meet the same face two days running. In the winter it is quite different. After a week of walking around Venice – and one does have to walk a lot – or of waiting at the landing stage for the diesel-run vaporetto, the same laughing students are there, the same solemn goodwives with their shopping bags and well-preserved fur collars, the same retired gentlemen with righteous blue eyes and brown hats. This is everyday Venice where the passers-by are sparse, where eventually they say good morning.

My first visit to Venice was on a cold, bright morning in February, with a friend who had been there before. However much one has read and heard about the visual impact of Venice, it never fails to take one by surprise. After five visits I still gasp. It is not merely the architecture, the palaces, the bridges and the general splendour, it is the combination of architecture with water, space, light and colour that causes amazement; especially, I think, the element of water. The first impression of the waterways of Venice is acoustic, so that normal sensations subliminally cease and new ones take their place. Voices, footsteps, bird cries, a cough from the window on the other side of the canal – all are different from the sounds of the land one has left. The traffic is entirely watery. A greengrocer's shop piled high with vegetables is a ship floating past your window.

After a few days of this estrangement from normal life I begin to feel at home with it. Some people tell me they can never settle down to a feeling of familiarity with Venice. Sometimes they are people who frequent the super hotels where everything is done to comfort and console the visitors who come with their usual bag of worries. I do not say that this is not a very good thing for a holiday. But the very nature of Venice is such that the things that usually preoccupy us, from which we are attempting to get away, undergo a shift of perspective after about three days.

I have known Venice in a mist and drizzle, where everything is depressed and soaking, every bridge is a bridge of sighs. But it is not the usual personal depression one is experiencing; it is something else, something belonging to Venice, it is collective. I think this is something like the reverse of Ruskin's Pathetic Fallacy in which he holds that artists and poets tend to attribute to nature our human responses; Venice would be 'brooding' or 'smiling,' according to how we feel. On the contrary, I think we are sad when majestic Venice is in gloom; and if we are depressed already the fine thing about those gloomy days of Venice is that you forget what you are personally depressed about. Venice is a very good place to be sad. On days of mist, it is like a trip to the Shades. But winter often sparkles and these are the days one can sit warmly in Florian's Café while outside the hardy musicians perform their nostalgic Palm Court pieces.

Venice has been declining for some hundreds of years. Decline is now of its essence, and I do not think it would be anything like as attractive to ourselves if it were on the way up in the modern sense and flourishing. The Venetians themselves talk little about Venice, never unless you ask. They are proud of their native city and attached to it, but it does not go to their heads as it does with the rest of us.

There was a time when wealthy foreigners like Milly in Henry James's *The Wings of the Dove* could take on a romantic palace, and play at princesses. Poor Milly got what she demanded, and this was, of course, how James made fun of his contemporaries in Venice:

> *At Venice, please, if possible, no dreadful, no vulgar hotel; but, if it can be at all managed – you know what I mean – some fine old rooms, wholly independent, for a series of months. Plenty of them, too, and the more interesting the better; part of a palace, historic and picturesque, but strictly inodorous, where we shall be to ourselves, with a cook, don't you know? – with servants, frescoes, tapestries, antiquities, the thorough make-believe of a settlement.*

Byron thought seriously of settling permanently in Venice to spend the winters there. Permanently is not a good idea; the city is bad for our bones, and also the sort of infatuation a foreigner feels about Venice cannot last. Henry James's American girlfriend, if one can stretch a phrase, settled in Venice only to throw herself out of a window one dark night, to her death. Byron's Venetian girl, who threw herself into the canal, was careful to be rescued.

However, it is difficult not to be romantic about Venice. Myself, I arrived on one of my visits – it was early in November – close to midnight. All the river traffic including the taxis were on strike in solidarity with the gondoliers who had notices up demanding that gondoliers' claims should be dealt with 'globally.' There was a squall blowing in from the lagoon. It was quite a plight for me, there on the landing stage, for my luggage was heavy with some reference books (I was correcting the proofs of my Venetian novel *Territorial Rights*). But it was really exciting to strike a bargain with some men on a coal barge which rocked and plunged in the wind and surge, with me and my books among the sooty cargo, up the Grand Canal where doges and dowagers were once wont to ride in state.

The night porter at my lodgings showed no surprise; he merely came down to the landing stage to collect me and my goods, dripping rags that we were, and to make sure that the men had not over-charged me. I will always remember that midnight journey through the black water, and the calling of the bargemen, wild seabird noises, as every now and again they passed another laden vessel. The palaces were mostly in darkness, with the water splashing their sides, the painted mooring poles gleaming suddenly in the light of our passing; the few lights from the windows were dim and greenish, always from tiny windows at the top. Nobody walked on the banks, and yet a strange effect that I can only describe as water voices came from those sidewalks and landing stages. Perhaps they were ghosts, wet and cold.

I usually stay at a charming, fairly old pensione near the Accademia, which sits on an angle of the Grand Canal and a side canal. In time, after I had taken in day by day all the sights and spectacles of Venice, the incredible St. Mark's Church, the happy square with its shops full of expensive junk, the Tintorettos, museums, and galleries and all those already hyperdescribed stones of Venice, I began to form a Venice of my own. It is rather as one does with acquaintances when one goes to live for a length of time in a new country – eventually one whittles them down to an affectionate few. These I visit again and again in my winter walks and excursions, well wrapped up and wearing boots like everyone else. Most men and women wear warm hats, too.

Since one of the advantages of an off-season visit is that there are no crowds, it is possible to sit without interruption almost alone in the church of the Frari looking at Titian's *Assumption*. I love to walk around the Ducal Palace to see those four charming Tetrarchs, timid and proper and quietly influential, modestly embracing each other in a formal half-huddle. Giorgione's mysterious *Tempest* in the Accademia is another of my best-loved familiars. And I remember a sunny winter trip, and also a cold bleak one, with a friend in the ferryboat to Torcello, one of the islands in the Venetian lagoon where very little goes on now except the magnificent cathedral, part Gothic, part Byzantine. There is a vast biblical narrative done in seventh century mosaics at one end, and a golden-backed mosaic of the Madonna behind the altar, hypnotically radiant. But going behind the altar to snoop we waded into a deep pool of water that had seeped into that glorious building. We were glad of our boots. In winter there are no restaurants on the smaller islands, no bars on the ferryboats. But sweet visitors do not care, and the sour ones do not matter.

The art treasures apart, what I return to again and again are the more homely friends of my walks through the windy *calles* and the placid, sometimes leafy squares of Venice. These include a men's hat shop standing all alone in a small square house on the canal near Santa Maria Formosa; in the windows, and piled up inside, is a vast variety of men's hats: straw boaters, Breton sailors' berets, felt hats, black velour hats, fedoras, stetsons, hats for hunting, hats for going to funerals.

Funerals in Venice, of course, are a stately procession. The city lays on a great show, with gilt-edged barges and coffins carved within an inch of their lives. In vain have the last two Popes set the example of being buried in plain pinewood boxes, there in St. Peter's for all the world to see. Venice sails on regardless. In Venice the ambulance service too is interesting: It provides a sedan chair to run a less-than-stretcher case down to the boat.

Often, in Venice, getting lost, as everyone does, I have come across a type of that high blank wall of James's *The Aspern Papers*:

> *. . . a high blank wall which appeared to confine an expanse of ground on one side of the house. Blank I call it, but it was figured over with the patches that please a painter, repaired breaches, crumblings of plaster, extrusions of brick that had turned pink with time; and a few thin trees, with the poles of certain rickety trellises, were visible over the top. The place was a garden and apparently it belonged to the house.*

I like the term 'apparently.' Because, in Venice anything can or might lie behind those high blank walls. It is well to say apparently. One never knows.

And the bridges on the side canals are something I can gaze at for hours. Sometimes they are set in groups, obliquely, for no immediately serviceable reason, and this is all the more enchanting.

It is true that, for myself, I never cease to feel a certain amazement that all that sheer visual goodness and aural sublimity was in fact based on commerce. Culture follows gold, somebody said. Indeed, in Venice, it apparently has done so. Today in Venice you could never live and follow a culture in the sort of style that gave birth to it. In a Venetian palace you could never live a modern life: You would have to be serving the walls, serving the servants, giving orders for your private riverboat to be repaired, the mooring posts to be painted, the crystal chandeliers to be cleaned piece by piece. To own a Venetian palace must be simply awful. Some people still do it.

It was only quite lately, in a much-travelled life, that I made my first trip to Venice. That was in 1975. I was vaguely saving it up for a romantic occasion. Special and romantic occasions were not wanting in my life but they never coincided with the possibility of a trip to Venice. So in the winter of 1975 I suddenly went. Venice itself was the romantic occasion: the medium is the message.

EUROPE'S HIGH NOTES

Harold C. Schonberg

So go to the Salzburg and Bayreuth festivals in the summer. Fight the crowds. Pay the absurdly overinflated ticket prices. Search desperately for a decent meal. Suffer the scarcely veiled insults when you complain about bad service.

There are better ways to enjoy musical Europe. Once the festival seasons are over, life resumes its normal course. The tourists go home, musical organizations start concentrating on what they really represent, which is the winter season, and the traveller experiences things as they really are. But even during the festival seasons it is not ordained On High that attendance is required, nor is it written that one must suffer to enjoy art.

Take Bayreuth. During the festival season, the little town is a madhouse, as it has been ever since the 1876 opening. (Tchaikovsky, who attended, complained not only about the difficulties of eating but also about the trouble he had getting drinking water.) But a canny traveller who wants to get the Bayreuth experience can visit there a few weeks before or a few weeks after the festival. Or in the dead of winter, for that matter. He will not be hearing the *Ring* cycle or *Tristan*. But he will be able, with no hassle or feeling of rush, to visit the great Villa Wahnfried, Wagner's house. (He knew how to live.) The visitor can look at the exhibits in the Wagner Museum. He can stroll through the gardens of Villa Wahnfried, paying due homage to Wagner's grave. And in another part of the town of Bayreuth is the grave of Franz Liszt, Wagner's father-in-law. The visitor can – as this one did – pick a flower off the grave and press it between the covers of a Liszt score.

The fun of exploring musical Europe is to take one's time, missing the more publicized events to search out the byways. As a matter of fact, the big centres of musical Europe can be pulverizingly conventional these days – conventional because ever since the jet plane, casts and soloists have become depressingly familiar. The same headliners jet from city to city, playing, conducting or singing much the same repertory. Everything has become standardized. Orchestras are even beginning to sound the same the world over. Why not? The same conductors are leading them. Why go to Vienna to hear Lorin Maazel and Isaac Stern do the Brahms Violin Concerto? Why go to London to hear Colin Davis and Vladimir Ashkenazy in a Beethoven concerto? You can hear the same conductors and soloists in the same repertory all over the United States.

Nor is there much difference on the operatic scene. La Scala, Vienna, London, Paris, Munich, the Metropolitan, Chicago, and San Francisco operas – all share the same soloists. The great singers give each opera house a couple of weeks, going elsewhere to sing the same repertory. Again: why go to Munich to hear a *Walküre* or *Nozze di Figaro* with much the same cast as that of the Metropolitan Opera?

No. Go instead to Prague, and go in the wintertime. The city is then uncrowded. It is relatively inexpensive. The opera house – the National Theatre – is on the Moldau, the river celebrated in Smetana's great symphonic poem, with St. Vitus's Cathedral looming in the distance. At the National Theatre in Prague, a steady diet of Czech operas is given. That means the operas of Smetana, Dvořák, and Janáček, most of which are not only beautiful but also unfamiliar to Western ears. Even the well-known ones, such as Smetana's *The Bartered Bride*, take on a different coloration and emotional feeling when heard in the original language.

In Prague there is also one of the world's greatest orchestras, the Czech Philarmonic. And since that is off the beaten track, you will not be hearing an overfamiliar figure as a soloist with it. Instead you will be getting one of the Russian hotshots, from Sviatoslav Richter down, or one of the superbly trained Czech pianists, such as Jan Palenka or Jiri Hubicka. Or you might hit the internationally acclaimed violinist Josef Suk, who plays in the West but not with any great frequency.

And Prague is also the home of the Artia publishing company. Serious music lovers can come home with suitcases bulging with scores and sheet music, or well-made art books. In all Soviet and Soviet-bloc countries, books and records cost a fraction of what they cost here. You can get orchestral scores of, say, the Janáček operas for fifteen dollars each. Here they would cost upward of seventy-five dollars.

Some years ago, in Prague, I was in a state bookstore rounding up pounds and pounds of music. When I asked for the bill, the proprietor took me aside, first glancing around to make sure that nobody was listening. He would give me a good deal on American cash or traveller's cheques, he said. But don't play around, no matter how much you may be tempted. The police don't think it's funny, and if they catch you in black-market currency transactions you can be in bad trouble.

A pleasant European musical holiday might involve visits to birthplaces and houses of composers. Many great composers are so memorialized. In Russia there is Klin and its attendant museum. Tchaikovsky worked happily there for many years. Outside Warsaw is Zelazowa Wola, Chopin's birthplace. There is a museum, as there is at so many of the other houses, and sometimes one is even allowed to touch Chopin's own piano. In Italy are Verdi museums, Puccini museums, Rossini museums. In Prague there is the enormous Smetana museum – he is a Czech national hero – on the banks of the Moldau, and there is also a much smaller Dvořák museum. And in Salzburg the focal point is Mozart's *Geburtshaus,* or birthplace.

There is something ironic about Salzburg and Mozart. Young Mozart hated the city, could not get out fast enough, went to Vienna and never returned. No matter. Mozart and Salzburg remain synonymous. The house in which Mozart was born has his clavichord and piano, the Lange unfinished portrait, oodles of manuscripts and memorabilia. In Salzburg it is not possible to escape Mozart. There is the big music festival, headed by Herbert von Karajan. There is the Mozarteum, the centre of Mozart research and concerts. There are Mozart candies, Mozart cookies, Mozart busts, Mozart souvenirs. But go there in the off season, if you can.

If you are a real opera buff, you don't necessarily have to fight your way through the publicized events to have a good time with opera. Most cities in Europe, and that includes the Soviet-bloc countries, have opera houses. Some are not very good, and so what? You can live off many an American hostess if you can tell stories of hearing *Madama Butterfly* sung in Bulgarian at the Sofia Opera. (It's quite an experience.) Or *Rigoletto* in Turkish, *Don Giovanni* in Swedish at the lovely Drottningholm Court Theatre outside Stockholm, *Aïda* in Finnish, and *Otello* in Estonian. In Kiev I caught a 'Faust' sung in Russian. It was frozen history. The costumes must have been patterned after the original Paris production of 1859. When is the last time you saw Mephistopheles wearing doublets and a hat with a black cock's feather in it?

Many of the small opera houses are lovely examples of eighteenth century architecture, complete with royal box, plush, and Biedermeier décor. Visiting them is its own reward. My favourite small house in all the world is the Cuvilliestheater in Munich, where Mozart's *Idomeneo* had its world premier in 1781. During World War II it was taken down brick by brick, rococo decoration by rococo decoration, hidden for safekeeping and carefully reassembled after hostilities ceased. But almost as nice are the Teatro La Fenice in Venice, the Margrave in Bayreuth, the Royal Opera in Stockholm, and the tiny Tyl Theatre in Prague, the site of another Mozart premier – *Don Giovanni*, in 1787.

We all know the fun of attending operetta in Vienna. But how many have gone to a *zarzuela* in Spain? The *zarzuela* is Spanish light opera, almost always composed in the last half of the nineteenth century in a style that mixes Rossini, Donizetti, and Bellini with some fainter Iberian characteristics. They are marvellous in their own genre. The performances start late, at 11:30 p.m. or so. Spaniards like to dine late, then go to the movies, the *zarzuela*, or other such popular entertainments.

Zarzuela performances feature singing actors, some of them with fresh, flexible voices. Every *zarzuela* has its stock figures: the doting husband, the lecherous old man, the two girls out to get the same boy and coming to blows over him. Business of rolling up sleeves and spitting on hands. Business of making a lunge at each other. Business of someone catching her skirts and pulling them back. Business of making up and cooing at each other – but with fingernails at the ready.

Every European city has its flea market, and there are stalls in every flea market that have something to do with music. There is not as much available as there used to be; since the war, too many visitors have picked everything over. What is more, dealers and stall owners who used to give their stuff away for next to nothing now know what it is worth, darn them.

Old records used to be a big attraction. In a Spanish flea market, about twenty-five years ago, I picked up two of the original Sarasate records, vintage 1906, and paid twenty-five cents each. Today each record is worth about seventy-five dollars, and they are not even mint copies. The record men in the big Paris flea market on the north side at Port St. Ouen are tough to negotiate with. They know the value of all collector's items, whether records, musical instruments, or art that has to do with music. About ten years ago I saw records by Planté there. Francis Planté was a French pianist who in 1929, at the age of eighty-nine, made several discs. They are rare, and the price on each was about twelve dollars. I turned them down – part of the fun is getting a steal – and have been kicking myself ever since, especially since I will have to pay about fifty dollars each if they turn up, which they don't.

Enterprising music-loving vacationers can follow any number of themes, depending on their sophistication. There could be a manuscript tour, in which the great repositories are visited and manuscripts of the great composers are examined. There could be an art tour based on paintings of musicians or great paintings on musical topics. There could be a flea-market tour in out-of-the-way places. Certainly there must be something grand in the Istanbul or Cairo bazaars. (I spent several days at the one in Istanbul and did come up with some nice items, notably a first edition of Liszt's solo piano arrangement of Schubert's *Divertissement à la Hongroise*, published by Simrock around

1840, with a lovely etching on the first page.) There could be a necrological tour – the burial sites of the great musicians, with appropriate tears shed at each one. And now that the People's Republic of China is opening up. . . .

ON THE ROAD FROM NAZARETH
TO BETHLEHEM

Malachi Martin

A fish. On a map that shows such things, that is what the topography of the land between Nazareth and Bethlehem reminds you of. A giant fish – or, more exactly, the skeleton of one – with its tail up there in the north, forked around the lower end of the sea of Galilee, and its head resting in the south on the sandy edges of the Sinai desert. The long ridge of mountains and high ground that runs down the centre of the land is like that fish's spine. Its ribs are splayed out on either side, creating ridges and valleys – called wadis in this part of the world – that on the western side lead to the coastal plain and, on the east, into the lush Jordan River valley.

That fish marks out country sodden with history, redolent of familiar biblical events. Assyrians, Phoenicians, Philistines, Egyptians, Greeks, Romans, Turks, British fought enormous battles in an unending seesaw struggle for land and empire throughout this area. And along its contours have walked the holiest men and women of the Bible, on journeys that have changed history forever. Abraham, Isaac, Jacob, Joseph, Joshua, Deborah, Samuel, Saul, David, Ruth, Naomi, Judith. These were but some who added layers of history like mantles over that land.

One such journey began with what is probably the most famous call for a census in history: 'And there went out a decree from Caesar Augustus that all the world be counted in a census . . . And all went to be registered, everyone to his own city. And Joseph also went up, out of the city of Nazareth, unto the city of David which is called Bethlehem . . . to be registered with Mary . . . who was expecting a child.'

Today, in the centre of modern Nazareth, you can see the traditional site of the house – by our standards, a hovel merely – in which Joseph and Mary made plans for the journey, as well as his workshop and the well where she drew water for the home.

In that time, there were three available routes for them to consider. Two traced the outer edges of the ribs of that geographical fish: one down the coastal plain, and one down the Jordan valley. Both of these were more dangerous and considerably longer than the third: the already 3,000-year-old trade route that threaded its way along the highlands. Customarily, for such periodic registrations, the Romans gave each tribe a deadline by which every member had to register in the tribe's principal town. Mary and Joseph knew that the Roman authorities brooked no delay or disobedience. At the same time, the child Mary carried was near its term. In these circumstances, they would have chosen the shortest, safest route from north to south in that land the Romans knew as their 'Syrian province.'

And so, shortly after the summons came to be registered, Joseph would have purchased places in the next caravan of pack-camels, ox-drawn carts, and passenger carriages heading south over the spine of the great fish. Many members of the caravan would have been rich merchants and traders travelling in their own covered, comfortable four-wheelers. Poorer folk such as this couple made it the hard way: She rode a donkey or mule, their belongings strapped behind her; he went on foot, leading the animal by a halter.

The distance to be covered was about seventy miles. A pleasant afternoon's drive by car today. That way corresponds rather closely, in fact, to the modern Routes 11, 33, 10, and 46. There is even a scenic railway now along certain lengths of the route. But in those ancient times, a ponderous caravan of men, women, oxcarts, carriages and animals would have covered five to seven miles on a good day, if the weather was fine and the spacing of trade stops and the condition of watering places did not alter plans. As these journeys went, the travellers probably reckoned seventeen to twenty days to reach Bethlehem. Their minds were certainly on the census registration, but they also travelled with increasing anticipation of the child to be born – the gift of the first Christmas.

Today, as you descend the Galilean foothills where Nazareth nestles, the first beauty that strikes your eye is the plain of Jezreel. Dominated on the northeast by the graceful serenity of the more than 1,000-foot Mount Tabor, the traditional site of the Transfiguration, Jezreel was called 'the garden of God' by its earliest dwellers. Fresh water gave life, then as now, to vineyards, fields of wheat and barley, orchards, farms, and carpets of many-hued wildflowers.

About ten miles west of this old route across Jezreel lies the thirteen-acre site of the once fortress-city of Megiddo where Solomon stabled the 500 horses of his chariot corps. There remain now only bare and silent ruins where once rose the daylong clang of armour in that vital stronghold. From there, according to tradition, the last battle for human salvation, Armageddon, will be fought and won by a heavenly army in the final days of earth's history.

Just before you leave Jezreel, nearly on the brink of your climb up to the spine of the fish, you will pass through what once was Nain, whose name means 'beauty': the town where David's prophet, Nathan, taught in his early years, and where, nine centuries later, Jesus brought a widow's son back to life. Like Megiddo, Nain lies uninhabited and unused today, mute witness of the past, still guardian of hopes and expectations.

Once you pass Kibbutz Jezreel, you are well on your way to the centre of the heartland region that was called Samaria, climbing to a high ground of 2,800 feet. To the east you can see, as Mary and Joseph did, the rising bulk of Mount Gilboa. Saul and his son, Jonathan, David's beloved friend, fell before the Philistines on those heights. David's lonely lament for their death seems still to linger there: 'No dew nor rain nor fields of corn let there ever be upon you . . . Mountain of Gilboa!' Death and disaster are etched by those words on the stark lines of Gilboa even today.

Almost opposite Gilboa, but on the western side of the route, is the bare land of Taanach. Sisera, an ancient oppressor of the Israelites, who led a corps of 900 chariots, was defeated here by the prophetess and judge, Deborah, who organized and rallied the Israelites. After that battle, it was another strong woman, Jael, who drove a nail through the head of the weary and defeated Sisera.

Just a few miles farther south and directly on our route is Dothan, where Joseph, Jacob's favourite son, was sold into slavery by his jealous brothers.

Today, trains and highway parallel the caravan route south from Dothan for some fifteen miles through a fascinating countryside of hills and valleys, all the way down to Shomron, the ancient capital of the northern kingdom of Israel. When Joseph and Mary's caravan stopped there – as it surely did, for it was a major trading centre – Shomron had been renamed Sebaste, and it had been refurbished by Herod the Great with Greek monuments and buildings. By their time, in fact, nation after nation had conquered and claimed this city over a period of 3,000 years. At Shomron-Sebaste, the travellers were half-way to Bethlehem, and had been perhaps as much as eight to ten days on the road.

While Mary and Joseph would not have taken any detours, as the traveller or pilgrim might, they were aware that about ten miles southeast of Shomron (along modern Route 10) there is a town on a small plain that lies between Mount Ebal (3,085 feet) and Mount Gerizim (2,890 feet). The ancient name of that town is Shechem. Today, it is called Nablus. It is one of the oldest religious and cultic sites of Israel. Abraham and Jacob each built holy altars there, and Joshua renewed the Covenant of Israel with God. There Jacob dug a well where, centuries later, Jesus would stop and talk with the Samaritan woman and promise her eternal life. Nablus remains the centre for the religious sect of the Samaritans today.

There is another place that, while not 'scenic,' will yet exert its pull on you for different reasons. Some six to seven miles beyond the modern town of Lubban Sharqiya – about another day's journey south for Mary and Joseph – if you let your eye travel two miles or so eastward over wooded hills, you can just spy meagre ruins of very ancient buildings. That is what remains of Shiloh. Now 'clad in eternal loneliness,' even as when David once sang of it, Shiloh was the home both of the Tabernacle and the Ark of the Covenant for a long time. Here the boy Samuel heard the voice of the Lord calling him to his ministry, and here the old High Priest, Eli, was struck dead by news of a disaster he himself had fed. In the evening, before sundown, Shiloh is a place that comes alive with strange presences conveying unsettling impressions – feelings of sadness at betrayal, and of some primal fear in us about ancient sacrifices, darkling fates, false gods, religious abominations, and the bloody destruction of Shiloh's temple by the Philistines, who bore the Ark away into exile as their trophy of victory.

Once you pass Shiloh, you might touch down briefly at Baal-hazor, if for nothing else than to visit the place where Absalom brutally killed his half-brother, Amnon, David's son by Ahinoam, in vengeance for Amnon's rape of Absalom's sister, Tamar. 'Henceforth,' the prophet Nathan warned David, 'bloodletting will never leave your family and house.' Indeed.

A few miles farther south and nearer the caravan route, not far from modern Beitin, is a holier place by far, and one where pious Jews such as Mary and Joseph would have paused for prayer: At the site of Bethel, now in ruins, Abraham built an altar and offered sacrifices to God, and Jacob dreamed of angels ascending and descending on the ladder between heaven and earth. 'Bethel,' Jacob exclaimed, 'is the House of God and the Gate of Heaven.'

Fittingly enough, you can catch the first glimpse of the highest buildings in Jerusalem from here. Today, the golden Dome of the Rock, sacred to Islam, glistens in the far distance. The caravan passengers of 2,000 years ago saw the golden points of Herod's magnificent Temple gleaming in the luminescence of Jerusalem's air. Yet there was one more stop before the caravan would reach Jerusalem.

Somewhere near the modern Ramallah, just ten miles and a good day-and-a-half journey from Jerusalem, caravans always halted; but not just for trade and rest. Here, you are 3,000 feet above sea level, and Jerusalem is in clear sight, sitting among its hills and clad in glory. Tradition tells us that those caravan passengers who were Jews would offer up thanks for this first clear look at the holy city, at its Temple and palaces, and for the chance to visit it. They recited David's Psalm, 'If I forget thee, O Jerusalem, may my right hand fall off.' And: 'One day in the House of the Lord is better than a thousand years in the palaces of sinners.' Surely, Joseph and Mary were among the worshippers on a late afternoon very near the first Christmas.

It would have been late the following day that the caravan approached the northern gate of Jerusalem and entered the city.

Joseph and Mary would have spent the night there, staying possibly with Mary's first cousin, Elizabeth, her husband Zachary, the priest, and their own newborn son, John, who would be forever known as the Baptist. But the Nazareth couple could not tarry in Jerusalem. The next day surely they were on their way southward, passing the tomb of Rachel, Jacob's wife, at Ramat Rachel, just outside the southern walls. Within a year of their passing by this place, all of the land from here to Bethlehem would resound with 'the voice of Rachel lamenting her children inconsolably,' as Herod the Great made his bloody attempt to find and kill the infant rival who, as the Three Kings told him, had been born King of the Jews.

Descending southward from Jerusalem today, you will not find the countryside much changed from Mary and Joseph's time, except for the greater areas under cultivation, the excellent new road, the many houses and farms, the usual signs of modernity. It was apparently nightfall when Joseph and Mary arrived at Bethlehem. In their time, Bethlehem was a very small town surrounded by a high protective wall. Inside that wall, the houses of Bethlehem huddled around the central square for all the world like brown-clad elders gathered for warmth around a fire. Facing that square on one side was the town's solitary public inn; by late day, it was already more than full, most probably with other members of the tribe of Judah gathered in for the same registration that had brought Mary and Joseph on their journey. Outside the town, the hills of Bethlehem are dotted with limestone caves that had for centuries been used by the shepherds of the region as stables and sleeping quarters during the hardest months of winter and early spring. It was in one such cave that Joseph found shelter for his wife and himself. And it was in that cave, and on that very night, that Mary's child was born.

To the south of the city lie pastures that have always grazed the flocks of Bethlehem. It was from those pastures that Samuel had summoned David for his anointing a thousand years before that night of Jesus's birth. It was those pastures that David had left behind him forever when he travelled to Saul's encampment and faced the giant, Goliath. And it was from those pastures that the shepherds came to see this newborn child announced to them, they said, by a chorus of angels.

The wall that enclosed Bethlehem is no longer there. The town is much bigger now, and quite prosperous too. That cave in which Jesus was born and cradled in a manger is known as the Grotto of the Nativity and is enclosed in the Church of the Nativity, zealously guarded by monks and priests and nuns. It is visited each year by millions of the faithful. Each one who enters that church must bend low to pass through its doorway. The Christians refashioned it so, in order to prevent the Moslem conqueror from riding his camel inside, in desecration, as he had the habit of doing with Christian holy places. After all, the monks of the time reasoned blandly with the Moslem, if God chose to be born in a stable, cannot ordinary mortals bend their proud heads to stoop their arrogant shoulders to enter there?

Just beside the Grotto, there is another cave where, 500 years after the travels of Mary and Joseph, Saint Jerome lived, kept a tame lion as a pet, and spent much of his life translating the Hebrew and Greek Scriptures into Latin.

It is unforgettable to follow the solemn and colourful Christmas services at the Church of the Nativity. There is, in fact, something about the Christmas atmosphere that hovers over all of Bethlehem, and clings to its countryside; something that overshadows all the hubbub and excitement and inevitable commerciality; something that invites you to reflect on the meaning of the words 'peace' and 'joy' at the place of that journey's end for the Nazareth couple. Something draws your footsteps to follow where the shepherds went, and to gaze upon the place where the Christmas child once lay. Something welcomes you to join the forever song of angels there, and to be warmed against winter's chill, as Mary and Joseph were, in the smile of Heaven's gladness.

FROM SPIRE TO SPIRE
IN YULETIDE LONDON

R. W. Apple, Jr

Probably none of the world's great churches bears the imprint of one man as clearly as St. Paul's Cathedral, London, bears that of Christopher Wren. But if that elegant Baroque masterpiece proclaims Wren's genius as a manipulator of volume and a synthesizer of contradictory details, his churches in the City of London demonstrate that he was a gifted miniaturist as well.

When the Great Fire of 1666 swept through the City – the congested area where London had its beginnings and where its financial activities are concentrated to this day – it consumed not only the old St. Paul's but also most of the ninety-seven parish churches. Wren was then thirty-four years old and teaching at Oxford; through his friendship with Charles II, he was commissioned to rebuild not only the cathedral, but also no fewer than fifty-one churches.

In lesser hands, the churches might have ended up looking alike; in his each looked distinctive. As Sir John Betjeman, the architectural historian and Poet Laureate, has written, they had only two things in common – prominent fonts and prominent altars with carved and painted altarpieces. 'Thus were emphasized,' says Sir John, 'the two sacraments essential to salvation, baptism and Holy Communion.' But in every other way, Wren's churches varied widely: some were brick and some were stone; some had lead-sheathed steeples and some had steeples of bare stone; some had domes and some did not; some had one aisle, some had two, and some had none. Most were built in what came to be known as English Baroque, but a few were frankly neo-Gothic.

Over the centuries, as more and more offices and fewer and fewer houses came to occupy the Square Mile, as the City is known, the churches lost their congregations. Many were sold. Others were destroyed in the German bombing raids of the Second World War and never rebuilt. Many were drastically modified, almost always with unfortunate results. But twenty-three Wren churches survive in their entirety, and the towers of several others can still be seen. Even more than St. Pauls, even more than Wren's other great buildings – the

Royal Naval College at Greenwich, the Royal Hospital in Chelsea, and the east front of Hampton Court – the City churches enable the modern visitor to explore the chaste, beautiful world of Christopher Wren.

But the Wren churches are not all the story. In a day's walk through the City one can see others, each with its special appeal, be it a magnificently carved font cover, a Norman chancel, or monuments to men long dead whose names live on in the tradition of the English-speaking peoples. Such a walk is especially pleasant when the churches are decorated for Christmas, and their carved festoons of wood or stone are echoed by garlands and swags of evergreens.

What follows is a modest proposal for such a walk. Each visitor can extend it, curtail it, or modify it to suit himself or herself; the more ambitious might want to do a bit of homework beforehand, for which I would recommend the appropriate pages in *The Cities of London and Westminster*, the first of two volumes that Sir Nikolaus Pevsner devotes to London in his monumental survey *The Buildings of England* (Penguin, available in Britain for about $23). I have here made a purely personal choice, based on long, fruitful hours of exploration during lunch breaks, *The Times's* London bureau being happily situated within a few minutes' walk of the best of Wren's handiwork.

A good place to begin is at **All Hallows-by-the-Tower**, which stands close to the Thames in the shadow of the Tower of London (you can get there easily by taking the Underground to the Tower Hill stop). Like many of the City churches, it is an oasis of calm amid the roaring traffic that often makes it hard to imagine that anything predated the internal combustion engine. It was from this church, spared in the Great Fire, that Samuel Pepys gazed out upon the smouldering ruins to observe, as he recorded in his diary for September 5, 1666, 'the saddest sight of desolation that I ever saw.'

All Hallows dates from Saxon times, probably from the seventh century. It was saved in 1666 by Admiral Sir William Penn, who ordered his sailors to blow up the houses near the church, creating a firebreak. (The Admiral's son, also named William, was baptised in the church and later went on to found Pennsylvania.) German bombers were more effective in December 1940, destroying all but the crypt, a few walls, and the tower, so that what you will see is mostly a reconstruction.

The visit is nonetheless worthwhile, largely because of the baptistery in the southwest corner, outside which stands a fine eighth century arch, and in which stands one of the greatest works of England's master wood-carver, Grinling Gibbons. It is a limewood cover for the font, showing three cherubs prancing around a pillar of grain and flowers, with a dove on top. Notice how Gibbons gave each of the cherubs an individual personality.

Emerging from the church, take the pedestrian subway to the other side of the street, turn left and then bear right on Great Tower Street. Two blocks farther along, recross the street and walk down Idol Lane. In a moment, you will see a church tower. Stop and look at it from there; the closer views are not as good. This tower, which is all that remains of **St. Dunstan-in-the-East**, is probably Wren's best work in the Gothic style, an airy confection of four tiers whose spire is poised on flying buttresses. Trees grow where the nave of the church stood before 1940.

Now bear right (you have no choice) into St. Dunstan's Lane and, after a few steps, turn right up the street called **St. Mary-at-Hill** to the church of the same name. Just beyond a clock projecting from an almost plain wall, you will see a blue sign marking a passageway that leads to a courtyard and to the door of the church – one of Wren's loveliest creations, with a great Palladian window at the east end and superb woodwork of the seventeenth, eighteenth, and nineteenth centuries (altarpiece, pulpit, staircase, organ case). A shallow dome rises above the centre of four intersecting barrel vaults, all in pale blue, white, and gold plaster that lends an air of ineffable serenity. It is in the style of Robert Adam and hence technically inappropriate, but never mind; it works. As Pevsner points out, the layout is that of many Byzantine churches, which Wren probably adapted from a church in Haarlem in the Netherlands.

Returning to the street, turn right, pausing first to look left at the tower of Wren's St. Margaret Pattens. The building in front of you as you walk down the hill used to be Billingsgate Market, the home of London's fish merchants, now unhappily moved to the Isle of Dogs. Turn right again along Thames Street when you reach it and walk a couple of blocks to the church of **St. Magnus the Martyr**. This church, distinguished by a 180-foot tower with a gold weathervane, was Wren's welcome to pedestrians crosssing the old London Bridge from the south, who passed under the arch in the porch. The interior, which T. S. Eliot said evoked the 'inexplicable splendour of Ionian white and gold,' is one of the architect's richest.

Make next for the tall monument to the north, walking up Fish Street. This is, in fact, **the Monument**, Wren's memorial to the Great Fire, which is 202 feet tall and stands 202 feet from the baker's shop in Pudding Lane where the blaze is said to have begun. Don't bother to climb the 311 steps; ugly office slabs now obscure the view. Instead, turn left into Monument Street, then right into King William Street, then left again (through the pedestrian subway) into Cannon Street. After two blocks, you will reach Abchurch Lane, which leads to a lovely little piazzetta next to **St. Mary Abchurch**, a tiny gem.

Here you can see Wren's sleight-of-hand at work. Squeezed into a site barely 80 feet square, the church is entirely anonymous, even drab, from the outside. But, as Pevsner says, 'the interior is a surprise, for though the area is small, it is made to look very spacious indeed by giving it one big dome on eight arches'. The dome cannot be seen from the street. The exquisitely detailed reredos, or altar screen, is by Gibbons; there are documents to prove it. This church, little visited, is sometimes locked; inquire at the public house nearby if need be.

Continue up the lane, turning left into King William Street (again) and following the sidewalk around to the left when you reach the big intersection ahead. The huge building ahead of you is the Bank of England; the church on your right is St. Mary Woolnoth by Nicholas Hawksmoor, another English master of the Baroque, and is well worth a visit if you aren't pressed for time. Turn left just beyond the Mansion House, the seat of London's Lord Mayor, into Walbrook, and you should see the tower of **St. Stephen Walbrook** rising just ahead of you.

This church is undergoing extensive restoration and will probably be closed at least until 1987; but it is worth checking, for here Wren designed a dome prefiguring that of St. Paul's, coffered on the inside in the style of the Pantheon in Rome, and here he demonstrated, in Betjeman's words, 'how to make a plain rectangle interesting and full of vistas.' It would never occur to you that the space was rectangular unless someone told you, for Wren has combined a basilical plan – an oblong with a projecting apse – with a Greek cross with a dome, filling the whole with a white forest of slender Corinthian columns that seem to lead toward infinity. For me, this is the most majestic and intellectually exciting building in the City – and that includes St. Paul's. I hope you see it.

By now it should be time for lunch. Walk straight out of the church and up a street called Bucklersbury, crossing Queen Victoria Street; when you reach Cheapside, turn left. On your left, just after crossing Queen Street, you will see **St. Mary-le-Bow**, our next goal, and right behind it, at 10 Bow Churchyard, the Bow Wine Vaults. Here they will give you a couple of glasses of decent beaujolais, homemade soup, an ample slice of rare roast beef, a salad and coffee, all for about $7, which isn't bad for London these days. (If you are feeling flush, Le Poulbot, a few yards farther along Cheapside, will feed you the City's best French cooking for about $45 a head if you order a simple wine.)

Bow church itself boasts Wren's most famous steeple, full of the gentle fantasy that this happy man loved. The church took its name from the Norman arches or bows in the crypt, so Wren embellished the architectural pun by putting stone arches at each corner of the balustrade topping the belfry. The belfry itself is the home of 'Bow

Bells,' which are woven into the folklore of Britain. A true Cockney, it is said, is someone born within the sound of these bells; during World War II, their recorded peal was broadcast worldwide by the BBC and came to symbolize liberation to millions of people in occupied Europe. The interior, completely rebuilt since 1941, is pleasant but less interesting. I would spend most of my time here standing at the foot of the nearby statue of Captain John Smith (of whom more later), studying the tower and the eight-foot-ten-inch winged copper dragon on the top.

Continue down Cheapside past Foster Lane, pausing there to enjoy the unaccustomed rear view of **St. Paul's**, then bear right into St. Martin-le-Grand. When you see a round building looming ahead (this is the London Museum, which should be visited on another day), turn left into Little Britain and follow it, bending first right and then left, until you stand on the edge of a great open square. On your right you will see a passageway leading beneath a thirteenth century gate.

The gate was originally the entrance to the nave of **St. Bartholomew the Great**, and the courtyard you cross was the nave itself. What is left of the church is the crossing and the chancel of the great abbey church, built in 1123 and mostly destroyed by Henry VIII in 1539, but even the stump is breathtaking – the most powerful of all the City churches, in my view, and the only one largely in the Norman style brought to England by William the Conqueror. The massive round piers, the plain but sensitively scalloped capitals, and the gallery above, with four arches within each larger arch, show Norman Romanesque at its most movingly sombre. The lady chapel behind the high altar, looks effete by comparison.

Walk south now, with the square on your right and St. Bartholomew's Hospital on your left. When you reach the Holborn Viaduct, turn into **St. Sepulchre**, architecturally the least distinguished church, perhaps, on our tour, but a fascinating place all the same. It is the biggest church in the City, an amalgam of pre-Fire and post-Fire styles that ends up looking Victorian.

For music lovers, the point of attraction is the chapel off the north aisle, with a book of remembrance devoted to famous musicians, kneeling cushions embroidered with their names, and the ashes of Sir Henry Wood, the much-loved creator of the informal, popular Prom concerts. The church also contains a superb old organ played by Handel and Mendelssohn. And Americans will not want to miss, in the south aisle, the tomb of Capt. John Smith, 'sometime governor of Virginia and admiral of New England'.

Next, cross Holborn Viaduct and walk down Old Bailey, the street that houses London's famous central criminal courts, turning left at Ludgate Hill, up which the royal coaches and horses toil for royal weddings and jubilees. The façade of **St. Paul's**, Wren's undoubted ecclesiastical masterpiece, towers above you. The present cathedral, the fourth or fifth to stand on the site, came to be a symbol of survival for London and the nation during the Blitz, defying even the smoke and flames of the raid of December 29, 1940, when the City and the docks were engulfed by fire. Against the pale dawn sky, serene and unmarked, the great 250-foot-high dome provided reassurance that Britain had lived to fight yet another day.

A few days before the Great Fire, Wren had visited what was then St. Paul's to see what could be done to save the decaying fabric of the thirteenth century cathedral, with the seventeenth century classical façade by Inigo Jones. The conflagration was devastating; after the fire, Wren wrote in his diary, 'St. Paul's is now a sad ruin and that beautiful portico now rent in pieces.'

What Wren put in its place – beginning on June 21, 1675, and ending thirty-three years later, when the architect, by then seventy-five years old, saw his son fit the top stone into place on the lantern – has changed relatively little over the years. An enormous structure, covering 78,000 square feet, it is dominated inside and out by the dome (by two domes, in fact; the one seen from the outside is not the one seen from the inside, there being three concentric shells).

Outside, the impression is of restraint, of a classicism that is just yielding to the Baroque. Inside, one is overwhelmed by the volume of enclosed space, by the warmth of the stone, and finally, as one reaches the crossing, by the gold and mosaic work. Even here, however, the English taste for understatement is evident – St. Paul's has little in common, for example, with the exuberant encrustations of Bavarian and Austrian Baroque churches.

Walk slowly down the nave in order to sense the full splendour of the crossing and the dome. If your taste runs to fantasy, you might try to imagine what it was like for Lady Diana Spencer, as she then was, to walk those 180 feet with the world watching. You can climb if you wish, to the Whispering Gallery, where the state trumpeters were placed for the royal wedding. Then spend some time studying the memorials to eminent Britons – the Wellington monument on the left of the nave, statues of Joshua Reynolds and Dr. Johnson, among others, by the dome piers, and a tablet marking the position of Churchill's casket during his state funeral on January 30, 1965. The work of Gibbons is all around, in stone this time, a profusion of cherubs and swags and garlands.

Before leaving, descend into the crypt. I had never seen it until the morning of the royal wedding, when the reporters were let out of the church by that route. It seemed eerily appropriate, somehow, to see there the dozens of tombs, memorials, and busts (tributes to Nelson and Lawrence of Arabia among them) after all the magnificence that had just unfolded overhead.

Emerging from the church, walk straight down the hill, under the railway bridge, across Ludgate Circus, and into Fleet Street. Turn left at the first intersection to **St. Bride**, which is of interest for two reasons: its wedding-cake steeple, with four octagons stacked one atop the other, at 226 feet loftier than any other Wren creation; and the list of its one-time parishioners. You cannot fail to see the steeple on your way down Ludgate Hill.

When you enter the church – the interior has been rebuilt since World War II – consider for a moment those who have stood on this spot before you: Chaucer, Shakespeare, Milton, Pepys, Dryden, Johnson and Boswell, Burke, Pope, Wordsworth, Keats, Dickens . . .

Since this is still the newspaper neighbourhood, there are plenty of pubs in which to rest your feet and slake your thirst; the Cheshire Cheese is in a courtyard just up Fleet Street. Down New Bridge Street towards the river is the Blackfriars Underground station, where you can catch a train back to your hotel.

In addition to Wren's ecclesiastical masterpiece, St. Paul's Cathedral, twenty-three smaller Wren churches survive within the precincts of the city:

St. Andrew Holborn (1686-87, 1704), Holborn Circus. The church, designed as an elongated rectangle with a projecting apse and two tiers of windows, was burned out in 1941; the square tower is a relic of the medieval church, to which Wren added a second stage with a cornice and balustrade, decorated with enormous vases.

St. Andrew-by-the-Wardrobe (1685-95), Queen Victoria Street. The church was gutted by fire in December 1940; only the walls and tower were left standing. It was restored to Wren's design in 1961; the red brick tower has stone quoins and a balustrade.

St. Anne and St Agnes (1676-87), Gresham Street. The red brick church, built to a domed, cruciform plan, was severely damaged by bombs during World War II and subsequently rebuilt; its small, stuccoed stone tower is surmounted by a little domed turret with an A-shaped vane.

St. Benet's Welsh Church (1677-85), St. Benet, Paul's Wharf. The small brick church has rounded windows decorated with carved stone festoons; extensive interior woodwork, including a high pedimented reredos and a balustraded communion rail. Inigo Jones was buried in an earlier church on the site.

St. Bride (1670-84, 1701-03), Fleet Street. The tall, pierced steeple is original; the rest of the church was gutted by fire in 1940, then restored to Wren's design, with rounded windows between pedimented doors and a line of oval clerestory windows. A museum in the crypt holds Roman and Saxon remains unearthed in 1952.

St. Clement Eastcheap (1683-87), Clement's Lane, Eastcheap. The previous church on this site was the first to burn in the Great Fire. The tower is red brick with stone quoins; the interior has good seventeenth century panelling, including a festooned and garlanded sounding board, and a fine plaster ceiling.

St. Edmund the King and Martyr (1670-79, 1706-07), Lombard Street. The façade has a central pediment and a round clock; the interior contains notable woodwork, including a swagged pulpit and a font with four gilded apostles; the square stone tower is topped by a lead-sheathed octagonal lantern and spire, terminating in a bulb and vase.

St. James Garlickhythe (1676-83, 1713), Garlick Hill, Upper Thames Street. Built to an oblong plan, the church was damaged in 1940 and 1941 and restored in 1963; the interior has seventeenth century woodwork and sword rests with lion and unicorn supporters. The tower is crowned by a spire, added in 1713, with a three-tiered lantern and a spirelet.

St. Lawrence Jewry (1670-87), Gresham Street. The church stands on the site of the medieval ghetto; its interior is largely modern, with a coffered ceiling after Wren's design. The tower has a pedimented lantern set out of alignment with the base; it is topped by a weathervane that incorporates a replica of the incendiary bomb that almost totally destroyed the church in 1940.

St. Magnus the Martyr (1681-87, 1706), Lower Thames Street. Tall modern buildings hem the church in today, so that only the tower and north side remain visible from the street. The interior was much altered in the eighteenth, nineteenth, and twentieth centuries, but retains an organ dating from 1712. The square stone tower supports an octagonal belfry, lead-covered cupola, lantern, obelisk, and vane.

St. Margaret Lothbury (1686-90, 1701), Lothbury. The square stone tower is topped by a lead-sheathed cupola, an obelisk spire and a gilded ball and vane. The interior woodwork includes a carved pulpit with a swagged and cherub-bedecked sounding board, a screen made to Wren's design, and a font sometimes attributed to Grinling Gibbons.

St. Margaret Pattens (1684-89, 1698-1702), Eastcheap. The plan is a plain oblong, with round clerestory windows; the interior is rich in seventeenth century woodwork, including a 'punishment bench' ornamented with a devil's head. The polygonal, lead-sheathed spire rises to become a needle supporting a golden vane.

St. Martin Ludgate (1677-87), Ludgate Hill. The interior is laid out as a square within a square; there is a gallery with coffered arches and door frames by Grinling Gibbons. The tower is topped by a lead-sheathed cupola and lantern, from which rises a sharp, needlelike spire.

St. Mary Abchurch (1681-86), Cannon Street. The domed interior has fine woodwork, especially the huge but delicately detailed Grinling Gibbons reredos. The inside of the dome was painted by Sir James Thornhill, probably in 1708 (since restored). The red brick tower is surmounted by a cupola, lantern, and thin lead-covered spire.

St. Mary Aldermary (1681-82, 1701-11), Queen Victoria Street. The church is perhaps the best of Wren's efforts in the neo-Gothic style; the interior has been remodelled on several occasions, but a Grinling Gibbons sword rest, pulpit and doorcase survive; the font dates from 1682. The tower rises from a sixteenth century base and sports pinnacles and gilded finials.

St. Mary-at-Hill (1670-76), Eastcheap. Wren's plan is almost square, with a shallow central dome; there is fine woodwork dating from the seventeenth (font cover) to the nineteenth centuries (organ case, pulpit, and sounding board, staircase). The brick tower is stuccoed on its east face, and has a Palladian window and projecting clock.

St. Mary-le-Bow (1670-83), Cheapside. The church was gutted by fire in 1941; its exterior was rebuilt to Wren's design, while the interior now follows a more open plan. The tower, with its dragon vane, is a series of visual and architectural puns on the "bow" theme. The crypt contains remains of a Norman church; Bow Bells ring from the belfry.

St. Michael Paternoster Royal (1686-94, 1715-17), Upper Thames Street. Burned out in 1941; the interior is now remarkable for its stained-glass windows, among them one showing Dick Whittington and his cat (Whittington lived in the parish and was buried in one of the earlier churches on this site). The tower is square; the three-tiered octagonal lantern and spirelet were added in 1715.

St Nicholas Cole Abbey (1671-81), Queen Victoria Street. The stone church was burned out in 1941 and completely rebuilt, with tall, rounded windows and a balustrade. The tower has a square base decorated with urns and an octagonal lead-sheathed spire that supports a vane in the form of a gilded three-masted ship.

St. Peter upon Cornhill (1677-87), Cornhill. The church is oblong, with a projecting apse and rounded and circular windows and rich woodwork, including a carved chancel screen sometimes attributed to Wren himself. The tower, with a copper dome and obelisk spire, topped with a vane in the form of a key, is visible from the churchyard or neighbouring Gracechurch Street.

St. Sepulchre (1670-77), Holborn Viaduct. The porch and the square, pinnacled tower date from 1450, and were restored by Wren, who also added the arcade. The interior is notable for a 1670 organ, a Musicians' Chapel and a memorial to Capt. John Smith, who is buried in the church.

St. Stephen Walbrook (1672-77, 1717), Walbrook. The interior is built to an oblong plan, with a dome that can be considered a study for St. Paul's and bays set off by freestanding Corinthian columns. The tower and steeple are stone, the steeple rising to two balls and a vane.

St. Vedast (1670-73, 1697), Foster Lane. The curving southwest wall survived the Great Fire and was incorporated into Wren's design; the interior is modern – the church was bombed in 1940 – although the ceiling follows Wren's design. The square tower is surmounted by a pilastered, three-tiered lantern, a ribbed spire, and a ball and vane.

Only the towers survive of six other City churches by Wren:

St. Alban (1697-98), Wood Street, a slender neo-Gothic structure of white stone with crocketed pinnacles.

St. Augustine and St. Faith (1680-87), Watling Street, a square tower with a bulbous dome and lead spire, rebuilt to Wren's design after World War II.

Christ Church (1704), Newgate street, a slender square stone tower with alternating closed and colonnaded stages and a turret and vane.

St. Dunstan-in-the-East (1697), Lower Thames Street, a four-tiered neo-Gothic tower of Portland stone, with a spire set on flying buttresses.

St. Mary Somerset (1695), Upper Thames Street, a slender, square white tower topped by a parapet with obelisk pinnacles. The main body of the church was demolished in 1871.

St. Olave Jewry (1670-76), St. Olave Jewry, a two-tiered stone tower with a notable vane in the shape of a fully rigged three-masted ship.

'BUON NATALE, ROMA'

Maureen Howard

'Merry Christmas.' 'Merry Christmas.' We sat in low easy chairs at Kennedy International Airport and toasted each other. It was Christmas Eve, and I could not quite credit that we would soon be on a flight to Rome. For twenty-five years I had put up a tree, roasted a turkey, mashed potatoes, baked pies (both pumpkin and mince) and steamed plum pudding (which no one liked).

Living abroad had been different. I had faked an American Christmas in England and in Italy, searching out cranberries and some queer root vegetable that approximated a pale yam, but to actually leave home, close the wreathless door behind us, and head off on holiday – that seemed a cool proposition indeed. My husband appeared delighted with our escape, but I was not at all sure I could pull it off – the sophistication implied in abandoning all ornamentation of the holiday including our worn record of Joan Baez singing 'Deck the Halls.'

Travelling at Christmas proved wonderful. It seemed, with the knowledge of hindsight, that I should have guessed that the holiday would regain significance for me in our peaceful walks through the undecorated streets of Rome, that we would hear glorious music in St. Mark's Basilica in Venice and that we would slow down to the luxurious pace that allowed us to pore over Waverley Root's *The Food of Italy* before going out to the next adventure of a meal.

We had allowed for the terrible crush of traffic on our way to the airport, but there was none. The Trans World Airlines terminal was calm, as unflustered as I've ever seen it, and I felt at once that all good people were already assembled in Dickensian scenes with holly, hot punch, blazing yule logs. As we took off, the lights strung on Queens looked predictably, sentimentally, like the twinkling essence of the Christmas we were leaving behind.

In fact, we were not without heart. We were flying to Italy to join my daughter, who had been studying in Rome for the semester. It had seemed a romantic idea when we saw her off on Labour Day – 'Christmas in Rome' – more a title than a stop on our itinerary. The scheme still lacked reality when I saw her waving to us at the customs gate and when we walked out to meet our rented minicar in the bright Italian sun. The muted winter greenery of Rome is such an immediate pleasure for travellers from the north – the umbrella pines and full hedges, the wildflowers along any scruffy patch by the highway as you approach the city.

The peculiar excitement of Christmas did not settle in until we were installed in our hotel on Aventine Hill, shutters thrown open to a view of red tile roofs and the bell tower of Sant'Anselmo, a stolid modern church tacked onto a Benedictine monastery. The little square below faced with the small-scale villas and embassies of this particularly private residential area was empty with that early hush of a holiday morning that I love in New York.

'*Buon Natale,*' we said to the boy who brought up our bags. '*Grazie,*' we said to each other when we exchanged our modest gifts. Knowing that we would shop together in Rome, I had simply brought my grown child Reese's Peanut Butter Cups from America. She had bought us gloves at a *sconti* (discount store) on via Nazionale, and mine were bright red, not for Christmas, but because red was the fashion that season. We were to see scarlet coats, shoes, bags, scarves all over Rome in the following weeks, and I had the nicest feeling as we went out in search of dinner, not only of being up-to-the-minute but of beginning to recall this city – that Romans are elegant, amused by the dictates of fashion yet somewhat too seriously addicted to '*la bella figura.*'

That Christmas dinner was a serendipity and a warning at once: travelling on holidays, beware the closed restaurants, museums, churches, palaces. Italians are observant of their major feasts. As often as we were disappointed (the Sistine Chapel, the Accademia in Venice were shut tight) we were charmed by something that came our way peculiar to the season – the shepherds playing flutes at the Pantheon, the sadly unconvincing Santa in a donkey cart in Piazza di Spagna posing with kids for *mille lire.*

Whether it was jet lag or the first seductive effects of the Italian scene, we telephoned a list of restaurants that were closed and strolled downhill without a worry. There we found a perfect neighbourhood trattoria, **Perilli** at 39 via Marmorata (57 24 15), which was totally booked but took us in anyway. We were served spaghetti carbonara, made as it should be with pancetta and a good dollop of pecorino, exactly as I had loved it in my neighbourhood trattoria in the late '50s, and the best capon grilled alla diavola, with irresistible potatoes roasted with sprigs of rosemary, a salad of tender radicchio (a wild chicory the colour of burnished mahogany). We sat happily in the midst of middle-class families trying to catch a word or two of what we thought to be holiday squabbles and holiday cheer.

My daughter had become an aficionada of Rome – its monuments, its paintings, its manners – and led us around quickly, efficiently. She had taken in much more of the city than I ever had when I drew into my writing and my Italian domesticity years ago. She knew the workers' restaurants with paper tablecloths, the bus routes, her favourite house done up in high mannerist style with eyes for windows and a late Baroque mouth for a door. She knew the most fashionable café in town. For some inexplicable reason the fanciest crowd frequented the **Sant'Eustachio,** off piazza Sant'Eustachio, which looked to us like any of a hundred bars, but the Alfa Romeos and Mercedes-Benzes were parked thick, the minks and Burberrys were elbowing in for a demitasse or cappuccino. All the kids got up to look mildly outrageous, new wave, were in piazza la Rotunda at a café that bursts into the square with a restless action.

As middle-aged tourists we would never have found the **Ivo Trastevere,** at 158 via San Francesco a Ripa (581 7082), filled with young people and natives of Trastevere. In the sedate times I'd passed in Rome I'd never seen such a true pizzeria (I'm not sure that one existed), good house wine, pitchers of beer, and all those Roman specialities that seldom appear on proper menus: *crostini, bruschetto, cuscinetti* – all variations on delicious, cheesy, toasted open sandwiches. You have to be sturdy for da Ivo: it's noisy, crowded, but the spirit and the food made one of our best nights. And after the pizzeria, I'm ashamed to say, we strolled on to the most sumptuous ice cream parlour, **Giolitti's** at 40 via Uffici del Vicario (678 0410).

It was not merely that my daughter could find her way around a European capital that was deeply satisfying to us. It was her response to Rome as a modern city, a working city withstanding the pressures of fashion and politics (it was, that Christmas, a heyday for the Red Brigades and in search of the terrorists roadblocks went up and down during the course of a Roman evening). Any tourist can find the Pinturicchios in Santa Maria d'Aracoeli, but it takes a traveller to sort out feelings of horror and compassion about the open drug scene – disposable hypodermic needles thrown outside cafés and in the corners of ancient ruins. There is more to bring home in an educated view than notes for the next art-history seminar. There are gypsy children begging as always, but they seem more professional, working the shops and restaurants. Unemployment, poverty, and a childish though familiar consumption of goods live side by side in the Eternal City.

A new energetic minister of cultural affairs had determined to use the sights of Rome. Abel Gance's *Napoleon* played to capacity crowds in front of an illuminated Colosseum. The Circus Maximus was to be used for films and modern games. During our visit the Palazzo

Venezia had a retrospective of Oskar Kokoschka, and the Villa Medici next to the Trinita dei Monti was fully enjoyed as a public place for the first time in many years. Now, that was the event of the season – le tout Rome turned out to get a look at the palace and at a striking exhibition of David's paintings and drawings of their city.

Some of my fond memories of Rome must be folded back in tissue paper. The Christmas bazaar in piazza Navona now has few toys or naïve crèche figures; it has gone all plastic. Taiwan baskets, cassettes, tricky T-shirts. The Presepio or Christmas crib is dolled up in many churches with corny lighting, taped music. Wanting to see what is current has its disillusioning aspects. We went to a touching hangout named Oz, run by kids trying so hard not to be Italian. They serve crêpes with fudge sauce and play awful pop music. Oz yearns to be in Ann Arbor or Northampton, cities as distant from Trastevere as an emerald palace. And given that it was a winter trip we missed our carefully planned New Year's Eve in Venice at Harry's Bar. The fog was so thick we ended up in a soccer players' establishment in Padua with an abysmal imitation of the Guy Lombardo show. But we ate good food, drank free champagne, retrieved a disastrous evening.

Ah, but on New Year's Day we came to Venice in a soft mist and walked right into a high mass in St. Mark's with Venetians in attendance and a Venetian choir singing in loden coats and wool hats in the marble loft. At the end of the mass there was a grand recessional with the cardinals, bishops, monsignors – all in white and gold – down to the final string of acolytes. The drama of it was moving and the procession itself amazingly simple compared to Bellini's elaborate ceremonial views of Venice. The holy day was captured. That mass at St. Mark's was so impressive that we could not help finding, a week later, the papal mass of the Epiphany a sorry media event. The tour buses all along the approach to St. Peter's might have warned us that there would be the constant flashbulbs, the necessary but distracting security, the manoeuvring of television equipment. Well, it was nice to see the altar in use.

To cheer ourselves that day we went for lunch to **Il Buco** at 8 via Sant'Ignazio (679 3298), a restaurant that is serious about its reputation, cooks game birds with distinction, and presents a lavish display of Tuscan specialities on a sideboard near the door. In the old days I had cooked at home in antiquated Italian kitchens, translating recipes out of Ada Boni's *Talismano della Felicità*, so it was new to me – the tourist business of always eating out. I was pleased to find that **Da Giggetto** at 21 via del Portico d'Ottavia (656 1105), the famous Jewish restaurant, had prospered without losing its verve. We treated ourselves to **Passetto,** 14 via Zanardelli (654 3696), for a special dinner that was absolutely up to the mark – fettuccine with butter and white truffles, and their version of Monte Bianco – a frothy confection of fresh chestnut purée and cream. The service was perfection and the meal half the price of comparable fare if it could be found in New York. A friend of ours suffering with intestinal gripes was served yoghurt so prettily it might have been a *specialité de la maison*.

On our last day we had a fine lunch at **El Toula**, 29B via della Lupa (678 1196), the only deluxe Italian restaurant I've ever set foot in. Indeed, there is fresh white linen underfoot at this pretty restaurant as you step down into the dining room, which is done up uncharacteristically with soft carpets and velvet chairs. The food I will inexpertly label Italian haute cuisine, and it was pricey for Rome.

Our hotel on the Aventine, the **Sant'Anselmo**, was chosen because it was near the cloistered convent of the Suore Comaldolesi in which my daughter and her friends of both sexes lived, surprisingly, in the logical cohabitation of the '80s. The Sant'Anselmo is a spotless, inexpensive hotel with stylish plumbing. Once a private villa, it is run by an obliging family. No elevator, no meals except the morning bread and butter, but it suited us perfectly. We parked our car with ease. We wandered the neighbourhood. I am an indifferent tourist (especially of a town I've lived in), and it was my sport to watch the children, deliverymen, maids and housewives of the prim Aventine come and go on their daily business. On any morning before we went forth to one of the prescribed sights, we could walk out to our own wonders down the block – the Villa of the Knights of Malta with its charming conceit, a brass peephole through which you see right over a tranquil garden to the dome of St. Peter's, or we could visit one of 'our' churches, **Sant'Alessio** belonging to the Benedictines, or **Santa Maria Aventina** remodelled after the design of Piranesi, or the very old, very beautiful **Santa Sabina**.

At Santa Sabina, our first stop on Christmas Day, I felt again the layers of history that are so demanding of foreigners in Rome. The delicate Corinthian columns inside the fifth century church are taken from a pagan temple. The old portico has carved cypress doors with one of the first representations of the Crucifixion. Bits and pieces of ancient carving and sarcophagi are stuck into the red-brown walls of the porch in that way the early Christians had of incorporating whatever was useful and decorative in their building, cleverly demystifying the fragments of Imperial Rome.

Each day walking down to via Marmorata on a real or made-up errand, we saw the same monastery walls, garden walls, remains of a castle's walls, until we began to remember slight variations in colour or contour of that old brick, this old tufa. The walls of the Aventine became one of our treasured sights. In his *Treatise on Painting* Leonardo advises us: 'If you look at old stained walls you will see on them the suggestion of landscapes, of battles, of lively figures, of strange faces and dress . . . by these confused impressions the fancy is aroused to new inventions.' I know that the spectacular wide-lens shot of Rome from the Gianiculum is much touted, but rather than the vast public roadway of the piazzale de Gianicolo I prefer to look out over the city from the belvedere next to Santa Sabina, with the fabulous implications of the Aventine walls at my back and at my side the cloisters with their insistence on an interior view.

Coming back to the Sant'Anselmo after our short trip to Venice, I began to hunker into the neighbourhood just as we were about to leave. Denied a kitchen, I tortured myself by discovering one of the best open markets in Rome just behind via Marmorata – blood oranges from Sicily, small, completely edible artichokes, milk-fed lambs. On our final day we walked our morning route, and taking a last look at Santa Sabina we saw a wedding. The bride, a stately woman in her thirties, marched in from the porch almost carelessly. She was wearing a little ermine jacket over her wedding dress against the chill of the basilica. Turning from his friends, her bridegroom smiled and led her to the priest. There was something so entirely unselfconscious about the way they used their church, an attitude of casual respect and possession that as a traveller, an American, I can never assume.

My daughter had returned to New York some days before us and she greeted us in her exuberant Italian, softening the reality of home. A year later she says that she has lost the language. I can only advise her that there is no way of assessing what remains of her months in Italy, but I know it is much more than being able to order fettuccine alla matriciana and a continuing interest in Caravaggio. It remains to be seen if I can possess the Christmas holiday this year with due reverence for tree and turkey, yet touch upon the religious nature of the season, that peace which I glimpsed away from home. Perhaps I will spend myself on five vegetables, wrap countless trinkets, but I may just walk across the street on the Nativity, through the old grey walls of Central Park, and wait under the bare branches for some shepherd from Juilliard to practise his flute.

THE JOIE DE VIVRE OF MONTREAL

Margaret Atwood

For 150 years Montreal was the only world-class Canadian city. When Toronto was a place where a snail was something you stomped on in the garden and where wine and legs, both frog and female, were viewed with puritanical horror, Montreal was dishing them all up with élan. It was the financial centre, the fur centre, the gastronomic centre, the centre. That it is no longer unchallenged is due not so much to its own falling star as to the rising stars of others. But for anyone who has ever lived there or spent time there, Montreal, with its mountain and rivers and history and ethnic mixture, will always be a special city: cosmopolitan, flavoursome, polyglot, vital, unique as a fingerprint.

You can't begin to talk about Montreal without tackling the language issue. Some travellers think they want to go to foreign places but are dismayed when the places turn out actually to be foreign. This can be especially true of Montreal, but there's no need to go into fibrillation just because the billboards are in French. The time has passed when you would be called a *maudit anglais*, or, worse, ignored, in bars, because you did not speak French well enough or indeed at all: The New Quebec language policy has brought with it a renewed sense of linguistic security. As in any foreign country you'll be appreciated if you make the effort, but no one will expect you to be other than you are. This is one part of the world where it's still an advantage to be an American, since Quebec has had a knees-under-the-table affair going with the States for some time. If in doubt, print the address for taxi drivers, which isn't a bad idea in any city. The fact is that most people you are likely to come in contact with speak English anyway.

Certainly in the hotels. There are many of these in Montreal, some distinguishable from one another, others not, still others with a touch of the bizarre. There are, for instance, the **Hilton Bonaventure,** with its plush horizontal layers and its attendants' costumes reminiscent in their hallucinatory extravagance of *The Confessions of an English Opium-Eater,* and the **Château Champlain,** which looks like a cheese grater but nevertheless houses several good restaurants. I'm told that the **Beaver Club** in the Queen Elizabeth (named after the eighteenth-century institution of that name, which was where the fur-trading gentlemen adventurers of the old North-West Company used to roister) is first choice for McGill University students when they've saved up for a special binge. I myself have a preference for the slightly musty but human-scale charms of the **Ritz Carlton,** where a wardrobe is still a wardrobe and the prevailing scent is not vinyl. May they never go modern. Their Café de Paris exists in a grand-style time warp.

In addition to the hotels, Montreal abounds with places to eat. Speaking of these is always risky, since everywhere has its off nights and chefs have a habit of playing musical kitchens. But for Montrealers food comes second only to language-and-politics as a topic of conversation, and for visitors it probably rates first. There are some cities in which you can eat well only if you have lots of money. There are others in which money makes no difference, since it's all awful anyway. Montreal, however, has a wide and happy range and a picky resident clientele. If you want to impress everyone, including yourself, with rich French cooking and equally rich atmosphere, try **Le St.-Amable,** which is a stone house in Old Montreal, that part of the city noted for its distinctive architecture. **Chez la Mère Michel** is a perennial favourite, also expensive but worth it.

The area around Crescent and Montagne used to be good for medium-range bistros and student cafés; it's now a little boutiquish, but there is still **L'Auberge St.-Tropez.** The Latin Quarter crowd has now shifted to the St.-Denis region, where you can eat very well for not as much. Try, for instance, **Le Bercail.** If you get too bogged down in hollandaise and crave something different and more informal, try **Ben's,** where the Montreal smoked meat is set off by walls full of equally smoked photos of the many luminaries who have eaten there. Greek restaurants everywhere tend to be solid for the price, and a good Montreal version is **Symposium des Dieux.** Native Montrealers in these pinched times are taking to bring-your-own-bottle restaurants, which with Montreal's excellent wine stores is no hardship. **Les Enfants du Pirée** is a successful example; it's on Duluth East, where many new restaurants are opening these days.

Note that the name of a restaurant is no longer a reliable indication of what you will find within, as all names now have to be in French – which is sometimes as if La Folie in Toronto were required to call itself The Stupidity. These regulations are enforced by a linguistic government flying squad known to resident Anglos as the Tongue Troopers.

But in a city of 3,000 restaurants it's futile to single out a few. Some help in choosing, for all price ranges, can be otained from *Where to Eat in Canada*, by Anne Hardy. This indefatigable author gobbles her way across Canada every year and gives quarter to none. It's important to get the latest edition.

No better place to purchase one – and any other book on the subject of Montreal or indeed of Canada – than in **The Double Hook/Le Crochet Double** in Westmount. This is one of those small, crammed, personally run bookshops, like Longhouse in Toronto, where you can browse, gossip, and be told what you ought to read. It was started by three Westmount matrons out of love, and has somehow flourished. It's as good a place as any to ask for advice of the where-to-buy-it variety, especially as concerns the town of Westmount. Westmount is the once-upon-a-time English-Canadian enclave of Montreal, where fur, railroad, and head-office millionaires used to progress through all the stages between ripeness and ossification. Some of them still do, and the mansions are extant and well worth a slow drive or a stroll – try the upper levels – though the area is now more linguistically diverse than it once was. Westmount is often overlooked as a place for visitors to shop for discretionary-income items, but ought not to be, since, being less tourist-conscious, it is sometimes better value.

But Montreal as a whole is good value as large cities go. It's still a place where you can walk instead of driving, where you can look without paying, where ambience is everywhere and not just in cute walled-off enclaves. For instance, explore the underground city, a useful thing to do, especially in winter, when a fur coat is anything but decoration. Montreal was one of the first cities to move to the caverns, and you can travel that way all over the city without freezing your nose. Tunnels link the many subterranean plazas, the foremost being the place Ville-Marie and the Complexe Desjardins.

Then of course there's the Metro. This ranks with that of Mexico City in the category of total-environment art-for-the-people. Toronto's subway is clean and brisk and slightly lavatorial; Montreal's, by contrast, is a luxurious visual sauna, an eyebath of muted lighting and glints of Byzantine colour, with the suave trains sneaking around on their sensuous pneumatic tyres. It's worth taking a trip to nowhere in particular just to look at the stations. My own theory is that Montreal Metro design – and much else in Montreal – is permeated with the spirit of the Catholic churches that for so long were the dominant force in Quebec. If this insight seems borderline, book a tour of the Radio-Canada building, the cathedral of Canadian communications. After you've immersed yourself in its vast, dim, reverent verticals and hushed catacombs, no doubt will remain.

For comparison purposes there are the real churches. Notre-Dame-de-Bonsecours in Old Montreal is the oldest, not to be confused with L'Eglise de Notre Dame on the place d'Armes, which is larger and ornate in the nineteenth century mode. If modern Gothic interests you, there's the Oratoire de St.-Joseph, where you may or may not see the embalmed heart of its founder, Brother André, depending on who has stolen or returned it lately. Quebec church styles, like Quebec antiques, are more baroque than their anglophone North American counterparts. If you would like to sample antiques, try the shop of Jean La Casse on Laurier West. You can have coffee afterward at La Croissanterie at Hutchinson and Fairmont and perhaps take a quiet look at Outremont, the attractive residential district that's the francophone equivalent of Westmount.

But any city is more than a sum of its architecture and furniture. Montreal is also Montrealers, and one of the best places to view these is at the theatre. Again there's a choice. The **Saidye Bronfman Center** is one of the few North American theatres where Yiddish plays are still performed. **The Centaur** is an English-speaking repertory company. Francophone theatres are legion, the classics being **Le Théâtre du Nouveau Monde** and **Le Théâtre de Quat'Sous. Le Café de la Place** has dinnertime theatre where Montrealers can do two of their favourite things at once. A visit to any of these will be more meaningful if you understand French, but if immersion makes you uneasy, sample a mime company or a dance troupe. Whether the performance is wordless or not, the facial mobility of the performers – and of their audience – is a scenario in itself, and a far cry from those twitches of the ear and tremors of the eyebrow used to signal emotion in the mature Westmount male. When you aren't watching the show, watch the audience: You'll find that the most immediately obvious thing about francophone Montrealers is that they enjoy enjoying themselves and are willing to share this pleasure with anyone willing to join in.

Montreal is one of those cities that inspire in their aficionados the kind of sentiment one feels for the other partner in a love affair that has been charming and perhaps difficult, but is not yet completely finished and over. Faded grandeur and remembrances of things past, true; but you keep thinking also that there's more to come. And with Montreal, there always is.

LODGINGS

The stately **Ritz Carlton Hotel** (514 842 4212) is at 1228 Sherbrooke Street West. Double rooms are about $110 (all prices are quoted in U.S. dollars). There are four breakfast menus served in L'Intercontinentale, with prices ranging from about $4 to about $7.50; dinner for two with wine will push beyond the $80 mark in the Café de Paris, which features an eight-course degustation menu with such specialities as galantine of duckling with chicken livers, quails with wild mushrooms, and panache of scallops with their roe and fresh salmon.

Three other major hotels are the **Hilton Bonaventure** (514 878 2332; doubles about $115), on the place Bonaventure; the **Château Champlain** (514 878 1688; doubles about $100) on the place du Canada; and the **Queen Elizabeth** (514 861 3511), at 900 Dorchester Boulevard, where doubles are about $90, and a meal for two, with wine, is about $70 in its Beaver Club restaurant. Specialities are steak and seafood, especially lobster.

QUINTESSENTIAL TABLES

Montreal has an abundance of restaurants, but four French establishments are quintessential: **Chez la Mère Michel** (514 934 0473), 1209 rue Guy, is installed in an old stone house and lists such specialities as *barquette alsacienne, tournedos béarnaise, rognons de veau*, fresh salmon, lobster soufflé Nantua; dinner for two, with wine, averages about $65.

Le St.-Amable (514 866 3471), 188 rue St.-Amable, is another converted stone house. Specialities include snails cooked with shallots in a champagne and cream sauce, rack of lamb, stuffed sole; dinner for two, with wine, is about $60.

L'Auberge St.-Tropez (514 861 3197), 1208 rue Crescent, specializes in Mediterranean fare, particularly fish (some of which is flown in from France); the fish soup with croûtons is highly recommended. There is a three-course table d'hôte dinner; a meal for two, with wine, should be about $50.

Le Bercail (514 288 4504), 1238 rue St.-Denis, has *quenelles de brochet*, tripes *à la mode de Caen*, rabbit, and sweetbreads. The table d'hôte dinners (about $7 or $8) are a good buy; an à la carte dinner for two, with wine, is about $35.

CHANGE OF PACE

Ben's Delicatessen (514 844 1001), 990 Maisonneuve Boulevard West, has all the usual deli snacks, although in unfamiliar guises: smoked meat means pastrami or corned beef, while corned beef is not smoked but boiled. A sandwich of any is about $2.

COSMOPOLITAN CITY OF
SMALL WORLDS

David Harris

When visiting San Francisco it must be remembered that the city's size hardly comes close to matching its notoriety. Both its newspapers and government stand out as ironic and occasionally embarrassing small-town counterpoints to what is otherwise an intensely cosmopolitan place. Having myself arrived here twenty years ago after an All-American adolescence in California's agricultural provinces, I must confess that those provincialisms did not meet my eye right away. I was taken by San Francisco's beauty, as is everyone, but more than anything else I was taken by its attitude.

To describe this city as 'tolerant' only scratches the surface. America's principal port to the Pacific, San Francisco has always been both the last touchstone for journeys to the unknown and a refuge for people seeking to be more different than they could have been anywhere else. Traditional mores here have always prescribed that people's civic value be calculated not so much on their activity as on the style with which they do it, and so San Francisco has a long history of lionizing eccentrics, being kind to drunks, tolerating tourists, nurturing aberrants, and giving serious consideration to even the most wacko of world views.

There is a strong case to be made that San Francisco could not live with itself without such an open-ended approach to reality. As is quickly apparent to anyone who visits, there is much differentness here. San Francisco has more Chinese, more homosexuals, and possibly more aspiring writers as a percentage of its population than any other city in the United States. It may also have more Nicaraguans, psychoanalysts, lawyers, Guatemalans, Filipinos, masseurs, M.D.s, free-lance philosophers, and natives of Samoa. Added to that are significant pockets of Irish, Italians, Pakistanis, Palestinians, Peruvians, Vietnamese, Greeks, Cambodians, Japanese, Russians, Koreans, Salvadorans and Eskimos. The consequent electricity is what gives urban life a good name. That it happens in such a small and pretty place is remarkable. That it happens with as much relative peace and mutual appreciation as it does is doubly so. For the tourist, that attitude makes San Francisco an easy place to see. It also explains why those of us who live here find it hard to leave.

A PLACE TO BEGIN

San Francisco is a succession of hills and valleys occupying the northern tip of the peninsula that forms the southern headland of San Francisco Bay. Each peak, slope, and gulch has a name and a distinct personality. None of them is by itself San Francisco, but you have to start somewhere. My favourite is the neighbourhood where Telegraph Hill and North Beach flow into each other in the city's northeast corner. Telegraph Hill was settled in the 1860s, and North Beach really used to be a beach until that indentation in the shoreline was filled in and San Francisco's financial district built on the fill. This neighbourhood is north of Chinatown, west of the Embarcadero, east of Russian Hill, and south of Fisherman's Wharf. Its best known intersection is Broadway and Columbus, but that particular corner has been given over for the last twenty years or so to tourists who are interested in 'he and she love acts' and should not be taken seriously.

The true heart of the neighbourhood is Washington Square, a small, grassy park bounded by Columbus, Union, Stockton, and Filbert streets. Late on a Sunday morning, representatives of all the neighbourhood's various strands usually put in an appearance in the square. Once a solidly blue-collar Italian place, the Filbert side of Washington Square is still dominated by the Peter and Paul Cathedral and the Union Street side by the Fior D'Italia restaurant (dinner about $7 to $15 a person without wine). The smoke shop next door to the Fior serves excellent espresso and cappuccino. The latest ethnic addition to this part of town is overflow from Chinatown.

Sandwiched between the waves of Chinese and Italians is a history of bohemianism kicked off by North Beach's beatnik era in the late 1950s. Today's incarnation of that tradition has drawn a population of young professional and literary types who use the square to walk their dogs or lie in the sun and read. Several times a year, the San Francisco Mime Troup and the Pickle Family Circus, two of the city's best outdoor entertainments, perform in Washington Square and, in October, the square houses the reviewing stands for the Columbus Day parade.

The nicest recent addition to the park's periphery is the **Washington Square Inn**, a former apartment house on the corner of Stockton and Filbert that has been made over into an exceedingly pleasant and fashionable bed and breakfast (croissants, coffee, fruit juice) establishment running $60 to $115 a day. My favourite restaurant in this part of town is the **Washington Square Bar and Grill** across Columbus. The crowd is usually sprinkled with journalists and writers of all stripes (lunch about $5 to $15 a person, dinner slightly more). The best Italian food is either the **Café Sport** on Green (lunch $4 to $6 each, dinner $8 to $16), the **North Beach Restaurant** on Stockton (lunch $4 to $9, dinner $12 to $22), or **Amelio's** on Powell, where a full dinner of appetizer, salad, entrée, dessert, and coffee, but not including wine, is about $32 to $35 a person.

Grant Avenue is the spine of the neighbourhood's street life and the best place to watch it from is either the veranda of the Savoy Tivoli or behind the window of the Café Trieste. If you are looking for something to do after dinner, walk down Columbus past Broadway to the City Lights Bookstore, the centre of beatnikism while it lasted and something of a historical landmark that still evokes memories of Ginsberg and Kerouac.

If it is before 9 pm, walk back up to Broadway and have a drink at **Enrico's**. Its outdoor tables afford a good view of tourists going next door to Finnochio's, the nation's oldest continuous transvestite floor show. If after 9 pm, proceed across the street from City Lights to **Tosca's**. The jukebox there plays nothing but opera. Its ambience has been somewhat diminished since a disco moved into the building's basement, but if you sit at the bar, it is still worth going. If after all this you want some exercise, walk back past Washington Square to Lombard and climb the hill to Coit Tower. It is as good a single view as exists in this city. The climb is arduous but the top of Telegraph Hill is an exhilarating place to catch your breath.

FOUR EXCURSIONS

Wherever you begin, San Francisco is a city made for excursions. Here are four I recommend.

1. **Stockton Street from Sacramento north**. Grant, one street east, is Chinatown's principal tourist thoroughfare, but on Stockton it is possible to get a sense of the Chinese as more than knick-knack salesmen. Chinatown is far and away the city's most densely populated region and the crush inundates Stockton every morning as residents jam the fish and vegetable markets. Crates of live frogs are stacked on the curb. At the Canton and Lee Sang fish markets, buyers stand four deep examining the day's catch and it is doubtful you'll hear any English spoken. In such an atmosphere, even the fish seem interesting.

If you get hungry, buy a box of dim sum to go ($1.50 to $3) at the **Asia Gardens** just down from Stockton on Pacific and proceed across Broadway to Washington Square and eat them on one of the benches. If you prefer Italian pastry, stop at the **Victoria Bakery** and do the same thing. If you've developed an appetite for a standard American breakfast, the **U.S. Café** near Stockton's corner with Columbus is good, relatively cheap, and will give you another look at the denizens of North Beach and Telegraph Hill. **Mama's**, on Washington Square next to the Cathedral, is cuter, but lacks the U.S. Café's character.

From Washington Square, keep following Stockton through the lower reaches of Telegraph Hill and on down the slope to the waterfront. At the end of Stockton Street, you will encounter **Pier 39**, the city's latest development to siphon off tourist money. A former shipping pier that has been transformed into two levels of shops, boutiques, fast-food stands, and restaurants, Pier 39 contains a plethora of options surrounded on three sides by water but, from a local's point of view—as is the case with most enterprises in this city targeted exclusively on tourists—almost everything at Pier 39 is overpriced and overdone. The fun house is the only permanent part of Pier 39 I can recommend, and that largely because the city's once great carnival, Playland at the Beach, has been long since torn down in a classic example of civic idiocy. If you walk as far as Pier 39, however, you will at least stand a chance of finding a cab for the ride back.

2. **The Hyde Street Cable Car to Aquatic Park**. I have not ridden a cable car in fifteen years, but you will probably want to. If you do, take the Hyde line that ends at a strip of grass on the city's northern shoreline.

To the east is the Cannery and Fisherman's Wharf. To the west is Ghirardelli Square. Go along Ghirardelli's lower edge and by the time you reach the end, you're at Aquatic Park, a strip of beach that curves around an inlet whose mouth is half spanned by the Muni Pier. Take the stairs between the grandstand and the Maritime Museum and, once down on the sand, take a good look at the museum. It is small and the exhibits uninspired, but the building itself has the cleanest of 1930s lines and is totally appropriate to its setting, so much so that my mind has almost ceased to distinguish it from the beach it borders. Following the walkway toward the pier, you may see swimmers training for the annual swim around Alcatraz. Don't be fooled into thinking about swimming yourself. The water is numbing, even on the warmest of San Francisco days.

The Muni Pier begins right after the Sea Scout clubhouse. You'll find no amusements here. This is an amateur fisherman's pier and a wide cross-section of the city's residents spend their weekends on Muni trying to beach a meal or two. The persistent succeed and, from my observation, the Chinese and the Samoans usually end up with the most fish. A walk along the pier provides a magnificent view of the bay and the Golden Gate. On any weekend, sailboats are racing and from 2 pm until the sun goes down beat their way back upwind toward the Marin County yacht harbours.

As you leave the pier, a paved trail leads up the hill to the right. If

you take it, you're in Fort Mason, a former Army base now incorporated in the Golden Gate National Recreation Area. Its former
warehouses and barracks have been given over to nonprofit groups
and the courtyards between them host events ranging from exhibitions
of historic farm machinery to Vietnam Veterans fairs. The westernmost row of buildings also houses **Greens**, one of the city's best
restaurants. Run by San Francisco's Zen Center, its breads and
vegetarian cuisine are among the finest in the country, its views of the
bay extraordinary, and it encourages diners to sit and talk long after
they've finished eating. Greens is also the hardest table in town to get
and currently is taking reservations with a two-month lead time. A
lunch at Greens is less than $10 and dinner, from a set menu on Friday
and Saturday only, less than $20. If you can't secure a table, return to
Ghirardelli Square.

Ghirardelli is a shopping and restaurant complex built on three
levels in and around an enormous old brick chocolate factory on the
side of the slope bordering the beach. It is an example of commercial
restoration at its best. The options are abundant and they are by and
large of high quality. Evidence can be seen in the large number of San
Francisco residents who frequent it. If you are at Ghirardelli and
hungry, **Modesto Lanzone's** on the main plaza has excellent Italian
food at $12 to $15 a person at lunch, $15 to $20 at dinner. If you'd like
to see the city's latest Manhattan transplant, try **Maxwell's Plum**, if
you can get a table by the windows overlooking Aquatic Park. (Lunch
$8 to $14, dinner $15 to $25.)

3. **Polk Street from Geary north**. San Francisco's tolerance of
open homosexuality is in the foreground of its current national image.
South of Geary, where Polk abuts the Tenderloin, is better to avoid,
but northward is a pleasant walk. As with the Castro district, Polk's
street life is constant and uninhibited. You will pass a couple of
excellent small bookshops and a mélange of restaurants, bars, and
clothing stores. If you want to eat on this stretch of Polk, try **Swann's
Oyster Bar** for seafood in an informal setting.

I like to keep walking north across Broadway where Lower Polk
gives way to Upper Polk. Upper Polk provides the shopping and
restaurant district for the western slope of Russian Hill. It has several
fine bars and a selection of French, Chinese, and Vietnamese restaurants. In the 2300 block, you'll find **Casablanca**, in my opinion the
best dinner spot on either end of Polk. Both the poached salmon and
pepper steak are as good as can be had anywhere in town. It serves
dinner only ($8 to $16).

4. **Rent a car for at least a day**. It is the best way to experience the
full sweep of San Francisco's natural setting. Be sure you have a good
map and don't be intimidated by the hills. They are easier to navigate

than you might imagine.

I would begin by driving through Golden Gate Park. Though more run down that it once was, it is still one of the world's premier urban green spaces. If you want to stop, go to the **Academy of Sciences**. It is tiny by international standards, but its exhibits are well done. Travelling national exhibits like Tut and Tiffany are shown at the **De Young Museum**, which faces the Academy across an open area crowned with a band stand at its west end. During the weekend, there are regular musical performances that make a pleasant background for a picnic.

From Golden Gate Park, follow 19th Avenue north toward the Golden Gate Bridge, take the last exit before the bridge itself, and wind down through the Presidio, following the signs to Fort Point. Part of the Golden Gate National Recreation Area, three-storey brick **Fort Point** was the main American defensive installation at the bay's mouth for the last half of the nineteenth century. It is now completely restored and a historical monument that hosts both permanent and visiting military history exhibitions. Once you've seen the fort itself, walk around its base to the westernmost edge of the rock plateau it sits on. This is an inevitably windy spot and the waves crashing below will give you strong hints about the power of the ocean opening up to the windward. Then look up at the bridge. This is still one of the world's loveliest spans. Driving across, it is easy to forget what it took to build and the perspective from Fort Point is the best reminder I know.

From Fort Point, get back on Highway 101 North, cross the bridge, take the first exit on the other side, and follow the signs to the Golden Gate National Recreation Area. This piece of the GGNRA was once a military reservation known as Fort Cronkhite and is entered through a long one-way tunnel controlled by a stop light. When you emerge from the tunnel, you will be in a valley that wriggles toward the ocean and is flanked by a high ridge of its left. Take one of the roads that climbs the ridge and explore. This is the bay's northern headland and the view from almost anywhere along it is panoramic. My favourite spot in this high ground is the abandoned concrete bunker complex and artillery emplacement designed to fend off the expected Japanese invasion during the first six months of World War II. The road that winds along the bay side of the ridge will take you back to the bridge and along it are vantage points commanding the entire north end of San Francisco, as well as the Golden Gate.

IF YOU HAVE TIME

Mission Street within four blocks either way of 24th was formerly working-class Irish and is now solidly Central and South American. The street life is continuous and the Mission District offers a wide variety of Latin American food.

The homes in Pacific Heights (Washington between Webster and the Presidio) are among the most imposing – and expensive – in the country.

The bay is truly impressive and any of the blue or red cruise ships or ferry lines from Fisherman's Wharf or the Ferry Building will do. Perhaps the best of the tours is the one of Alcatraz, but it is often booked up weeks ahead. Call 415 546 2805. If you have time on your hands afterward, tour the Balclutha, an old square-rigger turned museum on Fisherman's Wharf.

Haight Street between Masonic and Golden Gate Park gave birth to the hippies and was the scene of the Summer of Love in 1967. By 1970, the hippies had left and the neighbourhood was buried under an onslaught of lowriders and methedrine addicts. It has revived itself over the last few years and seems destined to be the next new shopping and eating thoroughfare.

INSIDE TIPS

If you don't want to sound like a tourist, don't call it 'Frisco.' If you say 'the City,' natives will know what you mean and may even mistake you for one of them.

Don't buy sourdough bread at the airport. It's a dead giveaway.

Give San Francisco its due. Those of us who live here are used to being dismissed at points east as no more than an outpost of oddities. Though being seen through the prism of our latest outrageous fringe is obviously something San Franciscans have come to expect, we resent it on our home turf. Being tolerant and being serious about what you do are by no means antithetical. Among the area's more recent contributions to the culture at large are the bank card, the space shuttle, the microprocessor industry, the artificial memory revolution, the physical fitness craze, *Godfathers I* and *II*, *Star Wars*, Mork, the heart-lung transplant, the human potential movement, the T- Formation, the video game, and the Sierra Club. We like to think the rest of the country would be lost without us.

QUEBEC CITY'S PRIME TIME

Mordecai Richler

In a Canada justifiably better known for its spaces rather than its places, we have for the most part built nondescript utilitarian cities (say Edmonton or Calgary), anchored against the wind rather than rooted in history, with little to delight the eye. There are two shining exceptions to this rule, Montreal, or what remains of it now that the developers have had their way, and Quebec City, still happily intact.

Rising out of Cape Diamant, an eight-mile-long plateau of solid rock, North America's only walled city soars over the narrows of the St. Lawrence, its Citadel and Château Frontenac – perched 200 feet above the shore – commanding the river and its approaches. Gazing down from its heights more than a hundred years ago, Charles Dickens noted the motley crowd of gables, roofs, and chimney tops and the beautiful St. Lawrence sparkling and flashing in the sunlight. 'It formed,' he concluded, 'one of the rightest and most enchanting pictures the eye can rest upon.' And so it does, even today. Especially in the winter, after a heavy snowfall has mantled the town, making it literally glow by night.

French and English Quebecers, currently at odds, have at least one thing in common – a punishing climate. Spring, such as it is here, can come and go in an afternoon. If you're not careful, you can doze right through it. One day the snows are blowing and the next everything has melted to mush, daffodils poking through here and there and the ice cracking up on the rivers. The next day it's summer. Short, sharp, and hot. Late in July (yes) the leaves have already begun to turn and the first blizzard can come early in November, bringing on our longest season, the six months of winter. If every country has a natural state, a season calculated to test its soul, then in Quebec it is certainly the winter. The most famous song by the province's unofficial poet laureate, Giles Vigneault, begins, properly enough, '*Mon pays c'est l'hiver.*'

Not to worry. In Quebec City, out of necessity, they have learned to thrive on winter, providing just the right mixture of sports and cafés and piano bars and hearty cuisine to take the sting out of it. Right outside the Château Frontenac, on the Dufferin Terrace, a gracious Victorian boardwalk overlooking the river, you can – if you are sufficiently intrepid – slide down the giant toboggan run, or skate on the outdoor rink. You can also skate, snowshoe, or sleighride on the almost two-mile-long rink on the frozen St. Charles River. Or, if you prefer, watch the dashing National Hockey League Nordiques skate at the Colisée. Or, if it's even thinner ice and fancier play that grabs you, you can take in a debate in the National Legislature.

Excellent downhill and cross-country ski runs are available less than an hour's drive from the city centre: Lac Beauport, Stoneham, Le Relais, and Parc du Mont Ste.-Anne, the last being the biggest ski complex in eastern Canada, as well as the only one equipped with four-passenger gondola aerial lifts. Mont Ste.-Anne also offers fifty miles of cross-country trails with 'eight heat refuges' and a welcoming post with a bar. Make that nine heat refuges.

After a day out in all that invigorating fresh air, your ears burning – your nostrils sticking together – your feet still there (if you look down to check) but now devoid of all feeling – there is nothing like a traditional French-Canadian meal to set you right again. Try **Aux Anciens Canadiens**, in a restored house built in 1675, on rue St. Louis. It offers *fèves au lard* (pork and beans), *soupe aux pois* (yellow pea soup), *tourtière* (minced-meat pie), and *tarte à la ferlouche* (molasses pie). Also highly recommended: hare stewed in apple cider and the duck in maple syrup.

If you are in the mood for something more formal, there is **Le Continental**, also on the rue St. Louis, or **Café Bonaparte**, housed in a beautiful stone building, circa 1823, on the Grande-Allée, the Upper Town's most stately street. Both these restaurants, reasonably priced old favourites – though the wine list can come as a shocker – specialize in haute cuisine. Snacks and more modest fare – say Gaspé salmon quiche – can be had at **Café le Rétro** on rue St. Jean, while the **Café la Siesta**, nearby on côte de la Fabrique, serves a fine salade Niçoise.

And available just about everywhere is a truly rare delicacy indigenous to La Belle Province. I speak of that dish now officially decreed here as hamburgeois, courtesy of the guardians of our linguistic purity – l'Office de la Langue Française, otherwise known as the Tongue Troopers – but still called hamburger elsewhere. Even, come to think of it, in France.

Quebec City is not only where our history begins, it is also at the core of our present problems. Some 20 per cent of Quebec's 6.2 million citizens would like the province to declare independence from the rest of Canada, while roughly a third of the Quebecois would settle for something called sovereignty-association, a nebulous concept unacceptable to the rest of Canada, which would be asked to guarantee the new country's currency and passports. The government in office in Quebec City at this writing, the Parti Quebecois, led by an increasingly combative Premier René Levesque, has pledged to fight the next election directly on an independence platform, something it hasn't dared to do before.

This, mind you, is a gesture more rhetorical than real. The political quarrel here, however deeply felt on both sides, does not impinge on the natural hospitality of the continent's only real French-speaking city. American visitors are welcome everywhere, and they will find the charming bilingual staff at the provincial tourist office in place d'Armes especially helpful in guiding them toward reasonably priced European-style pensions.

Quebec City, originally an Indian village called Stadacona, was discovered by a happy fluke. When Jacques Cartier, the seafarer from St. Malo in Brittany, landed there in 1534, it was a direct water route to India and Cathay he was after, not beaver pelts or *whisky blanc*. The city proper was founded in 1608, a fur-trading post established by Samuel de Champlain, and from here – and later Montreal – the legendary *voyageurs* ventured by canoe as far as Hudson Bay, the great Mackenzie River beyond the prairies, and the shores of the Arctic, in search of beaver pelts. Another official, the astute Jean Baptiste Talon, first intendant of the colony, conceived the idea of importing shiploads of orphaned girls from France for the settlers, *'les filles du roi.'*

'After the regiment of Cartignan was disbanded,' a French officer wrote home, 'ships were sent out freighted with girls of indifferent virtue, under the direction of a few pious duennas, who divided them into three classes. These vestals were, so to speak, piled in three different halls, where the bridegroom chose his bride as a butcher chooses his sheep out of a flock. There was wherewith to content the most fastidious; for here were to be seen the tall and the short, the blonde and the brown, the plump and the lean; everybody, in short, found a shoe to fit him. The next day the Governor caused the couple to be presented with an ox, a cow, a pair of swine, a pair of fowls, two barrels of salted meat and 11 crowns in money.'

'*Je me souviens,*' the melancholy motto of the province, is inscribed in flowers in Quebec City in the gardens of place d'Armes. And what the Quebecois remember above all else is the conquest of 1759 and the struggle on the Plains of Abraham, their Wailing Wall. After a two-month siege, but a battle that lasted only twenty minutes on the windswept plains on September 13, 1759, General Wolfe's army, having scaled the cliffs under cover of darkness, took the city for the British, settling a country's fate. Both Montcalm, the French commander, and Wolfe were slain in the battle. Now they share a common monument in the Jardin des Gouverneurs, just below the Château

Frontenac. Its inscription reads: 'Valour gave them a common death, history a common fame, posterity a common monument.'

Quebec City's skyline is dominated by the green copper roof, the spires, the portcullis, dormer windows, castlelike turrets and uncertain plumbing of the Château Frontenac. Before the turn of the century the hotel was built on the site of the Château Saint-Louis, once the residence of the governors of New France, among them Louis de Buade, the fiery comte de Frontenac.

Poor Frontenac. He abandoned the pleasures of the court of Louis XIV at the age of sixty-two once his beautiful wife, a grudgy type, denied him access to her bed. After he died, at the age of seventy-eight, his heart was carved out and sent to Madame la comtesse. But she spurned the little silver casket, saying she had never had her husband's heart when he was living and didn't want it now that he was dead.

The celebrated Château Frontenac is not the only first-class hotel in Quebec City. There are also the Hilton, Loew's and Auberge des Gouverneurs, but they lack the Château's special sense of place, its lofty baronial lobby, its dark-panelled walls, its splendid bar overlooking the river, and its unrivalled location. The Château Frontenac, after all, is Quebec City, and, speaking for myself, I can't imagine staying anywhere else, though I've never checked in, as Charles Lindbergh once did, swinging two parachutes after having landed a small plane on the Plains of Abraham.

The hotel reeks of recent as well as old history. In 1943, Churchill and Roosevelt both stayed there, allowing our very own wee Willy, that is to say Prime Minister William Lyon Mackenzie King, actually to sit next to them for photo opportunities. The fifteenth-floor Fontenac Suite, good enough for Emperor Haile Selassie of Ethiopia and his little chihuahua (they dined alone, the dog sitting in an upholstered chair opposite his master), did not suit Charles de Gaulle. De Gaulle, who had an aversion to lifts, attended a state dinner there in 1967 but laid his head to rest elsewhere.

Most of the historical sites in town are within a calèche ride or walking distance from the hotel. And immediately above it looms the Citadel, built on the ruins of seventeenth century French fortifications against the threat of an American invasion. Fortunately, the Citadel, once considered to be impregnable, has never been tested under enemy fire. However, should the uppity Americans ever take into their heads to attack, let them be warned that, in the event of a siege, acid rainwater can still be stored in protected reservoirs.

Lower Town, the old city hard by the base of the cliff, can be reached by descending the Breakneck Stairs of Mountain Hill or by taking a lift from Dufferin Terrace, just in front of the Château. From the lift, a brief walk through charming, narrow, 300-year-old streets will lead you to the place Royale, meticulously restored to its seventeenth and eighteenth century grandeur. Notre-Dame-des-Victoires, one of the oldest stone churches in North America, dominates the square. There is also a restored inn, Maison Chevalier, now a museum, with a splendid collection of early French-Canadian pine furniture and Beaudoin house, where the founder of Detroit, Antoine de la Mothe Cadillac, lived.

Lower Town, it should be remembered, is the site of Champlain's original settlement. Once it was a thriving port and a centre for fur trading and lumbering, a town whose wooden houses were razed by winter fires again and again. In those early days, the settlers were convinced that steep cliffs could never be populated. Then, the conquering British Army engineers came along and they began to build in brick and stone. The lives of the working class in Lower Town, during the years leading up to World War II, are celebrated in two rambunctious novels by Roger Lemelin, *The Town Below* and *The Plouffe Family*.

In Upper Town, avoid the main commercial streets, thick with garish souvenir shops, pathetically crude wood carvings of 'merry habitants,' and incredibly bad paintings by local 'artists.' Instead, plunge into the narrow back streets, wandering in any direction, and find yourself in what could be a very handsome French provincial town. Across the street from the City Hall, at the corner of Buade and côte de la Fabrique, there is the Basilica of Notre-Dame, built in 1647. The Upper Town also boasts the first cathedral of the Church of England ever built outside the British Isles, the Anglican Cathedral of the Holy Trinity, completed in 1804 at the personal expense of King George III.

Unless you have a taste for unbridled whoopee, a word of warning. If Quebec City is at its best in the wintertime, it should be avoided for ten days starting the first Thursday in February, Carnaval de Quebec time, when the hotels are overcrowded and the yahoos are out whooping it up everywhere, guzzling *caribou*, a potent mixture of cheap red wine and distilled alcohol, usually carried in fifteen-ounce plastic canes with removable tops.

To be fair, however, during Carnaval there are parades in both Upper and Lower Town, boat races across the ice-clogged St. Lawrence, costume balls, and dog-sled races. There's a ten-kilometre foot-race, stock-car racing in the snow, and a international snow-sculpture competition that draws teams from such unlikely places as China, Mexico, and Morocco. And, of course, there's the huge snow palace in the Parc de l'Esplanade. But there are also drunken, jostling crowds everywhere and Quebec City, to my mind, was not made for forced, desperate gaiety decreed by a chamber of commerce, but for the quiet contemplative walk.

Wandering through the exquisite twisting streets of Quebec City, head tucked into my collar against the punishing wind, I had to allow, grudgingly, that for all its present political silliness – the vengeful and tribal Parti Quebecois, their perverse language laws – I couldn't live anywhere else in Canada but in this province. Without Quebec and Quebecers, this Canada – this root cellar of a country – if not exactly an empty house, would certainly lack for a salon. So far as one can generalize, the French Canadians are among the most cultivated and spirited people in the country.

Quebec City is a very special place.

'The impression,' Charles Dickens wrote, 'made upon the visitor by this Gibraltar of North America, its giddy heights, its citadel suspended, as it were, in the air; its picturesque steep streets and frowning gateways; and the splendid views which burst upon the eye at every turn, is at once unique and lasting.'

PRIME TIME HINTS
Grand Hotel
Château Frontenac (reservations: 418 692 3861) has double rooms for an average of about $100 (all prices listed are in U.S. dollars); those with river views are somewhat more expensive, and should be requested in advance. One-bedroom suites are about $220 a night and two-bedroom suites are about $310. The Frontenac Suite, which has a king-sized bed and a sitting room with both river and city views, is approximately $320 a night.

FRESH AIR AND EXERCISE
Parc de Mont Ste.-Anne, twenty-five miles east of Quebec City, opens for the season in mid-November. Lift tickets are about $15 a day, or about $30 for a weekend pass, good Saturday and Sunday. Information: 418 827 4561.

FOOD AND DRINK
Aux Anciens Canadiens, 34 rue St. Louis, has table d'hôte meals for about $15 a person for four courses, without wine. Open daily. Reservations: 418 692 1627 or 418 692 0253.
Le Continental, 26 rue St. Louis, has specialities that range from sweetbreads madère to flambéed steak au poivre. A three-course meal for two, with wine, averages about $40. Closed on Sunday from November to February. Reservations: 418 694 9995.
Café Bonaparte, 680 Grande Allée, lists on its menu such seasonal specialities as game dishes and medallions of veal with wild mushrooms. A meal for two, with wine, averages about $40. Open daily. Reservations: 418 522 4704.

THE
OUTDOOR LIFE

CLASSIC TYROL

James Salter

There are places one loves without ever seeing them, usually because they have been written about. There are pages that never fail to stir the blood. 'Sizzling down the long black liquid stretches of Nationale Sept,' as Cyril Connolly once wrote of France, 'the plane trees going sha-sha-sha through the open window, the windscreen yellowing with crushed midges, she with the Michelin beside me, a handkerchief binding her hair . . . ' Very few writers can appeal to the senses so, and of course Hemingway is one of them. It was he who introduced me, I think, to the idea of long, secluded winters and the mountain villages in which, during the 1920s, he spent them.

Hemingway wove his cloth with names. The race tracks – San Siro, Enghien, St. Cloud. The cities – Milan, San Sebastian, Key West. In the late autumn, he said, when the bad weather came, he would leave Paris with his wife and small son and go to a place where the rain would become snow, coming down through the pines and creaking beneath their feet as they walked home at night in the cold. He spent his winters in Schruns, which is in the Vorarlberg, the part of Austria closest to Switzerland. He wrote about skiing there and in the Silvretta, at Kitzbühel, and in the Engadine. He worked on *The Sun Also Rises* in Schruns. He made me like skiing although I never dreamed I would really ski.

That was some time ago.

It's astonishing how things change if you live long enough. Restaurants that were absolute fixtures in New York like Chambord and the Café Chauveron are gone and so are galleries like Peter Deitsch's, hotels, theatres, even stadiums and streets. A whole new crowd comes in and is standing at the bar in new places, arrogant and stylish. Meanwhile, schools have disappeared, barbers, doormen. One looks around for things that are still there. There are some. One of them is the mountains in Austria where the good skiing is, in the Tyrol, the province just after the Vorarlberg, where skiing as we know it got started.

There are two great skiing places in the Tyrol, one at the very west end of it and one at the east. They are St. Anton and Kitzbühel, the beginning and end of skiing. This is in more than the figurative sense since St. Anton was where, in 1907, Hannes Schneider first instructed tourists in the system which became known as the Arlberg technique, the basis of modern downhill skiing. One of the largest and probably the best ski schools in the world is still there, with about 300 instructors at the height of the season, most of whom speak English.

As for Kitzbühel, it was a mythic resort of the 1930s and at the cost of very little of its charm has become the largest and best ski station in Austria. The medieval town is still there with its narrow streets and sturdy houses, the cable car is just a short walk up, skis over your shoulder and boots biting the crisp snow. A day of utterly simple things lies ahead, sunlight, icy pure air, the exhilaration of dropping effortlessly down trails through the black firs and larches; these pleasures, as Colette said, that one lightly calls physical.

The Tyrol is made up almost entirely of mountains cut by small Alpine valleys. An ancient farming area, much of the skiing is through upper meadows that have been cleared of trees. For a long time, until the eighteenth century, it was isolated and virtually pagan, and farmers on the inhospitable heights were exempt from taxes and military service. The people are honest, hardworking and independent, deeply rooted in their heritage. Tradition is powerful.

I learned to ski in St. Anton, at least I suffered my first humiliations there. At the end of those two weeks I knew something, mainly how difficult it was. The next year I went back and stayed in St. Christoph, a village nearby. With an instructor whose name I still remember after twenty-five years, I felt for the first time the thrill of what it could be like and went with him down pitches at the top of which he warned, Don't fall here or you'll go all the way to the bottom. The sweetness of hearing him behind me saying '*Ja, ja,*' as I did something right was overwhelming. He was a country boy as so many of them are, quiet and even-tempered, and from that time on I knew how to ski, although I had to work fifteen more seasons before I came to feel that I would never be getting any better.

Skiing, like sailing, is a world unto itself. Its glories are nearly indestructible. It embraces one entirely. It is a journey that follows a journey and leads one through days of almost mindless exertion and unpunished joy. Though countless skiers have been down the trails before, it seems they are still unconquered. Often as you stand looking down some steep pitch you have never set foot on, stoically preparing yourself, someone else or a pair will flash by and start down on a line even more difficult than the one you have nervously been considering, doing it in short, expert turns and suddenly giving you the confidence to do the same, now, before the mountain recovers itself, so to speak. And then miraculously, down the fall line, finding the rhythm somehow, leaving everything behind, the slope vanishing like silk beneath your skis – the hardest part is over. The sense of triumph is overwhelming.

It would be perfect if it were not for the crowds but, except in cross-country skiing, these you find everywhere now and with civilization. The days of meeting woodcutters in mountain towns and staying at undiscovered hotels for the winter are over; the disillusioned, less populous Europe of between the wars will not come back. Filled with people as it is, the Tyrol still has three great virtues which promise happiness: It is beautiful, friendly and cheap. Rooms, meals, lift tickets, taxis, discothèques all cost about half of what they are in the States.

In the hotels the rooms are clean and comfortable, especially in the older ones, and the linen crisp. There are still large staffs. They are young, most of them, waiters and busboys. In the off hours they are usually sitting in the kitchen or in a room just outside it. The eternal relationships exist. At the front desk a couple of years ago a tall, well-made girl was working. She was from another town. She wore flowered dresses and her hair was done with the careful elegance of cheap magazines. From the office she was visible to the owner, seated at his desk. He could see her reach back for a key or lean over to read a bus schedule on the counter. He kept the door ajar and pretended to be at work. Occasionally he would find some reason to admonish her. He was forty, the age of longing.

The Tyrol used to be much larger, but the southern part was ceded to Italy after the First World War. In their hearts the Austrians have never given up the lost portion. Almost all of them have relatives there and many still own land or houses. South Tyrol is wine-growing country and when you have a bottle of wine in Kitzbühel or St. Anton they call it 'our wine.'

It was the English who discovered the Tyrol and, as they did in so many other places, first made it fashionable. Since the last war and the waning of their fortunes they have retreated and been replaced by the Germans, many of them from around Munich, which, with the fine new roads, is just a few hours to the north. A few English are still around, of course, with their distinctive faces and pale complexions. There is a certain class of them that never changes. I was sitting in the bar one evening when a young English couple came in. She was wearing a very tight cloche hat. She had a wide jaw and eyes with a lot of black, very striking. She was talking about the Austrians and right away she used the word 'enigma' several times. She wasn't just a mannequin, you see. She had her own ideas and was expressing them in a clear voice, the way the English do, as if their language as well as their customs were impenetrable.

I like Kitzbühel for many reasons. One is the feel of it. Like ancient seabeds it is made up of many layers. There are the fashionable visitors from Munich and Vienna, the French and English, the families, the single men who are there for the winter. There is the centre of town with all its activity, the sporting-goods shops, boutiques, Café Praxmair, the large hotels, the sled ponies waiting patiently beneath their blankets, frozen breath rising slowly above their heads. But there are also the small, cosy pensions lost in the snow, with their rooms, as Proust said, whose odours indicate a whole secret system of life. There are the quiet hotels up by the cable car – the Alpina and Hahnenhof – the many moderately priced places like the Eggerwirt, the Tyrol, and the Klausner at the railway station. Kitzbühel lies in a large loop of track that carries, along with more ordinary trains, the Arlberg Express, which stops at St. Anton, Innsbruck and here on its way down from the Channel and Paris. Unfortunately it reaches Kitzbühel in the afternoon when you are up on the mountain. There are not many things as evocative as the sound of a crack train passing the hotel at night. It is something distinctly European that simply does not exist at home, like cathedrals, concierges and currency exchange. If you have never known it, your life is the poorer.

The vast, linked system of ski runs and lifts covers two separate mountains, the Hahnenkamm on one side and the Horn on the other. The Horn has easier runs and fewer people. The Hahnenkamm, for which the most famous downhill race in the world is named – it is held here every year in January as part of the World Cup – has lift connections with a number of neighbouring mountains as well and some unforgettable runs that go for miles, like the Fleck, and end up in other villages from which the return is by bus or taxi.

St. Anton is somewhat different. Like Wimbledon or St. Andrews, it is nearly a shrine. Far smaller than Kitzbühel, it has only about 1,700 inhabitants, though in the winter it seems the whole world is there. There are many who are learning to ski, those who ski very well, and others who return every year. So it has great crowds, animation, the Post Hotel and some of the most demanding runs in Europe. It is higher up than Kitzbühel, though not high by the standards of the American west, and has a greater vertical drop. The Galzig and the Valluga rise above with their classic runs, and there is the Grampen, which is somewhat easier. Around the corner from all this, as it were, is St. Christoph, not particularly pleasing to the eye and consisting mostly of hotels. The lifts connect to the St. Anton network. Although it is a village that was a haven for travellers caught in storms on the pass as far back as the fifteenth century, St. Christoph does not possess either the style or charm of St. Anton but does have excellent skiing and fewer people.

There is New York in winter, crowded and cold, 'narrow and tall on all sides, full of traffic, accident, commerce and adultery,' as Delmore Schwartz described it, 'its belly veined with black subways, its towers and bridges grand, numb, and without meaning.' Only hours away in this new age, a night's doze across the ocean, and you are driving out of Zürich in the morning, in winter silence, the trees white in the fog. Soon you enter a different world, calm and unchanging, barns with stones on the roof, towns built around churches. Roads lead off through the snowfields to distant farmhouses, their serenity lasting through generations.

Man occasionally makes something beautiful, God nearly always. It seems that these mountains are like that. The ski towns lie at the foot of them, coming to life in the dusk. Tomorrow you will be kicking off your bindings after the last run of the day, legs weary, lungs and soul purged, and trudging slowly downhill to comfort that is like a timeless dream of home. Then there is the next day and the day after that and on and on until two weeks are up, or three, and suddenly it's time to leave, that soon. People are driving into town as you depart, fresh faces glimpsed through the windshield, those for whom it is just beginning.

'And we'll do all that and Saint Moritz, too?' as someone in Hemingway says.

'Saint Moritz? Don't be vulgar. Kitzbühel you mean. You meet people like Michael Arlen at Saint Moritz.'

KITZBÜHEL TRADITIONAL
Tyrol Through the Night

Kitzbühel hotels may be booked by writing to the hotel in care of A-6370 Kitzbühel, Austria. Rates quoted are for demi-pension, a room with breakfast and one other meal.

Visitors to Kitzbühel for whom skiing is the thing may wish to choose from a number of simple, often family-run accommodations. Rates are about $30 a person at the rustic **Hahnenhof** (5356 2582), just outside town; about $20 a person at the **Gasthaus Eggerwirt** (5356 2455), in the centre of the old town; a bit more at the **Tyrol** (5356 2468), also in the centre, and about $25 a person at the larger **Klausner** (5356 2136), near the railway station.

The **Zur Tenne** (5356 4444) is *the* meeting place in town. About eighty guests can be accommodated in several contiguous pastel-coloured houses. Rooms are about $75 a person, including breakfast; ten have open fireplaces.

Schloss Lebenberg (5356 4301), a restored castle just outside town, is a self-contained resort with a glass-enclosed swimming pool, a restaurant and live music at night; about $60 a person, including breakfast.

AFTER SKIING HAHNENKAMM

The best dining in Kitzbühel is a combination of French and Austrian food. Meals for two with local wines should run to about $25-$30 at the following restaurants. The Grill at the **Goldener Greif** (5356 4311) is popular and good. Also in the centre of town is **La Cave** (5356 3435), mostly French dishes, with prices that run higher than the others on this list (figure $45-$75 or so for dinner for two), and **Zinnkrug** (5356 2613), mostly Austrian. **Unterbergstuben** (5356 2101), in a Tyrolean house, offers excellent versions of Tyrolean specialities. Reservations must be made several days in advance. Another restaurant housed in its own country house is **Schweden Kapelle** (5356 5870), eight minutes by car from the centre of Kitzbühel, with international and Austrian food, at about $40 to $50.

NOUVELLE VAIL

Peter Benchley

I was sitting in my garret, composing vanity licence plates for panjandrums (a part-time enterprise for which I am kept on a modest retainer by a mogul of my acquaintance) when the door was slammed open and the portal clogged by a giant of a man – at least, I assumed there was a man concealed somewhere inside the cocoon of pre-moulded plastic and polyester wimples.

The horrid vision spoke, in a voice that sounded like a Utah mud slide: 'Word has come down the lift line that you are preparing a paean to Vail, Colorado.'

I was stunned, like an ox felled by a maul. How could he have known?

When I did not reply, this anthropophagite strode in his custom-made Strolz ski boots across the forlorn parquet with tread so heavy that the girders trembled and, with a Rossignol down-filled fist that must have been imported in a tin from Westphalia, flung upon my escritoire a calling card.

'Captain Snowplow, Righter of Wrongs,' he said redundantly, for precisely thus did the card peg him.

'*Sans blague,*' I ventured, gazing up at where a face might reasonably have been expected to reside but where, in this case, I saw only my own visage reflected in Carrera goggles.

'It has come to my client's attention,' he began, and instanter the stench of litigation filled the room. My fingers danced impulsively toward the Touch-Tone to alert my solicitors.

I stayed my hand, however, and instead inquired with studied insouciance, 'And who is this client, Captain?'

'I represent . . .' he paused for melodramatic effect '. . . skiing. The winter wonderland. Purple mountains' majesty, from sea to shining sea.'

'I bet that's worth a couple of bucks,' I said, scrambling to recall if my umbrella policy covered class actions by an entire way of life. 'And what's your beef?'

'We are led to believe that this valentine to Vail, this nauseating encomium, will appear in the pages of the public gazette.'

'Nauseating! See here, Snowplow . . . ' I was bristling like a stoat as I rose to a level with his Fila sweater. 'My work has been dubbed jejune, vapid, even utterly without redeeming social value. But nauseating, never! Sir, you have gone too far.'

'I have gone too far,' he agreed, deflated. 'It's the heat. To have to wear a Bogner parka in an overheated garret . . .'

I relented. 'Why not take off a few layers and join me in a cup of Take-A-Break herb tea, and we'll discuss this man to man?'

'I can't,' he mewed. 'I am Bogner and Fila, Strolz and Rossignol, Kaestle and Head and Lange. Without them, I don't exist. Don't you see, poetaster? I am skiing.'

I could sympathize. After all, Barry Manilow got some distance claiming he is music; Helen Reddy bruits it about that she is woman. And truth to tell, there have been days when I know for sure that I am gin.

'The point is, scribe, skiing is the world! To write about one mountain is intellectual fiddlesticks. Skiing is the sparkling meadows of Switzerland, the glacial plains of New Zealand, the serpentine trails of Vermont.' Thinking he had me in rhapsodic thrall, the captain shifted gears into Jesuit low. 'To single out one mountain for praise is like choosing one wine as the world's most piquant, one painting as art's paradigm, or to descend to a level where, perhaps, you feel more at home, like selecting one automobile as the grooviest on the planet.'

I was warming to the Socratic fencing and so ignored the attempted kulturschlock. 'I would compare it, rather, to the selection of a tennis racquet. The variety seems infinite – of style, of shape, of weight and resilience and feel. But for each player there is only one with a perfect sweet spot. In skiing, for me . . .' – the grace with which I was about to score a knockdown dazzled even me – '. . . the sweet spot is Vail.'

'But why?' he reeled.

'It's huge. Sixty miles of trails . . .'

'Mammoth is bigger.'

'. . . eighteen lifts, more runs than a bear has hairs, 435 certified instructors, 225 acres of snowmaking . . .'

'Philistine! Is that all it is with you, the bigger the better? What about challenge? Come with me to Snowbird, and I will show you pain.'

'I want to live, Snowplow! In Vail, we can all live according to skiing's golden rule: *chacun à son goût*. I got kids who like to go down a slope like a lift shaft with zits, they have fun. I got houseguests who like a long lunch with a flagon or two of bubbly at the Cook Shack at Mid Vail and then maybe ski down on their schnozzolas, they have fun. Me, I've had enough of the East, where getting your jollies means screeching down a vertical ice tray and shouting shibboleths like

'Hoo-Hah!' or 'Barnes & Noble!' to ward off the meemies. In Vail, I can float down runs named the Meadows or Christmas – gentle names, Snowplow! – and can fantasize that I'm turning with the grace of a petrel. I can swoop along Cappuccino and Espresso, trails redolent of the good life, and can think of myself as Cary Grant absconding with Grace Kelly's bijoux. If my juices are flowing, I can challenge Prima or the Black Forest – no-nonsense chutes chiselled out of the rock by the hammer of Thor – and in a trice become Robert Redford going for the gold.

'You see, Snowplow, no matter how I feel, Vail makes me look good to myself.'

'And when day is done?'

'Come again?'

'Après-ski. Don't you feel like you're living inside a cuckoo clock? Instant Switzerland! The town's barely twenty years old. It has no history, no traditions, not like Aspen or Crested Butte or even Squaw Valley.'

'If I want a museum tour, I'll go to Florence. At least Vail doesn't look like a shopping mall. It has a film theatre and a hospital and restaurants that serve everything from tacos to fondue to raw clams, and more bars per square inch than any place outside Manhattan, including one where they serve something called a Kamikaze, which is a ticket to a mano a mano between you and your liver.'

'Tack-y!' Snowplow sniffed. 'Who'd want to frequent such a fleshpot?'

'Who? Biggies of all nations, that's who. Mexicans in flight from the peso, Venezuelan oil tycoons, Texans with bread to burn and most of the tsars of Tinseltown. You want film stars? We got supernovas.'

'Big deal. Dress Cliff Robertson in ski clothes on a cold day, he looks just like Jascha Heifetz, who looks just like Bo Derek. On a blustery day, buster, everybody bundles. You know what you are, scribbler? An élitist.'

'*Au contraire, mon capitaine.* Vail is the very temple of democracy. True, a classy condo in core Vail will set you back that million-plus you've been trying to find a home for. But entire houses, nestled at the very foot of this affable alp, can be let for a paltry three Gs a week. True again, them as wants to spend a grand a day for the Pooh-bah Suite in the new Westin Hotel can *épater* the bourgeoisie to their hearts' content. But such as dabble in the less remunerative professions can plop their pates upon a pillow for a C-note, more or less. And a day's lift ticket at Vail goes for less than a ducat at Sugarbush.'

Had he had eyes, Snowplow might have shed tears of frustration, for his quiver was empty. 'It's not fair!' he ululated. 'All those moms and dads at all those other spiffy joints who work so hard to give all people of all races and creeds such a good time, regardless of national origin, are they to be dismissed in your contumacious chronicle?'

'No one said life is fair, Snowplow.'

He turned to go, squeaking like the Tin Woodman. At the door, he stopped and said sourly, 'You've won a Pyrrhic victory, you money-grubbing typist. In your words will be the seeds of your own destruction. The hordes will read you and will flock to Vail, and pandemonium will be your reward. May all your lift lines be eternal.'

His words lingered, like spring slush, long after he had gone, and though he will never know it, they carried the day for him. The Muse and I, as we shared a twilight cordial, conceded his point: Why foul one's own nest?

Why tell the world about Sweet Basil, where the food is fine, the prices are just and the service is the stuff that dreams are made of ? Or about Cyrano's, a step up the decibel ladder, where locals and instructors and visitors gather in convivial congress to minimize the amount of blood in their alcohol?

Why sing the praises of instructors like Linwood Newton, known fondly to my offspring as 'Mad Dog,' a Pied Piper who enchants the young, delights the old and can beguile rank stumblebums like me into believing ourselves to be but a rung away from the World Cup?

Why reveal the whereabouts of the cosy town, snuggled like a cub in the bosom of Vail Mountain, where the only traffic is pedestrian, where everything from mink to minestrone is within five minutes' walk, and where none but the crapulous can lose their way?

Why indeed?

NOUVELLE VAIL
Life Off the Slopes

Vail has accommodations in all categories, from the new and luxurious to the small and homey. At the top of the list are the **Lodge at Vail** (303 476 5011), 174 East Gore Creek Drive, with doubles for about $135 (all rates given here are for the February-March high season); the **Kiandra Lodge** (303 476 5081), 20 Vail Road, with rates that range from $125 for a standard double to $350 for a fully equipped penthouse; the **Westin Hotel, Vail** (303 476 7111), with doubles from $150 to $175 and suites from $250 to $300, and **Marriott's Mark Resort** (303 476 4444), 715 West Lionshead Circle, with doubles for $120 to $155, suites from $220 to $480, and full health-club facilities for all guests.

Condominiums are available at the Lodge at Vail, the Vail Village Inn, Montaneros, and the Mountain Haus. One-bedroom units range from $160 to $250 a night, two bedroom units from $260 to $375. Booking information from the Vail Resort Association, 303 476 1000. For reservations, call 800 525 3875 or 303 476 5677.

AFTER THE LAST RUN

Dining in Vail ranges from French and expensive – the **Left Bank** (303 476 3696) in the Sitzmark Lodge is one example (about $60 or $70 for a three-course meal with wine for two) – to unpretentious (the **Cook Shack,** for lunch on the slopes; about $15 for soup and salad for two; reservations required, 303 476 6050). Restaurant fashions change quickly, but some current favourites are **La Tour** (303 476 4403), for such specialities as quenelles de brochet, mallard duck breast with Calvados, and striped bass (about $50 to $60 for two including a house wine, reservations essential); **Cyrano's Too** (303 476 1441), with snails and artichoke hearts in puff pastry, fresh seafood, and grilled duck breast (about $50 for two); and **Sweet Basil** (303 476 0125), for prawns with pesto sauce, pepper steak with port sauce, and veal with wild mushrooms (about $50 for two).

SKIING IN NEW ENGLAND'S NORTH COUNTRY

David Shribman

Weekend after weekend, all season long, the winter ritual would repeat itself: In the old days, when skiing was young, New Yorkers would gather in Grand Central Station, baggage in hand. All Friday night they would travel, east and then north, and by morning, often sleepless, they would spill into a small New Hampshire town. For two days, on wooden skis with leather bindings, they would ride the hills, sleeping in farmhouses and small inns, and then, as dusk gathered on Sunday afternoon, they would meet again, return to the trains and pull into New York by six-thirty Monday morning.

The Skimeister and the Eastern Slope Express, as the snow trains were known, are gone now; their passengers have grown grey and the sport they sampled on those quick weekend dashes to New England's North Country has grown fancy and sophisticated. Today, skis are made of space-age materials and metal bindings are made of super-light metals. But in the far northern reaches of New Hampshire, beyond the Washington-to-Boston quiche corridor, there are re-minders of the way skiing used to be.

This is a return to purity in the sport. It is not that the burghers of New Hampshire mountain towns have set out to purge winter sports of frills and frivolity. It is only that the style of these villages, with their municipal ice-skating rinks and church suppers, almost always has tended to be frumpy rather then fancy. This is true even today, when the southern part of the state has drifted into Boston's orbit.

Simplicity is the beauty of it all. There is a freshness to skiing on the slopes of Wildcat, the frosty peak near Mount Washington, and on the trails of Loon Mountain, off the Kancamagus Highway. The same spirit is found in the modest lodge at the base of the Dartmouth Skiway, where the talk runs to midterm examinations and Winter Carnival dates. Ski operators know that the skiing is the thing, not elaborate lodges and glittery discothèques, and they know that the atmospherics geology and biology gave to the state – mountains, vistas, trees and clear skies – are better than anything man could devise. Skiers who, each morning, load into station wagons and head for the mountains are more interested in their style of skiing than in their style of dress.

People have been skiing one way or another in New Hampshire since the 1870s, but today few people use rake handles for poles. Rope tows that were strung up hillsides in the 1930s have all but disappeared, replaced by chairlifts and gondolas and such. And yet there is something 'not quite about skiing in New Hampshire. Most of the mountains are not quite high enough. Most of the ski runs are not quite high enough. Most of the ski runs are not quite long enough. The snowfalls are, from time to time, not quite bountiful enough. Many of the ski lifts are not quite efficient. The ski towns are not quite glamorous. New Hampshire, in short, is not quite Vermont or Colorado. That is the main attraction.

For many New Englanders, skiing began where American skiing came of age, at Mount Cranmore, a mile from the centre of North Conway. One of the most famous ski towns in the country, it lies just west of the Maine border. In 1939, Hannes Schneider, an Austrian skier who brought the Arlberg method of teaching skiing to America, settled in that small New Hampsire community. There, the artistry of Mr. Schneider combined with the genius of Harvey Dow Gibson, a local businessman, to produce one of the first of the major ski areas, and perhaps the first real American ski boom. The feature attraction was a complicated ski tram known as the Skimobile. Today's sophisticated transportation engineers would call it a people mover: a series of small, individual green and red cars mounted on a wooden roadway that leads through the woods up the mountainside.

The Skimobile is still there, its cars still clanking up the mountain; there is nothing particularly efficient about it, but its very quirkiness lends a certain charm to bright winter mornings. So does the fact that the attendants at the three double chairlifts and the Poma lift recognize many of the skiers (and not just those from the nearby towns). Two, sometimes three generations of skiers have learned the rudiments of the sport from the same instructors at the Hannes Schneider Ski School. There are, to be sure, youth ski races and the occasional gimmicks, but sensible folks ignore them and concentrate on the wide slopes and the carved trails. Mount Cranmore is, above all, a family sort of place, where skiers share picnic lunches in the lodge and, on a few special afternoons each year, sit on a second-floor porch in oversized green wooden chairs and enjoy the winter sunshine. It is a peculiarly New England form of sunbathing.

Not far away are a number of other major ski areas, many of them a bit shorter on folklore but longer on snowmaking and trail variety. One of the most popular is Wildcat, with its gondola speeding skiers 6,800 feet up the mountain, two double chairlifts, two triple chairs and seventeen miles of trails. The mountain, with its north-northwest exposure, is legendary for its howling winds, but it is also known for its long trails and views. From a handful of trails and from the gondola, skiers can see the formidable bowls and, in winter, the forbidding reaches of Mount Washington, the Northeast's highest peak.

New Hampshire is a state of little jewels and treasures, small villages tucked beyond the next hill. One of the loveliest of these lies at a turn in the road. The town was once a summer meeting spot for such New England luminaries as Daniel Webster, Ralph Waldo Emerson, Henry David Thoreau and Nathaniel Hawthorne. It is known to the world, and in the history of economics, as Bretton Woods. Four decades ago, the world still gripped by war, financiers from forty-four nations gathered in an elegant old rambling hotel, strolled along the quarter-mile porch and, under glittering chandeliers, organized the World Bank and chose the American dollar as the international currency standard. The price of gold is no longer $35 an ounce, but Bretton Woods remains a magnificent mountain retreat, especially in winter.

Its ski facilities – a triple chair, two double chairs and a T-bar – are the newest in the state, but the setting and the feeling are as old as the hills. There is, from the summit, a magnificent view of the White Mountains and, nestled in a grove of trees, the Mount Washington Hotel, dowager of the mountains. The hotel is open only from May until the end of October, but the cross-country trails that spindle by it in winter are among the very best in the state.

The fourth major ski area in Mount Washington Valley is Attitash. If the New Hampshire winter does not provide ample snow, then the snow engineers of Attitash always manage to compensate, filling sixteen of the area's twenty slopes – 125 acres in all – with machine-made snow. Even when other New Hampshire peaks are brown, Attitash is cloaked in winter white. The area limits ticket sales in order to keep the lines short; there is a guarantee that it will take no more than fifteen minutes to get on the lift.

Over in Franconia Notch, which in the nineteenth century attracted a set of American landscape artists known as the Hudson River Valley School, stands a forbidding peak known as Cannon Mountain. As early as August 1934, members of the New Hampshire legislature had their eyes on this mound of evergreen and granite, and even held hearings on the possibility of building an aerial tramway for skiers. The idea was somewhat fantastic for the time, and so, it must be said, was the result, for by the early summer of 1938, North America's first aerial tramway was dedicated.

Today Cannon, still owned by the state, has seven lifts and thiry-six trails (including eight for experts), with fifty miles of ski-touring trails that wend past the sorts of sights that Asher B. Durand, Thomas Cole, and John Frederick Kensett committed to canvas.

Farther south, in Lincoln, three miles from the intersection of Route 93 and the Kancamagus Highway, stands Loon Mountain, home of a four-passenger gondola that streaks 7,000 feet into the hills. Loon and Waterville Valley (which, with its nine lifts, can take more skiers up the mountain per hour than any other area in the state) also offer limited ticket sales.

There are many memorable elements to time spent in the hills of New Hampshire: The variety and challenge offered by an area like Waterville Valley; the long, winding trails of Wildcat. But most memorable of all are the fresh winds and the old pines and jagged peaks where, in winter, no man goes – the quality of place that led artists into the area to paint the meadows and the streams, the peaks and the plateaux. For as long as people journey into those hills, they will feel that they are, as Benjamin Willey put it in 1856 in his history of the area's people, 'not in any namable latitude of this rugged earth, but in the world of pure beauty.'

GETTING THERE

The most direct way is to charter a plane. Two companies – L.J.L. Airway (telephone 603 356 2097) and Medicair (207 935 2999) – fly out of Eastern Slopes Regional Airport in Fryeburg, Maine (207 935 2500), about eight miles from North Conway, New Hampshire. L.J.L. will also fly groups from airports near New York City direct to Fryeburg. There is one town taxi or you might arrange, in advance, to be picked up by your hotel. Pilot Pal rents used cars for $25 a day; reservations should be made through Eastern Slopes Regional Airport.

You can also fly to Portland, Maine, via People Express, Bar Harbor Airlines, or Delta. It is about a two-hour drive to North Conway. Car-rental agencies at the airport include Avis, Budget, Hertz, and National.

TRAILS AND LIFTS

Skiers in the Mount Washington Valley may choose from a wide selection of facilities. **Attitash** in Bartlett on Route 302 often offers well-packed machine-made powder. At **Black Mountain** in Jackson, the skiing is modest but picturesque. There is an exceptional view of the western flank of the Presidential Range visible from the upper reaches of the well-groomed slopes of Bretton Woods. **Cannon Mountain** (603 823 5563) is the state's largest ski mountain, while Dartmouth Skiway (603 795 2143) in Lyme is a small, family- and student-orientated area. **Mount Cranmore,** with its challenging and beautiful Kandahar Trail, is as much a part of the village of North Conway as the fire station and the post office (603 356 5544).

In Lincoln, three miles from the interesection of I-93 and the Kancamagus Highway, **Loon Mountain** holds special appeal to the intermediate skier (603 745 8111), while **Waterville Valley,** also off I- 93, offers a wide assortment of varying levels of trails (603 236 8311). **Wildcat,** on Route 16 in Pinkham Notch, often offers skiing well into spring, because of the area's elevation and north facing exposure (603 466 3326).

ACCOMMODATIONS

New Hampshire is one of the centres of a special rural institution known as the inn, and for skiers the possibilities are limited only by time. (Unless otherwise noted, rates at these inns are daily rates, based on double occupancy during the winter season. Breakfast and dinner included, tax and gratuities additional. In high season, including holidays and February 'break,' rates are often increased; however, most inns offer special ski-week packages that include rooms and lift tickets at reduced rates.) In the Mount Washington Valley, **Cranmore Mountain Lodge** in Kearsarge (about $30 to $40 a person; telephone 603 356 2044) has its own skating pond, a toboggan hill, the ubiquitous guest living room and modern rooms in an adjacent barn loft.

Whitney's Village Inn in Jackson, at the base of Black Mountain Ski Area, has its own skating rink and is close to the other ski areas (about $50 or $60 a person; 603 383 6886). Other favourites: the **Dana Place Inn** in Jackson (double rooms, about $70 to $85, include breakfast only; 603 383 6822); the **New England Inn** in Intervale (a fireplace cottage for two is about $130, double room about $115; 603 356 5541), and the **Wildcat Inn and Tavern** (double room about $65, including tax, gratuities and breakfast only; 603 383 4245).

One of the most popular spots in the state is the **Balsams/Wilderness Grand Resort Hotel** in Dixville Notch (about $60 to $80 a person, including breakfast, dinner and ski tickets at the resort's own ski area; 603 255 3400).

For more modest skiing but a spectacular setting in the western part of the state, stay amid the antiques and the elegant rooms of the **Lyme Inn** (double rooms from about $50 to $65, including breakfast only; 603 795 2222) and ski at the Dartmouth Skiway.

There are also more modern accommodations. (Rates do not include meals.) In Bartlett, there is the **Attitash Mountain Village** (a two-person unit with a kitchenette is about $65 a night; 603 374 2386), or the **Red Jacket Mountain View Motor Inn** (double rooms from about $60 to $80; 603 356 5411), with an indoor pool, sauna, and Jacuzzi. Near Loon Mountain are the townhouses of the **Village of Loon Mountain** (rates for two-bedroom units begin at about $300 for the first two nights; 603 745 3401). In Waterville Valley, there are the **Inns of Waterville Valley** (double rooms begin at about $65; 603 236 8366) and the **TriPyramid Town Houses** (one-bedroom condominiums, sleeping two to six people, rent for about $200 for two nights; 603 236 8211). These lodgings also offer special ski-week packages.

IN SEARCH OF WINTER'S ESSENCE

Adam Nicolson

Going north in winter is like pouring cream on cream cheese. It is redoubling the effect, adding too many adjectives in a vulgar extreme. The day I left for the north of Finland, a friend of mine went south to Provence. We divided at the airport like a hinge, two equal halves folding out to their opposites. The South of France is where Europe concentrates as an essence, where you can't move without disturbing the stuff of an old culture. But in the snow-drooped forests of the northern winter, Europe begins to run out. It dilutes into wilderness there, merging with an independent Arctic world that circles the earth like a halo, independent of the continents that trail southward from it. My friend went to Aix to deny the winter, and I flew to Helsinki to exaggerate it.

From the windows of the plane, looking out over Denmark and southern Sweden, I saw the last evening light redden the western sides of the houses, and on the northern sides of woods a grey moon-shaped efflorescence on the ground, where shadow had preserved the frost all day. As the light finally disappeared, the landscape five miles below me sorted out into the black and white of lakes and snow, the polarities of a subpolar existence.

I waited in Helsinki airport for the flight northward to Ivalo. The yellow snowploughs drove in echelon up and down the runways like harvesters on the prairie, watched through the plate-glass walls of the airport by the Finns waiting for departure. It is the clothes that strike you first, their sheer bulk and comprehensiveness. Each extremity is muffled and padded by hats and gloves, and each trunk sheathed in an insulating roll of cloth. In the airport's discreet lighting it is as though a population of flippered and upholstered robots were moving around each other with as much recognition as a collection of old tyres.

The individuality, which is stifled by the volume of clothes, siphons out through the head and into the hats. They reveal as much of their occupants as cars do elsewhere in the world. Some were enormous, pale grey puffballs, like prize marrows gone spherical, medicine balls with subsidiary wing balls attached for the ears. Endless variations on the bobble and the pompon, the tassel and the tag. Some were modelled on the cartwheel, others on the toadstool, working elaborate mutations on kempt and unkempt, bushy and svelte, the hat as hair and even, in one remarkable instance, the hair as hat. It was obviously a question of when in Rome, and I bought one myself. It was made of bear fur, and when suitably arranged, came to resemble a piece of Mongolian armour, the earflaps folded down but curving outward like the bottom of a graph, and the attached strings hanging downward in a relaxed vertical. Only then was I inconspicuous.

The plane landed at Ivalo airport. This was the true north, 150 miles above the Arctic Circle, 26 degrees below zero Fahrenheit. The night was incontrovertibly black, blacker than any night I had seen, and the trees surrounding the apron, suffering from the elephantiasis of a heavy snowfall the day before, were flattened cut-outs in the white airport lights. It was four in the afternoon, and this was the year's midnight; night as a place, not a time. Fine snow hung and revolved in the lit air, moving upward as much as down, a sort of crystalline dust. And the cold gagged in your throat like something else mixed in the air, spiking at your insides as you swallowed. This cold pulls at your skin, plucks at it and pulls your face away from your skull. All this was what I had come for, what I was excited by: a place where the extremes of cold and lightlessness and the surrounding forest were in control, where a sense of necessity alone decided what was possible. I hoped to find no freedoms here.

Europe's wilderness, its green belt, is more complicated than I had imagined. I had expected a shed for an airport, but Ivalo's reception building was designed as a pastiche of a log cabin. Long ago it had made the journey from shed to slick plastic modernity, and now it was on its way down the other side, its concrete walls covered in unvarnished split logs left splintery for effect, and with stubby red candles burning smoothly on the bar tables. The signs on the lavatory doors were not, as they are everywhere else in Finland, pictures of a little girl and a little boy with potties, but tasteful, muesli-style diagrams of Lapps in Lapp hats, male and female. Places like this, where sophistication of urban design has run two or three stages ahead of the tastes of the people who use them, are among the more revealing in the world.

I was once in a bar in the Cevennes in France that had recently been decorated with fibreglass beams and wrought-iron lanterns, when a farmer turned up for a drink there driving a bullock cart full of dung, which he parked outside. No one seemed to notice the extraordinary short-circuited congruity, least of all the farmer himself. Nor did they here in this concrete log-cabin airport, where two old Lapp women waited to board the plane to Rovaniemi. Both were dressed in ordinary western European clothes, except for their hats, which had thick Davy Crockett foxtails hanging down on either side of their sagged skin faces. They held the ends of their fingers with nervousness, and were out of place in this fakery designed to imitate what other people imagined them to be.

A holiday brochure lay on a side table. 'Lifesee among the Lapps,' it said, 'where the heartfelt welcome of the wilderness lies in the warmth of our five star plus hotels.' I was in need of something more essential. I spent a night in a boardinghouse in Ivalo, and the next morning took the bus to Kirkenes in Norway. It was an eight-hour ride through the forest, always farther north, imagining that the farther up I went the better it would be, the higher the purer. The bus began full of people, and over the length of the journey gradually emptied until at the Norwegian border I was the only passenger left.

There can be few better ways of seeing the stage-set landscape of the northern day. By about ten o'clock in early January, the world is light, the sky mildly blanching up from the stained horizon. Nothing of the sun is visible, and beneath the snowed-in trees, their branches held down like a ballerina's arms at the end of a performance, the glareless snow absorbs all the light. It is unexpectedly beautiful, this grey and empty monotone of a dawn that lasts all day, in which the headlights of the bus are the only yellow. Or at least so I thought, until, cresting a rise, we faced a hill that some layer in the atmosphere had turned a butter yellow too. Absurdly, above it, a pink-melon moon was rising, the lower tip hinged to the yellow crest. Southward, where the daystain had shifted from left to right, you could look at the rim of the lit world.

It was dark by two in the afternoon. Children and grandmothers had been dropped at anonymous places *en route*, indistinguishable to a stranger from the endless repeated miles of birch and pine between them. No meaning, apparently, was invested in the details of this emptiness, and I wondered in an upside-down way, thinking of penguins in a penguin colony, how people could find their own nests.

We arrived at a café. It was full of foresters, the day's work necessarily over, drinking. Civilization was spread brittle and thin here. It was an all-male and all-plastic place; there were no layers to life. When genuinely near the wilderness, there is no self-reflection and no self-consciouness of style. In the middle of this great forest there were plastic wall panels patterned to look like strips of pine. The only food to be had was packaged hamburgers, the only drink coffee or beer. Tinsel bobbles hung in the windows. A forester, still in his working quilts, stared at me out of shameless curiosity, leaning backward in his chair, twisting his head around and up at the same time, somehow revolving his eyeballs in their sockets and simultaneously raising his half-drunk glass with its goo-smeared rim, in the heartfelt welcome of the wilderness. This was not metropolitan behaviour.

But even Kirkenes, when we got there, was not the far edge I was looking for. It is rough enough, a mining town and a small port, where the ironworks on the hillside dominates the neat wooden houses. Its shafts, lifts, and conveyors, all neon-lit and snow-covered in a constructionist dream, are arranged below chimneys where white smoke stalks out and floods the sky. Not a suburban landscape, but still with camera shops, comfort, the wash of international culture. It was warmer than Ivalo, only 2 degrees below zero, because it was nearer the sea. Kirkenes is farther east than Istanbul and as far from the southern tip of Norway as from there to Siena. But a farther place remained. Thirty-eight miles northeast of Kirkenes on the edge of the Barents Sea and on the border of the Soviet Union, a hamlet of only six people called Grensejakobselv. In winter it is accessible only by snow-tractor. I hired one with a driver – or chauffeur, as he insisted on being called – from the bus company. It was a red and yellow metal frog with rubber tracks and no doors. You climbed in through the window. It was a military vehicle with no concessions to even a macho beauty.

Until about noon – low moon – on the morning we went to Grensejakobselv, the day was washed in a feathery fox-fur light, but it turned worse, and snow thickened the sky like flour in a sauce. We stopped at a house in the middle of nowhere, and the chauffeur telephoned to find out about snow conditions. I was left with the man of the house, a solitary human goat with milky breath that blew all over me from only four inches away. He shouted a history of Germany at me and bellowed the family story into my pores, all of it couched in a laugh that gradually caught up with itself until in a sort of sonic boom he could burp out a whole globule of undigested laughter in a terrible convulsive hiccup. And then start again. He was a milk farmer, lived all alone, this was his uncle's farm, his mother's sister's husband's farm, Oskar's, and did I like cows and had I heard of the fish or was it walrus that ate men and what about his sideburns? 'And the ice madness! The Northern Pole! You get ice in the head!!' he gurgled. '*Idiooot!*' It was too much, and the great length of the man began to fold and buckle, until choking with delight at his own lunacy the cow farmer kicked over an entire bucket of milk. We left.

It was nearly two hours in the snow-tractor to Grensejakobselv, with only the wrenching of the gears and the clacking of the tracks underneath the van. The wind made moiré patterns on the blown snow and swirled up spirals of it in the headlights. Little else could be seen in the blizzard until we arrived at the valley of Jakobselv itself. There, on the edge of the Arctic Ocean, the day lightened to a sudden dark clarity. The land was white and the cliffs sheathed in a skin of ice, but the sea itself, with ten-foot rollers, was an unconditional black warmed up by the Gulf Stream and washing the snow off the rocks to a regular line. There was no colour. It was pure polarized monochrome, the untrammelled polarity of the deep North. It was the landscape I had been looking for, in which I was the only anomaly.

SKIING PEAK TO PEAK IN UTAH

Clifford D. May

Imagine a Rocky Mountain ski area with thousands of acres of open slopes and labyrinthine glades, with 126 trails and more than thirty-five lifts capable of hauling 43,600 skiers an hour to peaks as high as 11,000 feet above sea level. Such a complex does not quite exist but it has advanced beyond the realm of mere imagination: five ski resorts in Utah's Wasatch Range have become partners in the Interconnect Adventure, a programme that combines a daylong sampler of many of the state's most popular runs – at Park City, Solitude, Brighton, Alta and Snowbird – with guided ski touring through tranquil back country.

At first glance, the idea of covering so much territory in a single day struck me as far-fetched. I had skied Utah before and remembered that the drive from, say, Alta to Park City took a good hour. My second glance, however, at the start of a preview of an Interconnect tour, was from the top of Park City's Jupiter Peak, from which I could clearly see that the mountains on the route are actually adjacent – though the only roads between them snake in and out of long, narrow canyons. Nowhere else in North America are there so many ski areas so close together.

'That next valley right there, that's Big Cottonwood Canyon, where Solitude and Brighton are,' a Utahn pointed out. 'And way back there you can just make out the top of Snowbird in Little Cottonwood Canyon. Not too nice a view, is it?' he said, using the ironic locution that seems to have become a hallmark of Western speech. 'I mean, this isn't too much fun, right?'

Part of the fun was just the idea of getting to ski so many areas in so short a time. Like most skiers, I enjoy being able to say, 'Oh, sure, I've skied there,' whenever a mountain, from the Berkshires to the Pamirs, is mentioned. At the same time, I am reluctant to devote a day or more of precious hoilday to an area that may turn out not to suit my taste.

The other part of the fun was the opportunity to spend at least a little time away from ski areas. After all, back-country skiing has become one of the strongest trends in the sport today. Most back-country skiers, however, are using the new 'Norpine' (also known as alpine touring) boots and skis, designed to combine features of both cross-country (Nordic) and downhill (Alpine) equipment. Norpine skis are lighter than the downhill variety but, unlike the usual cross-country type, have metal edges. The boots are more substantial than those generally worn for cross-country.

In fact, the idea for Interconnect evolved over the last few years as a growing number of local Norpine skiers began using the expanding lift facilities of the Wasatch Range resorts as access to remote countryside, where they can meander as they like – far from groomed trails, madding crowds, and long lift lines – among the mountains and dales.

Beyond formalizing this approach to back-country skiing, the programme is designed to make it safer. 'You don't want skiers who aren't very experienced going out of bounds on their own,' explains Raivo Puusemp, formerly president of Ski Utah, the inter-resort association that organized the Interconnect Adventure. 'There's too great a danger that they'll wind up getting hurt and stranded far from any ski patrol, or being caught in an avalanche. With seasoned, professional guides along, however, this kind of adventure needn't entail much risk.'

'Interconnect won't give skiers the same kind of experience that helicopter skiing provides,' said Greg Smith of the Wasatch Powder-bird Guides, an outfit that has been involved in helicopter skiing for ten years, and which was instrumental in setting up the Interconnect programme. 'People shouldn't expect that. What we hope it will offer is a taste of several very different ski areas, as well as a chance to see a whole lot of great scenery in the Wasatch Range. And they'll be able to do all of that in a single day.'

Groups of four to fourteen skiers are taken on each tour. Though they needn't be experts, skiers signing on for Interconnect should be confident of their ability to handle a wide variety of terrain and snow conditions at a moderate pace.

They are issued a single ticket good for all lifts at all areas visited, with the right to cut lift lines everywhere except at Alta (which will only allow line cutting if a group falls behind its schedule). The programme is aimed mainly at downhill skiers, and no special equipment is needed (downhill rentals are, of course, available at all the local resorts; alpine touring equipment is not usually rented) but each skier will be lent an avalanche rescue beacon, a tiny electronic transmitter and receiver.

The tour groups generally board their first lift at nine a.m. and make their last christie around four p.m. Ground transportation back to the starting point is included in the price of $30 to $60, depending on which of three different routes is taken. The guides will decide which route to take, according to snow conditions and the level of skiing of the particular group.

On a preview of Interconnect Adventure one warm December weekend, I tagged along with Ski Utah's Mr. Puusemp and three of his friends. Using regular downhill boots and skis, we started off at ten a.m. from Park City, which, despite the vaguely urban-sounding name, is a large area served by eight double chairlifts, three triple chairs, and a four-passenger gondola. Though known primarily as an intermediate's resort, the recent opening of the Scott and Jupiter Bowls has given Park City several expert runs.

A twenty-minute ride on the gondola took us to the top of Double Jack, a mogul-covered run that provided a less than gentle warm-up. 'Not too out of shape, are we?' said one of my companions. Next, we rode the chairlift named Thaynes, then made a long traverse to the Jupiter chair, which took us to the top of Jupiter Peak. We spent a while just gazing at the mountains and feathery clouds in the distance and discussing our intended route. An easy schuss along a high ridge led to the ski area boundary.

There was something deliciously naughty about crossing that border and moving into the unpatrolled territory beyond. Suddenly, the snow was no longer a ski-beaten track but deep and unpacked powder. The five of us let loose, making wide, sweeping turns and leaving smoky rooster tails hanging in the air behind us.

Working our way down into Big Cottonwood Canyon, we glided past groves of aspen and Douglas fir to enter a broad meadow where the snow was carpeted with hoar-frost – tiny, glassy leaves of ice that glistened in the sun, lending a fairytale look to the landscape. Beyond the meadow, we passed a pair of Norpine skiers coming from another direction.

Though such skiers provided the inspiration for Interconnect, many of them are less than enthusiastic about it. 'The whole point of going out of bounds,' one told me later, 'is to get away from the tourists in their stretch pants.' Downhill skiers often show at least equal disdain for their back-to-the-earth counterparts, referring to them as 'granola-eaters' and 'Friends of the Squirrels.'

Not long after, the base of Solitude came into view. A favourite with local skiers, Solitude is rarely mentioned outside of Utah. But its five chairlifts serve a varied and interesting mountain, one that deserves more consideration, particularly on weekends when better-known areas are building up long lift lines. Just next door to Solitude is Brighton, which has four chairlifts and is thought of as a family resort. (Skiers can now buy a lift ticket good for both areas, using Solitude's new Summit lift as a link.)

Having started out late, we decided not to make the detour to

Brighton at this point. Instead, two chairlifts later, we reached the top of Solitude where we slid past a sign that read: ENTERING BACK COUNTRY AREA. NO SKI PATROL. NO AVALANCHE CON-TROL. ENTER AT OWN RISK. A shingle rated the day's 'Avalanche Hazard' as 'Moderate.'

The group dropped over the back of the mountain and began a traverse across a steep slope toward Twin Lakes Pass. In the distance, a rumpled bed of white mountains extended to the horizon. This was the most dangerous part of the journey, the most likely place to encounter an avalanche of a 'slab slide' – a sudden movement of large chunks of wet snow. To minimize the risk, we crossed one at a time, moving as quietly as we could.

Next, we began the most arduous part of the adventure, a climb of about eighty vertical feet to the saddle of the pass. It had become so warm that we were wearing only sweaters and ski vests, other layers having been peeled off and deposited in backpacks. Trudging through the sun-dampened snow in what was beginning to seem like subtropical heat, we suddenly found ourselves seriously discussing the merits of the granola-eaters' light and skinny skis.

At the top of the pass, we stopped to catch our breath. Then we began a graceful descent through Grizzly Gulch where we found another cache of soft, unbroken powder, the kind of snow for which our downhill skis were invented. The run took us into Little Cottonwood Canyon and to the base of Alta, noted for both the quality and quantity of its snow. Geographic and meteorological conditions combine to give Alta an average of 500 inches of dry, light powder each winter. Connoisseurs from as far away as the Swiss Alps and the Canadian Bugaboos come to sample it.

After a lunch of chilli, burgers and beer on the open-air deck of Alta's Alpenglow Lodge, we relaxed with some fast cruising on packed intermediate trails, then rode the Wildcat lift to the top of Peruvian Ridge, which we traversed to Punch Bowl. We cut left to Wildcat Bowl where deep, untouched snow was again found hiding among the trees. Dropping beneath a craggy cliff, the group made a long swing to the bottom of Snowbird, a challenging area with seven double chairlifts and a 125-passenger aerial tram. From the summit of Snowbird we looked down on Salt Lake City, swamped in grey-brown clouds. 'People don't believe how nice it can be up here even when the city is socked in with smog,' Mr. Puusemp commented.

At this point, we could have skied back to Alta, and from Alta there is a route leading back to Brighton. But taking into account the state of our muscles and the promise of strawberry daiquiris at Snowbird's Lodge Club, we all agreed that another couple of runs at Snowbird would be more than enough to make us feel we had put in a full day's skiing.

'What you didn't really get to see today,' Mr. Puusemp said later, 'is the potential for growth involved here. Taking all these areas together, we already have the most terrain and lift capacity in North America. We just need a few more lifts to really complete the system, to eliminate most of the walking and to make the connections between the areas even faster, simpler and safer. Several of those lifts are already planned. I mean, there isn't too much terrific skiing here, is there?'

In time, he added, other nearby resorts, including Deer Valley, Park West and the still undeveloped White Pine Area, could also be hooked into the Interconnect system, forming a mega-ski area unlike anything that now exists in the United States. Whether that leap can be made will depend largely on how popular and successful this first important step turns out to be.

All five ski areas on the Interconnect circuit are thirty-two miles or less from Salt Lake City International Airport, which can be reached directly from most major cities in the continental United States. A dozen major carriers serve the airport. It's worthwhile to shop around for the best fare and to look into package deals. Buses, limousines, taxis, and rental cars are available for the trip from the airport to any of the resorts. All five rent downhill equipment. For further information on Utah skiing in general, or for reservations for the Interconnect Adventure, contact Ski Utah, 307 West 23rd South, Salt Lake City, Utah 84103 (801 534 1779).

TAOS: A SKIER'S MARTINI

Donal Henahan

Every skier has a recurrent nightmare and here is mine. It has been snowing heavily for days. The ski area of my choice reports a 300-inch base and a foot of fresh powder. But I am not there. I am sitting on my baggage in an airline terminal in Denver, or Boise, or Montreal, or Salt Lake, or Munich, watching the snow pile up on empty runways and listening to a public address system telling of cancelled flights and impassable roads. With heaven only a few miles away, I am in limbo, snowbound while precious holiday time ticks away.

If you decide to ski Taos, in the New Mexico highlands, that particular nightmare will be spared you. There are Taos nightmares – the plunge called Stauffenberg, for instance, with its 37-degree pitch, or the heavily mogulled free-fall known as Al's Run – but getting there is not one of them. Fly into Albuquerque, where snow has not been a serious problem since the last ice age, then drive by bus or rented car the 142 miles north to Taos Ski Valley.

It is on the whole a blessedly boring trip, unless you are enchanted by vistas of sagebrush and yucca trees. The only panic you will encounter will be the slowly rising concern, if this is your first visit, that you have bought yourself a ski week in a desert. Over arrow-straight highways that must have been laid out by a particularly single-minded crow you zip through Santa Fe, Espanola, and the town of Taos, with still nothing in view that looks like snow.

But, have faith, somewhere well along the winding eighteen-mile mountain road from Taos to Taos Ski Valley a comforting whiteness appears. After all, you tell yourself nervously, this is a ski area that over the last ten years has averaged more than 300 inches and in a good season has gone to 580.

But then, one more curve in the road and your fate looms above you. There stands what appears at first to be a gigantic egg carton that someone has stood on edge: Al's Run. This and a couple of neighbouring snow chutes (gullies between rocks) that hover menacingly over the base area make such a daunting sight for the unprepared newcomer that Ernie Blake, who founded and still commands Taos Ski Valley,

has erected a sign over the lift-ticket booth that tries to be reassuring:
DON'T PANIC. YOU HAVE ONLY SEEN 1/30TH OF THE
MOUNTAIN. WE HAVE MANY EASIER SLOPES, TOO.

True. But Taos is mainly for serious skiers, and especially for those
who love powder in the trees. Even the so-called easiest trails can
surprise you in unexpected places by their steepness, and when snow
has been scarce the narrow runouts can turn perilously icy. On the
whole, however, Taos does a scrupulous job of overnight and spot
grooming. The runs on which the mountain's reputation depend, of
course, are too steep for any grooming machine. The powder bowls,
glades and chutes of the upper mountain can make certified experts
fall back on their snowplough and sideslip techniques. Even experts
are warned not to go alone into the Wheeler Wilderness area, which is
not swept by the ski patrol and where avalanches are not controlled.

Never mind, an aggressive intermediate can have a hairy enough
time on such a tree-studded drop as Walkyries Chute, one of many
forested runs that teach edge control in a hurry when the powder is
skied off. Walkyries, I noticed, seemed especially attractive to nature
lovers, many of whom spent much of their descent time fervently
embracing pine trees and bushes.

Taos, as Ernie Blake is proud to proclaim, is not for everybody. It is,
in comparison to areas farther north, neither posh nor celebrity-
conscious. The mountain is, at 11,819 feet, not especially high (Colorado's Aspen Highlands go over 14,000, for instance). Its vertical
drop is 2,612, compared to about 3,000 at Aspen and Vail and 4,200 at
Jackson Hole, Wyoming.

Still, Taos has a personality that many discriminating skiers find
irresistible, mixing as it does art-colony sophistication, powder-hog
machismo, and Tex-Mex culture. The Taos area is, of course, D. H.
Lawrence country, but the decidedly tacky shrine to his memory is a
letdown, and may not be worth a side trip (about twenty miles). It
may help the visitor bear the disappointment to know that Lawrence's
cowboy hat, typewriter, and leather jacket, formerly displayed in the
tiny hilltop temple, have vanished, pinched by literature-loving tourists. More fun by far is a slow drive through Espanola, where low-rider
cultists can be seen pavaning through town in their improbably ornate
and underslung cars at excruciatingly slow speeds, for who knows
what reason.

Even first-time visitors become possessive about Taos. They like its
refusal to act like the average Rockies ski resort. There are at least as
many pick-up trucks in the car parks as sports cars. The dialect most
frequently heard in the lift lines seems to be West Texan, which is close
enough to English so that an Easterner can understand a few necessary phrases in a short time. ('Hee-yo, ah'm goan for it!' is a good one

to recognize, and so is 'Godamighty, lookie out, ah'm comin'
through!') Friends, however, can be quickly made, if that is one's
intent, in spite of language barriers.

Taos Ski Valley itself, which is eighteen miles from town, can bed
down only 800 skiers at any moment (many visitors lodge in town).
Even on prime weekends in good seasons, when as many as 4,800 lift
tickets may be sold, lines are tolerable at the base and virtually
non-existent at the upper levels – except perhaps on an especially
powdery Saturday. Virtually everybody takes class lessons (half-day,
morning or afternoon) and signs up for the NASTAR (National
Standard Race) runs on Tuesdays, Fridays, and Sundays. The average daily crowd in 1983-84, a vintage season for snow throughout the
Rockies, was about 4,000. At Sun Valley, which has seventeen lifts,
compared to eight at Taos, weekend crowds can reach 6,000. At Aspen
and Vail, you never are quite sure on busy days if you are skiing or
being skied on. Death by trampling, at least, is rarely a hazard at Taos.

The bigger resorts, of course, do have something that is not easily
found at Taos: round-the-clock fun. At Taos, après-ski action does
exist, for those who are not too exhausted to hunt it down, at several of
the lodges (the Thunderbird, the St. Bernard and the Hondo have
disco music or live bands), and there are Western-style bars in Taos
itself where you might strike up a conversation about the style of either
Franz Klammer or Georgia O'Keeffe. There are respectable restaurants, such as the Casa Cordova, midway between Taos and the ski
area, and the pleasant little Apple Tree Restaurant in Taos itself. But a
little disco, a little restaurant-hopping, and that is about it. What you
do at Taos is ski hard all day, quit when the lifts shut down at four
p.m., and then struggle to stay awake at least until nine-thirty. It is
rumoured that young Atlases have been known to follow up a day on
blitz and El Funko with an evening of tennis (the Tennis Ranch of
Taos is fourteen miles from the slopes), but that must remain rumour
until some responsible person stays awake long enough after dinner to
confirm it.

The embodiment of the Ski Valley is Mr. Blake himself. Ernie, who
started his skiing career at St. Moritz in 1917 when he was four years
old, commands his ski area's personnel with a quasi-military discipline that derives from his World War II days in the Swiss Air Force
and the United States infantry. Ernie still skis every day, 'except when
the light is flat – I have cataracts and have to wear hard contact lenses.'
He prowls the mountain daily, king of his hill and the scourge of
unwary instructors. He is a proud, self-mocking, nostalgic, whimsical
man whose personal stamp is on every slope.

The name of virtually every run is connected to Ernie's colourful
past. There are, to be sure, conventional names of the sort to be found

at any ski mountain: Fanny Hill, for instance, is the baby slope and Porcupine is one of the pricklier intermediate runs. Psycho-path as you might easily grasp, is a somewhat scarier run. However, even Taos regulars might not know that the dread Stauffenberg is named for one of Ernie's war heroes: the German colonel who planted a bomb under Hitler's map table on July 20, 1944. Hitler escaped, of course, but Ernie has memorialized Colonel von Stauffenberg's good intentions. Oster, another expert run, is named for the second-ranking officer in the Hitler plot. Fabian and Treskow, similarly, are named for other would-be assassins of Hitler. Ernie was born in Germany, of a German father and a Swiss mother, so his interest in the war years is more than academically historical.

It is not necessary to know any of this to enjoy Ernie's Taos. As you ski the long, ego-building Totemoff, for instance, you might be mildly amused to think how apt the name is for a good intermediate run from which mangled bodies might have to be carted away periodically. But in fact Pete Totemoff is an Alaskan Indian, now retired from the Forest Service, who helped Mr. Blake lay out the slopes early in the 1950s. Pete, now sixty-six and skiing regularly, is still one of the Blake inner circle. In fact, most of the lodges, restaurants and other enterprises in Taos turn out to be owned or run by old friends of Ernie or by members of his family.

Among the veterans is Chilton Anderson, who has been an instructor for twenty-seven years. He is an amateur cellist and a leading figure in Taos's lively musical life the year round: a summertime chamber music festival has been operating for nineteen years. Another veteran is Jean Mayer, an instructor who has been at Taos for twenty-six years, owns the Hotel St. Bernard and has his own superexpert run named for him: Jean's Glade.

Perhaps the skier who best symbolized the independent spirit of Taos, however, was Dr. Albert M. Rosen, the Al of Al's Run. Dr. Rosen suffered a heart attack in 1970 and doctors told him it would be dangerous for him to continue even living in Taos, with its 7,000-foot elevation. However, at age sixty-seven Dr. Al was still skiing there twice a week – with an oxygen tank strapped to his back. He died in 1982, after a decade of bonus skiing, at sea level, while playing golf in Florida.

No report on Taos would be complete without mention of the fabled martini tree, which Ernie discovered in the winter of 1958-59. He was skiing with a woman who found it impossible to continue down the slope because the light had gone bad. Ernie says he suddenly thought of a 'great medical innovation' that might cure the trouble: He sent his fifteen-year-old son down for a Mexican porron filled with his favourite remedy, the dry martini. It worked miraculously and since that time Taos skiers have come to know that on certain days, if they look diligently, they might find martini-filled bottles hanging from trees along their way. Ernie insists that the spraying of martini into the mouth is not only therapeutic but entirely safe. 'It is aerated and very relaxing.'

In this, as in almost everything, Taos begs to differ with the majority. Ernie does not go along with the current nostrum of the slopes, white wine. 'White wine is dangerous,' he says with the air of a man whose authority is rarely challenged. 'It makes the knees buckle.'

GETTING THERE

The carefree way is via Albuquerque, then by rental car to Taos. The alernative route through Denver is a bit cheaper. 'Skierized' cars – equipped with snow tyres and ski racks – are available from Avis, Budget, and Hertz. Or take a Trailways bus (Albuquerque and Denver, both ways, each three times daily; reservations advisable, 505 776 2295). The shuttle bus service (505 758 3410) to and from the slopes from Taos motels is useful because parking space at the mountain is inadequate.

The number of skiers is limited on busy days, so ticket, lessons and equipment reservations are suggested (505 776 2291). Accommodations range from luxurious, at the slopeside Thunderbird Chalets, to spartan, at Abominable SnowMansion, dorm housing nine miles away. For all Taos information, call 505 776 2295.

Good bets for dining: Casa Cordova, Hotel St. Bernard, Apple Tree.

CROSS-COUNTRY:
THE POETRY OF SILENCE

Nelson Bryant

More than a decade ago I awoke at dawn in Manhattan and looked out from my hotel window at a wondrous, marvellously still and immaculate world of white – nearly a foot of snow had fallen in the night – and beheld a skier making the first tracks of the new day on Madison Avenue.

It may have been that he was merely being practical, getting to work in the best and fastest way possible, but I like to think otherwise, that he had a hunger to be alone in a quiet world, to feel underfoot the risings and fallings of the land so long buried beneath asphalt and concrete.

Within an hour his tracks were obliterated by less imaginative pedestrians, by buses and skidding taxis with blaring horns, and harried snow-removal crews. The day became usual, but he had celebrated its unusual birth.

Although reasonably social creatures, there are some of us who from time to time have a craving to be alone or with a carefully chosen companion only, in a world where the loudest sound may be the song of a chickadee balanced on a jouncing spruce branch, or the wind-created creaking of bare hardwood boughs high overhead.

Cross-country skiing is a splendid way to achieve this. It may be enjoyed as soon as there are a few inches of snow underfoot, and without – a major reason for its appeal to many – elaborate gear and preparation, without waiting one's turn at a ski lift, and on a wide variety of terrain, from city parks to wilderness areas.

When there is only a light covering of snow on the ground, one generally has to stick to trails, meadows or unploughed dirt roads, but as the snow deepens the opportunity for woods travel increases. Three or four feet of snow – the more the better – covers much of the undergrowth, the fallen trees, the debris left by logging operations, and a region that was a horror to the autumn upland bird or deer hunter is readily negotiable. And when all, or nearly all, the leaves are off the deciduous trees, a trail that in summer or early autumn seemed to lead one through a nearly impenetrable jungle often provides a clear view of distant hills or the twisting course of a brook.

The essential shapes of deciduous trees, which vary greatly, may be clearly seen in winter. The classic eastern white oak, for example, has a rounded crown with wide spreading branches, as does its cousin, the northern red oak, but the branches of the former spread upward, and sometimes horizontally, in a fairly symmetrical manner, while those of the latter are stouter, less regular, and often turned down. With a twelve-power pocket lens and a good text – William Trelease's *Winter Botany* (Dover Publications) is first rate – one can identify nearly all the trees and shrubs one encounters in this country. The *Audubon Society Field Guide to North American Trees* (Knopf) – one for the Eastern region and one for the Western – is superb and has illustrations of trees in their leafless stage.

I prefer to be abroad the morning after an evening's snowfall because every track I spot at such a time can be no more than a few hours old. If the snow has fallen most of the night, however, most of the animals will have remained holed up and tracks will be scarce until the following day. On old snow, new tracks can be distinguished from old, but this takes a little expertise.

Ponds, lakes, and streams will be on the topographic maps you should always bring with you – as well as a compass – when engaged in off-trail ski touring, but most beaver ponds will not be marked because they are too short-lived: Once the available food is gone, the animals move on.

More often than not, a visit to a beaver pond in the heart of winter will reveal nothing but the snow-covered, frozen-over pond and the animal's lodge, from the top of which, in bitterly cold weather, one can see the beaver's breath rising like smoke. Although beavers strive to get in enough food to last them through the winter, they sometimes fail at this and when a thaw allows them access to land, they will forage out through deep snow.

Cross-country skiing at night under a full, or nearly full, moon is an intoxicating experience, but it had best be confined to meadows or well-defined trails. Although the snow-moon combination makes it nearly light enough to read by, one's sense of distance, of variations in terrain, is not entirely adequate.

Moonlight skiing is an excellent opportunity to learn the constellations. Carry a so-called star wheel and a small flashlight with you. There is, for many, a special pleasure in recognizing stars and planets, and, should you lose your direction and be without compass, you will be able to find the North Star and your way home.

If you can make your way through the trailless summer wood with map and compass, you will be able to do the same, with less attention to maintaining direction, in winter. Running a compass course in winter is simpler because one can see more distant landmarks. The beginning ski tourer who is also a novice at orienteering would do best to remain on marked trails or well-defined unploughed roads or abandoned railway beds.

The New Hampshire Publishing Company, 9 Orange Street, Somersworth, N.H. 03878, has published a series of ski touring guides listing trails, often associated with inns or ski centres catering to cross-country skiers, in New England and the Adirondacks, and the New York-New Jersey Trail Conference, Inc., has published *A Guide to Ski Touring in New York–New Jersey*. The conference's address is 15 East 40th Street, New York, N.Y. 10016.

A family ski-touring expedition can be a lot of fun, but remember that youngsters – particularly those not yet in their teens – usually get cold faster than adults and often aren't aware of what is happening. If you are carrying a child on your back, err on the side of over-dressing it and watch it for signs of frostbite or chattering teeth or shivering. If your trip will carry you off the beaten track, make sure to tell some competent person – it is best to show them on a topographic map – where you will be travelling and when you expect to be back.

One bad spill on a downhill run can result in a broken leg or ankle and if that happens ten miles into the woods what was an exhilarating experience can become a test of your survival skills. If you are caught in a snowstorm that reduces visibility to near zero or if you underestimate the time needed to return and are caught out in the dark, your best bet may be to stay put, erect a crude shelter, or get out of the wind in a hole in the snow, and await the dawn.

A recently published and excellent paperback, *Cross Country Skier's Trailside Guide* (Stephen Greene Press, Fessenden Road, Brattleboro, Vt. 05301), covers all aspects of the sport, including equipment, conditioning, preskiing warm-up exercises, and safety rules. Written by Craig Woods, Gordon Hardy, and the editors of *Cross Country Skier*, it also contains an appendix listing cross-country skiing organizations and agencies serving skiers, and another devoted to suppliers of cross-country ski equipment.

YELLOWSTONE: FIRE AND ICE

William E. Schmidt

The first hard snow usually comes to Yellowstone in October, and by Thanksgiving most of the mountain passes and the roads into the interior have been surrendered to winter. As the snow deepens in the high country, the park's thick herds of bison and elk begin to cluster in the lower valleys that are their winter range. The animals stand out sharply against the white landscape, their shaggy flanks flecked with snow, as they push through belly-deep drifts in search of forage.

Behind them, where the great geysers fume, columns of steam climb against a brittle sky. It is the cold winter air that makes the geysers appear to boil so furiously, instantly condensing their vapours into thick plumes of steam that glaze nearby trees in a ghostly veneer of ice. Along the warm, geyser-fed rivers that meander through the snow, a perpetual fog swirls over the water, shrouding the surrounding forest and turning the afternoon sun into a luminescent pink ball.

The short, brutally cold days of winter are an extraordinary time to see Yellowstone. It is a season of almost primeval beauty, when the bison emerge from the mists like creatures from another time and 300-foot waterfalls are frozen into pillars of milky ice. Deep in the forests, the only sound is the muffled thump of snow falling to the ground from the tops of towering fir trees. Until spring, when maintenance crews begin to plough out the roads, travel inside most of the park will be limited to snowshoes, skis or tracked snow vehicles.

In winter, nature seems to have reclaimed the 3,400-square-mile preserve as her own. After the crowds of summer have gone, the animals recapture the ground where once the tourists roamed, and deep snow and ice enfold the forests.

There is a special kind of intoxication in all of this. It is a heady mixture of both excitement and apprehension, the powerful sensation that you are passing through a place where man clearly does not belong, an uncompromising land that has changed little since the first explorers discovered the Yellowstone region more than a century and a half ago.

The cold and the wind and the snow remake Yellowstone. The

gentle landscape of summer, with its wide green meadows and lolling rivers, is transformed; the asphalt parking lots where hundreds of camper trailers baked in last summer's sun are now buried beneath thick drifts of snow, broken only by the tracks of passing rabbits and elk. During January and February, night-time temperatures commonly drop to 20 degrees below zero. In the higher elevations, temperatures drop to as low as 60 degrees below zero, causing trees to explode as the moisture inside their trunks freezes and expands.

Less than a ten-minute trek from the Old Faithful area, the ski trails wind through towering forests of pine that absorb even the nearby drone of snowmobile engines. Elk browse along narrow streams, within a few feet of the trails. They do not move when you pass. It's almost as if you aren't there.

For those willing to brave it, the best way to see Yellowstone in winter is on skis. Without exception, the park offers the premier cross-country-ski experience in the lower forty-eight states. There are nearly seventy-five miles of groomed trails inside the park, as well as tens of thousands of acres of untracked wilderness. Here, serious back-country skiers not only break their own trails, but also sometimes camp overnight, bundled against the wind, the cold and the snow inside sleeping bags and tents.

For less hardy souls, even the novice trails are laid out so that they skirt the major thermal basins, which afford a close-up of the geysers and the mist-shrouded thermal pools. The meadows and wide valleys surrounding many of the park's thermal basins also provide the best opportunities for viewing park wildlife, which during the winter tends to congregate near the geysers and the hot pools. This is because the heat from the underground thermal activity helps melt the surrounding snow cover, making it easier for elk and bison to forage. The warm, open water also attracts a variety of birds, among them Canada geese and trumpeter swans.

Many of the animals, especially elk and bison, are much more conspicuous in winter than in summer, when they are spread throughout the park. Park naturalists estimate that during the winter months there are probably 15,000 elk, 2,000 bison and more than 400 bighorn sheep inside Yellowstone. (There are also several hundred mule deer and moose, as well as a variety of bears, but the bears are seldom seen once the snow starts falling.) During the hardest winters, the weakest individuals do not survive, and in spring, when the snow melts, the park is sometimes littered with their carcasses. As part of a formal National Park Service policy not to interfere with the natural order of things, the dead animals are left where they fall, to provide a feast for Yellowstone's thriving population of coyotes and other predators.

There is such an abundance of wildlife that it is not uncommon for skiers or snowmobilers to find their path blocked by herds of bison or elk. Not long ago, a woman skiing through the park crested a hill only to find herself on an unavoidable collision course with a 2,000-pound bison grazing in the snow on the other side of the slope. It was only after the skier skidded to a full stop beneath the shaggy belly of the beast that the buffalo decided it was time to move on, presumably in search of a less trafficked spot to browse. As it did, the animal stepped on the skier, breaking three of her ribs.

Snowmobiles, as well as skis and snowshoes for back-country touring, can be rented within the park. Visitors can also sign on for guided tours in a heated Snowcoach, a ten-passenger contraption resembling a cross between a bus and a tank that looks like something salvaged from the Russian front.

The policy to allow snowmobiles inside the park has aroused some controversy – among some environmental groups, snowmobiles are about as popular as nuclear power plants. A snowmobile cutting across country can wreak havoc with wildlife nesting areas, uproot plants and seedlings, and destroy forage needed for winter animals.

On winter weekends there can be as many as a thousand snowmobiles at a time within Yellowstone's boundaries. They are restricted to a network of trails laid out over 150 miles of the park's existing road system, and rangers argue that as long as the machines are so confined, they are no more disruptive than automobile traffic through the park during the summer months. (The same rangers also concede that one of their principal chores during the winter months is policing the snowmobile trails – accidents are not uncommon, and neither are citations for leaving the market trail system, an offence that is treated most seriously and can bring a fine of up to $500.)

The debate over snowmobiles illustrates a recurrent dilemma facing the park service. That is, how to provide for the greatest possible public access to the park without damaging the very features that make Yellowstone unique in the first place. One recent winter, for example, rangers had to crack down sharply on what is called 'hot potting.' Hot pots occur in several places throughout the park, where scalding water boiling off a hot spring or geyser basin will mix with the swift, cold currents of a nearby river and form a sort of natural hot tub. At one location, along the steeply terraced banks of the Gardiner River near Mammoth, so many people were stripping down and plunging into the tepid river that the surrounding area was being worn down by pedestrian traffic, and there were increasing instances of drunkenness and bawdy behaviour. Food and drink are now banned from the area, and swimming after dark is outlawed. Ideally, hot potting is an idyllic adventure. There is nothing more intoxicating than soaking in the steam of a geyser-fired river somewhere in the silent heart of Yellowstone. But it is best to ask the rangers for advice on where to go. Some rivers are closed to hot potting because of the fragile ecology of the surrounding area; others are just too dangerous. The water in many thermal areas is at a temperature of about 200 degrees.

For those who live year round inside Yellowstone, winter defies any single, simple description. It is a season of the contrasts, a time of immeasurable beauty and of iron cruelty. 'On a windy day, standing in the Hayden Valley, the landscape is so bleak and hard that sometimes I feel I am somewhere above the Arctic Circle,' said Tom Hobbs, the park's chief ranger. 'You sense strongly the struggle for survival among all the natural elements.'

But in other places, at other times, when the plumes from the nearby geysers drift over the forest like low clouds, and the wind off the mountains polishes snowbanks into soft, shifting sculpture, Yellowstone becomes a secret place of fire and ice where silence rings louder than sound.

THE PARK IN THE COLD
Finding Shelter

One recent season, a record 100,000 people visited Yellowstone National Park between mid-December and late March, nearly twice the number of visitors who wintered there in 1980. The increase reflects in part the efforts of TW Services Inc., the private concessionaire under contract to the National Park Service, and the park management itself, to expand wintertime facilities inside Yellowstone.

Mammoth Hot Springs: in recent years, this 100-room hotel, which is accessible by automobile, has been open during the winter. From the airport in Bozeman, Montana, travellers head east to Livingston on Interstate 90, and then straight south along U.S. 89 to Mammoth Hot Springs, which is about five miles inside the park's northern boundary. The road is kept open through the winter.

The hotel was constructed in 1936; it's not luxurious, but there is a newly remodelled restaurant and bar, decorated in a sort of North Woods Art Deco. Entrées in the dining room include steaks, duck, and trout and range from about $5 to $15; wine is also available. Breakfasts are about $4, and there is a fast-food restaurant next door with such standards as hamburgers and hot dogs.

Snow Lodge: this eighty-five-room establishment, about a quarter of a mile from the Old Faithful geyser, can be reached only by a snowmobile or Snowcoach, which makes regular daily runs from Mammoth Hot Springs, as well as from the park entrances.

There is a lounge with an open-hearth fireplace and a restaurant that offers a similarly priced but slightly more limited menu than that at Mammoth Hot Springs. An adjacent snack shop lists hamburgers, hot dogs, and the like.

Tariffs: rooms at the Mammoth Hot Springs Hotel are about $40 a night with bath, less without, single or double. Only rooms without bath are available in the Old Faithful Snow Lodge itself (about $30 a night, single or double), although there are standard cabins, with bath, nearby (roughly $40 a night, single or double).

The Mammoth Hot Springs Hotel is open from late December to late February, Snow Lodge from mid-December to mid-March. For reservations, telephone TW Services Inc., at 307 344 7311, or write to them in care of Yellowstone National Park, Wyo. 82091. Brochures and maps are also available.

SKIING AND SNOWMOBILING

Cross-country skis, boots, and poles can be rented inside the park. Group and private ski lessons are available at both Old Faithful and Mammoth Hot Springs.

Snowmobiles can be rented inside the park for about $70 a day, a fee that includes the use of the machine as well as a helmet, boots, mittens and an insulated snowmobile windsuit. Rates are somewhat cheaper if the machine is rented from private outfitters in the communities just outside the park's boundary.

SNOWCOACHING

Snowcoach tours run from the park's south entrance to Old Faithful (about $25 a person, one way), West Yellowstone to Old Faithful (about $20 a person, one way), and Mammoth Hot Springs to Old Faithful (about $25 a person, one way); round-trip fares are double the one-way rates; children between the ages of five and ten are half-fare, and children under four ride free. There is also a tour to the Grand Canyon of the Yellowstone River for about $50 a person, round trip, from either Mammoth Hot Springs or Old Faithful.

WINTER IN ITS PLACE

Peter Viertel

The Swiss are a fortunate people. Winter, which brings gloom to the soul of the Londoner, the Parisian, even the Madrileño, finds them in their element. Their small, industrious country, with its cosy inns and predictably efficient services, seems made for it. Like much else in Switzerland, winter has been tamed, put at man's disposal.

Wherever you happen to begin your trip, in Basel or Bern or Zürich or Geneva, you have only to take your car, or buy a ticket on an immaculately clean train and in a couple of hours you will find yourself in a pure white world that seems like a part of another planet, where the sun, if there is any to be had, shines down on God's children. The Alps are the country's proudest possession. They are unique among all the mountain ranges in the world, not only because they are so easily accessible, but also because they are the most civilized and well prepared to meet man's need to play in the cold season. No wilderness peaks, these; the region has been cultivated by man over the centuries.

This is a country is which the shops open at eight in the morning, the streets are virtually free of violent crime, the highways are safer from accidents than those of neighbouring countries, the telephone system is modern and dependable, and the national tourist bureau is almost as well organized as the national airline, which is one of the most efficient in the world (and operates at a nice profit). This orderliness is at no time more apparent than during the colder months. In Switzerland, winter is kept in its place. And there, like a fine Swiss watch, it works with precision.

It is not that Switzerland is spared bad weather. In Zürich the fog clouds begin to form over the lake as early as mid-October, and Geneva, although benefiting somewhat from the warm winds of the Rhône valley, has very little sun to offer its residents once the cold weather has set in. But a large area of the topography lies high above the level of the sea, which is proven at first view to the approaching guest who arrives by air. While the rest of the Continent is socked in, much of Helvetia is sticking up through the clouds. Parts of Austria, Italy, and France are similarly blessed, but it is Switzerland that first comes to mind when one thinks of a country and a people that are out to vanquish winter.

It was probably the English who first discovered the joys of winter in the Alps. Skiing was the key. The Scandinavians, and even the gold miners of northern California, had used skis to move about when walking became too laborious because of a deep snowfall, but downhill skiing as we know it today was first widely practised as a sport by upper-class Britons not long after the end of World War I. Even then, the Swiss railway system, equipped to operate in winter, made things easy for the pioneers of the new sport.

A Swiss tourist industry had existed for generations to serve summer visitors. These specialists in hotel-keeping were easily able to convert both modest inns and more luxurious establishments to winter use. Mountain guides, who in the past had spent their winters oiling hobnailed boots and coiling ropes, soon became expert at the new game of running down the crystal-covered meadows, and, since they were well acquainted with every rock and pine along the way, they became an invaluable asset in seeing to it that the guests made it back to shelter by the end of the day, to be comforted with blazing fires, mulled wine and sausages and other indigenous delicacies.

In less than two decades, winter tourism had begun to bring in respectable amounts of foreign currency during what had previously been a dead season, and soon, after the end of World War II, the skiing boom was well under way. By the early 1960s, a great many people had come to realize that the ideal winter holiday was to be had by going off to a small mountain village, where you could live quite reasonably in a cosy hotel, eat delicious Continental food and spend the days on the often sunny slopes. Davos and Zermatt, among other towns, grew into winter-sport centres, well organized to receive thousands of enthusiasts in a season. But even those who did not choose to ski could partake, and at other resorts – particularly St. Moritz – après-ski became as important as the sport itself. The town, and others like it, became an outpost of cosmopolitan glitter, complete with branches of Zürich banks and jewellery stores.

I myself first learned to ski a little before World War II in the mountains of Southern California. In November 1946, after a stint in the United States Marine Corps, I was hired to write a script for a Swiss motion-picture company. The Swiss producer, thinking rather naïvely that the city of Zürich offered too many distractions, sent me to Davos so that I could work undisturbed in the peace and quiet of the mountains.

An early snowfall made it possible for me to resume my skiing career. I found an instructor, a patient Swiss, and every afternoon we would make our way to the beginners' hill on the outskirts of the town, where we practised sideslipping and making turns in anticipation of the start of the season. The Parsennbahn, the local cable railway, began operating only in mid-December, and when the great day finally arrived, I made my first run down to Klosters, a neighbouring village about eight miles away. It took me nearly two hours – an expert skier can make this run in twenty minutes – since I must have fallen at least fifty times, but once there, I realized that I had discovered a small paradise.

Klosters was then, and is now, a paradigm of Swiss resorts. The village was picturesque, to say the least. Not one ugly building was then to be found in all the town; not one ugly building is present there today. Virtually all construction is in the chalet style, so that architecturally the village has not been spoiled by modern monstrosities. There was, and is, a charming, small hotel called the Chesa Grishuna, where for less than five dollars a day, room and board, a young screenwriter, even at a pared-down Swiss salary, could live and work in luxury (a room at the Chesa now costs about $100 a day, meals included). The people of Klosters were friendly, starved as they were for tourists, and the scenery was some of the most beautiful in the world. Needless to say, it was hard to leave Klosters once the script was finished.

I returned every year, and friends soon appeared on the scene. Robert Capa, the photographer, Irwin Shaw, Anatole Litvak, the movie director, Kirk Douglas, Gene Kelly, Arthur Stanton, James Jones, Gore Vidal. There was a tax benefit to be had by living seventeen out of eighteen months abroad, and Klosters became known as Hollywood on the Rocks.

The Gotschnabahn, a small cable car that joined Klosters to the Parsenn, was completed in 1949, and the village flourished. But it has been the automobile that has brought about the greatest – and, to some old residents, the least desirable – change. The main road to Davos runs straight through the village and from Friday afternoon to Sunday evening one has a distinct feeling that entire nations are on the move, either fleeing from an enemy army or moving up into the highlands where a new Mother Lode of gold has been discovered. They are no less of a nuisance when they start back into the valley at the end of the weekend. But there are also advantages to this popularity: There are now more good restaurants to be found in the town, and indoor tennis courts are only about five miles away. The ski runs, too, are better kept because of the large number of piste-making machines operating in the area. (But there is less powder snow to be found for the expert, and the runs are infinitely more crowded than ten years ago.)

For Klosters, and other Alpine villages, the high seasons are at

Christmas-time and from the middle of February to the end of March. Then it is crowded with skiers who come up from the adjoining Swiss and German valleys and give the place a Brueghel-like look, bright, tiny figures in a white landscape, skiing, skating, curling, eating.

Klosters, and Verbier – which has a new cable car that will take you to dizzying heights – are the places to go if you are an expert skier. But you don't have to be an expert, or even a skier, to enjoy winter in the Alps. Other pleasures are available for the earthbound and nonathletic. Walking paths are cleared for the use of strollers, and excursions by sleigh are organized. You can sunbathe on a sunny terrace in the midst of snow scenes, or you can take a cable car or lift to the top of a mountain, join the skiers for lunch at the restaurant that is almost sure to be at the top, then take the cable car or the lift back down. You can take scenic train rides – the Glacier Express, which runs between Zermatt and St. Moritz, is the most luxurious option, offering sumptuous meals and spectacular views. (Wine is served in 'leaning' glasses set at an angle to their bases; the idea is that you rotate the glass to prevent spilling as the train ascends or descends sharp gradients.)

There are baths to be taken at such spas as Bad Ragaz, where you can cure a variety of acquired ills, from rheumatism to liver ailments. Near Davos, at the end of an exhilarating downhill run, you can take off your boots and skiing togs and enjoy the natural curative waters of Bad Zerneus and be ready for the mountains again on the following day, with your muscles relaxed and bones almost as good as new. The resorts in eastern Switzerland offer a variety of indoor tennis and squash courts for the days when avalanches threaten. And all of these places, with the exception of Zurs, have excellent cross-country skiing, a sport that is less dangerous if you have set a high value on your bones and still want to trim off excessive winter weight.

For the man or woman who delights in the glamour of social life, St. Moritz and Gstaad have no winter equal. St. Moritz caters more to the German and Italian aristocracy, while Gstaad is frequented more by the French and Spanish titled rich (indeed, King Juan Carlos of Spain broke his pelvis skiing there one recent January).

In addition to royalty, these are the two Swiss ski resorts that attract the jet set. The winter migration of this not particularly rare fauna adheres to a schedule that is not influenced by the weather, because only a small percentage of them ski. They arrive early in February and depart early in March. Snow or no snow, icy moguls or deep powder, the cocktail and dinner parties follow one another in relentless succession. Hostesses vie for the right dates on the calendar, and are careful not to have their festivities conflict. No one has to get up early in the morning to be on the slopes, so that while the skiers sleep, you will be able to dance until dawn, and court the more or less attractive members of the opposite sex who go there for no other reason than to be wined and dined – and, of course, seduced.

St. Moritz offers better skiing and Gstaad a less dangerous altitude for the elderly of the blue-blooded, who may or may not be troubled by palpitations. The hangers-on of the rich are to be found in both spas: the jewel thieves – it has been said that Gstaad, St. Moritz, and Monte Carlo are the only places left where people are not afraid to wear real jewels – the professional backgammon players, and general layabouts, as well as the high-class ladies of doubtful virtue (if such a thing still exists).

In both Gstaad and St. Moritz, your average social climber will see as many wearers of expensive fun furs on the street and in the fashionable tearooms (Hanselmann's in St. Moritz is one example – don't let them seat you upstairs) as ski-booted sportsmen. The fur pedlars and jewellers of the world have shops there, as do the major fashion houses of Paris, so if you want to spend the million dollars your aunt bequeathed you, there is no better place to do so than Switzerland during the cold season. You don't have to be a gamesman to enjoy yourself and fritter away your cash.

If your heart is still set on skiing – and if you do not have a million dollars – you should know that in almost any Swiss resort you will be able to rent virtually new equipment at a modest price, thereby avoiding the need to pack the cumbersome gear that is an essential part of the sport. The railway system is the envy of the Western world, so you won't have to rent a car. The trains run on time and are clean and safe. You can buy a ticket in most Swiss resorts that will take care of the lifts and the trains taking you to them. Most areas are well patrolled, and if you obey the rules, you will not run into serious trouble with avalanches or snow slides.

Wherever you go, you will eat well. One of the continuing miracles of Switzerland is this small country's ability to sustain and protect three cultures and three languages – and three cuisines. Nor is this pleasant asset limited in any way to the specific regions. In Zürich, the German-Swiss capital, there are, for example, a number of excellent Italian and French restaurants, as well as those places offering Swiss-German fare. Swiss national delicacies are available in all of the resorts, as they are in the major Swiss cities. Fondue bourguignonne, fondue chinoise, and just plain old fondue are to be had for the asking. And don't miss a raclette party, where you eat a special variety of melted cheese served with boiled potatoes, onions, and sweet and sour pickles galore. The wide variety of regional sausages, the *bundnerfleisch* – smoked and dried beef served in thin slices – and rösti potatoes, the speciality of German Switzerland, should all be sampled.

But for all the amenities applied by man, it is the mountains themselves that are still the big thrill to this ageing, Alpine strap-hanger, and the slipping and sliding, the fast, free ride that they have to offer. There is very little in life as exhilarating as the silent, swift descent into the valley, with the cold air brushing past your goggles, and your well-trained legs and feet guiding you past the bumps and other obstacles, man-made or provided by nature. If you are not young any more, it will revive you, and if you are less than fifty, it will make you feel, for half an hour or more, that you are immortal.

And if you are jaded, and already considering Russian roulette as a winter pastime, you can bring your hang glider along, or rent one for a princely sum, on the spot. Swiss hospitals are as clean and efficient as everything else in this well-organized country.

THE QUESTION:
TO SKI OR APRÈS-SKI?

Enid Nemy

The photographs always look wonderful – an enormous room with sink-into chairs, a blazing log fire that makes even wrinkles look glamorous, and carelessly sophisticated men and women lolling around in various carelessly sophisticated attitudes. Oh yes, there's one other thing. The clothes, from the furry slippers to the chic sweaters, somehow indicate that these are people who have spent their day between ski lifts and slopes.

The truth about après-ski life in the internationally known resorts is somewhat different. This is not to say that no lolling is done in the big hotels and lodges but the fact is that after four or five hours of schussing and wedeling, most experienced skiers prefer more informal surroundings.

'You can either ski or you can après-ski but you can't do both,' said Felix Rohatyn, senior partner of Lazard Frères.

Robert S. McNamara, the former Secretary of Defense and president of the World Bank, who has been skiing at Aspen for thirty-five years, said, 'After skiing all day, what I like to do is have a good dinner and go to bed.'

Mr. McNamara is generally on Aspen's slopes about five hours a day, skiing into and out of his house for lunch. When he goes out for dinner in the evening, he likes Abetone's and Charlemagne and, in nearby Snowmass, Chez Grandmère. 'Chez Grandmère is run by a couple and it's expensive but the food is good and attractively served,' he says. The restaurant is also one of the few that has only one sitting, so diners don't feel rushed.

'One thing I would like to see,' Mr. McNamara adds, 'is a ski trail between Aspen and Vail so that skiers could, if they wanted, ski from one place to the other and stay overnight in huts, as they can in Switzerland. I've had two huts built, in memory of my wife, and I've skied up to one of them. I'm working with Fritz Benedict of the 10th Mountain Trail Association in Aspen on the whole idea.'

Mr. Rohatyn, Austrian-born and a skier since he was six years old, says his programme in Alta, Utah, where he went for ten years, was 'skiing, hot tub, nap, early dinner, and sleep.' However, more recently, he and his wife, Elizabeth, have been going to Sun Valley, Idaho, where they are slightly more active after a day's skiing.

'When we come down from the slopes, we may go to the Konditorei for Viennese coffee and pastry,' he said. 'And for dinner, Trail Creek Cabin is fun. You go in big sleighs and by the time you arrive you're both numb and hungry but you run into a lot of people there. Once it was Jane Fonda and Tom Hayden and that gave it a kind of glamorous aspect.'

Like Mr. McNamara and the Rohatyns, most serious skiers come off the slopes and either head directly for home or for cafés and restaurants, preferably with terraces, where they can collapse with a hot chocolate or cup of tea. Then, after a shower and a nap, it's off to a bar or restaurant, or combination of both, with less glitz and more atmosphere than that provided by tuxedo-clad waiters and white tablecloths. As for food, good Mexican dishes, barbecued ribs, a steak or raclette are apparently in far greater demand than nouvelle cuisine.

One skier with rather special ideas about relaxing when the lifts close is Seiji Ozawa, the music director of the Boston Symphony Orchestra. Mr. Ozawa, his wife, and their two young children ski both in Japan and at Alpine Meadows, near Squaw Valley. 'I take skiing as a family affair because I travel so much during the year.' Mr. Ozawa continued, 'In Japan, we go to Akakura, near the Sea of Japan, about four and a half hours by train from Tokyo, and we stay in an old-fashioned Japanese inn. Both our children were born in San Francisco and this is a chance for them to get lots of snow and also see old Japanese life.

'After skiing, we jump into the hot tub. In Japan, in the hot spas, you just call service and they bring you steamed or boiled peanuts and sake or cold beer while you are in the tub, which is just fantastic. You eat a little and get a little drunk. Then it is the custom to have dinner in your own room and maybe after that you join friends or people you have met, and the children play video games.'

Nan Kempner, a New York socialite who's been skiing for almost half a century, is more familiar with raclette than sushi. The best raclette, she says, is at Le Cerf, a small restaurant in Rougemont near Gstaad, Switzerland. In Vail, her restaurant choices are the Antlers Room in the Gasthof Gramshammer known as Pepi's, where the speciality is game, and the Tearoom Alpenrose for tea and breads, cakes and doughnuts.

Cynthia and Charles Olson of Chicago – he's chairman of the insurance brokerage firm – have been skiing in Vail since 1967. 'If there's anyone in town, you'll see them if you sit on the terrace at Pepi's,' Mrs. Olson says. 'They have to walk by there; it's like being in an outdoor café in Paris.' Their favourite restaurant, she says, is the Left Bank, in the centre of town, which has French country décor and consistently good food, particularly the seafood Provençal. For barbecue, Robin Cook, the author of such books as *Godplayer*, *The Sphinx*, and *Coma*, chooses the Shaft in Aspen, where the walls look as though they were carved from a vein of coal ore.

'I only eat ribs once a year and that's where I eat them,' said Dr. Cook, who has also been skiing since he was a child. 'You eat with your fingers and it always brings back images of the movie *Tom Jones*.'

The Cooks also go to the Ute City Banque, a restaurant that once was a bank and still has vestiges of the vault and tellers' windows and, for a drink immediately after skiing, the Timber Mill in Snowmass.

The Ute City Banque is on the preferred list of another literary figure, Larry Collins, the co-author of *O Jerusalem*, *The Fifth Horseman*, and *Is Paris Burning?*

'The Ute City Banque is congenial and you meet half the people you know,' Mr. Collins said. 'We also like Little Nell's, where everyone hangs out, and André's, which is a vertical pleasure dome, a bar, restaurant, and discothèque. Then there's the Crystal Palace, which is noisy and full of laughter. The food tends to get thrown at you with a certain air of careless disdain but it's done in good fun and with style.'

Nicholas M. Sands, a real-estate developer who has interests in Idaho, makes for the Duchin Room or Silver Creek Saloon in Ketchum after a day of skiing in Sun Valley.

'For dinner, I like La Provence because it's charming and quaint and the food is good,' he says. 'I also go to Chez Russell, and Louie's Italian Restaurant, which is in a wonderful setting on the Snake River.'

For Diahn McGrath, a television actress, and her husband, Thomas, a lawyer with Simpson, Thacher & Bartlett, the important consideration for an after-ski spot is somewhere suitable for their five-year-old daughter, Courtney.

'We like Casa Che at Snowmass because you can ski onto the terrace from the slopes and there is a wonderful barbecue, terrific salad bar, and great soups,' Mrs. McGrath said. 'And nobody minds if Courtney falls asleep on a banquette.'

Tiffany Green, in Snowmass, also meets with her approval, again because of a long and good salad bar and 'a harpist who plays during dinner and who absolutely mesmerizes the children.'

Leonard Lauder, president of Estee Lauder Inc., and his wife, Evelyn, a corporate vice president, alternate their skiing between Aspen and St. Moritz in Switzerland. For barbecue, they also like the Shaft in Aspen. 'But probably the best restaurant in town is the Abetone,' Mrs. Lauder said. 'It's modern and cool-looking and has consistently good food and service. Then there's a darling little restaurant called the Parlour Car, which is in two railway carriages said to have been the personal cars of Theodore Roosevelt. We also like Little Nell's where all the young kids congregate and your food is served in a miner's pan.'

When they are feeling up to it, the Lauders ski cross-country, about thirteen miles, to the Pine Creek Cook House, 'sort of Swiss and big as your thumb,' for such things as red cabbage and bratwurst, and to the Cross Country Cookery at Snowmass. 'There's a wood-burning stove and you eat in the kitchen and that's all there is,' Mrs. Lauder said, and added thankfully, 'and it's not quite as long a ski.'

When William F. Buckley, Jr., author and editor of the *National Review*, and his wife, Pat, take up their annual residence in Switzerland, they usually dine at home or at the chalets of friends. When they venture out, they like the Hotel Christiania dining room in Gstaad for lunch, the Hotel Garni in nearby Saanen, the Hotel Ermitage, and Hotel Alpenrose in Schönried, and the Hôtel de la Poste in Bulle.

'We also love lunching in the sun on the terrace of the Hotel Golf and Sport at Saanen-Moser,' Mrs. Buckley said. 'You're surrounded by mountains and it's the most beautiful valley in the area.'

Steve Garvey, first baseman for the San Diego Padres, is a relatively new convert to skiing but he now has a condominium at the Stein Ericksen Lodge in Park City, Utah, and divides his time between non-treacherous downhill slopes and cross-country trekking.

'When you're a professional athlete, you have to be a bit careful,' he explained.

One of his favourite after-ski activities is looking at the view from one of the lodge terraces or from his own balcony. 'As the light fades I like the stillness of the cold night air and the view of the mountains while I'm sipping hot chocolate on my balcony. It tapers the day down gently. There are mountains on one side and ski slopes on the other.'

Another after-ski diversion is the Jacuzzi followed by a few laps in the heated pool, which also has a mountain view. 'When I've wound down, I like some wine and cheese and then an early dinner. One of the restaurants I like is the Mariposa, which has really excellent food and desserts.'

Nannette Cavanagh, an expert skier who has, she said, skied everywhere and everything, likes the Hotel Jerome in Aspen and its bar, which looks like a Western saloon.

When she's skiing in Europe, she heads for the King's Club in the Palace Hotel at St. Moritz 'to see everything that's going on,' and the Hotel Post restaurant in St. Anton, Austria, for venison and lingonberry crêpes with powdered sugar.

But her first and foremost love is Bugaboo Lodge in the Canadian

Rockies. The Lodge, the only place to stay if one is skiing in the Bugaboos, maintains contact with the outside world via a weekly helicopter.

'It's in a glacial valley and the porch looks out onto the glacier. There's nothing to describe how you feel when you get in there at four or five p.m., put your feet up, drink steaming mugs of hot chocolate or cider, and look at the sun going down over the great expanse of green-blue ice. It's paradise untouched.'

WINTER · LEAVE IT
SOUTHERN ROUTES

FLORIDIANA

Artists and writers have their own Floridas. Alison Lurie chooses Key West, at once an old-fashioned small town and a setting for lively street theatre. For Roger Tory Peterson, Florida means Sanibel Island, where bald eagles soar overhead. James Rosenquist's Florida is a remote bay on the Gulf Coast where the intensity of the sunlight has caught his painter's eye. *The Sophisticated Traveller* asked a dozen part-time Floridians to write about the areas they know best; their insights illumine special worlds that may elude the casual visitor.

Key West: Neverland with Palms

ALISON LURIE

James Barrie, in *Peter Pan*, imagined an island that would contain all his childhood fantasies: pirates, Indians, mermaids, wild animals, fairies; a lagoon, a forest, and a cave. Key West, for me, is the same sort of supernatural assemblage. It is simultaneously a quiet small town; a warm, flowery, tropical paradise; a gathering of cosmopolitan restaurants and cafés and a writers' colony. And what is best of all, it actually exists and can be reached by flights from Miami as easy and almost as scenic as the one Peter Pan escorted Wendy, John and Michael on to Neverland.

To picture the island, forget your stereotypes of south Florida. Imagine instead an old-fashioned New England or Midwestern town with tree-lined streets and gingerbread-trimmed white houses. Then remove all the tame Temperate Zone flora and replace it with palms, banyans, figs, orchid trees and a riot of brilliantly flowering vines and shrubs. Imagine that in this magical small town it never snows, and you can swim in the warm turquoise sea twelve months of the year.

Yes, I've been to places like that, you may say; but I got tired of the hotel cooking and there was nothing to do in the evening. Don't worry; this will not happen in Key West. After you have sampled the native dishes – bubbling conch chowder and fritters; huge, incredibly fresh pink shrimp steamed in beer; and Key lime pie made with real Key limes from someone's backyard – there are many other possibilities. There is fine Italian cooking at Fiorini's, nouvelle cuisine – and celebrity watching – at Claire's, and Cuban roast pork and black beans at the Fourth of July. At Las Palmas del Mundo, hidden away in the historical preservation district, you can eat strange and delicious varieties of fresh-caught fish in an overgrown tropical garden; or you can lunch at La Terraza de Marti (known locally, with good reason, as the La-di-da) and watch – or if you are daring, join – the topless and sometimes bottomless swimmers in the heated, flower-bordered pool.

At sunset, on Mallory Dock, you can see the singers, jugglers, and clowns who keep alive the ancient tradition of strolling players. Later there are cafés and discos where you can hear – or dance to – hard rock, soft rock, classic swing, jazz, bluegrass, folk, or country and Western music. Around midnight, the local and visiting pirates, Indians, and so on – less disguised than you might think – come out.

As for myself, however, I go to Key West not so much for relaxation or entertainment as to work. And for a writer it is ideal. The island, as almost everyone knows, is haunted by authors of every sort, and there is always someone interesting to have supper with. The design of the houses, most of which have walled gardens surrounding a deck and/or pool, guarantees quiet and privacy almost as well as Peter Pan's underground cave. If I like I can unplug the telephone and write for days without interruption. Then, when I re-emerge, all the attractions of this contemporary Neverland are waiting.

The Everglades: Water Wilderness

BUDD SCHULBERG

For some forty years I've been drawn to the Everglades, the poetically but aptly named 'River of Grass' that overruns South Florida beyond Alligator Alley and the Tamiami Trail. The grass is sawgrass, mean to the touch but beautiful to the eye, stretching for trackless miles to the subtropical tip of the continent. It is a river without banks, fifty to seventy-five miles wide, imperceptibly moving south to Whitewater Bay and the gleaming, isolated sands of Cape Sable.

Here is an ecosystem unlike any other in America, more than a million square miles of shallow but never stagnant water, interspersed with cypress swamps, deep ponds, hummocks (or islands) rising from the grass, and great rivers that twist through the maze of mangrove on the western border, rivers with names that tell stories, like Lostman's, Shark, and Barron, for the far-seeing Barron G. Collier, a New York advertising man who discovered the Everglades when it still belonged to the Seminoles, the squatters, the gators, and the exotic plume birds that attracted feather merchants and Audubon protectors alike.

For this writer, a favourite holiday would begin at the Rod and Gun Lodge, once an old-fashioned retreat for adventurous millionaires, who came for the abundant tarpon and snook and to hunt panther, black bear, deer and game birds. The Lodge is a rustic and historic hotel on the Barron River in Everglades City (population: about 600), a sleepy backwater fishing village only fifty miles west of Miami, though it seems a million light years from the glitter, glamour, and clamour of the Beach.

Not far from the Rod and Gun Lodge (and recently built and far more comfortable Captain's Table) lies the western entrance to Everglades National Park, where early Federal protection has helped time stand still. Cruise the Barron River to the west and you are into another wonderland as singular as the sawgrass country, the ten thousand islands that stretch from once primitive, now condo-skylined Marco Island just south of Naples to the great bird rookeries of Florida Bay.

Some years ago my brother Stuart and I made a motion picture, *Wind Across the Everglades,* in which our protagonist, a young Audubon warden, described his impression of the Glades:

> *It's the way the world must have looked on the first day . . . just grass and water and islands and clouds, the fattest, whitest clouds, in the biggest, bluest sky I ever saw – and the life – it's all around you – under the water, in the shallows, in the trees, winging overhead – egrets and herons as white as the clouds – blue herons that melt into the sky – and roseate spoonbills the colour of twilight . . . Nobody who goes deep into that country will ever forget it. You've got to see it for yourself.*

Years after that was written, the pull of the Glades is as strong as ever. But man, as usual, has been tampering. Developers have filled in hundreds of thousands of acres to the east and north of the Park. The airboat, an ingenious device for rapid transport through the once impregnable wilderness of sawgrass and cypress swamp, is now used to excess, destroying natural crawlways, disturbing rookeries, battering the silence. And – more trouble in paradise – the Glades are God's or the devil's gift to drug traffickers. I know fishermen who used to scrounge for mullet but now own their own jets.

Happily, a vast water wilderness can hardly be changed into a jetport or a condo cluster overnight. The Florida Everglades, receiving the fresh water that still flows down from Lake Okechobee in Central Florida, is a work of pure genius that needs a great deal of help now to stand off the impurities of human greed and mindless despoliation. Oh, it will be there next year, and the next and the next. But, as our

Audubon agent said, 'You've got to see it for yourself.'

Whether you fly down to Naples or Fort Myers, motor in from Miami, or cruise over from Key Largo, Marathon, or Key West, seize the moment while the wild orchids bloom, the gators blink in the sun, the roseate spoonbills wade the flats, the herons perform their slow-motion cakewalk, and the limpkins cry.

Miami: Distant Echoes

ELIE WIESEL

Having spent all of my youth in the shadows of the Carpathians, I am always drawn to mountains, for I love their silence and their dizzying mysteries.

They're not like the sea, or rather, like the seashore. A wretched tourist, I am not made for holidays. I don't swim; I don't play tennis; and I know nothing of golf. Sunbathing, endless conversations about tans and the weather and the price of rooms and hotel service, about low and high politics and the news of the day; all this holiday chatter, this forced restfulness and programmed, commercialized 'happiness' is not for old-fashioned puritans like me.

And yet – don't laugh – I never leave for Miami without a certain keen pleasure. I manage to spend a Shabbat or Passover there, or give some biblical or Talmudic or Hassidic lecture in some synagogue, or offer a course on literature and philosophy at some young and enterprising university. Why not frankly admit it? They never have to beg; I accept invitations from Miami more readily than those from many other places.

The reason is that I have close friends there, one of them a childhood friend. We went to the same schools, we endured the same trials, until we were separated by war and I lost touch with him. For many long years in Paris I knew nothing of what had become of him except that he lived in the United States and owned an ultra-Orthodox hotel.

Our reunion? It was in 1965. I had come to Miami for a weekend. Barely settled in my hotel, I began to feel ill. Could it be the horrible décor of my surroundings? I shook from fever, my head felt as if it would explode. How could I possibly deliver a lecture on the morrow? And where could I turn for help, since I knew no one?

Suddenly I recalled my friend the hotel owner – how to find him? I riffled through the telephone book under kosher hotels. Which one belonged to him? There were so many. I decided to dial at random and in a stroke of luck, I got him promptly on the line. I gave my name and he exploded, 'What are you doing in a hotel for the idle rich?' I told him I was sick, that I needed a doctor. 'Don't budge!' said my friend. 'I know the personal physician of a great Hassidic rabbi. I'll bring him right over.'

I protested that I wasn't that sick, but fifteen minutes later they knocked at my door, the doctor performed a miracle, and so did my friend: He won me over to Miami.

I returned a few months later and stayed at his hotel, and now my family and I spend one winter week and a few days of spring there each year. My friend and I, isolated if not excluded from the present, often evoke the muffled world of our childhood, whose sounds and memories claw at us from far away to haunt us – and also to drive us forward. We are back home, back in time, before the storm.

Naturally, I have other friends there, too. One teaches at the university, the other is a state senator. There are the parents of a girl who took my course in literature at Boston University: Her father, a prosperous businessman, is active in the Republican party. They are all our new friends, and how to imagine Miami without them? With them, we discuss modern art, the Côte d'Azur, Israel and the Administration's Middle Eastern policies.

But, you'll ask me, what about the other side of Miami? The rising violence? The fear? The crimes, assaults, the racial riots? I am aware of all that, of course. Like everyone else, I am troubled, concerned. Rumours reach me – so-and-so is moving out. A loss of confidence in the future? A wish to start over somewhere else? But my Miami friends are still there, and I still love to visit them.

Could I some day settle in Miami for good? Yes, without a doubt, if – if only Miami were girt with the shimmering crests of soaring mountains like my distant, innocent little city.

Lauderdale: Now a Dream

FRANK CONROY

When I was a boy Fort Lauderdale was a small town. We lived in a little frame house out in the pine woods, and I'd ride my bike two miles through a still deserted landscape of palmetto scrub and sand soil to the city limits, which were marked by the railroad tracks. A mile or so beyond, houses began, then a petrol station or two, and, suddenly, downtown. Stores, the five-and-ten, four cinemas (splendid palaces of fantasy!), the old civic building, the Route 1 drawbridge – you could cover the whole town in an hour. Then out Las Olas Boulevard, with its towering palms, to the beach. Fort Lauderdale beach in those days was a mile-long strip with a public pool, seven or eight hotels, a YMCA, and six-block boardwalk. To the north, pine trees right down to the water, to the south, the same. A small, cautious town, a place that just barely survived the collapse of the 1920s boom, and wasn't about to make the same mistake a second time. If it was to grow (and indeed it was, past the wildest dreams of anyone in the '20s or for that matter, the late '40s), it would do so carefully.

I've been back several times. Once I rented a car and tried to find the frame house I'd lived in. It was impossible even to locate the area – the old grid of coral roads cutting through the pine woods was gone. The woods were gone. In their place, curving roads with unfamiliar names, tens of thousands of suburban homes stretching inland as far as the eye could see. It was a different place.

Flying above the east coast of Florida, one now sees a continuous built-up beach front – Miami, Fort Lauderdale, and on to the north – a huge metropolis running both along the ocean and deep inland. There are no more small towns in this part of Florida.

There is still the hot sun, the huge white clouds over the Atlantic, palm trees, and the special semitropical scent of the air. But there are a lot more people, drawn for various reasons to the fastest-growing area in the United States, many of them drawn by the old promise (the one that had fuelled the abortive '20s boom) of the good life. Temperate weather, swimming, fishing, golfing, and tennis year-round. If Travis McGee can enjoy a cocktail on the back of his boat in the Fort Lauderdale Marina, so can a lot of other people. Lauderdale seems now to offer almost anything you might want. You can barbecue in the backyard, or you can plunge into an increasingly international night-life. You can live on a pension, or you can blow a fortune. It is part of a vast new city – the South Florida coast – made up of forces as diverse as those in any city in America. It used to be fairly sleepy and fairly simple. Now it is complex and bursting with energy. Hard to believe how fast this country changes.

Sanibel Island: Focus on Birds

ROGER TORY PETERSON

Given a choice, most nature-oriented people would prefer to live on the west coast of Florida rather than along the eastern perimeter. Certainly, if I were to single out the number-one hot spot for wildlife photography, it would be the J. N. 'Ding' Darling Wildlife Refuge on Sanibel Island. For sheer variety it exceeds even the Audubon Society's Corkscrew Swamp Wildlife Sanctuary near Naples and the Park Service's Anhinga Trail in the Everglades.

Resting my Nikon with its 400-millimetre lens on the lowered window of my car, I have taken innumerable frame-filling shots of half a dozen kinds of herons and egrets as they fished along the canals that border the road. Anhingas and cormorants perch on exposed snags and spread their wings to dry. Skimmers, gulls and terns, resting on the sand, scarcely move out of the way as the car approaches. During the cooler months, ducks of a dozen sorts swim in the lagoons and flee in panic when one of the local bald eagles cruises over. Ospreys, perched on their bulky nests, seem to be posing for pictures.

In fact, all of the bays and beaches that surround Sanibel and Captiva islands are literally one big sanctuary where birds and other wildlife know they are safe. Pelicans compete for fish guts when the fishermen clean their catches. Laughing and ring-billed gulls fearlessly hover and take food from the hand.

Florida has changed greatly since the bad old days of plume hunting at the turn of the century. Not only have the birds come back, but people's attitudes have changed too. Killing has been replaced by love.

Boca Raton: Fish Galore

MARK J. SOSIN

While most people think of Boca Raton as an oceanfront city with grand houses, a labyrinth of estuarine waterways, and one of the highest per capita incomes in the land, fishermen view it as a gateway to spectacular sport.

Charging northward through the Florida Straits at a velocity that sometimes approaches five knots, the Gulf Stream pushes its warm waters closer to the white sand beaches of Boca Raton than anywhere else along the Atlantic Coast.

Residents talk in whispers about the sailfish, king mackerel, dolphin, wahoo, and other sport fish that lie beyond Boca Raton's front door, almost afraid that someone might hear them and uncover a closely guarded secret. The second reef rises from a sandy bottom in 60 feet of water and peaks at 45 feet before falling off into 90 feet of water. Sailfish prowl the back edge out to perhaps 180 feet of water, with the greatest concentrations present during the winter months. The colder the weather and the stronger the northers, the better the fishing. When tourists complain about the weather, that's the time for fishermen to be out on the water.

For those who enjoy the simplicity of bottom fishing, the reefs hold the answer. One can anchor and chum, or drift, the area. A variety of snappers from yellowtail to mangrove and muttons will surely please. Groupers also make a home in the coral and barracuda lurk in ambush waiting to grab an easy meal. Schools of bonito swim back and forth on either side of the reef and an occasional amberjack will crash a live bait intended for something else.

Almost as soon as a boat clears the narrow inlet at Boca Raton, the lines are put over and fishing begins. Kingfish enthusiasts work from the inlet to a half mile south, while most of the other boats troll to the north. Anglers have the option of lures or natural baits. One of the favourite techniques for catching sailfish is first to catch balao (pronounced ballyhoo) in fifteen feet of water over the patch reefs between the inlet and the Deerfield Fishing Pier and then slow troll them. Balao can be chummed around the boat with uncooked oatmeal and caught on tiny hooks baited with shrimp.

The Boca Raton Hotel serves as home base for charter boats. Arrangements can be made by calling the hotel (305-395-3000) or Brandy Marine Enterprises (305-368-5244), which manages the docks. Bait and tackle are furnished on a charter and each boat will accommodate up to six fishermen. The cost is around $400 a day and $205 for a half day. You'll be fishing in less than fifteen minutes after you leave the dock.

If you fish these waters successfully, be sure to tell people you caught the fish off Palm Beach. The folks who live in Boca Raton would prefer it that way.

Palm Beach: The Big Rich

CHARLOTTE CURTIS

Comes the forbidding grey sky along about Thanksgiving and that nip in the air that won't go away, and the big rich, like so many exotically plumed migratory birds, pack up their old and new money, abandon their luxe but chilly northern purlieus, and head for sunny Palm Beach, there to winter in their palatial houses among their orchids, their paintings and their big diamonds. Somehow, they fit tennis, golf, polo, croquet and even the uncommon thrill of a visit to a supermarket around their routinely exquisite lunch parties. By evening, they are suited up for the third time in a single day, and off in their Rolls-Royces and Mercedes, ready for that marathon of charity balls and private black-tie parties they so adore.

'It's like a stage set,' T. Bedford Davie, sportsman and collector, said, one balmy, star-bright night as he gazed out over a turquoise pool surrounded by artfully lighted palm trees. 'I sometimes wonder what the real people are doing.'

Aside from the purveyors, chauffeurs, waiters, maids, and others who serve the rich, the real people are tourists. Rich tourists stay in hotels or condominiums and have little or no contact with the powerful regulars. Since no bed comes cheap, the less affluent are daytrippers, in from West Palm Beach across Lake Worth, or travellers intrigued by the drive along the Atlantic with the serene but empty beach on one side and high hedges on the other. The greenery protects the great houses from frequent winds and curious eyes.

The dilemma is a curious one: How does one exhibit to one's peers an excellence of architecture, gardens and surroundings without also alerting the tour buses? One answer is ornamental iron fences, gates and private security forces.

Only a few denizens are Old Guard aristocrats. They are unfailingly polite, even to tourists. The others seem to be constantly getting in and out of ballgowns, aeroplanes, and gossip columns. Third- and fourth-generation millionaires and their second and third wives mingle democratically with new hotshot tycoons, Junior League volunteers, internationally celebrated philanthropists, retired diplomats, nobility (affectionately if derisively known as 'the Euroflux') escaping high taxes and weak economies, and refugees from such summer resorts as the Hamptons and Newport.

Observing the rarer birds at close range is no easy task. Walk down Worth Avenue, and those sockless, deeply tanned gents in their pricey pastel shirts and pants and big gold Omega watches could be the merely imitative rich tourists. The same applies to the bediamonded women buying $10,000 bracelets at David Webb. Befriend a news photographer or a portrait painter, and he will point out the real thing. Or sit in the lobby of the Breakers Hotel along about 7.30 p.m. when the black-tie biggies and their formally clad ladies are either arriving for a charity ball or departing for the private parties. Stay at the Colony Hotel, which caters to the regulars. They crowd croquet matches and opening nights at the Royal Poinciana Playhouse, and prefer their houses and clubs to the routinely poor restaurants. If they do turn up at a restaurant, they're the ones with the handsome flower centrepieces they had delivered ahead.

Critics tend to call Palm Beach the stamping ground of dinosaurs. If that were true, then how come a phone call from Palm Beach can buy or sell a huge company? Settle which city gets the next big shopping centre? Clinch the decision to move a corporate headquarters from New York to the Sun Belt?

Like it or not, Palm Beach was and still is a version of the materialistic American dream, excesses and all. It is the product of the entrepreneur's imagination and ability to raise money. It wasn't much of an island. The palm trees were imported. The houses were designed to lure the rich who mattered. Above all the place had to be beautiful and private, and it is. What the outsider sees today is not the real Palm Beach, but its public exterior.

Ybor City: Cigars and Politics

JOSÉ YGLESIAS

Is it permissible to recommend spending any part of one's holiday in a
shopping mall? Ybor Square, my favourite place in Tampa, is one. Not
in Tampa proper but in a section of it called Ybor City. My home-
town. A place to which a hundred years ago Spanish, Sicilian and
Cuban cigarmakers followed the siren call of Vicente Martínez Ybor,
a Spanish cigar manufacturer already established in Key West and
New York. He himself had been wooed by the tiny town of Tampa,
languishing inland on the bay in weather so dismal that it was a perfect
open-air humidor.

Martínez Ybor persuaded other manufacturers to build factories,
too, and enjoy the atmospheric and fiscal amenities. Yet his factory
was not the first to produce cigars. The cigarmakers he hired went on
strike before the official opening, immediately displaying the kind of
organizing talent that later led them to build the Cuban and Spanish
and Italian and Asturian social clubs – solid, handsome buildings with
ballrooms, canteens, gymnasiums and theatres – as well as two
hospitals that throughout my childhood were the best in Tampa. They
were the first workers to conceive of hiring a man with a trained voice,
or one naturally capable of reaching all corners of the factory, to read
them newspapers and books for four hours each day. It was from my
barely literate parents and grandparents that I first heard of the great
European writers.

The clubs, but not the industry or the readers, have survived, and
there are still some long-retired cigarmakers playing dominoes in their
canteens. You can walk from Ybor Square to the canteen that the
old-timers most frequent, in the basement of the Centro Asturiano,
three blocks away on Nebraska Avenue; stand at the beautiful long
marble bar drinking espresso and watch the players; or talk to them –
they're all historians of Ybor City's past. You can also walk east from
the square, peeking in first at the Cuban Club one block down, and
then, continuing along Seventh Avenue, at the Spanish and Italian
clubs. On the way you can stop at Fifteenth Street and buy the
wonderfully roasted Colombian coffee beans at Julio's Coffee House
that to this day my family still supplies me with. Or wait until you get
to the Naviera Coffee Mills at Twentieth Street. By then you might
have a lunch of Cuban ham-and-pork sandwiches at La Tropicana
Café on Nineteenth Street or go on to a first-rate Spanish meal at the
old Columbia Restaurant at Twenty-second Street. In the streets you
will see mostly American blacks who have moved into the old shacks
not bulldozed for the freeway, but the new Ybor City State Museum at

the end of your walk is full of photographs of what the old town and the insides of the factories looked like.

As you may have guessed, Ybor Square is entirely made up of Martínez Ybor's factory, a splendid group of deep-red brick buildings. It enfolds little shops, an Italian restaurant (the Spaghetti Warehouse) and a paradigmatic cigarmaker producing handmade cigars. But it is not these things that should draw you there, not even the designer/restorer's care in exposing the structural details of the old buildings with awe; it is rather the feeling one gets standing inside them that the cultural ambience that was created by Mr. Martínez Ybor's enterprise with a luxury product and by the radical activities of his cigarmakers, so vital when I was a boy, lingers there still, a heartening strain from the American past.

St. Petersburg: Gulf Sunsets

EUGENE C. PATTERSON

A stranger to Florida must see Disney World and Epcot Center, of course, but I would not maroon myself in swampy central Florida, far from the beaches, to be near these attractions. Sand and saltwater are still the main point of it all to me, especially since a couple of hours by interstate from barefoot lodgings by the sea will get you to the interior.

I am partial to the relatively unspoiled beaches of the state's western coast, with their window on the matchless sunsets over the Gulf of Mexico. If I were a winter visitor to Florida, I would fly into Tampa, rent a car and drive forty-five minutes west by causeway across the silvery reaches of Tampa Bay to St. Petersburg Beach. Having made reservations well in advance, I would check in at the Don Cesar Beach Resort hotel, a happy pink pile of exuberant architecture reclaimed from the 1920s. (I can yet summon the vision of Babe Ruth clumping down the Don's grand corridors with his Yankee team-mates of other springs.) From the oceanfront rooms you see beyond the pool and tennis courts to the curving white miles of beach and blue gulf swells running to the horizon.

A mile's walk south from the Don along the water brings you to Pass-A-Grille, the young set's beach. Fishermen can drive a half dozen miles north to the Florida sportfishing centre of Madeira Beach and charter a deep-sea vessel with knowledgeable skipper and mate for under $400 a day.

The King Charles at the Don is one of Florida's better restaurants. For other choices, follow the coast three villages north to Redington Beach and feast at the Wine Cellar, where the coquilles St. Jacques and the grilled freshwater trout are memorable. Or drive an hour south across the Skyway Bridge, still partially broken by the ship that hit it in 1982, turn west at Bradenton to the coast, and proceed south down scenic Longboat Key to shop the boutiques at St. Armand's Circle in Sarasota. *En route* along the Key you'll encounter four first-rank restaurants – L'Auberge du Bon Vivant, Far Horizons, the Colony, and Café l'Europe. Across the causeway in Sarasota is the St. Georges restaurant, perhaps the finest of them all.

Sailors and art lovers should drive the half-dozen miles east across the Pinellas Peninsula to old downtown St. Petersburg on Tampa Bay. At the pretty municipal marina sailboats can be chartered, bareboat or crewed, for a turn around the broad bay. Then surprise yourself, particularly if you've not cared much for Salvador Dali in the past, by spending an hour in the new bayfront Dali museum where one of the largest collections of his works is permanently exhibited.

My return route to St. Petersburg Beach would be through south Pasadena with a stop at Ted Peters' Smoked Fish. Rest barefoot on the outdoor benches and eat smoked mackerel or mullet, hot from the smoke-house, with an ice-cold stein of beer.

Disney World, Epcot, and Busch Gardens in Tampa are an easy drive away. But base camp for me will always be the soft sand of St. Petersburg Beach, lapped in moonlight when the sunset dims from gold to crimson.

Indian Bay, Aripeka: In Full Colour

JAMES ROSENQUIST

It's 95 degrees and I'm sitting in a petrol station near the Weeki Wachee Spring with a hot stalled motor, so when a better time to start writing about Florida? I'm a painter and Florida has sun. The sun in Florida allows an artist a full spectrum of colour quite unlike New York. People ask me why I moved here and I tell them that Florida is so bright that when you cry your tears either turn to broken glass or diamonds, but they never get soggy.

In the winter of 1954 I hitchhiked to Daytona Beach to see the 200-mile motorcycle races. The races were ferocious and so was the sun. I saw Joe Weatherly take a terrible crash. I achieved a terrific sunburn and was trying to hitchhike off the beach back to Daytona when on a lonely highway I heard a voice from the bushes say, 'Hey buddy, come in, you look fried.' I was invited to iced tea, chicken dinner and Key lime pie under a ceiling fan in an old white house. After dinner, the family showed me their never-pet alligator in the backyard, which led off into a swamp. Back in Daytona I bought a bus ticket and headed for Miami and Key West. Palm fronds covered old

U.S. 1 then and oranges dropped off roadside trees. I had my watercolour kit with me. Inspired by Winslow Homer and John Pike, I painted black shantytowns, harbour marinas, and the light on the palmettos. I stayed a few days and made my way back to Minnesota.

Seventeen years later, I was invited to the University of South Florida to make lithographs. While the lithograph tusche was drying I took drives up the Gulf Coast. Much to my surprise, it looked like the east coast of Florida in the '50s. It was sparsely populated and wild. I saw bears, deer, a bald eagle, mockingbirds, rattlers, and alligators. I drove off the highway on a back road to a secluded peninsula on the Gulf. It was beautiful.

Paul Simmons, a local resident, walked up. I said, 'It sure is nice out here.'

He said, 'It's paradise.'

I said, 'I sure would like to buy this land.'

He said, 'It's a great place but we're due for a hurricane. The last hurricane blew the neighbour's roof into your yard.'

I said, 'I don't own it yet.'

He said, 'If you stay here through the hurricane season, your blood will turn to watermelon juice.' Now I know what he means.

In 1975 I bought the land and designed a house with Gilbert Flores based on a Seminole Indian chickee. As it was being built, I became fascinated by the local people. I asked the man who was working on my house if he wanted a beer. He said, 'I don't drink, I don't smoke, I don't make love to women. I just fight the chickens.' I said, 'What?' He whispered, 'You know, cockfighting.' I started collecting colloquialisms: 'It rained so hard, it was a lighter-knot floater and a toad-frog strangler.' 'It's twice as nice as snuff, but not half as dusty.' 'It won't fester overnight, will it?'

I live on Indian Bay, a little bit north of Aripeka, a little bit south of Weeki Wachee. Chief Aripeka, a medicine man and a battle planner, but not a warrior, was known to the whites as Mr. Sam Jones. Billy Bowlegs, a noted Seminole Indian chief, might be buried in back of my studio. I've found nine arrowheads digging for a foundation.

I love Florida, and I'm glad that it's in the same time zone as New York.

Canaveral: Blasting Off

JOHN NOBLE WILFORD

On the day and night before a space shuttle launching, the crowds converge by the shores of the Indian River and Titusville and along the roads and causeways approaching Cape Canaveral. Cars, tents, recreational vehicles of every description, the ubiquitous pedlars of souvenirs. Cameras and telescopes on tripods, radios tuned in to the countdown, portable privies everywhere. The American family is waiting to see a select few of its own go off on a distant journey.

Several hundred thousand people attend the embarkation of each shuttle to space. A few thousand lucky ones, with special badges, see the launchings from visitor sites inside the Kennedy Space Center or from the press site, which is only three miles from the launching pad. They not only see the flames at ignition but can feel the powerful vibrations that rumble through the ground they stand on, a sensation no television coverage can convey. For others the action is more removed, but still impressive. Those in boats out in the Indian or Banana rivers can often see just as much. Those along the causeways may miss ignition, the low trees and palmetto scrub blocking their view, but with binoculars or even the unaided eye they can track the shuttle as it climbs into the sky and arcs out over the Atlantic Ocean. They share the hushed, expectant moments of the final countdown and perhaps some vicarious thrill at being closer than the rest of humanity to a daring adventure.

The spectacle lasts, at most, two or three minutes. On a clear day you can see the shuttle's two boosters when they stop firing, break away and fall to the ocean. Then it is all over. The shuttle, a tiny speck, disappears behind its own contrail, beyond the clouds, or simply beyond the resolving powers of the human eye.

But that need not be the extent of one's visit to America's foremost space port. Outside the gate, on the entrance road to Titusville, there is the Visitors Center, with an array of rockets from the earlier days of space flight and exhibits of other space ware and past achievements. Tour buses leave the centre frequently, except for a few hours before and after a launching, to give people a closer look at the shuttle – if it's on the launching pad – and at the other facilities that call to mind the days when astronauts went to the moon. No lesser attractions to many are the pelicans, eagles, alligators and other wildlife to be found in the shadow of high technology.

In the towns nearby, oddly enough, there are few manifestations of the activities that have made the name Cape Canaveral synonymous with space flight. The motels, condominiums and fast-food establishments could be anywhere in Florida, almost anywhere in America. The restaurants have mercifully restrained themselves from offering dishes like Apollo appetizers, Saturn salads or Voyager vichyssoise. Several of the best restaurants, Bernard's Surf, Captain Ed's or the Phoenix, could be anywhere in Florida.

One restaurant, however, is manifestly part of the space port scene – Ramon's in Cocoa Beach. The walls are covered with the emblems of aerospace contractors and NASA projects as well as large plaques listing the names and dates of most of the missions that have been launched from Cape Canaveral. But the food, beef and seafood, is better than at most museums. And the martinis are, as they say in space lingo, hypergolic. That means fuels that are combustible on contact.

This is where, on the evenings before and after a shot, the old space hands get together to revive memories of when missiles often as not fell ignominiously into the ocean, when old so-and-so drove his car into the surf and when men went to the moon. Don't be disheartened to hear someone from an adjoining table declare that as launchings go, the space shuttle is hardly in a class with the mighty Saturn 5, the moon rocket. Old space hands are like that. They think nothing in the world will ever compare to the Saturn 5.

Never mind. You, too, after a launching should be taking home a brief but incomparable memory.

Cross Creek: Gator Tales

HARRY CREWS

When I get a case of the black twirlies, or free-floating anxiety, or just the need to cool out from the typewriter, I go to Cross Creek. People from up North come there with their Airstream trailers or Winnebagos for a while during the winter months, but the people who live there year round number only about three hundred.

As most people know, Cross Creek was made famous by Marjorie Kinnan Rawlings, who lived there from the time she was about thirty-two. Her house is now a historic site, maintained by the Florida Park Service. She left the house to the University of Florida, which is in Gainesville, where I live, for the use of young and promising writers. It is for that reason that my association with Cross Creek goes back some twenty-odd years. It is furnished now as it was then, and is filled with all the memorabilia of her working life: her writing table and replicas of her manuscripts, books, and the cast-iron stove she cooked on. For those of us who know her work and revere her memory, the Creek is still haunted by her slightly tipsy ghost. But I don't go to Cross Creek for that reason. No, I go there for the people I know and love, and for the fine restaurant that is at the centre of the hamlet, a restaurant named after her most famous novel, *The Yearling*.

My day goes like this. I first stop at the little grocery store, the only one in the Creek, run by Jim Rimes. He is from Bacon County, Georgia, where I am from, and after I buy a pack of Red Man chewing tobacco, a couple of six-packs of beer and two quarts of Gatorade to go with the vodka I have thoughtfully brought along, we stand and talk for a while, I enjoying the sound of the English language as it was meant to be spoken. Then I drift down to the Yearling and go in the back door and talk a while with one of my dearest friends, Junior Jenkins, while he butchers cooter – what we call a freshwater turtle in the South – and frogs, and alligator tail and quail and all of the other fine fare that will be served in the restaurant that night. Mr. and Mrs. Herman own the restaurant, but it is Junior who has made it famous throughout the state, or so I believe. He is a big black man who has spent his life in and around the Creek, and whose grandmother was a friend of Marjorie Kinnan Rawlings whom she wrote about in the book *Cross Creek*.

After I've had a cup of coffee with Junior, and he has told me where the fish have been biting and what kind of lures or fresh bait to use, I go across the street to the Cross Creek Lodge and get a stump-knocker boat with a seven-and-a-half horsepower motor and head out to some of the most beautiful water God ever made. When I leave the lodge, if I turn right, I go to Lochloosa Lake, 12,000 acres big and filled with bass and bream that every fisherman dreams of. If, coming out of Cross Creek Lodge, I turn left, I go to Orange Lake, 18,000 acres big and filled with the same kind of fish.

But mind you, I'm not a fisherman. Sometimes I take bass and bream and perch. Sometimes I take nothing. But that is not really the point. Once I'm out in one of those beautiful clearwater lakes, I can't get a telephone call and I can't get a letter. I sit out there and watch my lure or bobber and think long thoughts about my free-floating anxiety and black twirlies and cool out from all that has been bothering me. By late afternoon when I get back to the Cross Creek Lodge, I am purified and holy, ready to deal with the world again. I walk to a great little house about a hundred yards from the Yearling restaurant where Rod Elrod, like a brother to me, lives. We clean the fish, have a drink together, and as often as not get to talking about horses and bulls and rodeos generally. Rod is twenty-eight years old and, until six years ago, was a bull rider on the rodeo circuit, but one day he drew a bull named Cassius Clay, the bull of the year on that circuit. Cassius Clay had been out of the chute eighty-nine times that year and had never been covered. He retired Rod from the rodeo circuit forever. Rod is healed up and whole now, but he still loves the sport and enjoys talking about it, and I enjoy listening. As likely as not, the two of us wander over to the bar at the Yearling restaurant, have a few drinks, and after a while sit down at a table to do some serious damage to several platters of what our buddy, Junior, has cooked up during the day.

All in all, it makes for a fine way to spend several hours forgetting what the world has been trying to tell you is important.

DREAMING OF SAVANNAH

V. S. Pritchett

Foreign place names are the Sirens of geography. They pull the armchair traveller to his feet. For me it is a matter of syllables that run like a tune and end in a consonant. Samarkand has luxury and a peremptory drum roll in it because of the final *d*. I am repelled by the insipid *ville*, even in France. Names that end in a plain *a* tell me nothing, though I was allured by *iana* when I was a dreamy boy, for it stirred the nostalgia for the faraway and limitless and the Utopian American dream: Huck Finn's longing to 'light out into the territory!' For the British islander there is no territory to 'light out into,' except the sea.

On the other hand, to have added that final *h* gave Savannah exotic allure and settling effect. I had wanted to go there since I was a boy reading Thackeray's *The Four Georges*. George II had given the colony a patent and a general had founded it. Thackeray had said it was a 'merry little place,' set in a wide savanna of forest broken by meadowy pastures and spacious plantations. There would be masses of flowers. From the decorative verandas of houses, even mansions, there would blow the pleasant, idle smoke of cigars.

In London I used to think how happy I would be if I had a prosperous and benevolent uncle in Savannah who would invite me there. I saw him as a retired merchant or planter, living in a white-pillared mansion. I would have drawling young cousins sitting in elegant drawing rooms among family portraits. And then, Savannah was a seaport. There was an incipient merchant in myself for, when I was sixteen, I became a clerk in bowler hat and white coat, often sent to work on Thames-side wharves on Pickle Herring Street, dodging between a dark office to the quay to report on the bales of hides from the barges. They came from abroad! My imagined uncle would have tallied bales of cotton in his time. The conjunction of land, sea, and trade was irresistible to my fancy.

Still later, I heard that Savannah had started as an eighteenth century town. I gave up my Ruskinian passion for the Gothic, for was not the eighteenth century the last when architects built sedate livable cities? When I heard that, like London, Savannah was a place laid out in a spreading chessboard of squares, I knew it would be my kind of place. No uncle of mine would tolerate mean villas or the high-rise apartment block. The very name also suggested that the traffic would be quiet.

It was spring when, in my old age, I at last saw this dreamed-of place. I had heard that it was one of the few beautiful cities in America and had arrested inner-city decay. From the plane as we passed over Georgia's red soil and hundreds of miles of flat pine forest and then came down, I saw I had made one extraordinary mistake. I had somehow turned Savannah into a steep Mediterranean city, pressed by mountains, close to the sea. How did I forget that savannas have no mountains and their towns are never pressed? The real place was flat, with one or two high and delicate spires rising from it. The forest stopped short at the long river estuary; Savannah was a wide, well-hidden haven and the sky was wide over its miles of outlying marshes.

We were soon in a town deep in shady terraces and square after square, in some ways like Bath if Bath had been a port and had no hills. The squares calmed the rush of traffic, which had to go around them. Savannah was a place for walking, and the only way to know a town is to walk in it. It was a city for flowers, for the oleander, the long beds of azaleas, the lilies, the rampant camellia, dogwood, and cherry, for balconies and secret gardens. One walked down avenues where that extraordinary tree, the live oak, with its long grey beards of Spanish moss, gave an air of almost eerie fantasy to a town that was ordered and yet various, where little was ugly. Yet it had been a traders' city; it had been spaciously planned and most of its plan had been conserved for 240 years. Happy eighteenth century, with its ideal of the useful and livable; century of Projects, Practical Benevolence, Patrons, and Trustees, for all its madhouses, its gamblers and adventurers. It is extraordinary that a mercantile colony had never been a haphazard camp, a huddle or a muddle, that it never scrapped its original pattern though several times its original timber-frame houses had been burned down.

Savannah was founded in 1733, by an unusual British general, James Edward Oglethorpe, a man who had fought against the Turks and had captured Belgrade. He was not only a commanding soldier but a practical idealist and philanthropist and he arrived in Savannah with a chessboard plan for a model settlement that would last. A Londonish city of shaded squares was in his mind, squares that did not exclude but led at short intervals from one to another, so that at the street corner one would look down a long vista of oases. Never was geometry so leafy or dignity so intimate.

And then, Oglethorpe's idealism was not Utopian. It was charitable. He had been shocked in London by the misery of the thousands of unlucky Londoners who were in prison for debt – the unfortunate pursuers of fortune. As a strong Protestant he was also concerned with Europeans who were the victims of religious persecution. When he sailed for the wooded haven of the Savannah River, insured by the Royal Patent, his 115 colonists included two groups of Jews from Central Europe, hardworking Moravians and persecuted Portuguese. On later voyages he brought in Highland Scots, Piedmontese who had known massacre, Greeks and some Irish Catholics. With him came his chaplain, John Wesley, who hoped to convert the Yamacraw Indians. The King's support also had a military motive: to protect the British colonists farther north in Georgia and beyond from the encroachment of the Spaniards in Florida.

In the early days there were no blacks in Savannah and indeed the town held out against slavery for a long time. Oglethorpe hated slavery. The early settlers were not allowed gin or rum. Wesley failed to convert the Indians and soon went home disillusioned, though later on Methodism and Whitefield's Baptists and Presbyterians dominated the city and all the South. One of the early difficulties was that the London colonists were city-bred and were no use with the axe and at clearing forests. There was trouble with the Malcontents – a traditional British product known by that name in the eighteenth century – who were disputatious in their Promised Land. The shortage of labour plagued the general. In the end the colony gave in on slavery and thousands of blacks came in.

We stayed in a small and charming hotel, the 17 Hundred 90 Inn, which had been discovered by an American friend and where the food and wine were excellent. We were given a simple frame cottage at the back with a large living room and pretty bedrooms. It had its lateral flight of steps to the stoop. The steep sideways flight of railed steps, wooden or iron, to most of the houses in old Savannah, leading up to the raised entrance floor, is one of the city's elegant but original idiosyncrasies. You supposedly arrived, free of street mud and sand, when you made your bow.

My first walk was to the harbour to see how trade was. The flat city ends in a fine long row of business houses and residential buildings called Factors Walk. There, in his time, the forebears of my imaginary uncle must have bid for cotton when cotton was king. The Walk is built on the middle level of a sloping bluff with warehouses beneath and Bay Street above. In fact, to get to the Walk you have to cross several curious iron bridges. Underneath them the trucks drive up the cobbled hill and the cobbles came from the ballast of the old sailing ships. Merchant vessels were in the harbour now; the port thrives on oil, lumber and paper, for the cotton trade moved to Texas.

On one of the fine squares up in the town is the Telfair Mansion, now an art gallery, in Greek revival style, with romantic statues of painters outside – Rembrandt is one – and there my unattainable relatives came to life in the family portraits. Perhaps my shrewd uncle would have married one of those dark-haired ladies. She would have a high bodice and long silk dress, with her solemn, round-eyed children, buttoned in velvet, around her on their best behaviour. You could hear her drawling voice, her talk of family connections, see her pride in her cabinets, chairs, her tables, her porcelain and her silver. She would be the traditional American hostess, eager for company all day. Perhaps she, or more likely her mother, had known the brilliant architects who built the city in stone and brick, especially William Jay, the young Englishman who had brought its Regency designs and fine style of ironwork from Bath itself. Perhaps her family had entertained Thackeray and given him a graceful four-poster to sleep in, and a neat desk to work at.

On Sunday she would go to church. The Sunday-morning congregation coming out of church is still one of the sights of Savannah. It is a city of superb churches, one denomination vying architecturally with another. Where did she worship? At the lovely white Greek Revival Christ Episcopal facing the spring flowers on Johnson Square, the keystone to the city? At the finest of all, the one whose high white spire dominates the city, the Independent Presbyterian? Or the classical First Baptist? Or the Roman Catholic Cathedral with its twin towers? She might have belonged to the Jewish congregation who came in 1733 and have gone to the Temple Mickve Israel.

Squares, rows, fine houses in brick and frame, verandas, balconies, where the wisteria and the creepers climb, spires and pillars, in a lacework of sun and shade, Savannah is delightful to the eye, and too lived-in to strike one as being a museum.

One had heard how so much of the South, being bemused by its past and then falling into desuetude, had been invaded by the property men and their bulldozers. By the 1950s Oglethorpe's Savannah was in danger. A famous market had been pulled down. To put a stop to this the remarkable Historic Savannah Foundation has had the financial skills and the taste that have aroused the pride of the city, especially in its old central part. The Savannah we saw was very much the result of the foundation's work. Threatened frame houses were even moved from derelict districts.

But it was soon understood the problem was not only aesthetic or historical. It was social. A new organization called Landmarks was formed to rescue interesting outer districts, notably the Victorian, which were becoming a slum. The poorer middle-class whites had moved out into the country suburb, the poorest of the blacks came in. The neglected place was going to pieces. The great danger to the rescuers was 'gentrification.' There was plain good architecture and a great deal of the decorative gingerbread style worth keeping. We know in London the troubles of gentrification. With the aid of Federal and other funds and the backing of a bank owned by blacks, it has been possible to do over a number of the houses and hand them back on subsidized rents to their tenants, counting successfully on the rise of communal pride. The movement is very much in the Oglethorpe tradition. American conservation owes everything to a canny mixture of financial skill, civic and domestic pride, and longsighted independent effort.

We were often in the company of an enthusiastic and experienced conservationist who knew every house in the city, a connoisseur who treated it even as his sacred collection. We saw his hospitable friends at his own fine house. With him we drove miles into the surrounding country, especially on the long roads from which one sees the vast stretch of marshes, where the cranes and the herons crack the shells of the oysters and tumble about in the sky, the long procession of pines. We went up that long straight avenue of old live oaks that approach the great house at Wormsloe. On that mile-long avenue one saw once more but now majestically the festoons of Spanish moss, which has a ghostly, weird, rather than melancholy, effect. It evoked sensations of what in Portugal they call *saudade*, a half-sad, half-romantic languor.

Back in Savannah we talked of white-faced, cynical, sentimental Thackeray, a man who liked eating well, who loved dining out and chattering about books, and the rising and falling families, over his wine. We felt sure he never wrote a line while he was there. Languorous towns are too alluring.

DOWN HOME IN ACADIA

Roy Reed

New Orleans has a French restaurant named Indulgence. It occupies an old cottage at the corner of Religious and Orange streets, a relaxed – some would say dilapidated – neighbourhood that fairly reflects America's most relaxed, well-worn city. As a metaphor, Indulgence is not bad for all of south Louisiana. New Orleans and the wet, subtropical Cajun country are territories of the senses.

A New Yorker went down for a visit one recent spring and spent days dashing everywhere to see everything before his holiday was over. His Louisiana friends finally persuaded him to stop: Stop and look, stop and talk, stop and nurse a drink in a homely bayou bar. He caught on, for a little while at the end. Even Southerners change for the better when they travel to southern Louisiana. We are all Northerners when we cross the Mediterranean frontier at Moissant Airport, and then Louisiana works its voodoo and pulls us in.

I drove down from the Ozarks recently. I spent a couple of days decompressing in New Orleans, then headed west into the bayous and prairies that have been the main home of the Acadians since Le Grand Dérangement of 1755. Spanish has replaced French as the second language of New Orleans because of a steady migration of Central Americans. But in the low rural parishes of the Acadian Coast and westward into the muddy verge of Texas, Cajun French is spoken widely and in some remote villages is still the dominant language. Because of the language, and because the Cajuns are a pool of distinctiveness, the visitor sometimes feels apart and fatigued. But if he stays long enough, he is restored and quieted and sucked into the humid Louisiana pace, which contests the speed of bayous.

I set about shedding the North by choosing a hotel in the French Quarter. Croissants and strong coffee were served in the courtyard, and I studied the new shoots of the banana trees. I spent half a day at Fair Grounds Race Track betting on horses, and studied the Gallic noses in the stands. I was told that the racetrack's restaurant, where people sip drinks and eat seafood during the races, is the largest restaurant in the world.

After two days of mellowing, I needed a puritan fix. I decided to learn something. I phoned W. Kenneth Holditch, professor of English at the University of New Orleans. Professor Holditch and Cynthia Ratcliffe, his partner, are the owners of Heritage Tours. For a modest stipend, they will guide you through every quatrain and corner of literary New Orleans.

I waited for them in the Napoleon House bar, sipping beer and listening to Berlioz. Through the high open doors I could see across the street and past the high open doors of another bar and café, Maspero's, which once was a slave auction house. Two pretty black girls sat eating lunch.

Holditch and Ratcliffe arrived and, to avoid appearing precipitate, drank a beer. Then we walked up Chartres Street to St. Peter, over to Royal and back to St. Louis. In those few blocks, with an occasional reference to houses and squares a short distance away, my learned guides pointed out the New Orleans connections of several dozen writers.

'*Scribner's* magazine found George Washington Cable here . . . William Faulkner lived in that apartment on Pirate's Alley. The house is for sale. We hear they're asking $575,000 . . . Truman Capote was born in New Orleans. His family lived in the Monteleone Hotel . . . Eudora Welty visits here often. One of her stories takes place in Galatoire's . . . John Galsworthy wrote a poem about the old St. Louis Hotel . . . Tennessee Williams had just bought the house at 1014 Dumaine and had it renovated . . .'

I remembered that the playwright had also spent many mornings in the courtyard of my hotel, Maison de Ville, drinking coffee and watchng the sparrows in the banana trees. His body is buried in St. Louis, but I think it pleases his ghost to reside in New Orleans with the cheeky urchins and marching jazz bands and Pete Fountain's sweet clarinet.

I drove west the next day, out through the cane fields and bayous. Every watery ditch is a plantation worked by egrets and overseen by hawks. The towns are blisters on the savanna. Houma, a rich little city of live oaks and mock French houses, is two hours west of New Orleans, and I stopped there for a couple of small indulgences – a restaurant, of course, and a cold, rainy, exhilarating tour of a swamp.

I went first to the Dusenberry family's restaurant, La Trouvaille, in a country house on Bayou Petit Caillou. They fed me spaghetti, homemade root beer, and bread pudding. Papa played the guitar and sang. Most of the songs were light, because Papa is a cut-up, but when he sang 'Ay-vahn-zhay-leen,' the story of the Acadian exile, people wiped tears, and I could not help thinking that the diaspora continues: Shoved out of Canada by the British; shoved from the best Louisiana land by the Anglo sugarcane planters, and now shoved back from the rich coastal marsh by the Texas oilmen, who are impatient with the oysters, muskrats and Cajuns that get in the way of the rigs. Bayou Annie Miller turns the tables on the oilmen. Mrs. Miller is a hearty country woman who used to trap muskrats and catch snakes for a living. When the oil companies dug canals for their workboats, she started a unique touring service. She runs her motorboat up the oil company canals into the swamps and points out the local colour – water birds, snakes, nutria, cypress trees.

'That's a blue runner,' she said, pointing to a snake on the bank. 'He'll stand up like a cobra and chase you. But if you get behind him and chase him, he'll run from you. You can have a lot of fun with that fellow.'

I shared the boat with a Swiss family, all of us huddled into windbreakers. We were amazed when Mrs. Miller stood in the open boat and called alligators by name.

'Candy! Baby Dee! Isabel! Come on, bay-bee. Hurry up, Bell!'

The gators were shy that morning, but Mrs. Miller was not. When she heard the Swiss speaking French among themselves, she joined them. '*C'est un grand héron bleu,*' she said in a hardy Cajun accent. 'Keep your hands inside the boat, Madame, *s'il vous plaît.*'

For the more subdued nature lover, there is Avery Island. I drove there from Houma, some ninety miles northwest on Route 90, and toured the famous McIlhenny Company Tabasco plant. Near sundown, I went into the island's Jungle Gardens and Bird Sanctuary and positioned myself at the rookery.

Thousands of egrets, ibises, herons, and other waterfowl arrived at twilight, ten or twenty at a time, and settled in the trees and bamboo. I stood watching until the flapping and grumbling stopped at dark. An alligator watched with me, collaborating in stealth, from the black water beneath the observation tower. Neither of us moved anything but our eyes for a long time. Then I blinked, and went to New Iberia and had an elegant, red-peppered crawfish Yvonne at Patout's Restaurant. The gator, I imagined, was having frog legs.

On my second day out of New Orleans I drove deep into the upper reaches of Bayou Teche, the remotest and least Anglicized part of Cajun country. The mailboxes announce Boudreaux, Le Blanc, Thériot, Broussard. The towns are called Breaux Bridge, Arnaudville, Grand Coteau. You pass an occasional symbol of the 'Texiens,' an oil-well pump flailing a sugarcane field to suck a different sweetness.

On the western bank of Bayou Teche sits the little town of St. Martinville, the spiritual capital of French-speaking Louisiana. More than 79 per cent of the residents of St. Martin Parish, or county, still speak the language their ancestors brought from Celtic Brittany by way of Canada.

I visited the Evangeline Oak on the bank of the bayou, where the tragic heroine waited in vain for her lover, then walked to the main street. I admired the wooden balconies and the grillework over the old stores. As I passed St. Martin Church, a bulletin board in the yard caught my eye. The notices read:

GOOD LENT — BON CARÊME

TURN AWAY FROM SIN — RECEVEZ BONNE NOUVELLE

DIEU EST AMOUR — GOD IS LOVE

Cajun French is more a spoken tongue than a written one. It is also used more often in the profane world than the sacred. After leaving St. Martinville I spent the evening at a restaurant and dance hall called Mulates, near Breaux Bridge. People go there to drink, eat crawfish, and listen to Cajun music. The couples danced a graceful, old-fashioned two-step, and many were speaking French.

French is widely used in songs and in radio and television programmes. One of the attractions in Lafayette, the largest town in the Cajun country, is Théâtre 'Cadien, which performs plays in French.

Almost all Cajuns except a few of the elderly speak English, but the outsider may be confused by it. I asked directions to a café in Houma and was told, 'Go down here five or four blocks and catch de bridge. You cross de bi-yo and go straight down that road about two mile. You can't miss it.' I went into a grocery in Gueydan looking for a famous Vermilion Parish rice that tastes and smells like popcorn. An amiable little woman of about seventy-five took me by the arm and led me to it. Then she told me, as I picked up a five-pound sack, 'People roun' here don't lack it. Me, I lack rice that tastes lack rice.'

The Cajuns are well known for their warmth. Strangers, no matter how presumptuous, are made welcome. For example, many of the sugarcane plantations and mills can be toured for the asking. The easy way to do this is to phone Thomas Warner, the information director for the American Sugar Cane League in New Orleans, and arrange a tour. But I once wheeled into the sugar mill at Breaux Bridge on an impulse, and the manager dropped everything for an hour to show the place to me and my friends and to explain the intricacies of sugar making.

I decided on my recent trip to visit a crawfish processing plant. The dictionaries spell it 'crayfish,' but why should an outsider who would shrink from peeling one be allowed to spell it?

Peeling happened to be the motive of my plant visit. I had peeled several pounds for lunch the day before and my thumb was sore from shell cuts. I was out of practice. I walked into Pat's seafood packing plant at Henderson, next door to Pat's famous restaurant, and asked to watch the pros.

A woman behind the table invited me to pull up a chair and go to work. When I declined, she said with a grin, 'You here to watch or learn?' I ignored her taunting and concentrated on her style. It consisted of two fast motions: off with the head, then off with the tail shell to expose the edible meat. I calculated that she could have peeled my entire lunch in ninety seconds.

When the outside world thinks of Cajun food, it thinks of crawfish, shrimp, oysters, jambalaya and gumbo. You learn of other, more primitive, foods as you penetrate the Acadian Coast and the bayous. On the window of the Bienvenu Cash Grocery at St. Martinville I saw advertising for hog lard, fresh hog cracklings (cooked skins), fresh catfish, garfish, turtle and alligator meat.

One of the least known and perhaps the most addictive of the Cajun dishes is boudin. Boudin (the last syllable rhymes with can, nasally) is a sausage containing rice, pork, and pork liver. Cajun children eat it like ice cream in a cone.

I have a friend in New Orleans who knows food, as well as politics, law and other Louisiana weaknesses. He had told me, with some show of confidentiality, where to find the world's best boudin. It was in the town of Jennings at a café named the Boudin King. I found myself within fifty miles of Jennings on the next to last day of my trip, so I went.

The Boudin King turns out to be not merely a café but also a man. Ellis Cormier, a royally built native of Jennings, started making boudin when he had a grocery store. Traditionally, the sausage is made from the scraps at *la boucherie*, or hog killing.

'I started using better pork because I didn't have enough scraps,' he said, 'and the business grew.' He claims to have created the boudin industry of Louisiana, although he admits that the claim is controversial. He uses his grandfather's recipe that originated in Nova Scotia. The seasonings include green onions, parsley, cayenne, salt and black pepper. Mr. Cormier has had customers from every state and several foreign countries. He sells 4,000 pounds a week.

I drove on to Eunice to spend the night and that evening, a Friday, I visited a bar called the Blue Goose hoping to hear a Cajun band. But the printed schedule of bands that I had picked up in Lafayette turned out to be a rather generalized guide, like Cajun directions on the highway. The Blue Goose had a band on Sunday, not Friday.

The barmaid, whose name was Jenny, pacified me by teaching me the rudiments of bourre, the favourite card game among Cajuns. She said her widowed mother earned her living at it. The conversation turned to food, and I mentioned that I had just that day eaten the best boudin in the world.

'Ah, now, *cher*,' she said, 'the best boudin is made here in Eunice. You go try the boudin at Johnson's Grocery.'

At seven-thirty the next morning I joined a fifty-foot line at the meat counter of Johnson's Grocery. All of us were buying boudin. The butcher sold me a pound wrapped in plain paper. I drove ten miles north to Mamou, where I was to spend my last half day in the Cajun country, and carried the boudin into Fred's Lounge. I ordered a beer and began eating my breakfast – Budweiser and boudin.

Fred's Lounge was an indulgence I had promised myself. I had once spend Mardi Gras in Mamou. Country Cajun towns celebrate Mardi Gras (which usually comes in February) on horseback. Young men dress as clowns, get drunk and ride the countryside begging chickens and other ingredients for a giant gumbo. In the excitement of *courir de Mardi Gras* I had somehow missed Fred's Lounge, and had since learned that the best radio show of country Cajun music originates in Fred's every Saturday morning.

Revon Reed, the host, plays records, tells jokes and reads commercials in the old-fashioned redneck French of the Cajuns. A live band plays string music as well, and the regulars crowd the dance floor. The bar is busy by 8.30 a.m.

The barmaid filled me in on the action, a kind of running soap opera. 'See that old man? That the riches' man in Evangeline Parish. He bought his wife a washing machine last year, first one she ever had in forty years, and it's a wringer machine. He comes in here every Saturday and chases the women.'

Another elderly man and his woman friend came in.

'What you have, *cher*?' the barmaid asked.

'Two Morgan Davids.'

She returned to me and noticed what I was eating. I explained that it was the world's best boudin, from Eunice. She lifted an eyebrow and said, 'Listen, *cher*, the best boudin in the world is made at the grocery store right here in Mamou, down the street here.' She pulled her own package of sausage from under the bar and cut a slice for me. 'Now you tell me, *cher*, isn't that the best boudin in the world?' I admitted it. She brought me another beer.

Two or three hours later I left the warm comfort of Fred's and went into the street, headed north. I felt a blush of the alienness that keeps the visitor off balance everywhere. The traveller's dignity is always in peril. He knows that his speech, his clothes, his gestures are all out of place and slightly preposterous. The Cajuns understand and work to make the stranger comfortable.

I was stopped by a middle-aged man as I walked toward my car. He wore a fine cardigan sweater and a British-style touring cap. It was clear that he saw in me a fellow traveller, and less chance of making a fool of himself.

'Pardon me,' he said in a cultivated accent from somewhere, 'can you tell me where to buy boudin?'

I directed him to the grocery store half a block away, and told him he couldn't miss it. I also told him that he had come to the right place. Mamou, I said confidentially, makes the best boudin in the world.

THREE DAYS ALONG EL CAMINO REAL

Robert Lindsey

In 1769 a band of Franciscan friars travelled north from Mexico on a mission to save souls. It was a journey that would take sixty years, and when it was over, the Spanish padres had not only converted uncounted thousands of Indians to Roman Catholicism but they had also planted the seeds from which grew the state of California.

Led by Father Junipero Serra, the padres built a chain of twenty-one missions, each a day's journey apart – about thirty miles. The missions were crudely made of adobe bricks and red tile and stretched up the coast from San Diego to Sonoma, a distance of more than 600 miles.

Spain called the road that linked the missions El Camino Real, the King's Highway. Small settlements, then towns and cities formed around the missions, and the King's Highway became the spine of California. These days motorists can traverse the entire King's Highway in a day. But for those with more time, there is no better way to explore California than to spend at least two days and preferably three following the path carved out by the padres.

The southern segment of El Camino Real around San Diego and Los Angeles and the northern segment around San Jose and San Francisco have been urbanized. In Los Angeles as well as in California's other major metropolitan areas, little remains of the placid scenes that the Spanish missionaries encountered more than 200 years ago. But there is a 240-mile stretch of El Camino Real, between Santa Barbara and Carmel on the Monterey Peninsula, that has refused to yield to urbanization.

It is, in many ways, what California used to be: expanses of rolling countryside inland and spectacular, unspoiled ocean vistas on the coast, small coastal communities and slow-paced mission towns that have retained much of the flavour of their Spanish past.

The autumn and winter are exceptionally attractive periods to visit the region. The summer crowds are gone and so is most of the fog that tends to shroud the coast during summer. Rainfall can be expected periodically but not often, and temperatures are generally mild.

A tour of the heart of the King's Highway can begin from either Los Angeles or San Francisco; its attractions provide a diverting contrast to the metropolitan areas. U.S. 101, which connects Los Angeles and San Francisco, is, with a few deviations, the same route that the padres took, and is the asphalt descendant of El Camino Real. Motorists are reminded of this every few miles by replicas of a green mission bell standing beside the road on a staff.

Those who visit the area by car and begin the tour from the south should make **Santa Barbara,** a drive of less than two hours from Los Angeles, their first stop. It is a beguiling seaside town, and one that as much as any in California has kept alive the heritage of its Spanish past with mission-style, red-tile-roof Mediterranean architecture and an easygoing way of life. It is a city with fine restaurants and beaches and some of America's most beautiful residential neighbourhoods, many hidden on slopes overlooking the Pacific among huge oak trees, themselves works of art.

A good way to get oriented is to take the thirty-six-mile Scenic Drive marked by signs around the city. An annotated map is available from the Santa Barbara Chamber of Commerce, 1301 Santa Barbara Street (805 965 3021), and at most hotels. The route takes you past stunning vistas of the city's beaches and harbour and the terraced mountains that rise east of the city. It passes many well-preserved adobe buildings from the Spanish and Mexican eras and elegant homes in the exclusive residential areas of Montecito, south of the city, and Hope Ranch, north of it. Extending the heritage of the city, many of these costly homes are designed in the Spanish style.

Santa Barbara, unlike many cities in California, is an appealing place for walkers. A good spot to start is the County Courthouse in the 1100 block of Anacapa Street. The building's 70-foot-high clock tower, visible for blocks around, is the most prominent feature of one of America's most attractive public buildings. It was built in the late 1920s after an earthquake destroyed the previous courthouse and much of the rest of Santa Barbara. At a time when architects elsewhere were borrowing ideas from ancient Rome and Greece for public buildings, the designers of Santa Babara's courthouse chose a stunning, castle-like Spanish-Moorish design that helps set the architectural tone for the city. The courthouse, including an observation deck atop the clock tower, is open to the public without charge between 8 am and 5 pm.

From the courthouse, visitors, strolling on sidewalks covered with Spanish-style red tiles, can explore the State Street shopping district and visit a number of old buildings from the time of Spanish, and later Mexican, rule. Much of the Santa Barbara Presidio still stands not far from the courthouse. At 715 Santa Barbara Street, for example, is the

167-year-old adobe building called Casa de Covarrubias. Nearby, at the northeast corner of State and Carrillo streets, is an adobe used by Col. John C. Fremont after the city was taken over by the United States in 1846.

A map detailing a 'Red Tile Tour' indicating the location of these and other historic landmarks is available at the Chamber of Commerce office, which is also a good source of other information about the area.

The Santa Barbara Historical Society Museum at 136 East De la Guerra Street, which is open daily except Monday from noon until 5 pm and weekends from 1 pm to 5 pm, contains a good collection of mementoes from the city's past. Admission is free.

Not far away, at Anapamu and State streets, is the Santa Barbara Museum of Art, which specializes in sculpture and American and Oriental art. Admission is free. Open daily except Monday from 11 am to 5 pm, Thursdays until 9 pm and on Sundays from noon to 5 pm.

Also worth a visit is the city's Museum of Natural History and Gladwin Planetarium. Situated on Puesta del Sol Road near the Santa Barbara Mission, the museum has exhibits exploring early years of the Santa Barbara region. It is open every day except Christmas, New Year's Day and Thanksgiving from 9 am to 5 pm Monday to Saturday and from 10 am to 5 pm on Sunday.

Santa Barbara is a good place for your first visit to a mission. **Mission Santa Barbara** is a striking building with twin bell towers that make it one of the most beautiful – and most photographed – of the twenty-one missions. Like most of them it still functions as a Catholic church, and you may encounter a wedding or other event during your visit.

The mission, situated atop a hill at the upper end of Laguna Street, was founded in 1786, rebuilt in 1820 after an earthquake and rebuilt again after another earthquake in 1925. It is open to visitors between 9 am and 5 pm daily. There is no charge to enter the church, but donations are solicited for admission to the mission museum.

As you drive north along U.S. 101, you will see frequent signs alerting you to the location of nearby missions, most of which have been restored. Each mission's architecture and interior are somewhat different from the others, and if you have a special fascination with the history of early California, you may want to stop at all of them; most people, though, find that a visit to two or three is ample.

At Buellton, forty-five miles north of Santa Barbara, as U.S. 101 passes through the bucolic Santa Ynez Valley, you may want to take a short drive east on State Route 246 to **Solvang.** It is a charming, if somewhat commercialized, village that grew up around a colony founded in 1910 by Danish immigrants. The immigrants' descendants have kept Old World traditions alive, with Danish architecture and a variety of Danish bakeries, restaurants and gift shops.

On Route 246 just east of Solvang is one of the best preserved of the old missions, **Mission Santa Ynez,** which was founded in 1804 and once had 12,000 head of cattle grazing in the nearby hills. Its operating hours are similar to those at Mission Santa Barbara.

About 70 miles north of Buellton, in the downtown section of San Luis Obispo, **Mission San Luis Obispo de Tolosa** has attractive gardens, an especially well-preserved interior and a comprehensive museum with old photographs, religious papers and other relics. The mission is open daily from 9 am to 4 pm. There is no admission charge, but donations are solicited.

At San Luis Obispo, travellers face a fork in the road. They can continue north to Carmel on U.S. 101 through the lush Salinas Valley and more mission towns, or they can head west on State Route 1 toward the ocean. (For travellers making the trip in a southerly direction, the choice of routes is made in Carmel.)

The inland route on U.S. 101 provides a chance to explore a region that is currently a source of excitement within California's wine industry. Traditionally, the state's premium wine grapes have come from a handful of regions near the coast, such as the Napa, Sonoma, Santa Clara and Livermore valleys, whose soil and climate rank, California chauvinists claim, among the world's best for wine.

But the growing demand by Americans for premium wines, and growing economic pressures to urbanize many of the state's traditional agricultural valleys, have forced vintners to look elsewhere for grapes, including some of the same hillsides along El Camino Real where two hundred years or so ago the Spanish padres produced grapes for sacramental wine. In the last decade or so, thousands of acres of premium grapes have been planted in San Luis Obispo County, near Santa Barbara, and in the Salinas Valley.

Most wine purists appear to feel that the region has not yet produced wines equal to California's best, but you can judge that for yourself. Several wineries along El Camino Real offer free tastings. In San Luis Obispo, **Chamisal Vineyard** (805 544 3576) is proud of its chardonnay. In Paso Robles, **Hoffman Mountain Ranch Vineyard** (805 238 4982), at Black Oak corner near U.S. 101, operates a tasting room from 11 am to 5 pm daily except holidays, offering chardonnay, riesling, and a variety of red wines. In Gonzales, a few miles south of Salinas, **Monterey Vineyards** offers free tours and tastings from 10 am to 5 pm.

If you decide to take the coastal rather than the inland route to Carmel, plan to add two or three hours to the trip. There are long stretches of twists and turns as the highway hugs a serpentine ledge hundreds of feet above a sheer cliff. But if you do not press yourself for time and do not drive at night, there is no reason to avoid the highway. Some people feel it is better to travel the route northbound, for then they are not driving along the cliff side of the road. Whichever direction is taken, you will be rewarded with beautiful vistas of ocean meeting land.

From San Luis Obispo, Route 1 swings through the colourful seaside towns of Morro Bay and Cambria. Near Cambria is a landmark that should not be missed: the estate in **San Simeon** of the late publisher William Randolph Hearst. He was a man seemingly obsessed with a drive to acquire everything he saw, and much of what he bought is here.

Hearst built a castle overlooking the Pacific that would have done justice to a medieval prince and stuffed it with artworks and artifacts; he stripped castles and European country houses of entire rooms and invited the rich and famous to visit him at this remote spot. People still argue about the quality of his taste, but Hearst Castle, which his family donated to the state of California in 1958, is a stunning monument to one man's wealth and acquisitiveness.

From San Simeon, Route 1 begins a ninety-mile course to Carmel, following the scalloped ledge of the mountains and passing **Big Sur.** The beauty, solitude and tolerance that Big Sur bestows on its visitors attracted thousands of hippies and wanderers during the '60s and '70s, and while they no longer come in such numbers, it still attracts, along with other visitors, a funky crowd whose beards, long hair, and attire curiously carry one back to the '60s.

From Big Sur, it is an easy drive to **Carmel,** a hamlet of about 5,000 people built on the side of a forested hill that slopes into the Pacific, where a sandy beach sweeps in one direction toward the golf links of Pebble Beach and, in the other, toward the rocky tip of Point Lobos. Carmel, which has a splendid mission a few blocks from Route 1 – it is the burial site of Father Serra – tends to get crowded on weekends. But people come nevertheless, drawn by a peculiar charm, a mixture of an English village, a rustic forest of windswept trees, quaint buildings, and scores of first-rate shops, art galleries, and restaurants. One notable antiques shop is Luciano's on San Carlos Street between Fifth and Sixth avenues.

If there is anything that takes precedence over shopping and dining in the Carmel area, it is golf. There are thirteen golf courses on the Monterey Peninsula, offering golfers more than fifty miles of fairways, some right above the pounding surf. Two of the more challenging are the 6,799-yard Pebble Beach course and the 6,810-yard Spyglass Hill course, both at the Lodge at Pebble Beach. For starting times, call 408 624 3811.

Between Carmel and **Monterey,** whose fisherman's wharf and Cannery Row are worth a side trip, are Pebble Beach and Del Monte Forest, a gated enclave of the affluent. For four dollars, which is refunded if you play a round of golf or eat at one of the restaurants at the Lodge at Pebble Beach, out-of-towners can tour Del Monte Forest on 17-Mile Drive.

The curving roadway covers much of the residential area and passes a spectacular stretch of coastline edged with monumental cypress trees sculpted by the wind. The 20th Century-Fox Corporation bought most of the remaining land in the forest a few years ago, and the residents are worried that Marvin Davis, a Denver oilman who recently bought the film studio, will try to speed development of the area by selling off the land for condominiums, spoiling its extraordinary beauty and charm. But right now it is as beautiful as ever.

STOPS ALONG THE ROYAL ROAD
Santa Barbara

For many years, the only place to stay in Santa Barbara was the **Biltmore** (805 969 2261), a complex of Spanish-style, white stucco, red-tile-roof buildings built in 1927 on twenty-one acres of beautifully landscaped grounds at the edge of the Pacific. The Marriott hotel chain took over the hotel at 1260 Channel Drive a few years ago and has renovated it beautifully. Some longtime visitors say they believe that the quality of service and some amenities that gave the hotel its special élan have declined and, as a result, the Biltmore no longer ranks as the world-class resort it once was. Still, many will choose no other place in Santa Barbara. Rates range from about $115 to $190 for one or two people in a room, with $155 for a cottage.

Not far away at 900 San Ysidro Lane, in the scenic suburb of Montecito, is the rustic but quite elegant **San Ysidro Ranch** (805 969 5046). Laurence Olivier and Vivien Leigh were married there; John and Jacqueline Kennedy spent part of their honeymoon there, and other celebrities have been coming to stay at one of its cottages for years. Rates, which vary according to the size and style of the cottage, range from about $100 to over $375; the latter is for a cottage that can accommodate four. The dining room is rustic, but the service and the Continental-style cuisine are tasteful. Dinner for two: about $80.

For palates craving an American-style menu there are two popular places that specialize in make-it-yourself salads, beef and seafood: **Chuck's Steak House** (805 687 4417), 3888 State Street, and the **Chart House** (805 966 2112), 101 East Cabrillo Boulevard. Neither accepts reservations.

The Big Yellow House (805 969 4414), 108 Pierpont Street, just off U.S. 101 about five miles south of Santa Barbara, is popular with families with big appetites. Good, hearty food (usually chicken and beef; the entrées vary nightly) is served family style with no limit on the servings. About $35 for a family of four.

Buellton

Pea Soup Andersen's (805 688 5581), at State Route 246 and Avenue of the Flags, is a restaurant that has become an institution by enshrining a single dish – pea soup. With a carafe of house wine, dinner for two in the main restaurant (including all the soup and salad you can eat) costs between $11 and $18; be prepared for a long wait, especially on weekends. Two people interested only in a bowl of pea soup and a glass of wine can eat for less than $7.

San Luis Obispo

Heritage Inn (805 544 7440), 978 Olive Street, is a bed-and-breakfast guesthouse in a charming old building furnished with antiques. Rates for two (no children, smokers, or pets) are about $50 to $75 including evening sherry and Continental breakfast.

Madonna Inn (805 543 3000), 100 Madonna Road, has 104 rooms, some carved out of rocks. Most rooms have unusual décor; one may be decorated as a cave, its neighbour with period furnishings. Some visitors do not care for the kitsch, and in places the inn is reminiscent of Miami Beach at its worst, but it is nevertheless a landmark on U.S. 101 and worth at least a stop for a cup of coffee, if not for the night. The rate for two in a room ranges from about $60 to $140.

Around San Simeon

Cavalier Inn (805 927 4688), on Route 1, is a modest motel close to Hearst Castle; some rooms have fireplaces and some have ocean views. Rates range from about $47 to $70 for two in a room.

Not far from the castle at 2905 Burton Drive in Cambria is the fifty-seven-year-old **Cambria Pines Lodge** (805 927 4200), a complex of cabins set amid a pine forest; some of the cabins show their age, although it is popular with families. Rates vary according to the size of the cabin, with the minimum about $45.

Big Sur

Along Route 1 are two places that combine exciting hilltop views of the Pacific and good, if uncomplicated food. About thirty miles south of Carmel and 800 feet above the sea, **Nepenthe** (408 667 2345) serves lunch and dinner at modest prices. At lunch hamburgers and other sandwiches are served with an attractive salad, cost about $6, and are almost big enough for two healthy appetites. Two can have dinner, with wine, for less than $25.

A few miles up the coast, twelve miles south of Carmel, **Rocky Point** (408 624 2933) occupies a site overlooking the ocean. Drawing cards are huge barbecued steaks, salads, and commendable garlic toast. Steak dinner for two, with wine, about $60. Reservations recommended.

Carmel

Vagabond's House Inn (408 624 7738), at Dolores Street and Fourth Avenue, distils the charm for which Carmel is famous; it is a complex of old buildings positioned around a landscaped courtyard. Rates for two in a room with breakfast range from about $65 to $85; it is best to book well in advance.

Nearby on Ocean Avenue, Carmel's main street, is the **Pine Inn** (408

624 3851), a dark, traditional place reminiscent of an English inn. Rates: about $50 to $110. Also on Ocean Avenue is the charming **Normandy Inn** (408 624 3825), which has a cluster of cottages. The atmosphere is country French. Rates average $75 a night for two.

The **Adobe Inn** (408 624 3933), at Dolores and Eighth Streets, is a conveniently situated modern inn with fireplaces in most rooms. For two persons, rates range from $75 to $94.

The Lodge at Pebble Beach (408 624 3811) is an elegant resort with beautiful ocean vistas. It is surrounded by golf courses, tennis courts and other recreational facilities. Rates for two: $160 to $175.

Club XIX (408 625 1880) at the Lodge at Pebble Beach offers excellent French food served well. Just about everything is good, but you cannot go wrong by choosing a Caesar salad, rack of lamb and soufflé Grand Marnier, which recently cost $85 for two, including a good bottle of California wine and the 15 per cent service charge added to all bills. Reservations essential.

Casanova (408 625 0501), on Fifth Street between Mission and San Carlos streets, is a restaurant that seems to have been picked up stone by stone from the French countryside and dropped intact onto its setting. In a dozen visits, I have never been disappointed. My highest recommendation goes to the scampi – a half-dozen large prawns served in garlic sauce on a bed of Casanova-made pasta – and, when it is in season, fresh salmon prepared in almost a dozen ways. Dinner for two, with a bottle of the good house wine at $8, runs about $55. No reservations are accepted, but there is generally no wait for a table for those arriving before 7 pm.

The Butcher Shop (408 624 2569), on Ocean Avenue near Dolores Street, has an early-bird special. Diners who arrive between 4.30 and 6 pm are offered a variety of dinners, including spare ribs, for about $7 to $110.

HEARST CASTLE
When to Go

Guided tours of Hearst Castle are offered daily, except Christmas, New Year's Day, and Thanksgiving, from 8.20 am to 3.20 pm. Visitors park near Route 1 and are transported to the castle by bus; three tours, showing different parts of the estate, are conducted, each lasting about an hour and forty-five minutes; the guides, whose fields of knowledge range from Hollywood in the 1930s to Renaissance art, seem especially well prepared for their jobs. They recommend Tour No. 1 to first-time visitors.

Getting Tickets

The tours are extremely popular, and it is best to buy tickets before arriving at San Simeon. Tickets can be purchased from travel agents or from Ticketron outlets. Adults are charged $8 for each tour and children between six and twelve years pay $4.

Information

A brochure and other details on the tours may be obtained by writing to the Department of Parks and Recreation, San Simeon Area, P.O. Box 8, San Simeon, Calif. 93452, or by calling 805 927 4621.

GRAND HOTELS, L.A. STYLE

Aljean Harmetz

Where do the top corporate executives, the international film stars, the Middle Eastern sheikhs, and the trendy rock groups stay in Beverly Hills? Where should you stay when you fly west to buy your $6,000 mink-lined, bulletproof bomber jacket at Bijan on Rodeo Drive, to sell Warner Brothers your first screenplay or simply to get a suntan in January? The choices:

The pink-and-green **Beverly Hills Hotel**, with its breezy informality and its history of Hollywood deal-making beside the pool. The sedate **Beverly Wilshire**, at the foot of Rodeo Drive, where Howard Keck, the oil magnate, and Marge Everett, owner of the Hollywood Park racetrack, are among the twenty-one year-round guests.

The busy **Beverly Hilton**, where the Academy Awards ball is held every spring. The crescent-shaped **Century Plaza**, where the astronauts stayed when they came home from the moon and which serves as President Reagan's stopping-off place between Washington and his Santa Barbara ranch.

The rustic **Bel-Air Hotel**, with its wooden bridges and swans and ten acres of some of the most expensive residential real estate in the world.

L'Ermitage, with a million dollars' worth of nineteenth and twentieth century European paintings in the dining room and a fireplace in every suite.

Or a dozen others: from the **Holiday Inns** and **Ramada Inns** to the tiny, $58-a-day **Beverly House** in the heart of Beverly Hills. If the Century Plaza and Beverly Hilton are sniffed at by their rivals as 'convention' hotels, the Beverly Hills described as 'somewhat sloppy,' the Beverly Wilshire considered 'too staid,' the Bel-Air 'too isolated,' and L'Ermitage 'too special,' there is agreement that each hotel will suit someone's taste.

'I can't think of a city where the concentration of good hotels is as high as here on the West Side,' says William G. Quinn, managing director of the Century Plaza. 'They're all within ten minutes of each other, and they're all well run and individual. After a while, a returning guest will simply go where he was most comfortable.'

Paul Newman, Ingrid Bergman, Henry Kissinger, Paul McCartney, and the late Shah of Iran are among the celebrities who have been comfortable at the Beverly Hills Hotel. Elizabeth Taylor literally grew up there, since her father had his art gallery in the lower lobby, and has shared one of the bungalows with her husbands.

'The orange juice is freshly squeezed,' says Burton Slatkin, president of the Beverly Hills Hotel Corporation. 'We don't precook the bacon. Our employees are people who have service mentalities, who enjoy making people feel at home. We try to avoid sharpie types. Our guests most commonly describe us as "friendly, warm and helpful" and say this place is like their own private club.' It's a brisk fifteen-minute walk from the hotel to shops, and taxis are often hard to come by, but, says Mr. Slatkin, 'we try not to say no to anything our guests want, and our bellman will pick up a package in Beverly Hills.'

Built in 1912, the hotel sprawls over twelve acres and has 315 rooms, including twenty-one bungalows that rent for as much as $1,300 a day. A few spartan singles are available for about $90. There are no conventions and no commercial discounts. Even Howard Hughes, who was a permanent guest for twenty-five years before he moved to Las Vegas in 1967, paid the full price of $250,000 a year for his twenty-three rooms. Marvin Davis, the Denver oil billionaire who recently purchased 20th Century-Fox for nearly $800 million, keeps a bungalow year round.

The hotel once sat amid bean fields and bridle paths; today it is surrounded by two-million-dollar homes. Even an unsuspecting businessman can be discovered while sunbathing around the usually empty pool. In 1956, Robert Evans, part-owner of Evan-Picone Inc., manufacturer of sportswear, was seen by Norma Shearer and chosen to play her late husband, Hollywood's 'boy genius' of the 1930s Irving Thalberg, in *Man of a Thousand Faces*. He later became a vice president in charge of production at Paramount. 'The pool and the Polo Lounge are all eyes and very little stomach,' he says, 'a Mecca for people looking to see who else is there.'

The writer Joan Didion once defined the Polo Lounge as 'the home of the Deal.' It is still, emphatically, the place where Hollywood executives eat breakfast, then jog three miles before going off 'to take a meeting.'

The Polo Lounge was named when Hollywood played polo. Now Hollywood plays tennis, but the Beverly Hills is the only West Side hotel with tennis courts. It is no accident that the title character in the film *American Gigolo* prowled the lounge's green banquettes for women who wanted his services. The bar also attracts high-priced prostitutes.

'The executives who stay at the Beverly Wilshire have no time for such things,' says Larry Mark, a Paramount vice president of production who stayed at the Beverly Wilshire every six weeks for two years when he was based in New York. 'The El Padrino room is full of executives with lots of charts, because the Beverly Wilshire is where work-loving executives stay. Play-loving executives stay at the Beverly Hills.'

The Beverly Wilshire prides itself on being a New York-type hotel. The lift operators wear white gloves, and special guests are welcomed with champagne – forty or fifty bottles are given away each day – or a box of Godiva chocolates. 'We are probably the largest deluxe hotel in the world,' says Hernando Courtwright, the seventy-seven-year-old proprietor of the 445-room establishment. Ironically, it was Mr. Courtwright who helped create the mystique of the rival Beverly Hills Hotel. He even named the Polo Lounge during the twenty-two years he ran the Beverly Hills Hotel after the Depression.

'There are three important things for a hotel,' says Mr. Quinn of the Century Plaza. 'Location! Location! And Location!' Situated at the foot of Rodeo Drive, the Beverly Wilshire has, unquestionably, the best location of any of the hotels. And Mr. Courtwright – who once greeted the Emperor of Japan with a fifteen-man mariachi band and spent $25,000 on daisies for the Queen of Denmark – has worked hard to help develop, beautify and publicize Rodeo Drive as one of the premier shopping streets in the world.

Mr. Courtwright likes to describe his guests as 'an élite group.' The actor Warren Beatty lived in a Beverly Wilshire penthouse for eleven years before he decided to leave in 1972 because construction of the hotel's new tower invaded his privacy. The hotel's rooms start at $100 a day, but there are corporate rates for 'good corporate clients.' Conventions are frowned on, but small meetings of stockholders are encouraged.

The new tower, with its bay windows, mission arches, wrought-iron balconies and central air-conditioning, has won architectural awards. Rooms in the original hotel have been redecorated. Until recently, some were dowdy, with noisy room air-conditioners.

Both the Beverly Wilshire and the Beverly Hills Hotel have their strong partisans. 'Just driving up to the Beverly Hills makes you giggle,' says Victoria Wilson, a senior editor at Alfred A. Knopf. 'Once you're there, everybody makes you feel cosy. Even the forty-year-old banana-leaf wallpaper is great. The Beverly Wilshire is like a Midwesterner's notion of a fancy hotel – it's stodgy and unfriendly. The Beverly Wilshire is self-important. The Beverly Hills doesn't pretend to be anything but what it is.'

But a financial editor from New York who prefers the Beverly Wilshire calls the housekeeping at the Beverly Hills Hotel 'wildly inefficient.' And Michael Maslansky, co-owner of a Hollywood public-relations concern, recalls that a desk clerk at the Beverly Hills would not let the actress Marthe Keller register because she was not carrying a credit card and 'someone had forgotten to say that the studio was paying her bill.' He says, 'I had to come down and give them my credit card before they would let Marthe have her room. In any great hotel, people are able to use their heads.'

Barry Diller, chairman of Paramount Pictures, spurns both the Beverly Hills and the Beverly Wilshire. 'In terms of personal service and privacy and caring about the people who stay there, the Bel-Air Hotel is one of the best hotels in the United States,' he says. Mr. Diller lived in the Bel-Air for seven years when he was commuting from coast to coast as vice president of the American Broadcasting Companies. The hotel is a Spanish hacienda of pink adobe with forty rooms that cost from about $160 to $250 a night and twenty-eight suites that range from $300 to $1,200. Hidden beneath a variety of tropical trees, the former stable of a California oil magnate has become a honeymoon hotel. Mark Spitz, the Olympic swimmer, Jay Rockefeller, now Governor of West Virginia, and Zubin Mehta, the conductor, spent their honeymoons there.

James Checkman, who was manager of the Bel-Air for seventeen years, described the hotel as 'restful' and 'beautiful.' It is several miles up a dead-end canyon road, has no shops or boutiques, and only a single restaurant, open from seven-thirty am to midnight. The lobby – where Dame Edith Sitwell once held court in a black cowl – looks like a comfortable living room, with ceramic and painted swans everywhere.

Every guest is welcomed with candy or nuts, but not with liquor. 'People who want what the Beverly Hills has to offer would feel a bit restless here,' said Mr. Checkman. Fervently loyal guests include David Rockefeller, Deborah Kerr, Robert Redford and some top executives for television networks.

With an occupancy rate above 90 per cent, although it spends less than $100 a month on advertising, the Bel-Air is, says Mr. Checkman, 'the only hotel I've ever heard of that doesn't overbook.' With only one change in ownership since 1943, it is a haven for public figures and businessmen who seek privacy; there is no need to go through the lobby to get to the rooms.

The eighteen-year-old Century Plaza and the twenty-nine-year-old Beverly Hilton are chain-owned hotels. The Century Plaza has 750 rooms and suites that rent from about $120 to $900; the Hilton has 625 that range from about $120 to $600. Both cater to conventions, with the Century Plaza serving half a million banquet meals a year.

Two of the Beverly Hilton's restaurants – L'Escoffier and Trader Vic's – were among the eight Los Angeles restaurants given top ratings in recent years by the Los Angeles Restaurant Writers Association, along with the Beverly Wilshire's La Bella Fontana. Charles Bolla, general manager for the Beverly Hilton, says the hotel was 'a favoured child' of its owner, Conrad Hilton, who lived in nearby Bel-Air. Barron Hilton, his son, still has the $11 fixed-price buffet for lunch each weekday in the hotel's 'Mr. H' room.

'You must make adjustments in your chain philosophy to suit your clientele,' says Mr. Bolla. More than a third of the Beverly Hilton's guests come from abroad, a figure that rises to nearly half in summer. 'The stars aren't here; they're probably at the Beverly Hills,' he says. 'But we get all the people who represent the film, television, and record industries in London.'

The hotel – which is at a busy intersection on the western outskirts of Beverly Hills – encourages comments. Mr. Bolla says he reads and responds to every complaint: He changed all the hotel's shower heads after European guests complained they were too small. Each room has a refrigerator and each suite has a bar; in the penthouse suites, the bar is fully stocked.

The Century Plaza's redecoration plan recently included telephones and scales in every bathroom, refrigerators and armoires in every room and king-size beds in nearly half the rooms. As this volume was on its way to press, the hotel was constructing a new $800 million luxury tower.

The Century Plaza's chief disadvantage is its location, surrounded by the office buildings of Century City, at least a ten-minute walk from Beverly Hills. But it is across the street from two cinemas and a major legitimate theatre that caters mostly to big Broadway musicals. A haven for businessmen, particularly from the Orient, the hotel is also used by the Dallas Cowboys, the New Orleans Saints, and for television networks' affiliate meetings. It is the only West Side hotel with a separate kosher kitchen.

A big advantage for the Century Plaza is that someone was clever enough to involve the Secret Service in its planning. It has penthouse suites designed for the needs of state visits, a bank of secure lifts and a locked underground entrance.

The result is that Lyndon B. Johnson and every President since have stayed at the Century Plaza and attended banquets there. 'Fifteen-year-old hotels search for a way to keep their name in front of the public,' says Mr. Quinn. 'We get national press coverage, and people perceive a hotel where a head of state stays to be a nice hotel.'

L'Ermitage, on a quiet street across Beverly Hills from the Hilton, has no rooms, only 117 suites. Each is equipped with separate showers, stoves, family-size refrigerators, and digital clock-radios. One employee, with a degree in agriculture, tends the dozen or more plants in each suite.

Even other hoteliers speak of the five-year-old L'Ermitage as 'Special,' and at about $200 a night for a one-bedroom suite, it is the most expensive of the major West Side hotels. But the charge includes everything; there are no surcharges, not even for twenty-four-hour room service. 'We don't believe in nickel-and-diming people,' says Peter Benassi, the hotel's marketing vice president. There is free limousine service throughout Beverly Hills, complimentary copies of the *The Wall Street Journal* and *The Los Angeles Times* to read during the complimentary Continental breakfast, and caviar and fresh strawberries with sour cream and brown sugar every afternoon. Guests who want their shoes shined leave them outside the door. An English guest is said to have hung kippers on the door next to his shoes, with instructions to broil in butter for seven minutes.

L'Ermitage – owned by two brothers, Severyn and Arnold Askenazy, who are real-estate developers – does not give out the names of its guests. But Lord Olivier is known to have stayed there, as he has at the Bel-Air. L'Ermitage's $900-a-night, three-bedroom penthouse suite with its four bathrooms and four television sets is often occupied by the same person for eight or nine months at a time, according to one official.

At L'Ermitage doors open only to a guest's own four-digit code, the Jacuzzi baths bubble mineral water, and only hotel guests are allowed to eat beneath the Dufys, Renoirs, and Vlamincks in the thirty-nine-seat Café Russe.

For avid swimmers, the Beverly Wilshire's tiny rooftop pool is impossible and the fabled Beverly Hills pool – locked at 5 pm – is a major disappointment. Yellow-and-white-striped cabanas in which to close deals alongside the Beverly Hill pool can be rented for $35 a day. It costs $10 extra for each guest even if they only come for a drink.

L'Ermitage's rooftop pool is small but well designed. For sunbathing or a private lunch, there are ten or twelve secluded solariums behind tall hedges, each with a telephone. There is a marble fountain with cherubs, and guests can bubble in mineral water or swim at midnight or at dawn.

The Beverly Hilton has the largest all-tile pool of any West Coast hotel. The Century Plaza's pool, suspended over the ballroom, is also large, and there is a separate shallow children's pool. The oval Bel-Air pool is perhaps not as large as a dedicated swimmer might like, but its setting is lovely. It is also the only pool that can be reached without walking through lobbies or taking a lift, and it is not subject to viewing from nearby hotel suites.

There are other hotels, of course, and film stars even stay in some of them. The 150-room **Beverly Hillcrest** costs a minimum of about

$85 a night and was a favourite of the the late William Holden, who liked its lack of fuss and its restaurant. The **Westwood Marquis**, where one-bedroom suites start at about $140, has a splendid Sunday brunch. The **Beverly Rodeo** charges about $100 for two persons and is in the middle of Rodeo Drive. The fifty-room **Beverly House**, which advertises itself as a European-style pension, has no restaurant but offers considerable personal attention. Dorothy Jeakins, a three-time winner of the Academy Award for costume design, stays there.

And where do the rock groups stay? Nowhere – if the hotels can help it. The Beverly Hills, for example, has 'a blanket rule' against them. 'They're not brought up to consider the rights of other people,' says the hotel's Mr. Slatkin. 'We frown on singers because of their behaviour,' says the Bel-Air's Mr. Checkman. The other hoteliers agree.

But they are currently being outwitted, because travel agents have begun to book the groups under the names of the individual musicians.

Bel-Air, 701 Stone Canyon Road (213 472 1211). Single/double rooms range from about $160 to $250; one- and two-bedroom suites from $300 to $1,200.

Beverly Hillcrest, Beverwil Drive at Pico Boulevard (213 277 2800). Single rooms, about $85 to $95; doubles, $94 to $106.

Beverly Hills Hotel, 9641 Sunset Boulevard (213 276 2251). A few singles available in main hotel from about $90 to $130; standard single, $135 to $195; twin/double, $155 to $215; one-bedroom suite, $265 to $525; two-bedroom suite, $430 to $755. Bungalows are also available: one-bedroom suite, $340 to $455; two-bedroom suite, $505 to $655; three-bedroom suite, $655 to $855; four-bedroom suite, $790 to $1,330.

Beverly Hilton, 9876 Wilshire Boulevard (213 274 7777). Single rooms, from about $100 for standard to $135 for deluxe; twin rooms, about $115 to $150; one-bedroom suites, $225 to $350; two-bedroom suites, $325 to $4,000. No charge for children, regardless of age, who occupy rooms with their parents.

Beverly House, 140 South Lasky Drive (213 271 2145). Single rooms, $58 to $68; double, $68 to $78.

Beverly Rodeo, 360 North Rodeo Drive (213 273 0300). Standard singles, $85; doubles, $100. Deluxe singles, $90; doubles, $105; suites, about $105 to $290.

Beverly Wilshire, 9500 Wilshire Boulevard (213 275 4282). Single rooms from about $100 to $170; double rooms from about $145 to $195; one-bedroom suite, about $205 to $290; two-bedroom suite, $345 to $400. Townhouse, $600 to $1,000.

Century Plaza, Avenue of the Stars (213 277 2000). Single rooms from about $120 standard to $300 deluxe; twin/king, about $140 to $160; one-bedroom corner suite, $300; two-bedroom corner suite, $400; one-bedroom penthouse suite, $500; two-bedroom penthouse suite, $600;

176 · WINTER: LEAVE IT

royal suite, $800, and presidential suite, $900. No additional charge for children eighteen and under in parent's room. Prices do not include 10 per cent tax.

Holiday Inn, 9360 Wilshire Boulevard (213 273 1400). Single rooms, $75 to $90; doubles, $90 to $105.

L'Ermitage, 9291 Burton Way (213 278 3344). One-bedroom suites, about $200 to $245; two-bedroom townhouse suites, about $400 to $500; three-bedroom penthouse suite, $950. All rates are for single or double occupancy. No charge for children under twelve. No pets.

HOLLYWOOD: THIS WAY IN

Aljean Harmetz

'Perrier is passé,' says Peter Morton. 'It's been replaced by a low-sodium Swedish mineral water, Ram-Losa. Jordan red wine is in. So are low-salt diets and yoga.'

As the proprietor of two successful restaurants in Hollywood, Mr. Morton has a good eye for what's in and what isn't. (According to his own estimation, only one of his restaurants is in, the other is merely extremely successful.)

In is more important in Southern California than in most places: Hollywood is a three-billion-dollar-a-year industry for manufacturing dreams, but it is also a state of mind. Whatever is trendy there today – personal nutritionists, hanging upside down, a single orchid instead of a floral bouquet, short hair, chocolate truffles – is likely to be sold elsewhere in the United States tomorrow.

The eternal sunshine, the edge of desperation that comes from living in a slide area at the end of a continent, the perpetual gamble to be first with something new but not too innovative that is at the heart of Hollywood film making, the unnatural necessity of remaining young and beautiful – all blend to create a fertile soil in which to grow fads and foibles.

It is watered, of course, by money. Money rains down incessantly. Million-dollar salaries are not common, but a clever producer or agent can combine perks and productivity for $350,000. And virtually every low-level vice president makes $100,000 a year, not to mention three expense-account meals a day.

There are 30,000 restaurants in Los Angeles, but only a dozen, more or less, are used by Hollywood for deals and relaxation. Not everyone goes to the in restaurants: Katharine Hepburn recently told a friend she hadn't set foot in any Hollywood restaurant for forty-five years, and Barry Diller, the chairman of Paramount Pictures, prefers to lunch on chilli dogs at Pink's hot-dog stand. 'But there is no middle- or high-level studio executive, studio head, agent, or entertainment lawyer who hasn't been to lunch at Ma Maison in the last few months.' says Michael Maslansky, a partner in PMK, a public-relations firm.

Mr. Maslansky is sitting at a table on the right side of the right room – the enclosed-in-plastic garden room – at Ma Maison, a French bistro so haughty that it has an unlisted phone number. Jack Lemmon is two tables away; Margaux Hemingway, Joan Collins, a dozen agents, and the powerful Hollywood lawyer Greg Bautzer are sprinkled nearby. As in almost all the in Hollywood restaurants, the tables are close together, the food is good but not superb, and the noise level is deafening.

'Any restaurant that serves superb food in an elegant atmosphere changes the focus,' says Jacki Applebaum, a canny Los Angeles restaurant publicist. 'La Toque has some of the best food in the city; it isn't in because although it's a fine dining experience, it isn't fun.'

What is fun? 'I was initiated into Friday lunch at Ma Maison by David Niven,' says Burton Monasch, executive vice president of 20th Century-Fox. 'That's girl-watching day. There were two beautiful girls sitting alone. Everyone tried to buy them a drink, but they refused all offers and got up to leave. Greg Bautzer followed them into the car park and returned in two minutes with both of them. Suddenly the restaurant burst into uproarious applause.'

'It is a rather boisterous, not exactly dignified crowd, a little bit on the vulgar side. But that matches the lack of pretension of the restaurant,' says Mr. Maslansky. 'Whenever I have a client come in from New York, I take him to lunch at Ma Maison. It's the best way to let important people know you're in town.'

It has been said that where lunch in New York is three martinis followed by a steak, lunch in Hollywood is Perrier and lime followed by a chopped salad. 'If you order a third martini, people look at you like you've done somethng disgusting,' Mr. Maslansky says. One transplanted agent who was used to the rhythm and pace of New York dealt with the problem by having his Ma Maison waiter feed him vodka in his water glass every time he lunched at the restaurant.

In Hollywood, eating out serves a multitude of purposes, the least of which is food. Public lunches by agents and studio executives are called 'romances': The agents are romancing studio heads; the studio heads are romancing actors or directors. 'If we're getting close to the deal, close to saying, "Let's have the lawyers in," I'll serve lunch in the conference room next to my office,' says one top executive. 'Those lunches tend to be very Spartan – diet cola and salads without dressing, and both participants trying to one-up each other by eating less.'

'You never close deals at dinner,' agrees Larry Mark, a production vice president at Paramount. 'Dinner is for nurturing relationships.' Often this pays off. One night Mr. Mark saw David Marshall Grant, a young actor enjoying an 'exposure dinner' (as in 'You need the exposure') with his agent, and made a note to suggest him for Paramount's film *Terms of Endearment,* then in production.

'I only go to four restaurants, places where people know me and I can negotiate the room,' says Mr. Maslansky. 'Mine is a service business. If I'm going to take clients out, I need to feel comfortable. On the other hand, when I'm being auditioned by a potential client, more often than not it's breakfast at the Beverly Hills Hotel's Polo Lounge.'

Starting as early as seven am one can hear the crunch of toast and the babble of gross points, percentages and up-front money from almost every table at the Polo Lounge. When Bob Cort, a production vice president at 20th Century-Fox, phoned an attractive female executive he was eager to meet, the lady suggested breakfast at the Beverly Hills Hotel. 'I want a date,' Mr. Cort replied plaintively. 'I don't want to talk a deal!'

'One thing people in Los Angeles should not try to do is eat well,' says Barry Diller. 'There's no good French food in Los Angeles. Los Angeles has great Mexican food and great junk food. A nice restaurant that also defines Los Angeles is Charmer's Market. It has as much style as one can cook into a place, but it's also easy, fresh, sunny, ridiculously casual, and you can eat and shop at the same time.'

Charmer's Market, near the ocean at the southern tip of Santa Monica, is a combination restaurant and fancy-food market beneath an orange-and-green stucco tent. 'I didn't set out to get the Hollywood crowd,' says the owner, Jane Erickson, who sports a modified punk haircut. 'I just wanted to create an environment where people could enjoy shopping and stop for a glass of wine or something to eat halfway through. But I guess there's a certain atmosphere of theatre here.' Ali MacGraw, Dustin Hoffman, Goldie Hawn, the screenwriter Robert Towne, who lives down the street, Jane Fonda, who also lives nearby, Rutger Hauer and Warren Beatty buy their Ram-Losa or imported gooseberries in rhythm with the blaring rock music at Charmer's Market.

The Old Guard is not to be found there. 'The Old Guard,' says Mr. Maslansky, 'will go to Tiffany's for their jewellery, Giorgio for their dresses, Cedars-Sinai for their births and Forest Lawn for their burials.' They will also, most often, go to Chasen's for dinner.

'Chasen's is a very proper chophouse,' says Miss Applebaum, 'the only restaurant in town that still finishes preparing every dish at the table, and it has absolutely the best service in the city. And it has good food. But it's passé; everybody in there is over fifty.'

Being over fifty is the kiss of death in Hollywood. 'Everybody is looking for a quick way to stay young,' says Wendy Goldberg, the bubbly wife of Leonard Goldberg, who made a fortune co-producing such television series as *Charlie's Angels* and *Fantasy Island.* 'It's kind of sad to want instant youth. What's so terrible about gaining a little maturity?' She pauses, then adds, 'Of course, I lie about my age.'

The search for instant youth and perpetual beauty has spilled over into a fanaticism about being physically fit. At six am any weekday morning (seven am on Sundays) San Vincente Boulevard from Barrington Avenue to the Pacific Ocean is full of jogging agents, actors and producers. Regulars include Elliot Gould, Valerie Harper, former California Governor Jerry Brown (who was once accompanied by his secret service escort), Arnold Schwarzenegger, and Meredith Baxter Birney and David Birney training for the New York Marathon.

There is almost no trendy place for a late-night drink in Hollywood, because most people are home and in bed by eleven. Jerry Weintraub, the producer of *Cruising* and *Diner,* goes to bed at eight-thirty pm and gets up at four-thirty am to run – only slightly excessive for a town where the early bird gets first crack at the freshest deal. Nor is Hollywood averse to combining long-distance running and deal-making; Berte Hirschfield, wife of the chairman of 20th Century-Fox, sometimes hears a whole negotiation during her daily half-hour run around the UCLA track.

The ladies who lunch to dispel boredom – frequently the wives of celebrities – often choose the Bistro Gardens in Beverly Hills. They tend also to go to nutritionists for personalized diet plans. Jane Fonda's Workout was briefly trendy but is currently unfashionable. Tina Sinatra is sure that bicycles are on the way back. 'A lot of us are buying bicycles and getting together in packs on weekends,' she says.

A lot of people are also hanging by their heels from gym bars. For $20 a half hour, you can 'swing your way to health' at Alex and Walter's, whose clients over the last decade have included George Hamilton, Sally Struthers, and Barbara Babcock of *Hill Street Blues*, even though the gym is located in an extremely unchic part of Culver City. 'When you're upside down, gravity pulls you, increases metabolism,' says Walter, a Russian-born gymnast.

Since gymnastics is now fashionable, half a dozen new gyms have sprung up in West Hollywood, within a few blocks of the trendy restaurants. The most star-studded belongs to Stephan – 'a sweet little studio on Melrose,' says Jessica Lange, her damp hair curling in ringlets after a ninety-minute workout 'stretching myself' on Stephan's rather old-fashioned machines.

None of the new gyms have quite the glittering clientele of Bikram Choudhury's Yoga College of India on Wilshire Boulevard in Beverly Hills. In a town where most exercise is done in private swimming pools, on private tennis courts, or at private lessons, Bikram offers only ninety-minute class lessons ($20 for a single lesson, $100 for a set of ten).

Presided over by Bikram, his body glistening in a black bikini, the classes are a mixture of inspirational monologue and hard work ('Lower spine supposed to hurt like hell!') in an enormous, humid room mirrored on three sides. Patrons have included Shirley MacLaine, Raquel Welch, Carol Lynley, Quincy Jones, Richard Benjamin and Paula Prentiss, Jill St. John, Candice Bergen and the director Louis Malle.

It is Rodeo Drive, a few blocks away from the Yoga College, that is the epitome of Beverly Hills to many people dwelling east of the Mississippi. Everything glitters on Rodeo Drive. At Bijan, where service is by appointment only, the store perfume comes in a Baccarat bottle for $1,500 and a mink glove hides a $10,000 .38-calibre revolver with a 24-carat gold-plated barrel.

'Who wants to shop at a place where you have to make an appointment?' asks Wendy Goldberg. 'Rodeo Drive is mainly for tourists.'

There are exceptions – including Linda Lee for dresses, the men's shoes at Gucci, and Jerry Magnin's and Dick Carroll's, two long-established men's stores – but Rodeo Drive, in general, is definitely not in. A new group of Rodeo Drive shops, the Rodeo Collection, sports an advisory panel that includes Gregory Peck's wife, Véronique, and Johnny Carson's estranged wife, Joanna. The backing of half a dozen such Hollywood socialites has given the Rodeo Collection a certain cachet. But there is also something of a backlash from other celebrities' wives over reports that the ladies get a discount on clothes as well as free parking.

The really in place for shopping has relatively unpretentious shops and acres of free parking for everybody. It is the Sunset Plaza area on the Sunset Strip. 'This is where the action was when I first started in the picture business in 1947,' says Marion Wagner, who as Marion Marshall played the ingénue in such films as *Halls of Montezuma* and *I Was a Male War Bride*. (She has since been married to the director Stanley Donen and the actor Robert Wagner.) 'The Trocadero and Macambo nightclubs were here. Don Loper had his first salon where Le Dome restaurant is now. The area went downhill like crazy in the '60s when the hippies came, but it's had a slow regrowth since the early '70s, when the hippies moved out.'

Marion Wagner Inc. is one of the trendy shops at Sunset Plaza. No well-known designer labels are carried; Mrs. Wagner specializes in handwoven and textured things, including a smashing $784 leather-and-beaver crocheted jacket. Customers include Stefanie Powers, Linda Gray, Joanne Woodward, Mary Costa, the opera singer, Raquel Welch, Olivia Newton-John, Sally Field and Fay Wray.

For young Hollywood – and most of the rest of young Los Angeles –

the real shopping place and time is Melrose Avenue in West Hollywood on Saturday afternoon. For a mile or two the sidewalks are so packed with people that it is hardly possible to walk down them. The merchandise ranges from 30's art deco, clothing, and collectables to 80's high-tech furniture. The clothes that can be found on the boutique-lined street are whatever is the trend of the moment; recently they were an update on the punk look, with the bright colours and shocking new young European designer clothes that could also be found along King's Road in London.

Although most Hollywood fads seem to spring up haphazardly, almost thoughtlessly, opening an in restaurant requires careful orchestration. There are three ways to create an in Hollywood restaurant, says Jackie Applebaum: acquire a group of important Hollywood backers, open your own restaurant after you have been chef or maître d'hôtel at some other trendy spot or hire a publicist to bring in the 'right' people. Le Dome is an example of the third method, Spago of the second, and Morton's of the first.

Le Dome, on the Sunset Strip, is all magenta and avocado with dusty rose tablecloths. Vaguely Chinese in décor, it seems more formal than the other in restaurants because it has no central room for table-hopping and intensifying the noise. Le Dome caters to the music crowd for late lunches and after-concert spaghetti-and-caviar, a dish introduced here by Rod Stewart. It opened in 1978 with twenty-eight sponsors, mostly Hollywood celebrities who put up $3,500 apiece and got $5,000 worth of food in return. 'That meant instantaneous use of the restaurant,' says Miss Applebaum, who was the publicist partly responsible for the strategy. 'Le Dome was immediately hot and you had to wait two weeks for reservations.'

Spago, a mile or so down the Strip, was the hot new restaurant of the moment five years after the opening of Le Dome. Owned by Wolfgang Puck, the former chef at Ma Maison, Spago has been called the fanciest pizza parlour in the world – the pizzas feature goat cheese, duck sausage, aubergines and blanched garlic. It is also generally agreed to have the worst service in town ('Hi, I'm Justin, and this is the sort of restaurant where if you eat with your fingers no one will tell on you') and a policy of overbooking that leaves anyone who is not instantly recognizable waiting at the bar for up to an hour. 'If you want to come on a Friday or Saturday night, you have to book four weeks in advance,' says Barry Krost, a producer and personal manager. 'Who wants to decide on a pizza four weeks ahead?' Still, at the moment everyone goes to Spago because everyone else goes to Spago. And things have improved somewhat since Mr. Puck replaced the reservations manager a while ago.

'People in the industry prefer to go to a restaurant where other people in the industry go,' says Peter Morton. No regular patron waits at Mortons, a wildly informal place dotted with huge palm trees in wicker baskets. 'And the best way to build a clientele is to take care of your regular customers.'

Patrick Terrail, Ma Maison's owner and host, has been known to make a point of it: When he once overheard Barry Krost telling his dinner companion that what he really wanted was 'a Big Mac,' Mr. Terrail sent out to MacDonald's for hamburgers and french fries. On a difficult day at Ma Maison, with such important regular customers as Freddie Fields, president of M-G-M, waiting for tables, Mr. Terrail gently nudged Mr. Fields into temporarily joining another party. 'One must pretend it is a big party and everyone is having fun,' Mr. Terrail says. 'So people waiting won't even know they're waiting any more.'

'My restaurant caters to the industry,' agrees Mr. Morton, who has at various times owned fifteen successful restaurants, mostly in London. 'I enjoy their company and I honour their reservations at difficult hours. If they were to go just for food, they'd go to Michael's L'Ermitage, St. Germain, but those places are not very exciting. There's an electricity in the air here.'

At Mortons, the food is basic American, music plays continuously, and the only light comes from votive candles. 'Macho food is in,' says Mr. Morton – grilled chicken, grilled fish, corn on the cob, down-to-earth back-to-basics. Some people don't come here because it's too noisy for them, but the noise reduces inhibitions. You can move freely from table to table; the service isn't formal enough to inhibit you. And the light isn't bright enough to make women feel unattractive.'

The chief backer of Mortons is Jerry Weintraub. Mr. Morton's newer Hard Rock Café, which has a Cadillac mounted on the roof and a motorcycle on the wall, is backed by Henry Winkler, Barry Diller, Steven Spielberg and Ned Tanen, the former president of Universal. The Hard Rock Café is even more aggressively American, serving Hamburgers, ribs and chilli – and even more noisy. Mr. Morton doubts that it will ever be in, despite its thoroughbred backers. 'It's not expensive enough to be in,' he says.

But what's in is relative, and the visitor to Hollywood had better be warned that it can all change in the winking of a strobe light. Not too long ago, cold pasta salads were in. But within a few short months, Tina Sinatra was heard to say: 'If I see one more cold pasta salad, I'll throw it on the floor.'

CHECKING IN FROM DAWN TILL DUSK
Breakfast

A day of watching the movers and shakers move and shake might start with breakfast in the **Polo Lounge** of the Beverly Hills Hotel (213 276 2251), 9461 Sunset Boulevard. Service begins at 7 am and the average bill for a meal of orange juice, eggs (perhaps scrambled with smoked salmon) and coffee is about $15. For those who wish to stay overnight to get an early start on the wheeling and dealing, double rooms are $155 to $215 a night, and bungalows are $340 to $1,330, depending on size. Comparable rates and accommodations may be found at the **Beverly Wilshire** (reservations: 800 421 4354), 9500 Wilshire Boulevard, or at the smaller, quieter **Bel-Air Hotel**, 701 Stone Canyon Road (213 472 1211).

Mid-morning Shape-up

Bikram Choudhury's Yoga College of India (213 276 1048) is at 9301 Wilshire Boulevard. Ninety-minute classes are held at 9 and 10.30 am, Monday through Saturday; there are also afternoon sessions at 4.30 and 6, Monday through Friday.

Alex and Walter's Gymnasium is at 3380 Motor Avenue. In addition to the private sessions, there are exercise classes, limited to six participants, for $8 an hour. Call 213 204 2550 for an appointment.

Stephan's Studio is at 8618 Melrose Avenue. Ninety-minute workouts are $17; groups are limited to eight participants. Call 213 652 9244 for an appointment.

Lunch Break

Bistro Gardens, 176 North Canon Drive (213 550 3900), has such luncheon specialities as choucroute garni Alsacienne ($13.25), grilled shrimp with mustard sauce ($15.75), and cold poached salmon with cucumber salad ($13.75); desserts include fresh fruits or berries in season.

A chilli dog at **Pink's**, at the corner of Melrose and La Brea, is $1.40 and available from 8 am to 2 am daily.

Afternoon Snack

Charmer's Market, 175 Marine Street, Santa Monica (213 399 9160), offers, in addition to such lunch and dinner specialities as scallops in raspberry sauce ($12.50) and hot barbecued duck salad with mango and papaya ($8.50), eat-in or take-out snacks and desserts, among them freshly baked croissants ($1.50), white or dark chocolate zephyr cake ($4 a slice in the restaurant section, $3.50 to go), and white chocolate champagne truffles or dark chocolate rum truffles ($1 each). A six-pack of Ram-Losa is $5.94.

Dining in (and out)

Ma Maison, 8368 Melrose Avenue (213 655 1991), lists lobster salad ($17.50), breast of duck with red wine and noodles ($19.95), and loin of lamb with garlic and roquefort ($18.95) among its specialities. A dessert of a puff-pastry shell filled with pastry cream and fresh berries, served with a light caramel sauce and fresh sorbet, is $5.50.

Le Dome, 8720 Sunset Boulevard (213 659 6919), has hot duck salad with wild mushrooms ($14.50), boudin noir ($11), and salad Niçoise ($9.50) among its specialities; its pastry cart is stocked with nine different fruit tarts every day ($4.75).

Spago, 8795 Sunset Boulevard (213 652 4025), has such imaginative grilled dishes as lobster ravioli and goat cheese salad; a full dinner for two, with wine, averages about $80. Its pizzas are topped with garlic and prosciutto ($8.25) and duck sausage ($9.50), among other things; one that is not on the menu, but can usually be whipped up by the chef, has smoked salmon, golden caviar, and sour cream ($20). Book well in advance; reservations are taken between 3.30 and 8 pm.

Mortons, 8800 Melrose Avenue (213 276 1253), specializes in such unadorned fare as grilled swordfish ($18), grilled chicken ($14), and Norwegian smoked salmon ($14). A side order of broiled potato skins, served with sour cream and chives, is $2.

Hard Rock Café, 8600 Beverly Boulevard (213 276 7605, but no telephone reservations accepted), has even simpler dishes: barbecued ribs ($6.95), chicken salad ($4.95), hamburgers ($4), and hot fudge sundaes ($2.50).

Chasen's, the bastion of the Old Guard, is at 9039 Beverly Boulevard (213 271 2168). The menu is à la carte, and lists fifty meat, chicken, and fish entrées; dinner for two with wine is about $100. Chasen's well-known chilli is not on the menu; ask for it ($7.50).

GETTING AROUND IN STYLE

Southwest Leasing and Rental on Olympic Boulevard (213 820 9000) will rent you a Rolls-Royce Silver Shadow for $225 a day, including fifty free miles. A Mercedes-Benz 380 SL or SEL is $50 a day, plus 35 cents a mile; the 300 Turbodiesel, $90 a day and 35 cents a mile.

ONE-DAY DRIVES INTO HISTORY

Marlise Simons

One of the true pleasures of Mexico City, its inhabitants like to say, is getting out of it. On weekends, those with the option flee to second homes in Cuernavaca or Valle de Bravo. For tourists, a day trip out of the capital is rewarded with rest from the urban bustle and enjoyment of the mountains and towns that surround the city. The best time to escape is during the week, when most Mexicans are busily jousting for space on the Paseo de la Reforma. They take their battles to the highways on weekends, and that is the time to be in Mexico City.

It is also best to drive yourself. And since Mexicans are notoriously bad at giving directions, a good map is an adequate substitute for poor Spanish. You can go by bus, but the trip, while memorably inexpensive, will probably be limited to a single destination. The visitor can also avoid getting lost by hiring a taxi for the day, but it will be cheaper and certainly more adventurous to rent a car. Hertz, Avis, Budget and other familiar agencies have offices in the city.

Driving is not as perilous as it seems, especially outside the city, although the driver should always be ready for the unexpected, such as buses that overtake – just as you are overtaking. Also, avoid driving at night, since donkeys and cows – and quite a few trucks – do not have lights.

The choice of where to go is rich. There are, for example, little outings, such as the drive west along the Toluca highway to La Marquesa, an unexpected valley trapped between pine-covered mountains, where aged – and therefore safe – horses can be hired by the hour for a quiet wander in the fresh air. On Fridays, the trip can be extended to a half-day by visiting the Indian market in Toluca or to a full day by driving up a nearby dormant volcano, the Nevado de Toluca, and picnicking in the crater.

Another route into the western hills outside Mexico City leads through El Desierto de los Leones which, in the absence of both desert and lions, is certainly misnamed. After turning off the Periferico South (the capital's main ring road) at Altavista and following the signs to El Desierto, the road winds through villages and pine forests, offering panoramic views of the entire Valley of Mexico (weather and pollution permitting). A ruined sixteenth century convent 9,000 feet above sea level merits a visit – it accommodates a simple but good restaurant run by a French couple – before the road slowly swings down to join the Toluca highway.

A trip to the pre-Hispanic ruins at Teotihuacan is a must of any visit to Mexico City. On this excursion tourists often prefer to share a hotel taxi with a driver-cum-guide, but a rental-car driver can be there in less than an hour by heading up Insurgentes Norte and following the signs to PIRAMIDES. The ruins, which date to around 200 BC, are dominated by the Pyramids of the Sun and Moon, both of which can be climbed by the energetic. In its days of glory, Teotihuacan controlled a vast area of the Mexican highlands and, with an estimated population of 200,000, was once the largest city in the world. Grass-covered mounds surrounding the main buildings are witness to how much of the ruins are still unexcavated.

For a full day – or more – away from Mexico City, the three main highways leading from the capital provide a framework for the options to explore:

CHOLULA AND PUEBLA
To reach the Puebla road, you have to cross much of Mexico City, taking the Viaducto almost to the airport, then following the signs to the right. The rewards come soon afterward as the highway heads up through pine forests into the mountains, with the two snow-covered volcanoes, Ixtacihuatl and Popocatepetl, suddenly making dramatic entries into view.

The first town reached is **San Martin Texmelucan**, which has a serape, or shawl, market on Tuesday mornings as well as the festival of the local saint on November 11. San Martin is the turn-off point from the highway toward **Huejotzingo**, a traditional Chichimec Indian town that became the site of one of the earliest – and finest – Franciscan monasteries in the New World. The sixteenth century church and monastery, with their well-preserved murals, are particularly worth a visit. The town itself is typically provincial, although it turns wild every May 5 when Indians in masks and colourful costumes noisily re-enact Mexico's temporary defeat of a French invasion force in the Battle of Puebla in 1862.

The road, shaded by magnificent eucalyptus trees, then leads to **Cholula**, perhaps the most important shrine at the time of the Spanish Conquest. Its demise, though, began even before Hernan Cortes reached Tenochtitlan, or Mexico City: Staying here on his way inland, Cortes uncovered a plot and ordered the slaughter of some three thousand Indian priests and followers.

Legend has it that there was one temple for every day of the year in Cholula and that a church was built above each of them to symbolize the victory of the Christian God. Today, several dozen churches survive and one of them, Our Lady of the Remedies, is perched 200 feet high, atop an ancient pyramid considered to be the largest man-made construction in the New World. Parts of the pyramid have been uncovered and restored and some of its five miles of interior passages can be explored in order to view long-hidden murals.

From Cholula, the spires of the churches in **Puebla** can be seen. Puebla is an entirely Spanish colonial city, founded in 1531 roughly halfway between Mexico City and Veracruz, the port from which the country's gold and other wealth was shipped to Spain. In foods, it is famous for the *mole poblano*, the spicy chocolate sauce now served all over Mexico, and *camote*, a candy made of sweet potatoes.

In Puebla, drive straight to the Zocalo and have a modestly priced lunch (why not try *mole poblano* and beer?) at La Espada under the plaza's elegant arches. Then, for digestion, enjoy a walk in the shade before crossing the square to visit the cathedral, one of the largest and most beautiful in Mexico. Puebla is a city of churches, but Spanish colonial architecture at its best is everywhere to be seen, notably in the Palafoxian Library and the Casa del Alfenique, or Barley Sugar House. By 5 pm, though, it is wise to start heading back to Mexico City along the main toll road in order to miss the worst of the rush hour.

CUERNAVACA AND ENVIRONS

A good deal lower than Mexico City's often chilly 7,500-foot altitude, **Cuernavaca** has traditionally served as the capital's spa. For hundreds of years, the Aztec kings, Cortes, and the Spanish viceroys, as well as the wealthy or retired of more recent days, have all kept homes there. On weekends, many Mexicans are to be found lounging by swimming pools in huge gardens behind high walls.

The driver setting out for Cuernavaca from Mexico City on the Periferico South should ignore the sign to Cuernavaca and keep going some five miles to the turning for Xochimilco, site of the 'floating gardens,' with their flower-covered punts. Continue through the town until you see a minuscule sign for Oaxtepec. The road then heads into the hills and, within minutes, the volcanoes come into view. Off to the left is the Cortes Pass through which the Conquistador's army marched on its way to Mexico City in 1519. On the roadside, there are little stalls selling delicious mixiotes, spicy meat or chicken cooked in the leaves of the maguey cactus. If you have a delicate stomach, though, perhaps it's better not to be tempted.

Once over the edge of the soup bowl of mountains that surround the capital, the road dips down into the Valley of Morelos – and the temperature rises steadily. The first town is **Oaxtepec**, a favourite retreat of Emperor Montezuma I, where some Aztec ruins are preserved. Then take the highway to Cuernavaca through the valley's sugarcane fields, stopping briefly in the little town of **Tlayacapan** to look at – and perhaps buy – some of its handmade pottery, temptingly lined up along the roadside.

Eleven miles before Cuernavaca is a favourite town among foreign residents of Mexico, **Tepoztlan**, which sits beneath a thousand-foot cliff. Around the town are myriad weekend homes, but Tepoztlan itself is distinctively Mexican, with its Sunday market and crumbling sixteenth century Dominican monastery. According to local legend, this is a surviving Aztec village – and it is true that the Nahuatl language is still spoken and superstitions remain – but the influence of the nearby capital is strong. The energetic visitor can climb the cliff to visit the remains of a pre-Hispanic temple.

On reaching Cuernavaca, stop for lunch amid the flamingos and peacocks and sculptures in the gardens of Las Mananitas. The restaurant's menu is huge and, for Mexico, expensive, ranging from simple steaks to explosive chilli dishes. The sauces that accompany the *filete de huachinango* (red snapper) are particularly good and there are some sumptuous desserts. No credit cards are accepted.

From there, head for the twin plazas downtown and, after tasting the mood, visit the museum of pre-Hispanic, colonial, and revolutionary objects now housed in Cortes's former palace (built on the site of Montezuma's old palace). From there, the sixteenth century cathedral can be seen up the hill, but the restoration of its original simplicity is worth a closer look. Across from the cathedral are the Borda Gardens, where an exhibition of Indian folk art is organized each year to coincide with the Day of the Dead on November 2.

As you drive out of Cuernavaca toward the highway to Mexico City, a huge bronze equestrian statue of Emiliano Zapata recalls that this region was the scene of some of the fiercest fighting during the 1910-1917 Revolution.

TULA AND TEPOTZOTLAN

After Teotihuacan, **Tula** is the most impressive pre-Hispanic site near Mexico City. In historical terms, it is even more important because it was there that the legend of the god-king Quetzalcoatl was born. He was forced to leave Tula by the warrior Toltecs, but he promised to return. The plumed serpent image of Quetzalcoatl appeared in numerous subsequent civilizations, and some five hundred years later Montezuma mistook Cortes for Quetzalcoatl and lowered his guard to the advancing Spanish troops.

For this trip, take the Periferico North toward Queretaro; then, after thirty-three miles, take the turning for Tula, which lies twenty-two miles beyond. Tula is a somewhat run-down town, subject to the pollution from a nearby oil refinery, but the ruins are special, particularly their *atlantes*, or carved pillars, which once supported the roof of the temple to Quetzalcoatl. The ruins of several other pyramids and temples can be seen, and the *pelota*, or ball court, has been well preserved. The site also has a dilapidated museum worth peeping at.

The return from Tula should be timed so that lunchtime – around 2 pm – coincides with arrival in **Tepotzotlan** (to be distinguished from Tepoztlan), an old Otomi Indian village twenty-five miles from Mexico City. It has numerous restaurants overlooking the huge square in front of the church, but the best place to eat is on the patio of the Tepotzotlan Convent (serenaded on Sundays by the town's brass band). The food is good Mexican and you can watch senoras 'clapping' corn paste into tortillas with their hands while you await your order. The convent's menu includes *mole poblano*, *mole verde*, roasted goat, *enchiladas verdes*, and *carne asada a la tampiqueña*. But you can also ask for steak or fried chicken.

The church and convent are now part of the National Viceroys' Museum and are well worth entering. The church, founded by the Jesuits, has an intricate stone façade and a dazzling gold-covered altar, while the museum contains paintings, furniture, vestments, and pottery from the sixteenth to eighteenth centuries. Behind the buildings is a vast walled garden offering shade for a siesta.

On Sundays, Tepotzotlan is a favourite place for Mexicans looking for lunch, which is fine if you like crowds. Those who visit during the week will find traffic pouring out of Mexico City as they drive back to the capital – a reminder that, when it comes to travelling, when in Mexico, don't do as the Mexicans.

LEGACY OF THE CONQUISTADORS

Gordon Mott

The Spanish Conquistadors who vanquished the Aztec Empire are better remembered for the riches they took out of Mexico than for what they left behind. But the colonists did give the country a legacy in the stately haciendas they built to re-create the glories of Spain. Hernan Cortes, the man who led the conquest, contructed some of Mexico's grandest haciendas, and other Spaniards also built New World castles to be near the source of their fortunes: the huge silver and gold mines, the vast cattle ranches and the sugar plantations.

Many of the haciendas have decayed or are privately owned, but a few have been transformed into hotels; not highly polished beachside resorts, easily accessible by air, but out-of-the-way places waiting for the adventurous traveller willing to test his driving skills on Mexican highways.

At least five can be reached in ninety minutes or less from Mexico City. Each can be a base from which to explore archaeological sites, national parks, and colonial towns.

In the vicinity of Hacienda Galindo and Hacienda la Mansion, for example, are the colonial capital, Queretaro, with well-preserved buildings and a bullring, and the town of Tula, site of some Toltec ruins. The haciendas were built in 1546 by Cortes just south of Queretaro. The estate covered 60,000 acres and had 9,000 head of cattle and 2,000 horses. Cortes is said to have granted the entire estate to his Aztec translator and mistress, an Indian known as La Malinche. The buildings lay in virtual ruins until the early 1970s, when Piero Ricci bought what was left after much of the land was divided among local farmers as provided in the 1917 constitution.

La Mansion has 108 rooms, bougainvillaea-filled gardens, thirty-foot-high walls, arches and long hallways. Many suites include a sitting room and a bedroom decorated with red tile floors, wood-frame beds with wrought-iron headboards, light fixtures also of wrought iron, chairs and couches made of finely carved wood and walls painted in bright oranges, blues and greens.

Hacienda Galindo recalls the aura of an old hacienda town.

Motorists must crawl along cobblestone streets past low pastel-coloured buildings decorated with wrought-iron bars on the windows and stone window sills. At the end of the tree-lined drive the street opens into a courtyard with a seventeenth century church on one side and the high walls of the hacienda bordering the other three sides.

The hotel is built around a series of courtyards and gardens overflowing with bougainvillaea, Spanish oaks and manicured lawns. The dining room is Baroque, with walls covered with decorative wood carvings and oil paintings, and the food is prepared with more skill than at La Mansion. Such dishes as *carne asada*, served with a thin piece of beef, peppers, beans, an enchilada and guacamole sauce, are worth trying.

Hacienda Galindo has six clay courts for tennis, La Mansion four. Both hotels offer golf on a nearby course and horseback riding.

Queretaro, less than thirty minutes away, was the centre of Mexico's independence movement against Spain in 1810 and against Maximilian I in 1867. Weekend bullfights attract visitors from all over Mexico. To the south on Highway 57 is San Juan del Rio, a wine and crafts centre, and off the highway at the San Juan del Rio exit is Tequisquiapan, a small spa where careful restoration has preserved the colonial atmosphere.

About halfway between Mexico City and the Galindo hotels are the Toltec ruins at Tula, best known for huge pillars decorated with carvings.

Two hacienda hotels afford the traveller the chance to view the ruins of Xochicalco or sample Taxco's silver shops. They are Hacienda del Cocoyoc near Oaxtepec and Ex-Hacienda del Cortes on the outskirts of Cuernavaca. (Why the Cortes adds 'Ex' to its name could not be determined. No one at the hotel had an explanation.) On a clear day, travellers heading for either the Cocoyoc or the Cortes get a view to the east of the two towering volcanoes that keep watch on Mexico city. The 17,845-foot Popocatepetl (Popo for short), or Smoking Mountain, lies on the right, and the twin peaks of Ixtaccihuatl, a 17,295-foot giant known as the White Lady or Sleeping Lady, can be seen on the left. The highway cuts across a 9,500-foot pass through Tres Cumbres and then begins a long descent toward the valley around Cuernavaca.

Hacienda del Cocoyoc provides nearly everything a visitor needs. An arch over an old wooden door at the entrance is engraved with a message 'The Door to the Paradise of America.' Considering that the temperature rarely varies from the high 80s at noon to the low 50s at night, the claim is not unjustified. Rains usually occur at night during the rainy season, which can run from late May or early June to October or November. The golf course is always green, and Popo can be seen from many of the tees.

The hacienda was built in 1560 to house the overseer of the cane fields in the state of Morelos. Following the outbreak of revolution in 1910 some of Emiliano Zapata's followers attacked it, causing serious damage. It was converted to a hotel in 1968. Some of the irrigation aqueducts remain on the grounds, and the swimming pool is surrounded by the walls of the old sugar refinery. Many of the 298 rooms are being remodelled, but there's nothing particularly outstanding about the furnishings. They are standard Mexican colonial with wooden bed frames, brightly coloured upholstery and red tile floors. The twenty-eight master suites have private pools, sitting rooms and king-size beds.

Cocoyoc attracts many conferences, but its nine restaurants, five bars and discothèque also cater to individual holidaymakers. The food is not outstanding, but such mexican dishes as *tacos de pollo* (chicken tacos) and *carne asada* (grilled meat) are well prepared. A word of advice: avoid ordering fish – it's a long way from the ocean.

The most charming hotel is **Ex-Hacienda del Cortes**, the Cuernavaca home that Cortes occupied during his years in Mexico. It became one of the most important sugar refineries in Mexico in the nineteenth century. The refinery building, with huge vaulted ceilings and big storage rooms, now houses the dining room, bar and conference area, and the pool is built around some of the old pillars.

The hotel has only twenty rooms, but each is a suite filled with carved-wood antiques. The décor varies but never strays far from Spanish colonial with wrought-iron light fixtures, tile floors and painted tiles in the bathrooms. The walls are painted in such bright Mexican colours as burnt orange, deep blue, pink, yellow or green. Several rooms have twenty-foot-high vaulted ceilings with a skylight, and the Imperial Suite, named for the Shah of Iran, who once occupied it, includes two rooms with adjoining Jacuzzi. Every room opens onto the garden, landscaped with ferns and palms, and small chairs and tables are carefully placed in the shade of the big trees.

Eating is a special experience at Ex-Hacienda del Cortes. The food is not exotic or exceptionally prepared, but the huge arches, the sound of an enclosed stream that used to turn a mill wheel, the strumming of a guitar and candles flickering in the evening breeze all combine with excellent service to make any meal an occasion. Those who enjoy spicy food should try *puntas de filete al chipotle*. It is prepared by cutting filet mignon into strips or chunks and cooking them in a sauce made from the chipotle pepper, a dark red pepper similar to a hot Indian pepper.

Along the highway to Cocoyoc, which exits off the Cuernavaca-Mexico City route at the seventy-kilometre mark, is Tepoztlan, where legend says the Aztec god Quetzalcoatl was born. A well-maintained sixteenth century Dominican monastery is open to visitors just off

Tepoztlan's main square. The town also has a small Aztec pyramid built in honour of the god of *pulque*, a cheap, foul-smelling liquor made from the maguey plant (unrefined tequila, one might say). The pyramid rests atop the Cerro de Tepozteco and requires a 2,000-foot climb along a rocky path into which stairs have been built. Those in good shape can go up and back in about two hours.

The ruins of Xochicalco may be the least known but most interesting in Mexico. The huge site lies about thirty minutes south of Cuernavaca, six or seven miles off the Cuernavaca-Acapulco highway at the Alpuyeca exit. The site links the Toltec and later Aztec kingdoms and also apparently served as a gathering point for the civilizations of Teotihuacan, Tula, Zapoteca, and the Mayan regions in southern Mexico.

Farther south and perhaps too far for a one-day excursion are the caves of Cacahuamilpa, a series of caverns stretching for nearly forty miles. On the way, visitors pass Tequesquitengo Lake, one of the largest bodies of fresh water in Mexico. The silver-mining and crafts town of Taxco is about a two-hour drive from Cuernavaca.

In Cuernavaca itself it is customary to start the day with coffee or beer on the Zocalo, the main square, probably in the company of some of the many retired Americans who live there. From the Zocalo, you can explore the Palacio de Cortes, the Borda Gardens, and the cathedral across the street from the gardens. Then for lunch most visitors stop at Las Mananitas, considered one of the best restaurants in Mexico.

A national park and a silver mine are two attractions in the vicinity of **Hacienda San Miguel Regla**, probably the most authentic of the hacienda hotels. It lies in the hills to the east of Mexico City above the town of Pachuca. Being more out of the way than the other haciendas, it is harder to find and making reservations is more difficult, since there is no Mexico City reservations number. The present number is Huasca 2, a number that tends to baffle most operators in the United States. The owner, Laurie Dalton, daughter of Jess Dalton, a lawyer who joined a group of other American investors in restoring the hacienda as a private club about forty years ago before it became a hotel in the 1950s, is trying to obtain a new number. (In the meantime, it helps to tell the operator that Huasca is in the state of Hidalgo.)

Huge iron doors painted red frame a stone driveway that leads to a chapel. The main square is filled with tall trees surrounding an old fountain. Renovated sections of the hotel contain modestly decorated rooms, each with a fireplace. Since nights can get cold, it's wise to tip the bellman 150 pesos (about a dollar) to ensure that he lights the fire every evening while you're at dinner.

Meals, served family style without a menu, consist of hearty, country food. The soups are delicious, and the entrées are simple preparations of meat or chicken with vegetables. In the morning the hotel makes some of the best *huevos rancheros* in the country. The sauce is a spicy combination of serrano chillies, tomatoes and onions – a real wake-me-up breakfast.

But San Miguel Regla's real charms are its grounds studded with oaks and pines, small lakes and paths through well-tended lawns and its location away from the hubbub of the modern world. There are no TVs or anything else to pollute the crisp mountain air. Horseback riding is available, and there is a heated swimming pool.

The drive to San Miguel Regla offers at least one unusual side trip. Near the summit of the mountain range that is encountered after leaving Pachuca is El Chico, a national park set among pine trees and interesting outcroppings. A mile farther down the highway is Real del Monte, one of the hemisphere's oldest and biggest silver mines. My favourite pastime in San Miguel Regla is to brave the cold night air and walk away from the lights to gaze at the stars. The sky shimmers with thousands of them.

Many of the buildings in the hacienda look out on a small pond, which used to feed the silver-smelting rooms. The hacienda, built by the Conde Pedro Romero de Terreros in the eighteenth century, is one of the country's younger hacienda hotels.

These lodgings offer something different for the traveller willing to take to the hinterland highways: the chance to glimpse the beautiful countryside and relive some of the grandeur that prevailed when hacienda dwellers were akin to lords ruling over their fiefdoms.

IF YOU GO
Car rental
To rent a car all you need is a valid U.S. driver's licence. It is advisable to take the full-coverage insurance offered by the rental agency. Rates vary, and all rentals are subject to a 15 per cent tax.

If you have trouble with your car, wait for the arrival of the Green Angels, who usually speak Spanish and English and are geared to give highway assistance. All roads leading to the haciendas are toll roads with fees ranging from 75 cents to $1.25, depending on whether it's a weekday or a weekend.

Driving directions from Mexico City Airport have been provided for each hacienda.

Hacienda Galindo/Hacienda la Mansion are run by the Exelaris-Hyatt chain. Reservations for either may be made by calling 905 533 3550 in Mexico City. In the United States, Hacienda Galindo may be booked by calling Hyatt (800 228 9000 in the eastern United States). At Galindo, junior and master suites have private Jacuzzis and cost about $90 a night for two. Regular rooms are well appointed, about $45 a night. At La Mansion, a junior suite for two costs about $50 a night; other rooms $25 to $30 a night. Rates do not include meals, but guests may sign up for a meal plan that provides three no-choice meals a day for about $16, or they may order from an à la carte menu, selecting such entrées as *carne asada* (about $4) or fish (about $3) and paying for each meal separately.

From the airport, follow exit signs for Viaducto Miguel Aleman, an east-west expressway often posted as plain 'Viaducto.' Just beyond the Insurgentes Street exit, watch for signs to Periferico and take the exit for Perinorte, which becomes Highway 57. La Mansion exit is at about kilometre 168. The hotel is fifty yards off the highway to the right. Hacienda Galindo is about five miles west of Highway 57; follow the signs.

Hacienda del Cocoyoc/Ex-Hacienda del Cortes are in the state of Morelos. Cocoyoc may be booked by calling 800 882 5001. The Cocoyoc is the most expensive of the resorts. A room for two costs about $70 a night; junior suites, $85; master suites, all with private pools, about $100. No meals included in the rates. The hotel restaurant menu offers such appetizers as chicken salad and shrimp salad and entrées such as enchiladas, *carne asada*, and fish. The Cortes has no United States reservations number, but it may be booked by calling 5 88 44 in Cuernavaca. A room or junior suite for two costs about $35 a night, a suite with queen-size bed is $40, the Imperial suite – two separate rooms with adjoining Jacuzzi – about $80. Meals extra. The à la carte menu includes avocado salad, shrimp cocktail, chateaubriand for two, *puntas de filete al chipotle*, fish.

From the airport, look for Viaducto-Churubusco signs and follow the ones to Churubusco. The divided four-lane street with frequent traffic lights winds around the southern end of the city. Watch for signs to Cuernavaca and Highway 95 and take Viaducto Tlalpan to Cuernavaca Cuota, a toll road that cuts at least an hour off the trip over the Ajusco Mountains. Tolls on weekdays run about $1, on weekends $1.50. After crossing the summit, take the exit to Cuautla and Oaxtepec. Oaxtepec is fifteen miles from the exit on a narrow but well-marked two-lane highway. In Oaxtepec follow signs to the Cocoyoc.

To reach the Cortes, take the Acapulco-Taxco bypass around Cuernavaca. On the southern edge of the city is a green sign for Ex-Hacienda del Cortes. Follow the small signs after going under the highway to the first traffic light, turn right and go about two miles. You may think you're on the wrong road – bumpy, rocky, full of potholes – but keep going, you'll get there.

Hacienda San Miguel Regla is the hardest to find. From the airport, take Circuito Interior Norte to Insurgentes Norte, which becomes Pachuca Highway. Follow the signs to Pachuca, not to Piramides (the pyramids at Teotihuacan). At Pachuca, follow bypass signs for Tampico, which lead around the eastern side of Pachuca to the highway to San Miguel Regla. Exit to the right at the fork at kilometre 118. Follow that road through the town of Huasca to San Miguel. The paved road ends about half a mile from the hotel. Take the first right on the dirt road and look for the red iron gates. Rates at San Miguel Regla include three meals. Rooms for two cost about $45; one-bedroom house about $50, two-bedroom house (three fireplaces), $70 for four people.

THE CAPITAL'S MANY MOODS

Alan Riding

Most of the many wonderful things about Mexico City were here last year or even 400 years ago. The capital's real appeal remains timeless, as if the future were frozen by captured moments from the past. After all, as Tenochtitlan, the city survived the Spanish Conquest in 1521 and, renamed Mexico City, it lived through three centuries of Spanish rule and subsequent occupations by American and French troops. The city took the chaos of the 1910–1917 Revolution in its stride and it continues to bounce through frequent earthquakes. Its history is recorded like wrinkles on its face.

But the city – and don't let anyone deceive you – is not easy to embrace. It is old and new, elegant and vulgar, complex and straight-forward. It is a collection of villages and it is the largest city in the world. And it takes a knack to survive its remorseless battering of body and soul. The secret, though, is simple: Look beyond the cacophonous traffic and crowded streets, and the Mexicans themselves retain the humanity that the city at times seems to have lost.

The Mexicans are of course so different from Americans that I often wonder whether any two neighbours in the world can have so little in common. And the people from the capital, the so-called *chilangos,* are the quintessential Mexicans. They are reserved, discreet, indirect, even insecure when a relationship is still formal. But they are also witty, sentimental and warmly affectionate as soon as trust is estab-lished. The family remains the dominant force in society because it is here that intimacy can be expressed without risk.

Soon after breakfast on a typical Sunday, for example, balloons in those bright Mexican pinks and greens were strung up between trees to stake out a claim to a little corner of Chapultepec Park. Nearby a large sheet of paper was pinned to a tree to announce LA FIESTA DE PABLO. And as the morning advanced, Pablo's cousins, aunts, uncles and grandparents joined the family for his ninth birthday party. Stones were gathered and a fire was started to keep the tacos and pork *carnitas* warm. Then there was a wild soccer game, with Granny as the goalkeeper, followed by a quick performance from a clown who wandered by looking for work. And finally it was lunchtime, the most important part of the day, when the tequila and the guitar appeared and the stories and the jokes began. Then all ended abruptly with the scramble to the cars as the seasonal storm arrived punctually at 5 pm.

Chapultepec Park on Sunday is as good a place as any for a first taste of Mexico City. The park, which now stretches in three huge sections up the western slopes of the capital, is crowded with museums, with entertainments, and, above all, with life. Thousands upon thousands of Mexicans of all ages and most classes seek refuge there each Sunday or holiday (of which there are many) to row on the lakes, to picnic in the shade or to attend open-air courses in everything from hairdressing to electronics. And where there are crowds in Mexico there are also street vendors – of balloons and books, of flutes and food – as well as artists, dancers, and musicians, all performing for small change.

Yet even with the crowds the park seems like an oasis of peace because the mood is so relaxed. Children run freely everywhere (where don't they in Mexico?), a clinch of teenage maids on their day off giggle as they pose before an old man with a box camera, a woman in Indian costume quietly stitches as she awaits a client for her little pile of limes, a group of boys coast by on roller skates. I sometimes feel I am in the nineteenth century, because it was surely little different then.

In a single square mile, Chapultepec Park offers a memorable collection of museums. The newest is the Rufino Tamayo Museum, a stunning sculpture that houses the private collection of Mexico's best-known painter. Nearby, across the Paseo de la Reforma, is the Museum of Modern Art, which contains works by such twentieth century artists as Diego Rivera and David Alfaro Siqueiros, as well as temporary exhibits by European and American painters. For those attracted by the colonial period, the museum to visit is in Chapultepec Castle, with paintings, costumes and furniture from the Conquest to the Revolution.

Mexico City has so many museums that an entire holiday could be spent visiting them. The Palace of Fine Arts has its own gallery. The Anahuacalli Museum in the south of the city contains the late Diego Rivera's own collection of pre-Hispanic art, while the new National Museum of Interventions recounts in documents, paintings, and even photographs the story of the numerous foreign interventions suffered by Mexico since its independence in 1810. The psyche of a nation that records its defeats in museums is, at best, unusual, although it does portray itself, as Oliver Cromwell might have said, 'warts and all.'

There is one museum that should not be missed even by those who regard museum-tramping as the antithesis of a holiday – the Museum of Anthropology. Contained in its splendid marble halls is, quite simply, Mexico's entire pre-Columbian history. A whole day – or more – can be spent retracing 3,000 years of civilizations from the early Olmecs to the late Aztecs through their jewellery, figures, stellae, and monuments. Artifacts from the Aztecs' recently uncovered Main Temple or Templo Mayor in Mexico City are also on view. The ruins of the Templo Mayor itself are to be found beside the National Palace in the capital's main plaza, or Zocalo.

The **Zocalo** is worth a visit, if only to enjoy a rare sense of space in this overcrowded city. Arrive on any of myriad political occasions, however, and you will understand why the square has no trees: almost a million people can gather here. On such occasions huge banners and coloured lights are attached to the sixteenth century cathedral and the fine eighteenth and nineteenth century government buildings that surround the plaza. The cathedral probably looks better from the outside, but the National Palace should be entered for a view of Diego Rivera's magnificent murals recording his tormented vision of Mexican history.

Once downtown, stick around. It was here, on an island in the middle of the now dry Lake Texcoco, that Tenochtitlan was founded, and the dozens of churches tucked among the narrow streets are witness to the temples that once existed. Echoes of Mexico City fifty years ago, though, are just as strong among the tailors, bookshops, jewellers, and Spanish restaurants of the area. Both the Stock Exchange and the Congress are nearby, spilling out men in dark suits who clump together over long lunches to exchange gossip.

The downtown section, which is almost isolated from the rest of the capital by the tremendous struggle of getting there, functions much like a village during the day. Ironically, the city's monumental traffic jams have had a similar impact on life throughout the metropolis. Mexicans who have a choice – a lucky minority – live, work and socialize in their own neighbourhoods. Not a few people will ask for the address before accepting a dinner invitation. Only tourists who travel outside the rush hour have the option of looking at each of these different villages.

One is the **Zona Rosa**, or Pink Zone, so named no doubt to suggest a respectable red-light district. This is the most cosmopolitan part of Mexico City, an area of boutiques, jewellers, hotels, and restaurants catering mainly to tourists and more affluent Mexicans. A typically Mexican character also makes his appearance here: the 'junior,' the teenage son of a wealthy politician or businessman who has too much money to spend and too much volume on his car stereo. At times, visitors to the Zona Rosa might forget they're in Mexico. But the zone, conveniently close to the Paseo de la Reforma, is a pleasant and safe place for an evening stroll or a coffee in a pavement café. Shopping is good, but prices tend to be high.

The Zona Rosa is a relatively new phenomenon; other urban communities are much older. In the 1930s, for example, **San Angel** was still separated from downtown Mexico City by fields. It was one of numerous Indian villages on the banks of Lake Texcoco and, like the city itself, was rebuilt by the Spaniards. To this day it retains the mood of a Spanish pueblo, with a sixteenth century church, narrow cobbled streets, beautiful homes hidden behind walls three feet thick, and now restaurants and shops. The best day to visit it is Saturday, when an open-air artisan market is held just off the Plaza de San Jacinto. But the colonial atmosphere of the neighbourhood can be captured any day at the San Angel Inn, an old hacienda, with patios overflowing with bougainvillaea, which has been converted into one of the capital's most elegant restaurants.

Not far away and also in the south of the city is **Coyoacan**, another pre-Conquest village that retains even more small-town atmosphere, because both rich and poor live side by side. There are massive mansions along Francisco Sosa Street, for example, but next door there may be a shop that sells tacos and tortillas. The twin plazas of Coyoacan, with church, bandstand, benches, ramblas, and other trappings of a provincial plaza, are a further reminder of the community's quiet independence.

Many of the new neighbourhoods that have sprung up in the past two decades are almost indistinguishable from American suburbs, surrounded as they are by highways and shopping centres. But a stronger spirit survives in older and poorer inner-city communities such as the **Colonia Guerrero** and **Tepito**. Tepito, which was the barrio described in Oscar Lewis's *The Children of Sanchez,* is the proud home of Mexico's smugglers. Most Mexicans only visit it to buy contraband liquor, perfumes and electronic equipment. And few tourists are ever to be seen there. But for visitors interested in seeing more than just the pretty face of Mexico City, Tepito is a fascinating contrast to, say, San Angel.

On Sunday mornings, a few blocks from Tepito, La Lagunilla flea market takes over several streets, bringing vendors from all over the city and offering everything from old records, books and coins to colonial swords and Indian masks. Both bargains and 'finds' are awaiting those willing to look slowly and negotiate patiently.

A different form of community is that which comes alive every night around the **Plaza de Garibaldi**, the home of the country's mariachi musicians and a shrine to the fiesta. People from all over Mexico and the world gather almost ritualistically to sing, drink, and dance in bars, on the plaza, and even among the counters of an adjacent market with 'fast food,' Mexican style. Garibaldi is intriguing because it offers the best insight into the happiness and sadness of the Mexican soul. Don't stay too late, though, because the Mexican soul can erupt as suddenly and wildly as the volcanoes that run down the country's spine.

For the visitor to Mexico City, then, the answer to confronting this sprawling mass of 15 million people is to do as the Mexicans: break up the city and take it in bites. In this way it becomes digestible and tasty. There is no need to try it all, to take those Mexico City-in-a-Day bus tours that leave you numb. Rather, once dropped by cab in one place or another, the best way of travelling is by foot, wandering around courtyards, looking over fences, finding new corners of life that goes on as it might have done ten or a hundred years ago. In this way, the city can be enjoyed as the truly great capital that only some visitors are fortunate enough to discover.

MEXICO: A WORLD OF DIFFERENCES

John Canaday

There are a lot of Mexicos, all inseparable from one another – ancient Mexico, colonial Mexico, provincial Mexico, metropolitan Mexico, wild Mexico, poor Mexico and rich Mexico, illiterate Mexico and intellectual Mexico, gentle Mexico and, I suppose, violent Mexico, although I have never met it. During our acquaintance of more than fifty years Mexico has never failed me, either in the delight offered by familiar places revisited or in revelations of its variety in new ones.

I first got hooked on the sounds, looks, smells, and tastes of things Mexican during my early teens, after my family moved to San Antonio, Texas, where the Mexican population made it the third largest Mexican city after Mexico City and Veracruz. San Antonio has, at this writing, a Mexican-American mayor, but at that time, during the 1920s, 'Mexican Town' was, if not exactly a ghetto, at least off limits for a kid who lived north of Military Plaza.

Nevertheless, I would go there of an afternoon – brief, solitary, and covert excursions during which I became a closet Mexiphile, standing outside phonograph shops listening to Mexican records on the loud speaker ('Rancho Grande,' 'La Cucaracha,' 'A Media Luz,' 'Ojos Verdes'), consuming great sticky slabs of crystallized pumpkin and, from a wary distance, staring at voluptuous females lounging in the windows. There was even a theatre, the Zaragoza, playing Mexican vaudeville, where, later on, I saw a wonderful clown who I like to think was the young Cantinflas.

Toward the end of the '20s and the end of my teens I discovered the raffish border towns of Nuevo Laredo and Villa Acuna, which, being only 150 miles from San Antonio, were accessible for a bit of a fling with beer (this was during Prohibition) and acquaintance with genuine Mexican, as opposed to Tex-Mex, cookery. The preparation was rough, giving no indication of the subtleties and variety of classical Mexican dishes, but I at least learned that Tex-Mex is little more than a tasty parody of the real thing. A major discovery was *cabrito* – grilled kid, still a favourite all these years later. Then, during the 1930s, I got as far south as Uruapan, in the state of Michoacan, and Mexico City.

Since then I have fanned out in all directions. I have missed Baja California, which is next on my list, and have avoided resorts like Acapulco and Cozumel. They are no doubt delightful, but when I travel I want to get to know the people of a country and see the monuments of its past.

This has brought me to some odd places, but the worst that ever happened to me was the theft of my car in Monterrey and the picking of my pocket in the Toluca market, which I later discovered is notorious in that respect. But on the other hand my pocket has been picked by the gentleman behind me boarding a bus on Sixth Avenue at Forty-fourth Street in New York, and my car has been rifled in Austin, Texas, one of the most civilized and safest cities I know of. This is going to sound impossible, but it is true that during all my visits to Mexico, which must add up to fifteen or so by now, I have never been spoken to rudely – at least not by any Mexican – rich, poor, illiterate, upper, lower, or middle class. By other tourists, yes, but not by any Mexican.

The wonder is that Mexico in all its aspects remains all of a piece. Its ancient, colonial and modern worlds and its wildly disparate social and economic groups are unified by a fusion of bloods and cultures that make it like no other place in the world, not even like any other Latin American country. Among all the countries of Central and South America that suffered the holocaust of Spain's criminally blind, cruel, and greedy conquest, it has been in Mexico alone that the roots of Indian cultures survived long enough underground to flower in hybridization with Spain's. For comparison, take Peru. Peru is almost as fascinating as Mexico in its colonial architecture, colonial painting and what little the Spaniards didn't destroy of its Inca monuments, and I hold the country in deep affection, but the Peruvian Indians, granting a very few exceptions, are an isolated people with no viable roots in their great Inca past.

The Peruvian mestizos – persons of mixed white and Indian blood – are hardly better off, leaving the country's wealth and power concentrated in the hands of the whites (15 per cent of the population), with old Spanish families at the top still breeding Peru's aristocrats.

Mexico also has its aristocracy-by-birth in the old criollo families, although the overwhelming majority of the population, the people we think of first when we say 'Mexicans,' are mestizos. Flourishing within this mestizo group, and increasingly dominating the aristocracy-by-birth (or by commercial success), there is an aristocracy-by-achievement made up of artists, intellectuals, and politicians who are aggressively proud of their Indian ancestry and play down any Spanish dilution.

Proud in the first place of being Indian, the artists particularly are doubly proud of belonging to ethnic subdivisions – Toltec, Mixtec, Zapotec, Tarascan, and others – that created the great pre-Hispanic monuments, sculptures, and ceramics. There are about two million Mayan Indians today, and you will find men and women in the markets and streets of the Yucatán with exactly the same regal profile that you find painted and carved in the ruins of their magnificent culture, which, for reasons still unexplained, disappeared long before the Spanish conquest.

No one can understand Mexico or get the fullest pleasure from a trip there without beginning with a recognition of the vitality of Indian culture as an equal – or dominant – partner in the Mexican hybrid. It bothers me that so few tourists approach Mexico with this awareness; the measure of excellence in Mexican colonial art and architecture is not the degree to which it succeeds in imitating its Spanish sources, but the degree to which it becomes an indigenous expression. It was the Indian genes that transformed and individualized a style that the Spanish thought to transplant intact. In certain major projects, notably the cathedral in Mexico City, the transplantation worked. That enormous edifice might just as well be in Spain, which makes it for me one of the least rewarding churches in Mexico.

In other buildings where the sculptural ornamentation and wall paintings, the altars, pulpits and screens, were done by Indian artisans and craftsmen rather than by imported Spaniards, the effulgent Baroque style of the Spanish models was transformed by eyes and hands that had neither direct acquaintance with the parent style nor the technical mastery to execute its fantastically elaborated forms. In terms of opulent gilding and bright colour, Mexican Baroque can out-Baroque Spanish, while at the same time the staggering complexities of the style are arbitrarily disciplined by the limitations of less highly developed techniques.

In extreme cases the chastened result takes on a naïve cast in the translation of the most sophisticated of European styles, and can ring with a true piety that to my taste is more desirable than the most deft professionalism.

The misfortune for the habitually Europe-orientated tourist is that an intensely Mexican masterpiece may seem to be a failed Spanish effort. Aesthetically it would make just as much sense to regard the Spanish models as examples of a preliminary style lacking the kind of discipline imposed upon their Indian variants. Neither premise is valid, of course, but it is always the Mexican product that suffers from comparison. Mexican Baroque is not simply provincial Spanish Baroque. It is in truth more individualized than are the various European national Baroque styles from one another.

Playing the painful game of eliminating all but one each in the categories of pre-Columbian, colonial, and modern Mexican sites for recommendation to tourists on a curtailed schedule, I would suggest Palenque, Oaxaca, and, of course, Mexico City. Palenque, still in the process of extrication from the jungle that had overgrown it, is the most evocative of all the ancient Mayan cities except Tikal in Guatemala. The trouble is, it's a little out of the way, but it is worth sacrificing a day to travel time. Oaxaca is easy – an hour's plane ride from Mexico City.

I like Oaxaca better than the usual choice of Taxco because it has withstood the tourist invasion with less adulteration of its natural self. Taxco has always struck me as a stage set in spite of its undeniable authenticity, while Oaxaca has somehow remained a lively little city, large enough to have excellent hotels on its charming town square, formerly rich enough to have inherited from its past a massively constructed and richly decorated cathedral along with half a dozen other fine churches and monasteries, and small enough so that you can amble around from one to another on foot.

There are another half-dozen fine churches in the nearby countryside and, if you are there on a Saturday, one of the best Indian markets in all Mexico. (There is also the pre-Columbian complex of Mitla within the immediate area – an atypical example for which I have never been able to work up any enthusiasm.)

The question is bound to arise: Is Mexico still tourist heaven? To that one I have to give a yes-and-no answer. Mexico as I first knew it had its share of tourists, but they were a small band and a special breed: hardy, adventurous, and few in numbers compared with the flocks that were migrating to France every summer. Air travel and Mexico's Government-sponsored tourist industry have made all the difference. It used to take longer to go to the Yucatán from New York by rail than it did to go to France or England by boat, and Mexican hotel accommodations, once you got there, could be disconcerting outside the largest cities. Things are better today in many ways if you are ready, as virtually everybody is, to trade off a little adventure for an increase in convenience.

I could wish that Mexico City, which I used to know as a quiet provincial capital where life was carried on at a gracious pace against an essentially turn-of-the-century backdrop, had not changed into an enormous, traffic-clogged, high-rise, polluted metropolis, but I have comparable regrets about changes in Paris and New York. On the credit side for Mexico City today there is the National Museum of Anthropology, one of the truly stunning museums in the world; it and Chapultepec Castle, Mexico's official colonial museum, would be worth the trip if you saw nothing else.

Hotels everywhere are better. On my first visit in 1933 to the little city of Patzcuaro – and here I have to resort to the adjective 'enchant-ing' – the only hotel had no hot water and very little cold; it also had lumpy beds smelling of mould and bathrooms that were long on picturesque ingenuity but short on efficiency. Today there are small motels just outside Patzcuaro and it would be folly to object to their bland, characterless comfort. You leave Mexico for Nowhere when you enter them, but that's all right; you are in the middle of Mexico again when you go out of the door the next morning.

And it is wonderful. I'll go back any time. And back. And back. And back.

THE RIO BEAT

Warren Hoge

Its name conjures up visions of long curving beaches, tall coolers in pastel swirls, and the charged mysteries of tropical nights. But Rio is many other things as well. It is a business, banking and communications capital, home to 6 million people. Though it is locally considered an unseemly detail, and can easily get lost in the dawn-to-dawn pursuit of pleasure, many people labour to make a living here. But the city's industriousness has become so intertwined with its dedication to enjoying life that conventional values have ended up delightfully twisted. In Rio, people who work hard can be heard apologizing for their behaviour more than those who play hard.

The city's development has set business areas and beaches within brief strolls of each other, and the pursuit of leisure and of daily bread coexist happily. Shopping areas are filled with people in nothing but bathing suits, while the beach is a bustling meeting spot, a place for hanging out, an extension of the city with its street-corner chatter and its sidewalk hawkers. Driftwood collectors and anyone longing for a good soulful stare out to sea should go elsewhere.

As a general rule, the reception of foreigners in Rio is very friendly and haughtiness is unknown. All mixtures of language are employed to communicate, and Spanish is widely understood. These ground rules apply everywhere that Cariocas, as they are called, disport themselves, whether on the beach or in restaurants, bars and what are technically private clubs.

Rio is nearly enveloped by nature. It is a city hacked out of a rain forest that the Cariocas have gone to great lengths and heights to tame. Untended, the land erupts in gaudy tropical profusion, which may also say something about the Carioca character. Anyone riding the funicular up to the Christ the Redeemer statue that overlooks Rio from the summit of Corcovado mountain will see how quickly the vegetation becomes a jungle fastness when it's not covered with concrete. Corcovado – the word means 'hunchbacked' in Portuguese – rises steeply in the city's midst, part of a jagged chain of peaks that soar up from the coastline, giving Rio the shapely figure that has become its tourist emblem. A series of tunnels connect neighbourhoods separated by these hulking rock faces, and a drive through one of them can sometimes take you from one climate to another. Rio's capricious weather often bathes one community in sunshine while it's pouring drenching rain on another, around the corner of the next headland.

Rio is blisteringly hot in all but the winter months of June, July and August, when the average temperature dips to 70 degrees. To escape the heat, Cariocas move as much of their lives as they can onto the beaches. That includes societal divisions.

Artists, musicians, writers and gay-movement activists can be found in stand-up clutches of animated conversation in front of Vinicius de Morais Street, named for the poet and lyricist of many of Brazil's best-known popular songs, who held forth in Ipanema until his death in 1981. (His name was actually spelled Moraes, but it's Morais on the street signs, and someone insisting on details like that in Rio ends up being called a bore.) Surfers and their groupies favour the far north end of the Ipanema beach called Arpoador where rock clusters and prevailing currents produce the mightiest breakers.

Rio's high society has staked out for itself the stretch in front of the Country Club between Anibal de Mendonça and Henrique Dumont Streets in Ipanema. There's no qualitative reason to choose that section of sand except that for those who belong to the club it's close to the bar and the changing rooms – and for those who don't, laying one's towel out there can give the impression that one does. Status isn't everything in Rio society, but it's way ahead of anything else. The visitor will hardly notice the difference. Stripping down to bathing suits has a way of making people look equal, and it's better to watch Rio's rich when they turn into beautiful people by night.

The visitor will find the best beach and the most dramatic visual setting in São Conrado, a neighbourhood isolated from the rest of the city by another of the rocky seaside escarpments. There bathers can follow the swooping descents of hang gliders off the heights or buy chilled coconuts from vendors who hack the tops off and offer them with a straw to sip the cool liquid inside.

The entire Rio shore offers a splendid display of *jeunesse dorée*. The tanned young women are revelations in their string bikinis, here called *tangas*, and the young men, veterans of the chinning bars and gym-nasts' blocks set up along the beachfront, have washboard stomachs and chests that could serve as moulds for armour breastplates. Late Saturday and Sunday afternoons the beaches are taken over by soccer teams who, while amateur, exhibit the balletic type of play that has made the Brazilian style the favourite of crowds around the soccer-playing world.

The joggers come out at dawn and dusk. Since the emphasis is on looking good, no one wears bulky sweatshirts or clashing colours. Rio's garment industry devotes a lot of time to sports clothes, and the jogging tracks have become fashion runways. (The only time I ever saw as much make-up on a jogger was one morning in Central Park when Lyn Revson ran by, and she, aside from bearing the name of the president of one of the world's major cosmetics firms, was doing a spot for television at the time.)

All this activity builds up a thirst, and there are two principal potions that Cariocas turn to. The first is the highly esteemed Brazilian draught beer served at corner bars and sidewalk cafés all over the beach neighbourhoods at a temperature that is locally known as 'stupidly cold.' The other is a wide-mouthed glass of freshly squeezed juice made from the country's abundant tropical fruits. Outlets are almost as numerous as beer halls, and they are easily recognizable by the clusters of gourds and melons hanging above the counter. Among the choices are mango, passion fruit, cashew, sweet-sop, strawberry, apple, pear, pineapple, honeydew melon, and a healthful mixture of avocado, fruits, and cereal called a *vitamina abacate*. Like everything else in Rio, the drinks are pretty.

Don't be bothered by the way Brazilians litter their beaches with paper wrappers, soft-drink cans, and other disposables. In the early evening, when the veil of mist from the surf and the fog off the mountains meet and soften the edges of vision, platoons of sanitation men in bright orange uniforms rake the beach of the day's debris. Aside from leaving things clean for the next morning, their gentle march across the sands is also a reminder that in Rio the most commonplace things can borrow grace from natural splendour.

With so much gorgeousness to occupy the day, it would seem unlikely that people here would dedicate so much time to filling the dark hours. But they do. There's no evidence that nights on the Tropic of Capricorn last longer than in counterpart latitudes in the northern hemisphere, but people in Rio make more of them.

Things start late. At nine o'clock, restaurants are the preserve of idle waiters, and the properly acculturated dinner-party hostess is just stepping from the shower. Four and five hours afterward, the same restaurant is feverish with activity and if her living room isn't likewise, the hostess will be in despair.

The best advice for the visitor who doesn't want to eat alone or surrounded by busloads of tourists is to adapt to local custom. When Cariocas make a downward adjustment in these timetables, the reason is almost always because a visiting American or European is involved.

Ricardo Amaral, owner of Rio's hottest nightspot, the Hippopotamus discothèque, rolls his eyes to the heavens at mention of the four am closing time in New York (he is also the proprietor of Club A in midtown Manhattan). Walk out of Hippopotamus at an hour when runners are already in the street, calisthenics classes have commenced on the beach, and vendors are setting up their stalls in the farmers' market, and, if you glance behind, you'll see that the frolic inside is still pulsating as if there weren't already a tomorrow.

The hostess at Hippopotamus, a former Jacques Fath model named Danusa Leão, and her philosophy of the night are so central to the local culture that she became a cover story in *Veja*, the country's leading weekly news magazine. 'The secret,' she said in the article, 'is to be happy. For me this is an obligation. There's nothing selfish about being happy. Only by being happy can you pass it along to others, and the night-time makes me happy.'

Bohemian figures in pursuit of this felicity are revered in Rio. Night-time eccentricities are not only forgiven, they're exalted. I have a friend from a respected family who remembers regularly seeing her father come home just as she was sweeping her book bag off the front hall table to go to school. The group with which he stayed up all night included leading businessmen, a leftist politician, a newspaper publisher, and an assortment of playboys.

Hippopotamus is a private club, but visitors staying at the Caesar Park, Inter-Continental, Meridien, Nacional, and Rio Palace Hotels can obtain cards from the respective managers entitling them to entry. People showing up unannounced have been known to get in, but there is no formula for impressing the doorman. Inside is one of Rio's best restaurants, its prestige dance floor, and the beautiful people of all ages who have given it its reputation.

Rio is informal to an extent that Americans or Europeans often don't properly anticipate. If you want to leave no doubt you are a foreigner, wear a necktie. Even the priciest spots in Rio do not require a jacket, and men generally go out in slacks and open-necked shirts. Since Brazil is a country run by and for men, women are not permitted the same liberties. Silky things, jewellery, clinging pantsuits and the like are expected.

There are no bastions of the Old Guard in Rio because there is no Old Guard. The emphasis is on youth, and older people follow the young people's lead. Even such people as soccer stars and numbers operators are getting onto privileged dance floors these days, a sign that the democracy that is creeping back into the country's public life may have spilled over into the Rio night also. 'This is the city that cares least about what a person does, has done, or might do,' says Mr. Amaral. 'In Paris they want to know what family you're from. In New York, it's what business. Here that's considered boring.'

Rio's neighbourhood names won't mean much to a new arrival, but think of Leme, Copacabana, and Flamengo as Manhattan's Upper

West Side, Ipanema as the East Fifties and Sixties, Leblon and Gávea as the Upper East Side, São Cristovao as Bay Ridge in Brooklyn and Botafogo, the only community to have preserved some of its old residences, as a little like Greenwich Village.

Entertainers, writers and their admirers have hung out for years at Antonio's in Leblon. It is, like many such establishments, small and not particularly comfortable. Its food, moreover, is undistinguished – and it's full all night long. Some of its more traditional clientele have recently moved on to a dressier restaurant called Fiorentino, also in Leblon, while others can be found these days at the Clube Gourmet in Botafogo, run by José Hugo Celidonio, the country's leading food writer and a personal friend of many of the well-known French chefs. (Mr. Celidonio recently opened a beef restaurant called Sir Loin overlooking the ocean in the Marina Palace Hotel in Leblon. It is likely to become as popular as his Gourmet because he breaks the mould of society spots and serves good food).

The film colony and friends in the artistic world have turned the residential neighbourhood of Lower Gávea into their haunt and its restaurant Guimas, run by a former Portuguese photographer, into their command post. The mating rituals of the golden youth are on display each night in Lower Leblon on the curb outside the Pizzaria Guanabara and the Caneco 70. Both are easily identifiable by the packs of motorcycles parked outside.

Singers often drop into Chico's Bar, on the lagoon behind Ipanema, for a surprise set after their shows elsewhere. A group of leading samba singers recently filled a gap in the Rio night by opening a Clube do Samba in Barra de Tijuca where honest Brazilian music is played. The Canecao Hall in Botafogo offers the best Brazilian popular singers in extended one-man shows.

Little of the music and poetry that Rio has produced in abundance ever gets written before midnight. The great bossa nova songs of Antonio Carlos Jobim and Vinicius de Moraes took shape in the half light of dawns over Ipanema. The tunes that set the rhythm for each year's Carnival emerge from the animated darkness of the city's hillside slums, while the parade that highlights the annual saturnalia only steps off in the evening and continues on through the night until noon the next day. (Visitors who want to get an idea of what Carnival is like can attend rehearsals of the samba clubs, known as samba schools. The Portella school is conveniently situated at 81 Clara Nunes Street in Madureira; beginning at about midnight, they strut every Friday night from the beginning of August through Carnival. A more touristic version of the dancing and singing is available all year at the Oba Oba nightclub in Ipanema and the Plataforma in Leblon.)

Lest Rio's hours take their toll, a whole support industry is at hand.

There is, for example, no shortage of places to get one's hair done for the night out. The beauty salons of Rio's best-known hairdresser, Jambert, alone take up a five-storey building in Leblon. For more fundamental touch-ups, Rio's night crawlers repair to the various clinics around town that have earned Rio the reputation of being the world capital of cosmetic surgery. The fact that there are so many of them helps answer the question of how people who stay up so late can keep looking so good.

GETTING INTO THE SWING
Hotels with Cachet
Caesar Park (287 3122), Avenida Vieira Souto 460, Ipanema, has a restaurant that serves a Falstaffian Saturday lunch of feijoada, the Brazilian national dish, for about $15 a couple. Double rooms with sea views cost about $150.

Rio Palace (521 3232), Avenida Atlântica 4240, Copacabana, marks the junction of Copacabana and Ipanema beaches. Its Pré Catalan restaurant was created by Gaston Le Nôtre, whose noted desserts are here confected with tropical fruits. Double rooms with balconies looking out on the beach and Sugar Loaf Mountain cost about $140.

Hotel Meridien (275 9922), Avenida Atlântica 1020, has a top-floor restaurant, Le Saint Honoré, inspired by Paul Bocuse, and double rooms with ocean view for about $150.

Inter-Continental (399 2200), Avenida Prefeito Mendes de Moraes 222, São Conrado, has rooms with balconies overlooking the ocean or grounds; double rooms cost about $120.

Hotel Nacional (399 0100), Avenida Niemeyer 769, São Conrado, a cylindrical black building designed by the Brazilian architect Oscar Niemeyer, has double rooms for about $45.

Copacabana Palace Hotel (257 1818), Avenida Atlântica 1702, Copacabana, the model for Fred Astaire's sound stage dance floor in *Flying down to Rio*, remains the city's most romantic tourist address. Double rooms with view cost about $130.

Dining à la Carioca
Leblon: **Fiorentino** (274 6841), at Rua General San Martin 1227, has a Continental menu with occasional added Brazilian specialities like *feijoada*. Dinner for two with Brazilian wine costs about $30. **Antônio's** (294 2699), Avenida Bartolomeu Mitre 297C, charges roughly the same and specializes in lobster tail in wine sauce and paillard of veal with fettuccine. The **Sir Loin** (259 5212), in the Marina Palace Hotel, Avenida Delfim Moreira 630, takes as its inspiration the American sirloin steak served for two with wine for $30.

Botafogo: The **Clube Gourmet** (286 6577), Rua General Polidoro 186, offers three different options for appetizer, fish course, entrée, and dessert nightly at about $30 a couple.

Lower Gávea: **Guimas** (259 7996), Rua José Roberto Macedo Soares 5, has such specialities as barbecued hen stuffed with ricotta and chestnuts and grated codfish served in a cream sauce. Dinner for two with wine costs $15.

And on into the Night

Hippopotamus: Guests at all the hotels listed above except the Copacabana Palace can request a letter that gives them entrée to dining and dancing at Hippopotamus (277 8658 and 247 0351), Rua Barão da Torre 354, Ipanema. The average bill for dinner for two with drinks and wine is roughly $40.

Golden Room: Ricardo Amaral, the entrepreneur responsible for Hippopotamus, has also made an effort to recall the palmy nights of Rio's old casino days by reopening the courtly Golden Room (257 1818, extension 479) of the Copacabana Palace, a monument of the 1920s that was once the scene of café-society black-tie outings.

Asa Branca: Another institution of Rio's past has been grandly revived at the Asa Branca (252 4428), Avenida Mem de Sá 17, in Lapa, a onetime Bohemian corner of the city that is now a nest of office buildings. Inaugurated by King Juan Carlos of Spain, the Asa Branca is a *gafieira*, a place where the samba that's played is the kind that calls for dancing cheek to cheek.

THE SORCERY OF THE AMAZON

Edwin McDowell

On the outskirts of the Brazilian Amazon village of Belterra one afternoon, I was stopped in my tracks by a bird call of such clarity that I wondered if perhaps I had stumbled upon the uirapuru, that songbird so melodious that other birds are said to stop and listen. But as I entered a jungle clearing, in pursuit of that rapturous melody, I discovered that the notes had issued from an Indian youngster who was lolling in a hammock, idly blowing on a hand-carved bird call.

That was almost a decade ago, and I have thought of that incident many times since. On return visits almost every year to various parts of the Amazon Basin – across which I have hopscotched from the mouth of the Amazon River at Belém, Brazil, to Iquitos, Peru, with stopovers at tributaries in Colombia and Venezuela – I have found that things are rarely what they seem in the tropics. For this is a region with monkeys that bark like dogs, beetles that hiss like steam engines, birds that moan, screech, or break into fits of laughter, and frogs that roar, grunt, trill, hammer, or whistle.

Nature is the major appeal of the Amazon, an area larger than Western Europe with a population less than that of Madrid. Almost the entire region is an ornithologist's delight, attracting birdwatching expeditions and individual birders from many parts of the world. Fishermen and hunters come from many nations, particularly during the waning moon from June to December, when fish and animals are most abundant. Many Europeans, still imbued with hopelessly romantic visions about the Noble Savage, come to see the Indians – whose numbers, unfortunately, are rapidly dwindling from contact with 'civilization' and its diseases, against which they have no immunity. While some Amazon tour operators offer visits to authentic Indian villages, others have established camps where Indians are trotted out to perform for visitors like aboriginal Rockettes.

Yet many visitors, myself included, enjoy particularly the sense of timelessness the region imparts in an unsurpassed and largely unspoiled tropical setting. On many of its hundreds of rivers, of which a dozen or so are more than a thousand miles long, there is time to sit idly atop a double- or triple-deck Amazon boat (a style known locally as a 'birdcage') and watch the world's biggest jungle glide by. Time to watch fiery sunsets over the mightiest river in all the world. Time to wander unhurriedly through the villages at night and watch barefoot children still at play. Time to observe the mothers and grandmothers in every village at practically every hour of the day or night who, like T. S. Eliot's 'lonely men in shirtsleeves,' while away the hours leaning out of open windows.

Travelling in the Amazon presents unique practical problems, among them that of lodgings – only the major cities offer anything approaching first-class hotels. Moreover, while air service to and among the region's major cities is generally frequent and dependable, air fares are expensive (about $1,250 round trip New York to Belém or New York to Manaus, Brazil). Launches and riverboats will carry passengers inexpensively from one Amazon city to the other, but accommodations are usually spartan and the food is better left uneaten. The best and safest passenger ships on the river are said to be those operated by Enasa, the navigation line owned by the Brazilian Government, which maintains a regular but infrequent schedule between Belém and Iquitos (first-class passage with meals runs around $125, second class $80). Several of my Brazilian friends swear by the boat trip, which generally takes eight days upriver and four down, but one or two friends have sworn at it and others have found it tiresome – at any rate, less interesting than wandering through the towns and villages.

Many first-time visitors to the Amazon expect to swelter in heat and humidity, but that combination is rarely as oppressive as it is portrayed. To be sure, humidity averages 78 per cent in Manaus, the unofficial capital of the Amazon, but the average annual temperature is a manageable 81 degrees Fahrenheit and the city's highest recorded temperature of 101.5 is well below the highest recorded in most American cities.

I myself thrive in that climate, but even those who don't tend to find the actual heat and humidity less troublesome than the uniformly warm days and nights. For example, the temperature range between the warmest and coolest months averages only about three degrees. And while the amount of rainfall is considerably more from January to June than from July to December (Belém averages seventeen inches in March and half an inch in September), even during the dry season it is a rare day that afternoon showers do not wash away the jungle dust, lowering temperatures and leaving the air redolent of flowers and moisture.

A mosquito net is a prudent investment aboard ship and in the smaller towns of the interior, but I have not found it necessary in the big cities. While it would be foolish to minimize the discomfort, inconvenience or potential health problems posed by gnats and mosquitoes, I have found them less of a problem than the swarms I remember from my South Jersey childhood. Some Amazonian friends recommend Cutter's insect repellent, my last container of which I left with a friend in Itacoatiara, a village on the banks of the Amazon 150 miles east of Manaus.

Health and hygiene in the Amazon are noticeably better than just a few years ago, but would-be visitors would do well to read and heed the health information section in *The South American Handbook* (distributed by Rand McNally), available in most major libraries. Finally, visitors who do not speak at least a smattering of Portuguese or Spanish should either stick to the standard tours available in the larger cities or consider arranging with the tour operators or local language schools to hire an interpreter.

Nevertheless, despite its remoteness, the Amazon offers many unexpected amenities. Belém has several excellent hotels, with a Hilton under construction. At Iquitos, an attractive Peruvian port city 2,000 miles from the Atlantic Ocean, visitors can stay at the modern Amazonas Hotel (originally a Holiday Inn) set incongruously at the edge of the jungle or at the clean, comfortable Hotel de Turistas facing the Amazon River.

The substantial and luxurious Hotel Tropical, set in flowery grounds on the outskirts of Manaus, presumably would have satisfied even the nineteenth century rubber barons, whose ostentatious striving for comfort and pretensions to culture transformed Manaus from a dusty, backward city into the so-called Paris of the Jungle. The Hotel Tropical in Santarem, 500 miles downriver from Manaus, where the blue waters of the Tapajos River flow into the muddy waters of the Amazon, is not nearly as luxurious, but it is modern, comfortable, has two swimming pools, and is quite ingenious: One entire side of the hotel is ringed by large slats which, although perhaps intended primarily to deflect the rays of the sun, also hide the dilapidated wooden huts in the distance.

And there are other attractions and amenities. Belém, for example, boasts the century-old Teatro da Paz, with its interior of red plush, crystal chandeliers, and gilded boxes, where Anna Pavlova danced. The city-block-long Emilio Goeldi Museum contains a small zoo, a vast botanical garden, and the Amazon's leading anthropological and research centre. The nearby basilica of Nossa Senhora de Nazare is famed for its stained-glass windows and its interior, made completely of marble except for the ceiling, which is of Brazilian hardwood. The city itself has numerous broad streets shaded by stately mango trees. The Ceart gift shop on Avenida Cerzedelo Correa has an outstanding selection of native handcrafts.

Santarem, halfway between Belém and Manaus, is no longer a village but a city of some 150,000 people that finally has a couple of traffic lights yet at the same time still manages to resemble Elizabeth Bishop's description:

> *The street was deep in dark gold river sand damp*
> *from the ritual afternoon rain, and teams of zebus*
> *plodded, gentle, proud, and blue, with down-curved*
> *horns and hanging ears, pulling carts with solid wheels.*

Situated on the southern bank of the Amazon at the confluence of the Tapajos, Santarem is a city in transition that still retains important links to the past. With luck, you may run into Chester Coleman, a native of Chicago who arrived in Santarem on the first ship that Henry Ford sent to the Ford company's Amazon rubber plantation. That was 1928, about fifteen years after the price of Brazilian rubber had plummeted in the face of competition from the then British colonies of Ceylon and Singapore. Ford's experiment lasted until 1945, when he admitted failure and resold his plantations to the Brazilian Government for a nominal sum. What remains of his dream can be seen by taking a bus twenty-five miles south to Belterra at kilometre 39. The old golf course is now a soccer field and the jungle has reclaimed much of the land, but many of the original white houses are fully occupied and the original hospital is still open.

Manaus offers an Indian museum and a small zoo on the outskirts of the city, stocked with animals captured by the engineering battalions that built and maintain roads in the region. Its floating docks, which rise and fall forty feet with the tide of the Rio Negro, are open to the public on Sunday mornings, as is the nearby Customs House, which was prefabricated in Europe, shipped across the Atlantic in blocks, and erected in 1906. Many tourists travel the ten miles down the Negro to watch its black waters empty into the muddy Amazon, then watch the two rivers run side by side for another several miles before finally mixing. But the major attraction in Manaus, today a centre of light industry, is the famed Teatro Amazonas, the opulent opera house completed in 1896 after fifteen years at a cost of more than $2 million and restored a few years ago.

This jungle pleasure dome has marble staircases and columns transported from Italy, pavement stones from Portugal, chandeliers from Venice and iron framework from Scotland. The 40,000 blue, green and gold ceramic tiles in its cupola were imported from Alsace. At the turn of the century, when the cost of living in Manaus was several times that of New York and electric trolley cars wound through city streets past tiled mansions and lush gardens, rubber barons in white suits and ladies dressed in the latest European fashions descended on San Sebastian square to view the Comédie Française, Italian tragedians and other performers bold enough to journey into the jungle thicket.

These days the theatre is open several nights a week for folklore shows or singers or dramatists who have recently appeared in Rio De Janeiro and Belém. But Margot Fonteyn danced there as recently as 1975 and, with luck, one of the English-speaking guides will show you her toe shoes and other remembrances of the theatre's grandeur that are kept in the private museum on the top floor.

Leticia, Colombia's only Amazon port, is a tropical polyglot adjoining the Brazilian city of Tabatinga (headquarters of the Brazilian jungle command) and facing the Peruvian settlement of Ramon Castilla several miles across the Amazon River. It is also the crossroads for the Amazon's thriving drug trade with Europe and the United States. A favourite local pastime is to sit at the sidewalk café outside the Anaconda Hotel on Leticia's waterfront, a café where at any moment one expects to see a perspiring Sydney Greenstreet sharing confidences with Peter Lorre, and watch the flashy drug dealers and their fashionable ladies drop by the casino for a night on the town.

Iquitos, Peru's principal Amazon city with a population of about 150,000, has lovely parks, a beautiful riverside promenade called the Malecon and a number of graceful tiled buildings. Several tour agencies offer a variety of excursions to jungle lodges, some for as many as four or five days. The city has a university, three cinemas and a tinny-looking iron building directly across from the Plaza de Armas that was supposedly designed by Alexandre Gustave Eiffel for a nineteenth century exposition in Paris and reassembled in Iquitos after it was shipped across the ocean.

All the above cities have good clean restaurants and Belém and Manaus have several. The best-known regional specialities are *pirarucu*, *tambaqui*, and *tucunare*, fish that are stewed, fried or roasted according to local taste. Any of the three are likely to be served in *caldeirada*, a fish stew served with farinha and a sauce made from onions and a local pepper called *murupi*. On my first visit to Manaus the Government had banned the catching of pirarucu during its spawning season. After I lamented to a resident that I had been eager to taste the giant fish, he knowingly replied, 'Don't worry, it is illegal only to catch pirarucu, not to eat them.'

Cupim, the meaty sack from the buffalo, is a favourite at barbecue restaurants (called *churrascarias*) in Belém. Guarana is a soft drink made from the berries of an Amazonian plant, while another soft drink, plus ice cream and liquor, are made from the juice extracted from the fruit of the acai. But perhaps the most famous Amazon food is *pato no tucupi* duck served in the broth of the manioc root. The tucupi is extracted from the soft white pulp of the manioc in which, according to legend, the body of Mani, the beautiful daughter of an Indian chief, was hidden after her death.

All the larger Amazon cities have waterfront markets, where herbs and aphrodisiacs are sold alongside fresh fish and vegetables – Belen, a neighbourhood in Iquitos, is the Amazon version of Hong Kong's floating city of Aberdeen, with a market both colourful and squalid – look but don't buy.

The Amazon has always attracted a variety of characters, native and newcomer. In the mid-nineteenth century the British botanist Richard Spruce passed the time playing the bagpipes in the middle of the jungle. When Spruce and the English naturalists Alfred Russel Wallace and Henry Walter Bates got together in Santarem, they met in the home of an old Scots trader who had been there forty-five years and who periodically received bundles of English newspapers which he read at random, completely confusing the chronology.

I have never run into anyone like the old Scots, but I have met Amazon residents who refuse to believe that men have landed on the moon. I have been introduced to women who believe that the freshwater dolphin, the *boto*, sometimes turns himself into a male seducer and impregnates young girls. A local dentist I met while sailing along the Javari River between Brazil and Peru insisted that many Amazon residents still believe in the curupira, the legendary jungle sprite whose feet are turned backward and who can imitate a variety of human and animal sounds. And the American manager of a plywood factory near Iquitos told me that his workers are scared to death of the tunche, the fabled owl-like bird whose name is spoken in whispers.

They are wrong, of course. At least I think they are wrong. But somehow in the Amazonian vastness the line between fact and fancy seems neither quite so clear-cut nor quite so important.

HOW TO GET THERE

Varig Airlines flies direct to Manaus and Belém from Miami, while Faucett Airlines flies nonstop from Miami to Iquitos. Santarem and Iquitos are served by flights among the various Amazon cities.

Belém, Brazil

Stay at the **Excelsior Grao Para** on Avenida Presidente Vargas across from the Praca de Republica, the **Hotel Regente** on Avenida Governador Jose Malcher, the **Equitorial** on Avenida Bras de Aguiar or the

Vanja on Travessa Benjamin Constant. Singles $25-$35, doubles $40-$50. The **Circular Militar** restaurant in the old town is highly recommended, as are the **Augustus** on Avenida Almirante Barroso and **La Em Casa** on Avenida Governador Jose Malcher. All serve local fish dishes as well as steaks. Figure on paying about $15-$20 a person for dinner. **So Delicias** at Nazari 251 is perfect for sweets, pastries and soft drinks.

The local beers are uniformly good throughout the Amazon: in Belém, try Cerpa.

Ciatur and **Turismo Bradesco,** both on Avenida Presidente Vargas, are reliable tour companies, offering half-day city tours, evening dinner and nightclub tours, four-hour excursions of the Bay of Guajara through the nearby channels and creeks, or eight-hour trips to Mosqueiro Island on the Para River.

You can fly or take a boat to Marajo, an island the size of Denmark in the middle of the Amazon River that is home to buffalo and crocodiles. Prices range upward to $200 for the one-and-a-half-day trip, including sea and air transportation, a canoe and jeep tour.

Santarem, Brazil

Don't settle for anything except the **Hotel Tropical** run by Varig Airlines ($22 single, $25 double). It is airconditioned, and has two swimming pools and a restaurant that specializes in *tambaqui* and other local fish dishes. The hotel will book city tours, tours to beaches, or a two-hour river excursion to the junction of the Amazon and Tapajos rivers.

Manaus, Brazil

The luxurious **Hotel Tropical,** about ten miles out of town, also owned by Varig, charges $65-$100 single, $80-$100 double. Otherwise, try the **Amazonas Hotel** downtown for about half that price. The **Taruma** restaurant at the Tropical is relatively expensive ($20-$25 a person) but good, specializing in giant *tucunare* and *pirarucu* fish. The **Monaco,** on Avenue Constantino Nery, also serves *tucunare* at its rooftop restaurant.

Selvatur Agency in the Hotel Amazonas and Amazon Explorers Tour Service in the Hotel Lord offer three-hour city tours. A six-hour excursion on the Amazon River and the Rio Negro includes a visit to where the muddy waters of the former and the inky waters of the latter converge. An overnight tour to Lake Januaria includes the river trip.

Leticia, Colombia

At one time the **Parador Ticuna,** with thirteen apartments and a swimming pool, was an enjoyable place to stay, as was the nearby **Hotel Colonial,** eighteen air-conditioned rooms with pool. But recent travellers report that new owners have allowed both hotels to deteriorate. Before trying either of them, try to book at the **Anaconda** (telephone 71 19), a forty-five room hotel facing the Amazon (or Solimoes, as the river is called in these parts). Plan to pay about $35 a night for a double, including breakfast.

Hotels here are often full, so if you can't find a room, ask the taxi driver to drive you across the unguarded border to the **Hotel Solimoes** in

Tabatinga, Brazil. Like everything else in that frontier city, the hotel is run by the Brazilian army but it is clean, modern and only ten minutes from the centre of Leticia.

Turamazonas and La Rana tours both offer brief trips through the jungle, all-day tours up the Javari River to a rubber plantation and visits to Yagua and Ticuna Indian villages. La Rana owns a camp about seven miles from Leticia in the Tacanas River.

Iquitos, Peru

Try to stay at the **Hotel de Turistas** ($15-$20 single, $25 double) overlooking the Amazon and the Malecon. The **Acosta,** a few blocks away, lacks the view and the charm but is also highly recommended (about $15 single). Otherwise, the air-conditioned **Amazonas** (single $45, double $60) just outside town boasts a swimming pool and a nightclub. The Hotel de Turistas and the Amazonas have above average restaurants, but permanent residents opt for **Don Giovanni** at Putumayo 168, which serves good barbecued chicken and fish, pizza and spaghetti. Amazon Lodge Tours, Explorama Tours and Artesanias La Chamita are all near the Plaza de Armas and all offer a variety of local and overnight excursions. For cruises to Leticia, Manaus or nearby jungle villages, figure about $100 a person a day.

THE ALGARVE: PORTUGAL'S PLACE APART

Enid Nemy

It is easy to do nothing in the Algarve, blessed as it is with one of the most beautiful climates in Europe, for a good deal of it is still not of this modern, rushing world. One can be almost anaesthetized by this special province at the southwest tip of the Iberian Peninsula, by its sun, its light, by air heavy with the scents of eucalyptus and maquis, and by a sense of timelessness. Inertia never bothers the conscience; there are few churches and museums of sufficient import to demand sightseeing, and although the ocean side is punctuated with new, sometimes obtrusive developments, there is, withal, a sense of the past.

To the Phoenicians, Greeks and Carthaginians, the Algarvian coast was a trade secret, rich in marine life, outside the Gates of Hercules. To the Romans and the Moors, it was the western limit of their disparate empires. To Islam, for four centuries, it was Al-Gharb, the west; and for almost six hundred years after the Moors were expelled in the thirteenth century, it was a separate kingdom under the Portuguese crown and all its kings and queens were 'of Portugal and the Algarve.'

It has always been a place apart, and the reason is partly geographical. The Atlantic borders the Algarve on the south and west. Its eastern border is Spain and the wide, sluggish Guadiana River. It is separated from the rest of Portugal by successive ranges of mountains. It is not large – only eighty-five miles from Spain to Cape St. Vincent and twenty-three miles from the mountains to the sea. Where there is water, the Algarve can explode into vivid blossoms and sustain the olive, the oak, the almond, orange, lemon and fig, but much of it is carob and cactus country. It lay slumbering for centuries, almost retired from history, until it was discovered by tourists and real-estate developers a few decades ago.

Its apartness is also cultural. The mountains have been more of a barrier between the Algarve and Portugal than the sea has been between it and North Africa. It has been called the mirror image of Morocco, and its villages and people prove the resemblance. The greatest monument of the Algarve is the Moorish fortress town of

Silves. The basic architecture is the whitewashed cube and wall, sometimes enlivened with splashes of North African colour, surmounted by characteristic chimneys, which often resemble minarets, and sometimes decorated with the tiles the Arabs brought with them to the Iberian Peninsula.

Typical Algarvian villages, which still exist in such places as Santa Barbara de Nexe, Cacela Santa Rita, Feiteira, and Alte, are almost as secretive as a casbah. There are few storefronts. When the doors are closed, the passer-by is often hard-pressed to know what is going on, what trade or craft is practised, behind the walls that line the street. Only occasionally a wine seller will proclaim his calling by mounting a traditional leafy bough over his door.

The people, too, are different from the Portuguese of the north: smaller of build, generally darker of complexion, although there is a leavening of paler skins and freckles from the Scottish Highlanders who were once there. The Algarvian is conservative; even today many cling to the donkey cart, wear black clothes and hats, and carry black umbrellas in the hot sun. The Arab legacy is strong, and the old description of the Algarvian still applies: 'a man of order, of peace; his heart is great, his dignity greater.'

There is, in fact, something almost biblical in the small villages as yet unreached by water mains. There, women journey to a central well for water and some balance pitchers on their heads to carry it back. A Roman would also feel at home, trudging along a road that he laid out, past familiar-looking vineyards, glimpsing bake ovens, water wheels, and the pink-tiled roofs of villas among the umbrella pines. Old customs are observed: The traveller has the right to one piece of fruit from any orchard and to a drink of water or wine from any household he passes.

The history of the Algarve has been a record of intrusions. The Romans, the Vandals, the Visigoths and the Arabs invaded. Prince Henry the Navigator didn't invade; he merely came down from the north at the start of the fifteenth century. At Sagres, a whisper away from Cape St. Vincent, he founded his school of navigation, which led to the great Portuguese discoveries in Africa, Asia and the Americas. Today, Sagres is the site of the Pousada do Infante, one of the most scenic of the government inns and a stark contrast to the modern architecture and activity at hotels in such places as Praia da Rocha and Vilamoura. At the nearby port of Lagos, scores of fishing boats leave each morning from the same harbour from which, for a short while, the Portuguese set sail on their early voyages of discovery. As discovery gave way to trade, the cargoes went north to Lisbon – although not before a Genoa-born seaman named Cristobal Colón clambered ashore there from a sinking ship.

History intruded again at the end of the sixteenth century, when the English stopped by to 'singe the beard of the King of Spain' and loot Faro, and when Jervis and Nelson made their marks by defeating the French fleet off Cape St. Vincent.

Much has remained unchanged but not all. Farmers have left the land, small businessmen have become entrepreneurs and teenagers live in jeans and carry transistors. The new world of high-rise resort hotels, packaged paradises, trendy restaurants and bars, boutiques, discos and even casinos lines the ocean side of the east-west highway between Faro and Lagos. But in this strip, there are, as well, excellent golf courses and miles of beautiful beaches, caves and grottoes. It is, however, on the other side of the highway, and back in the hills, that the old Algarve still exists.

One morning, during the height of the Portuguese revolution in 1974, my husband and I were sitting on the terrace of a house we owned in the Algarve, tucked away in the hills behind Santa Barbara de Nexe. The sun was brilliant, a few bees droned overhead, the cuckoos were calling over the next hill, yet the silence seemed absolute and we were bathed in fragrance and contentment.

My husband looked up from one of the British newspapers we bought each afternoon and saved to read with coffee the next morning. 'You may not know it but, according to this paper, we're in a state of unbearable tension and thinking of leaving the country,' he said. We laughed simultaneously, the ripples echoing across the stillness.

We were not naïve; nor were we, as foreigners, isolated from the changes taking place throughout Portugal. Soldiers with rifles had patrolled the airport in Lisbon when we arrived a week earlier on our way south for our semi-annual stay. Some Portuguese, particularly the wealthy, had left. The bank clerks had suddenly become servants of the people and had stopped wearing ties. Tourists had stopped coming. Foreign residents who had lived in the country for some time were apprehensive. No one could pretend that nothing was going on. The country was taking a full turn from right to left.

Nevertheless, we and a few thousand other house owners in the Algarve – mostly British, with some Americans, Scandinavians, Germans, and Dutch – never really believed that we would have to flee. We spent hours repeating rumours and gossip and trying to identify political factions whose acronyms baffled even the Portuguese. But most of us were convinced that somehow life would go on pretty much as it had before.

The experience of the old Algarve and the instinct that bloodshed and violence were not part of the Algarvian character, were, in fact, among the strongest of reasons why the revolution could be taken in stride by so many foreigners. The revolution itself was a pretty strange one, with more carnations than bullets poking out of gun muzzles, and even the burglars who twice broke into our house in the months following displayed traces of typical conservatism and courtesy. They took exactly half our flatware, two of the three alarm clocks, and two of perhaps eight pairs of old shoes we had left behind. (Our local postmistress, who previously had been all business, was so undone when she heard of the burglaries that she presented my husband with a free stamp.)

The revolution is now history; many who fled have since returned, and the country today is either right of centre or left of centre, according to who is doing the talking. But for us the events and conduct during that time of comparative upheaval were important because a good part of our love affair with the Algarve is due to our affection for its people.

The affair began a decade ago with a decision, for no good reason, to buy property and build a house. It was gloomy and raining as we set out with the real-estate agent from Faro for Santa Barbara, and until we left that village, all was fairly normal. Our route then took us through the backyard of a farm, to the consternation of several howling dogs and what seemed to be hundreds of cackling chickens, and onto a rock-strewn ribbon of dirt that wound upward through what can be best be called scrub. The car finally called it quits. We emerged to climb, ankle-deep in red clay mud, to the top of the hill. The view was hazy – we could barely see the car below, let alone Faro and the Atlantic Ocean in the distance. The property was a strange shape, studded with boulders, puny trees and scratchy shrubs, but we stood there like fools, completely at peace with the world.

'We'll take it,' we said. Few contractors were willing to undertake building in an area that remote, with no road fit for trucks with building supplies, no electricity, no telephone lines, no water. The agent said she would guarantee everything except water and, despite pitying looks from friends, we believed her. Within the year, it was all there, except the water, which never was found and had to be bought and brought up by truck. Within two years, the house was finished.

We learned a lot about the Algarvians while the house was being built. The first discovery was that no matter how short our visit was, there was no point trying to hurry a business discussion, a throwback, perhaps, to the Moorish influence. When we met with the contractor, we drank coffee, discussed America and Portugal, reviewed books and music and, several hours later, finally got down to fireplaces, water cisterns and tile. Sometimes we were so exhausted after a few days of talk that we would say we had to return to America and take ourselves off to a hotel at the other end of the Algarve. There we would live in silence, laying down our British mysteries only long enough to stuff ourselves with *cataplana* (clams and pork) and grilled sardines.

But the experience stood us in good stead and is useful even now when, having sold the house, we return as holidaymakers twice a year. We know that most Algarvians are virtually unmoved by demands, reasonable or not, and turn to stone when anger is exhibited. On the other hand, an appeal to help solve a problem will usually bring forth results. A market woman, who resents a customer's picking through the tomatoes, will take over the picking herself it one professes ignorance and appeals to her expertise, an exercise that requires no language but shrugs of the shoulder and a woebegone look. A motorist, appealed to in pidgin Portuguese, will make a complete turn and spend fifteen minutes leading a stranger to a desired road.

If there are negative features to the Algarve, as there must be even to the infatuated, the most serious is the quality of the driving. Many Algarvians and, in fact, many Portuguese, become devil-may-care, macho creatures when behind the wheel of a car, apparently oblivious to its lethal capabilities. A recently instituted safety campaign may curb some of the recklessness, but it is not uncommon to see cars passing one another on blind curves or for one car to cut in front of another to make a turn. Portugal has some of the best-marked roads on the Continent, replete with warning signs and speed limits, but the warnings are virtually ignored. Motoring can be a frightening experience; it is always a watchful one.

Fortunately, even if a wary eye is needed for other drivers, the other eye is still free to enjoy the profusion of nature that blankets a good deal of the countryside. Oleanders and bougainvillaea flourish, poppies punctuate open fields, iris, geraniums, and small white daisylike cistus add patches of colour to white cottages, umbrella pines and cork oaks frame highways. In the square in Faro, where visitors and residents alike sit reading their newspapers and drinking their morning coffee, purple-flowered jacaranda trees reach for the sun.

And early in the year almond blossoms lay a mantle of white over the landscape. Legend has it that the almond trees were planted by a prince for his Scandinavian princess, who pined for the snow of her native land. No matter if it is apocryphal. After a few days in the Algarve, it seems quite possible.

COMING OF AGE IN KENYA

Peter Maas

Twilight had enveloped our tent encampment by a stream on the great Serengeti Plain just outside the protected park of the Masai Mara game reserve in southwest Kenya. We – my son, John-Michael, and I – were sitting in front of the campfire while dinner was being prepared. Behind us a huge, blood-red equatorial sun was touching down on a cloudless horizon. To our left, some thirty miles away, a giant storm moved slowly west. It looked like one of those A-bomb test blasts, only infinitely magnified.

Still, in the vastness of the African sky, you could see it all, self-contained, from one side to the other. The mushrooming thunder-heads, pink and mauve in the setting sun, must have reached up to 50,000 feet, maybe more. Beneath them, in the grey mass of rain, enormous lightning bolts shot out endlessly, eight, ten at a time. You could hear the reverberating peal of thunder ever so faintly. Coming from so far off made it that much more awesome. The ground under my feet seemed to shake.

Directly above us the first stars had started to appear. And to the south, on our right, a second great storm was passing by, with the same tinted thunderheads, the same jagged flashes of lightning, the same earth-shaking booms.

Meanwhile, just as the sun vanished in a burst of crimson afterglow, a full, shimmering yellow moon was rising in the velvety blue eastern sky.

This simultaneous panorama of sun and moon, of the two storms, the stars glittering overhead, lasted perhaps fifteen minutes. Then abruptly, in an instant, I would think, the land around us turned pitch black. Even the moon, as brilliant as it was, couldn't dent the darkness past the campfire for a while. There was an absolute, utter silence.

I had never felt so small. Or so close to my son, who was then almost thirteen. I had this desire to clutch him and hold him to me. But I didn't. He, like me, had said nothing during the spellbinding celestial light-and-sound display we had witnessed. Indeed, it had been beyond words, and I really wasn't sure precisely what was going on in his mind. In the next second I realized that my impulsive yearning for physical contact with him wasn't at all necessary. We had shared an extraordinary moment that evening in Africa, and we both knew it.

Hyenas began wailing. Somewhere to the northeast a lion bellowed, and then another. A troop of olive baboons nesting in a big acacia tree at one end of our campsite acted up. John-Michael glanced nervously in their direction. The tree was closest to his tent, and, the night before, he'd been awakened by the baboons foraging around. 'Did you take a look outside?' I had asked, and he replied, 'Are you kidding? I was afraid they were coming in for me.'

He walked down to the cooking fire to see what our Kikuyu chef was concocting. From the first, J.-M. had been fascinated by our key piece of safari kitchen equipment, nothing more than an iron box with a hinged door plunked down in the glowing embers, out of which had come delectable meals – ham, turkey, chicken, and duck. I was sipping an ice-cold martini when J.-M. returned. 'Hey, it looks good,' he said. 'Roast beef.'

We'd been on other trips. To Disney World in Florida, for instance, and the Universal Studios tour in Southern California, and on holidays in the Caribbean to snorkel and fish. But he'd been a kid then, and I had made certain that there was a pal of his along, or at least plenty of kids his age in the immediate vicinity. His mother had died when he was eight, and I had always been apprehensive about going off with him one-on-one, wondering how I could possibly keep him entertained on my own.

Now, though, he was getting to be not a kid any more, edging hesitantly into young manhood, and so I decided to chance flying practically halfway around the globe with him to spend ten days viewing African wildlife close up. There'd be only the two of us. Besides, it wasn't planned solely for my son's benefit. It was for me, too. As a reporter and writer, I had seen a great deal of the world, but I had never been to the big-game terrain of Africa. I wanted the experience while there was still time. In every sense of the word, I had been told, that kind of Africa was an endangered species.

As safari neophytes, we were on an equal footing we hadn't known before, and almost at once I started observing new things in J.-M. from this perspective. Things I liked. It was on our third day, I think, up in the Aberdare Range north of Nairobi. We had been searching for a leopard, the most elusive of Kenya's Big Five game animals – the others being the lion, rhino, elephant and buffalo. Suddenly our guide, Tony Seth-Smith, spotted some fresh claw marks on a tree. Then as we inched along in our Range Rover, we saw the leopard, not more than fifty feet off the trail, hunched down under a tree, almost lost in the dappled sunlight, eyes fixed on us.

In his excitement, J.-M. was a little slow focusing his camera and setting the correct exposure. 'Come on,' Seth-Smith snapped, 'it's not going to stay there forever.' Then the leopard was gone. I thought Tony had been a little harsh, and I was about to say so. But something made me wait to see how my son would react. His upper lip trembled. Tears looked to be next. He pulled himself together, however, and quietly said, 'I'm sorry. I did the best I could. The important thing is I saw it myself. Anyone can look at a picture.'

I became aware of a new, relaxed camaraderie between us. We had come down to lake Nakuru to view the flamingos. At Nakuru, when you've seen a flamingo, you've literally seen them all. They cluster by the acre across the lake, like great floating pink gardens. Perhaps a thousand, ten thousand, will take off at once, and it is as if a portion of the earth had lifted itself to the sky. At dusk we were coming around the southern end of the lake. I was talking to Seth-Smith. Out of the corner of my eye I spied what appeared to be a log lying across most of the dirt road ahead of us. Tony swerved to the left. J.-M. behind me in the Range Rover, yelled, 'Snake! Snake!'

I detected considerable glee in his voice. If there's one thing I can't stand, it's snakes.

I stared grimly forward while J.-M. and Tony went back to inspect what turned out to be a python, apparently in postdigestive somnolence.

'You should have seen it,' J.-M. said. 'It must have been ten feet long.'

'That's nice,' I said, happy that on this one night, at least, we would be staying in a lodge instead of tents.

'Tony, how big do they get?'

'I once saw one that measured more than twenty feet.'

'About right for swallowing a medium-sized boy,' I said.

'Oh, Dad,' John-Michael said.

Our safari had begun in the Aberdares, then on to Lake Nakuru, and to another lake, Naivasha, teeming with bird life – eagles and ospreys, herons and hawks, even the first storks I'd ever seen – and, as always, with a complement of animals – waterbucks, reedbucks, gazelles, zebras, hippos.

Of all the animals I would see, though, it was the African elephant that got to me. We were in the Aberdares. We had rounded a corner to go up a mountain trail just wide enough for the Range Rover. And there one was, advancing toward us, a majestic male, with long, curving tusks. I was surprised by its brownish colour. All the prancing elephants I'd seen in circuses were distinctly grey, but later Tony explained that they were the more trainable Asian variety. We stopped. Nobody said a word. I vaguely heard J.-M.'s shutter clicking behind me. I felt as if I were face to face with some elementary, primordial force. About 150 yards had at first separated us. Now it was perhaps forty yards. I found myself looking at the massive, wrinkled head looming over me, ears flaring, trunk raised, and I knew that in one frozen moment I had connected with another time. It remained as motionless as I was. Then, with unexpected quickness, the elephant turned away into the forest. I saw the treetops flailing.

Travelling farther north through the Aberdares, we saw across a narrow valley three more of these behemoths making their way along the flank of a hill. I watched, mesmerized, through my binoculars. They were moving in parallel formation, about fifty yards apart, heedless of what lay in their respective paths. Three great brown hulks crunching through green. They seemed so indestructibly ageless. But, of course, they weren't, and I listened to Seth-Smith describe the carnage being wrought by poachers in unprotected areas of the bush, and a profound sadness swept over me. Suddenly, it had become very personal.

There was wildlife to be seen wherever we went, but nothing approached what we encountered on the last leg of the safari – in the rolling savanna country of the Masai Mara. Where before we had spied a dozen or so zebras at once, here were herds of hundreds. Impala and topi and wildebeest surged past us beyond count. Lions by the dozen. Then a solitary rhino. Hippos churning up the Mara River. A crocodile, as sinister as advertised, stretched out on a rocky spit. Giraffes silhouetted against the horizon. Ostriches racing across the grassland. Overhead, eagles and falcons dipped and soared continually – and vultures.

But it was there in the Masai Mara, for all of its animals, that I was struck by the physical immensity of Africa, the endless vistas, the immeasurable sweep of the African sky, all of a piece, making miniatures of even the elephants in its grandeur. The air was so magically clear, turning distance into an illusionist's trick.

My first morning in the camp where I would see the two enormous thunderstorms I noticed a line of hills to the south.

'Maybe we could take a quick drive over,' I said to Seth-Smith.

'They're across the border, in Tanzania.'

'I didn't know we were so near.'

'Well, actually, those hills are ninety miles off, you know.'

The Masai Mara reserve is divided into two parts. The inner, protected section with its park trails is set aside exclusively for viewing animals. The rest of it, much larger, remains reasonably close to what it has always been, inhabited by nomadic Masai tribes, Kenya's warrior class equivalent to the Zulus. Camping outside the protected park made a difference. Within, there was a general air of tranquillity.

Outside, however, the tempo quickened – a gazelle was far more skittish, a lion far less approachable.

All one night we heard lions. Seth-Smith reckoned that they were in a clump of low-lying hills about five miles northeast of us. We would try to track them.

Tony used to lead hunting parties. Now hunting was outlawed. He made a pretty persuasive case, though, that the results had been counterproductive. Professional hunters like him, more than anyone else, had a vested interest in the preservation of game. But poachers were having a field day because district game wardens couldn't possibly monitor the huge tracts of territory assigned to them. Hunters, licensed for strictly limited bags, could play a critical role in helping to police indiscriminate, illegal killing.

We had an immediate example. We had left camp at five-thirty am. Several times Tony got out of the Range Rover, examining droppings, searching for tracks. 'They're not far,' he said. We came over a rise, and found we had company below. Masai tribesmen had also heard the lions. Bows in hand, they were circling a scrub thicket. Their arrows, Tony said, were treated with fast-acting poison.

He began palavering with the tribesmen, who suddenly didn't appear too picturesque any more. But he managed an impressively officious bearing, and after some give-and-take, the Masai retreated. We waited for a while, nosed around the thicket and saw what they had been stalking – a pair of lionesses and five cubs.

Driving around in a Range Rover observing game isn't the height of danger. The idea, indeed, is to get as close as possible to the animals before they take off. But stepping out of the Range Rover and walking in the bush, as we occasionally did, brought new elements into play. Then you heard Africa. The steady insect hum. The cry of birds that the Range Rover's engine had drowned out. The wind. And you sensed a certain menace in the great landscape. The possibility of the unexpected.

One afternoon Tony, John-Michael and I were lined along the bank of a tributary running into the Mara River casting for catfish for an evening fry. These big African catfish are tough. Landing them was only half the battle. Then they had to be stunned with a small club or else they would head right back into the water.

We were so intent on the thrashing fish we were hauling in that nobody noticed the buffalo until it snorted. It was to our left, beyond where Tony was standing, on the far side of a tree. Practically the first animal we'd seen on safari was a buffalo. But they had since become such a common sight that, from the Range Rover at least, they had begun to remind me of nothing so much as herds of cows you might see grazing on a Wisconsin dairy farm.

Suddenly this particular buffalo, about thirty yards away, snorting and stamping its front hoofs, jerking its curved horns back and forth, didn't look so bovine any more. Using the tree to screen himself, Tony edged forward. He picked up a dead branch, shouted, and hurled it toward the buffalo. But the buffalo didn't budge. Instead, the snorting and horn-tossing increased. I didn't want to think about what could happen next.

Tony called softly to us, 'It's been raked by a lion. It's hurt and confused.'

I backed slowly to John-Michael. 'If we have to, we'll dive in the water,' I said.

'Suppose there's crocodiles?'

'We'll worry about that later.'

We watched Tony pick up another dead limb and throw it with more shouts, and this time the buffalo spun half around. Then it charged past the tree. I saw it stagger and almost fall, and then veer off into the woods. We could hear the crashing. Tony said that one of the buffalo's hind legs had been damaged by the lion.

On our final safari day, it was dusk and we were returning to camp in the Masai Mara. A fairly large herd of wildebeests was stationed on a wide, sloping section of grassy plain. It was a lovely scene in the last rays of the sun, the kind that would have made a perfect ending for one of those old travel films when the narrator says, 'So now we say goodbye to . . .'

All at once Tony braked the Range Rover and pointed to two hyenas that had come over a rise and were trotting toward the wildebeests. I had always thought that hyenas were only scavengers, living off the kill of others. I was wrong.

As the hyenas moved in, the wildebeests broke into a frantic fragmenting gallop. Within minutes, the hyenas had isolated one. It tore down the plain, a hyena in apparently hopeless pursuit. But the second hyena had circled around and was boring in at an angle to cut it off. The wildebeest skidded to a stop, turned, and started back. The two hyenas instantly switched roles. Twice more this occurred. Now all the distances were shortening – the distance the wildebeest would run before turning, the distance between it and the hyenas. Then each of the hyenas was alongside the wildebeest, leaping at it, jaws snapping, and it went down.

We continued on to the camp in a sombre mood. 'I didn't like that,' John-Michael said. 'I'm glad it was dark.'

After leaving Nairobi, once again in the familiar confines of a Pan Am 747, I gazed down at a Congo River that was as big as five or six Mississippis, while John-Michael buried himself in comic books. I wondered if I had read too much into this trip with him. For these past ten days at least, I had ceased being an all-knowledgeable authority figure, and I thought that I had glimpsed in this shared adventure the sort of man he would become. But, of course, I couldn't speak for what was in his mind. Perhaps it had just been another visit to a different Disney World as far as he was concerned.

The photographs he had taken were developed. Friends dutifully dropped by to view the slide shows. I was especially pleased to note that he had, in fact, got a terrific shot of the leopard, but I thought how right he'd been. Having actually seen it was more important than the picture. Then the slides were stored away.

That was more than three years ago. My son is now well past sixteen. The other day, when I began this memory of our safari together, I asked him if he remembered much about it. He looked at me solemnly and said, 'I'll never forget it.'

CHOOSING A SAFARI
Safari programmes of almost any length, price, and type are available from a number of packagers, among them **Abercrombie and Kent International, Inc.; Four Winds Travel, Inc.; Hemphill/Harris Travel Corporation; Lindblad Travel, Inc.;** and **World Travel Consultants, Inc.,** which specializes in individualized safaris. Some sample prices: about $1,800 to $2,300 a person, double-occupancy and exclusive of airfare, buys a basic sixteen-day animal-watching trip; $4,500 a person and up, a luxury tenting expedition of similar length, and about $3,000 a person, an eighteen-day air safari. All may be booked through travel agents.

Custom-tailored safaris may also be arranged through such specialists as **Mackey Travel**, 250 West 57th Street, New York 10107 (212 757 0722), which represents Ker & Downey Safaris Ltd. of Nairobi, and **Certified Travel Consultants/Safari and Tours**, 500 Fifth Avenue, Suite 1821, New York 10110 (212 354 0007).

In Nairobi itself, there are several agents who will arrange for guides and book you a safari on the spot. Some of these are **Abercrombie and Kent, Ker & Downey, Bruce Safari Limited**, and **Njambi Tours** (in the Inter-Continental Hotel).

VAST, STILL, TIMELESS, AWESOME

Colleen McCullough

For Americans, Australia is a new world. Easier transportation has helped double the number of American visitors in recent years. They find an island continent of contrasts, from the vast silences of the outback to the richness of the waters of the Great Barrier Reef to the brash sophistication of Sydney.

For many Americans willing to make the long and arduous journey to Australia, the first stop is Sydney, a city I love – and loathe. What I love is the beauty, the climate, the atmosphere. But it is a city, and cities tend to be the same the whole world over – crowded, riddled with industrial disputes, tied up with traffic, expensive. Three days in Sydney is always enough for me; then I get out, dying to taste the essence of Australia.

What is that essence? I can answer for myself without even pausing to think. Vastness, loneliness, stillness, timelessness, an utter lack of people. That is the real Australia. There's no sense of milk and honey, no conviction that the country is simply waiting to be tilled and tended. It is not at all antagonistic: It is indifferent, as if the land that existed unchanged for aeons before any man set foot on it will exist unchanged for aeons after the foot of man has forever left it. I love that. But it is unsettling. Man is reduced, humbled. If you can take that salutary experience in your stride, you will love Australia, the real Australia.

Rent a car, and head anywhere. Within half a day's drive of Sydney the timelessness is already there. Forests that stretch on and on into the haze of distance, sheer cliffs with their flanks drowned in yet more trees, the spindle of a thin white waterfall tugged sideways in a stiff wind, and such a silence. Not a mere soundlessness, but the absence of sounds of men. A vast pervasive murmur from tossing leaves in billions, the calls of birds, the shrilling of cicadas, and, on a very hot day, a dull thrumming, which is the land itself vibrating in the heat.

Australia is the land and its trees, its plants, its birds and its animals and its fish. But in a city they are not Australia; alongside a busy road they are not; in a zoo they are not. I like to drive up into the Watalgans, a mountain range only two hours north of Sydney, and find a spot beside a shallow musty pool where the bell-birds tinkle and chime incessantly. For hours I just sit and watch and listen. Such beautiful birds, such wonderful insects. And a quality and a clarity about the light that defies description. Like a long golden dream.

In August and September the bush will be drenched yellow with the wattle blooming, and in the grasses at that time of year are multitudes of native flowers, frail and vivid. There is a smell to the bush, of eucalyptus oil and hot dust and, after a heavy shower, the overpowering scent of wet earth, ecstatic and numbing. After dark the animals come out: wombats and wallabies and kangaroos and, lithe and agile as monkeys, koalas swinging on high from tree to tree. During daylight hours Australian animals are very shy, but in the night they walk.

West of the Great Dividing Range the country changes, becomes much drier and browner, the Australia of foreign imagination, until toward the middle of the continent the desert encroaches. It is superb desert. I shall never forget the long hot ride out from Alice Springs to Ayers Rock, three hundred lonely miles. The track, for it is no more, winds back and forth beneath a sky so lofty and richly blue it almost pierces the eye, and on all sides lie the sand dunes, scarlet dust heaped in great undulating waves, their redness splashed with the brilliant emerald of spinifex tussocks.

When the rock comes into sight, it stalks the approaching car like some sullen ominous monster, changing its position so quickly and so radically that the mind cannot believe it is truly rooted to one spot. How can a rock be so awesome? It is. Eaten away with caves all around its eleven-mile base, it is so smooth and dangerous to scale that a visitor attempting the climb any later in the day than dawn is flirting with death. And when the sun sets, the rock follows the colours in the clouds as if on fire from within.

There's coastal Queensland, lush and tropical, with the Great Barrier Reef flanking its luminous shallow waters, keeping the might of the Pacific at bay. The stretch between the towns of Proserpine and Mackay is gorgeous, for the coast there is bright with flowering trees and shrubs, hilly and lapped with enchanting inlets, while the waters for a hundred miles are dappled with tall, satisfyingly tropical islands. For sailors, this part of Australia is a sheer joy. Around Cairns, which is considerably farther north, the reef itself is accessible, so this is where the scuba divers flock and, in season, the big-game fishermen.

Behind Cairns lie thousands of square miles of mountainous jungle, but there are spots where the visitor can walk through carefully mapped areas to sample this exotic vegetation, its orchids and ferns and flowering vines.

I have always wanted to go to Thursday Island, off the northern tip of Queensland. Like Broome, on the west coast, this was a great pearling centre, and there are still relics of those glamorous days. Places like Broome and Thursday Island remind me that the Orient is closest of all other land masses to Australia. Many of the pearl divers were Japanese and the pearl traders Chinese, and their influence remains: joss houses, graveyards, shops.

My pick of the mining towns, and Australia has many interesting ones, would be Coober Pedy in South Australia. It lies amid a desolation hard to visualize, a flat, stony, utterly barren off-white desert. Here they mine the opal, in conditions so inclement that it has become a troglodyte community, where the dwellings are beneath the earth, only a tin chimney and corrugated iron around the privy indicating the underground site of a dwelling. The life is rough and fascinating, the population polyglot and almost entirely male. So much wealth comes out of this sterile glaring desolation that the settlement has an air of suppressed violence, and in the pub the furniture is all securely bolted to the ground. Here the visitor can fossick, as it is called, for his own opal, or buy it at cheaper prices than in the city. Coober Pedy is well worth a visit.

Everyone seems to overlook the island of Tasmania. But if as a visiting American you can only find the time to go to Australia during December, January, February, or March, then Tasmania is the ideal place to head for. Right in the path of the roaring forties – the stormy oceanic areas between 40 and 50 degrees latitude – it is cool compared to the rest of the continent for the remainder of the year. But these are the summer months, when in the north the monsoons come down, and in the centre the heat is stupefying. Even Sydney in summer can be daunting.

Tasmania is wild, beautiful, rugged, heavily forested. The clouds rise up off the mountains in ragged curtains, the ranges glow violet, and the lakes are lovely and many. In the highlands the forests are unearthly, weighed down with lichen and long drifting fronds of pale mosses, the tree trunks and rocks mottled orange and yellow with fungus, and a tenuous mist in the hollows.

In Tasmania the best-preserved convict settlements outside of Norfolk Island can be explored. Hobart is an exquisite little city, and very old for this part of the world. On the western side of the island there is an old copper-mining region centred on Queenstown, where the ranges pulsate with colour and the rain melts the landscape into sad but vivid softness.

A boat trip along the Gordon River out of Queenstown yields the most perfect reflections I have seen anywhere in the world. The boat seems suspended at the exact centre of the universe, which goes on below in a mirror-image of the world above, and it is impossible to tell where one world ends and the other begins.

I don't mind sitting in a dry riverbed somewhere in western Queensland, either. One of the best lessons Australia can teach is to respect rain and water. Many times I have gone without a bath for days, in areas where there is no water (and no hotel). Then suddenly I have come upon a still deep pool fringed with reeds and low mottled red cliffs, and had a bath more memorable than Cleopatra's. It is mostly safe to camp out there. For me the best part of Australia is to lie snug in a sleeping bag looking up at the complete vault of a sky so clear that nebulae seem spun out of clouds, and Venus washes the land with light like a minimoon.

BY THE SEA

AN INN ON THE PACIFIC'S EDGE

Herbert Gold

Ventana means 'window' in Spanish. The Ventana at Big Sur, California, is variously called the Ventana Hotel, the Ventana Inn, and the Ventana Retreat. Lacking the quasi-mystic aura of the nearby Tassajara Zen guest facility, lacking the countercultural improvementalism of nearby Esalen, the Ventana seems to be merely a tasteful, luxurious, expensive, hot-tubbed, advanced-sybaritic, getaway, red-wood-and-cedar lodge on its magnificent site up a slope of the Santa Lucia mountains just above the bravely foaming Pacific Ocean.

Merely?

On a recent visit I discovered that the big news at Ventana was not the deer or occasional mountain bobcat visible from the open terrace of the Ventana Restaurant where I sunned myself on a bright December day (fresh mountain trout, a bottle of beer, a small salad; bliss). Since I had last been there, management had changed and the slide disasters of the winter of 1982-83 had temporarily closed the coastal highway in both directions. Big Sur became a frontier again.

While the Ventana was isolated, the temporarily unemployed staff busied themselves constructing a footpath, with lights, leading the eighth of a mile from the inn to the restaurant. Crunching along gravel that makes a sound underfoot like that of fresh snow (though of course snow is unknown here), one can contemplate one's moral priorities and one's appetite while observing the native wildflowers, the California poppies and clarkias, the wild hyacinths and lilies, the birds, the occasional deer, fox and coyote under the redwood and across the two handsome little wooden footbridges that span the creeks.

That's the big news at Ventana. The regular news is that this decade-old realized fantasy of a Hollywood millionaire still has no crowds, no conventions, no tennis courts, no golf ranges and will not have them. A handsome pool, hot tubs and walking in the woods and on the beach are the social distractions. Cable television in the rooms proves that the real world has not been fanatically rejected, but the place was designed for those who like to be lonely or alone, with a significant other or without, and cultivating both inner and outer landscapes. The external beauty is undeniable. Internal beauty is a local option.

After my lunch, I headed through the grasses up the hill, but the bobcats did not welcome my company and disappeared. I circled back to speak French with the young French student of Japanese who visited Big Sur 'for a cup of iced tea' and now works in the Ventana Store (books, handicrafts, mountain clothing). I passed the fountain and rock pool to reserve my table for dinner with the young German scholar of I-know-not-what who works in the restaurant. After this diligent tour of cosmopolitian downtown Ventana on its hill, I returned to my room for a swim, a tub, a sauna, and a nap. I had done a half-day's hard duty. There are no disco delights available. This negative, for many, implies a sweet-scented, bird-chirping, soul-restoring positive.

In the role of relentless muckraking journalist, I also chatted with Bob Bussinger, former stockbroker, then '60s protester, then Ventana waiter, now the resident manager, who uses (correctly) words like 'hideaway,' 'intrigue,' and 'place for dreaming' to describe Ventana. The original visionary developer was a co-producer of *Easy Rider*, and visitors have included Jack Nicholson, Candice Bergen, Alec Guinness, Suzanne Somers, Pat Benatar, Chevy Chase, Goldie Hawn – the group of devoted labourers in the factories of rock and film who occasionally nourish their spirits in this benevolently isolated cul-de-sac. The Big Sur coast has always attracted the slightly offbeat, who wended their way from San Francisco, Los Angeles, or Paris, but it never had a luxury hotel. It still doesn't have a typical one. Ventana was designed by unhotel experts for their own pleasure.

At one point, in the way of such matters, bankruptcy loomed. Professionals took over – but professionals who seemed to understand the nature of an unhotel – and now the place, like its cedar greyed by salt winds, has worn comfortably, perhaps even profitably, into the special world of Big Sur.

Ventana remains a discreet window toward both the Santa Lucia mountains and the Pacific Ocean, which meet at Big Sur in a rare symbiosis: foaming sea and misty mountain wilderness. With the new studios and rooms, Ventana can now accept sixty guests comfortably.

The rooms can be darkened with lattice shutters, but can be best enjoyed when thrown open to the light, in order to enjoy the details: folkwork baskets to hold kindling at the fireplaces, wicker settees, window seats piled with pillows, quilts from Nova Scotia. The feeling is country-house guest room, and that each room is the best room in the house, with terrace, view, and its own wicker furniture. The fireplaces and latticed porches of the inn, the use of congenial redwood and glass, the wicker and natural fibres, the private terraces and

Japanese baths, the choice of mountain or sea views, or sometimes both, are all, well, appropriate, as is the breakfast served with fresh fruits, pastries baked in the Ventana kitchen, honeys and varieties of baroque silence. The circumnavigating paths toward slope or beach, restaurant, or store use the setting so that both the going and the getting there are pleasures.

I enjoy many hotel lacks: the lack of video games, Muzak, convention groups, bustling lobby. Ventana is a place for reading, walking, getting acquainted or avoiding acquaintance, and yet it includes a fine restaurant with a good wine list. The windows of the restaurant are open to a fifty-mile view of the Big Sur coast. The décor is airy, simple, pure, defined by the cedar colours and fireside warmth. Tablecloths are deliberately short, to show off the wood. Lunch is best taken in the sun on the expansive apron of terrace; dinner is candlelit and slightly more formal.

The food is California mélange – fresh fish, veal, chicken, clever pastas, costing about $15 a person at lunch, perhaps $20 or $25 for dinner, not including the wine collection. Rewarding the visitor for any calorie-burning hiking he may have done or imagined, dessert pastries are exceptionally fine, light, fruit-endowed, made in the Ventana kitchen. The crew runs a tight ship as to towels, room arrangements, service, comfort. The facilities almost tempt a person to become a millionaire, so that he could afford it more often.

Breakfast, for example, deserves emphasis. Included in the room charge, it is served buffet style in the lobby in front of the fireplace – pitchers of fresh orange juice, platters of fruits, melons, strawberries, pineapples, papayas, whatever is available, a choice of pastries and hearty dark Ventana breads, coffee and herbal or non-herbal teas, honey and preserves and tapes of baroque music.

I picked up my morning *San Francisco Chronicle* at the door to my room, had my swim, refused the offer of a breakfast tray delivered to my room because I intended to spend a good part of my future returning to that buffet table. I recognized the variations on Corelli's 'La Folia.' Already I stared at the hills in deep grief because one day I would have to leave, driving the three and a half hours north along the ocean to San Francisco.

After breakfast, I strolled down to inspect the sea up close. There were one or two others poking at kelp or waiting for their appointments with the sea lions and whales. The gulls and hawks either ignored the few beach strollers or swooped close. I looked west, but, being nearsighted, could not make out the coast of Japan. I saw a horse and a lovely girl riding it bareback on the beach. They looked at me and saw a man riding a notebook.

Surf and mountains, surf creatures and mountain ones; here is an arena apart from struggle, except for the traditional one of pelicans trying to swallow a wriggling fish, which was the only creature in these parts that surely wished itself to be elsewhere.

Time for a few more laps in the pool.

Ventana is thriving again, with the coastal highway, California Route 1, finally clear both from San Francisco to the north and Los Angeles to the south. Some of Ventana's faithful clientele fly in to the Monterey Peninsula airport, about thirty-five miles away.

I found the hotel unscarred by its climatic trials. In a time of silvery rain, I enjoyed the hot tubs and sauna, the sight of the California grey whales off the coast, the hospitality of the new special rates for 'Artists' Retreat,' the exhibits of Big Sur area paintings, the fireplaces in the new rooms. Neither success nor travail nor changed management seems to alter the basic Ventana devotion to elegant ease, excellent food in a roughneck world, a place for honeymooners, good friends or lonely brooders. This is the 180-degree opposite of a busy convention or resort hotel. It is exactly the vision of a mountain seaside country inn that a 60s-style entrepreneur might create, provided he had gone to a fine university and read a little Zen. Surprisingly, it works. It ticks like a sundial.

Double rooms at Ventana (408 667 2331) begin at about $125, and a two-level suite with fireplace and ocean view costs about $250. Room rates include a large breakfast as well as wine, cheese and fruit in the afternoon.

CARMEL

Robert Lindsey

Shortly after dawn, the sun has lifted itself above the Santa Lucia Mountains, but most of the town of Carmel is still sleeping. The streets are quiet, the beach is empty, and smoke from the chimneys of a few early risers has begun to fuse with droplets of morning fog to form a luminescent blue haze in the highest branches of the pine, cypress, oak and eucalyptus trees that cover much of the town with a lush green canopy.

This is the time I treasure most. Carmel, a village of fewer than 5,000 people on the Pacific coast 130 miles south of San Francisco, is best seen on foot; the best time to see it is in the morning, walking the streets or strolling the beaches. Away from the business district, the I. Magnin store and the shops on Ocean Avenue that sell forty-dollar neckties, you walk along the edge of the continent, sprayed by the foam of breakers pounding hard against a rocky shore, along a beach as white as crushed alabaster. You observe gulls diving for their breakfast and watch the frolicking sea otters, now making a comeback after decades in which it was thought they had been hunted to extinction. You swear that some of them are looking right back at you.

Often in the morning, before the sun manages to cut through the mists, a low fog casts a grey ceiling over Carmel. Rhododendrons and begonias flourish in this climate, and there are so many gardens blooming behind fences that it's easy to think you are in a rural English village.

For more than a century, writers – Richard Henry Dana, Robert Louis Stevenson, Jack London, John Steinbeck and Robinson Jeffers among them – have sought to capture the essence of the Monterey Peninsula and to explain the hold it can exert on visitors. And for almost as long, local people have been fighting to preserve its beauty against the inroads made by commerce. The battle is still going on. Despite some setbacks, beauty, on balance, is still winning.

The early history of Carmel and the Monterey Peninsula was shaped by two groups: the Spanish padres, who came in the eighteenth century to convert the Indian population, and the hucksters and land developers who followed them a century later. In 1602, a Spanish explorer, Don Sebastian Vizcaino, sailed into the large bay that he named for the Count of Monterey. Two Carmelite priests who accompanied the expedition were granted permission to name a smaller bay and an adjacent valley for their order, and the name 'Carmelo' first appeared on Spanish maps.

In 1770, Father Junipero Serra, the best known of the Franciscan missionaries, founded Mission San Carlos Borromeo de Carmelo not far from Carmel Bay. A little more than a century later, a real-estate promoter named S. J. Duckworth, convinced that Carmel's old mission, then largely decayed, could help him sell land to Catholics, founded a church-orientated colony similar to nearby Pacific Grove, which had been developed as a retreat for Methodists. He called it Carmel City.

Duckworth subdivided the area into a grid of 40- by 100-foot lots and tried to sell them for twenty dollars apiece. A few people immigrated here, including some poor Mexican squatters whose neighbourhood was sneeringly referred to as 'Tortilla Flat,' and which later became the setting for a Steinbeck novel. But without a railway or easy access by road, the project was an economic disaster. In 1902, Duckworth's holdings were purchased by another developer who renamed the small community Carmel-by-the-Sea – still its legal name.

The projected town of Carmel-by-the-Sea was laid out on a series of hills that rolled toward the ocean. But the grid plan, which seemed on a map to be a good idea, presented grave problems when the developers tried to build straight roads over steep slopes, ravines and gullies; at many points, they just gave up, either ending the streets haphazardly or snaking them around the terrain. More significantly, the hills and gullies made it difficult to drain rainfall away from town and the merchants who had begun to open shops on Ocean Avenue, then as now the main street of Carmel, complained of flooding every winter.

The city fathers thereupon made a decision that was pivotal in the town's evolution: Hundreds of additional pine trees were planted on the slopes of Carmel in the hopes that their roots would trap some of the rainfall; and it was further ordained, in 1916, that no tree could be cut down without municipal permission. These decisions did not just solve the flooding problem. They created what Carmel officially calls an 'urban forest,' a rich woodland of trees that, starting with a stand of gnarled cypresses overlooking the beach, marches up the slopes of the town and scents the air with a pervasive aroma of pine. (The no-cutting rule is still rigidly enforced; not a few houses have oak trees as an integral part of their structure, and if ever there is a choice between moving a road or cutting a large oak, the road is moved.)

Drawn by this planned natural beauty, artists and writers began moving to Carmel en masse, and by the 1920s the town was known as an artists' colony, a reputation it has jealously preserved.

Carmel today is made up of two separate communities – the residential district and the shopping village. The two have rarely coexisted in peace; in fact, for as long as anyone can remember, Carmel residents have looked with suspicion at the shopping village, where most of the stores are run by out-of-towners. In 1926, Perry Newberry, the editor of *The Pine Cone*, the local newspaper, ran successfully for the office of city trustee with the slogan: 'Don't Boost ... If you truly want Carmel to become a boosting, hustling, wide awake lively metropolis, don't vote for Perry Newberry.'

In 1929, the city council passed a resolution declaring that 'The City of Carmel-by-the-Sea is hereby determined to be primarily, essentially and predominantly a residential city ...' In 1946, a planning commission was established to 'guard against undesirable development'; a new general plan adopted recently called for a reduction in the number of 'restaurants, bars, art galleries, real-estate firms, gift shops, jewellery stores,' and other services not designed to serve the needs of residents.

The town has managed to confine its commercial district to about twenty square blocks, although old-timers still remain apprehensive about what they regard as too much commercialism, too much catering to the appetites of tourists. They can be heard at almost any meeting of the city countil trying to erect new barricades to change. Yet most visitors to Carmel are unaware of this infighting; the truth is that the old residents have done a pretty good job of preserving what is best about Carmel. The beaches, the trees, the twisting streets and architectural eccentricities haven't changed much at all. The big difference is that more people now come to enjoy them.

The heart of the commericial district, Ocean Avenue, is divided by a median strip planted with tall pines. Along Ocean and its side streets there is one shop for every four residents, more than seventy restaurants, dozens of art galleries and jewellery stores, bakeries and antique shops, and more than fifty hotels.

The residential district is a tree-shaded architectural mélange beyond the shopping village where a modest bungalow on one of the original 40- by 100-foot lots can cost $300,000 or more. Examining the photographs of houses for sale displayed prominently in the windows of brokers on Ocean Avenue has been a pastime for visitors for decades; inspecting the 'open houses' that are listed each Thursday in the *The Pine Cone* is equally popular.

Many of the 'Houses for Sale' listings refer cryptically to a 'Carmel Charmer.' The late Fran Mauer, who probably sold more houses in town than anyone else, gave this definition: 'A Carmel Charmer is a house that puts its arms around you when you walk inside.' The classic Charmer, possibly built in the 1920s and expanded and modernized several times since then, is a cosy brown cottage with redwood siding, a pitched open-beam ceiling, a shingle roof, an obligatory fireplace and a garden. But the prevailing architectural ethic of Carmel is eclectic; virtually every style – Spanish adobe, glass-and-stone contemporary, colonial, thatched-roof cottages, gingerbread houses straight out of 'Hansel and Gretel' – is represented along the tree-shaded streets.

Then there are the beaches – the main town beach at the foot of Ocean Avenue, a mile-wide swathe of white sand, and another wide crescent of sand, almost as appealing, about half a mile to the south, where the Carmel River empties into Carmel Bay. (Because of frequent riptides, swimmers are warned to be extra cautious at the Carmel River Beach.) The heavy storms of recent winters have left their scars, but some of the many tons of sand taken away by the storms have now been swept back by the tides.

Children, surfers, and dogs (which have the run of the beach without a leash) brave the churning surf the year round; others should take note that the water tends to be chilly except on the hotter days of summer. But even on the most crowded weekends (with the possible exception of the Fourth of July weekend, Carmel's summer peak) it is possible to find a quiet spot of your own in which to sunbathe, read a book, or daydream as you watch the waves roll in.

Carmel is what you make of it, but perhaps more than anything it is a place for romance, which seems to thrive against its backdrop of cypress trees, sunsets, and quaint buildings. Not long ago, I was passing the Church of the Wayfarer when a bridal party emerged in a profusion of flowers and happiness. 'She didn't want to get married anyplace else,' the maid of honour told a friend. 'She said she and Steve fell in love here and that her grandmother and her mother and all of her sisters were married in this church.'

Even more recently, I went for a walk on Scenic Drive, the twisting, promenade-like road guarded by cypresses, set on a bluff above the two beaches. I passed the square tower of Tor House, the stone house that Robinson Jeffers built by hand in 1918-1919, and nearby, a Frank Lloyd Wright house on the edge of the bay. The sky sparkled above the blue and green water and, in the distance, the rocky shore at Point Lobos and the Santa Lucias.

As I tried to soak up the beauty, I spotted a couple in their thirties walking along the beach hand in hand, their young son a few steps behind them. Carmel, I reflected once again, is a lovely place for romance.

SMALL HOTELS

Small, charming hotels abound. Among the best are **Vagabond's House Inn** (408 624 7738; double rooms are about $65-$85); **Lobos Lodge** (408 624 3874; $75-$85); **Normandy Inn** (408 624 3825; $75); and the **Sundial Lodge** (408 624 8578; $60-$70).

The **Pine Inn** on Ocean Avenue (408 624 3851; $50-$110) is reminiscent of an old hotel in the English countryside. The conveniently located **La Playa Hotel** (408 624 6476; $95-$115) has recently been extensively remodelled. The **Highlands Inn** (408 624 3801), which cascades down the slopes of a hill overlooking the Pacific a few miles south of Carmel, has also been remodelled extensively, although in the remodelling it has lost some of its old charm. Rates for two at the Highlands Inn, including two meals daily, are $135-$250.

Reserve early; accommodations are often difficult to find, especially on weekends. The Carmel Business Association, P.O. Box 4444, Carmel-by-the-Sea, Calif. 93921 (408 624 2522), can supply you with a complete list of hotels and motels.

INTIMATE DINING

Scores of restaurants, often tucked away on side streets and in lofts, offer a wide range of culinary styles. Some of the more interesting, where dinner for two, with wine, generally costs around $40 to $50, are:

Shabu-Shabu (408 625 2828), in the basement of the Carmel Plaza at Ocean Avenue and Seventh Street, a reconstruction of a small Japanese inn, specializing in dishes prepared before you on a hot plate.

Casanova (408 625 0501, no reservations accepted), on Fifth Street between San Carlos and Mission, which serves such Continental specialities as *cannelloni calabrese* and *involtini di petti di pollo* on an outdoor terrace (lunch here is a bargain, about $20 for two, with a large glass of wine).

The **Mission Ranch** (408 624 3824), 26270 Dolores, a tradition for decades, with a wide range of simple beef and seafood served in generous quantities against a backdrop of grazing cattle and a view of the Pacific. Dinner for two is about $30, with a large carafe of good California wine.

French restaurants include **La Bohème** (408 624 7500, no reservations), a bistro at Dolores and Seventh with a different three-course menu nightly, and **L'Escargo,** Mission and Fourth (408 624 4914), where the chicken with truffles, fresh mussels, and local salmon are recommended.

SHOPPING THE VILLAGE

Almost every visitor buys something at the **Dansk** factory outlet store at the corner of Ocean Avenue and San Carlos (they'll pack and ship the items, dicounted by as much as 50 per cent.). Many male visitors also take home one of the silk neckties made locally by the **Robert Talbott** company, which has two shops on Ocean Avenue.

The side streets off Ocean Avenue are rife with art galleries. The **Carmel Art Association,** on Dolores Street between Fifth and Sixth, is owned by local artists and is a good place to sample their work. **Luciano's Antiques,** on San Carlos Street between Fifth and Sixth avenues, is one of more than a dozen first-rate antique shops.

SAMPLING THE VARIED WORLDS
OF JAMAICA

Barbara Crossette

What's a dedicated traveller to do about the Caribbean? The restless breed of holidaymaker who needs more than a beach, a bar, and a book – the one who likes to move around, change scenes, discover things, and kibitz with strangers – hears boredom and claustrophobia alarms ringing in the names of little islands. Give us sun and sea, of course, but also give us space and choice, a few open roads, and a couple of general stores that don't stock suntan oil, postcards or pastel T-shirts.

There are ways, usually expensive, to avoid regimented resort life, like chartering a yacht to island hop or flying off on one's own to the bigger islands, looking for destinations or hotels not on the package circuit. Over the years we've tried freelancing our way around a number of larger islands, with mixed success. Cuba was off limits, and Trinidad (even with Tobago thrown in) was mostly a scruffy disappointment. Puerto Rico would have been fine, if muggers hadn't been stalking some of the loveliest secluded spots. Haiti was fascinating, if sad. And Jamaica – well, Jamaica had British cooking and a mood, people said, that was inhospitable. We never really gave it a chance. Then a writing assignment provided an excuse to travel the length and breadth of Jamaica, and the island turned out to be a happy surprise. Jamaica, the Caribbean's third-largest island (144 miles long and more than 50 miles wide), has a variety of terrain: savannas and marshlands; small coves and long, empty beaches; rivers and waterfalls, and some of the highest (7,400 feet) and coolest mountains of any island. It also has a wide variety of places to stay, ranging from campsites, private homes and small inns to fully staffed villas, golf clubs and glitzy hotels with nonstop activities.

Jamaica is a tropical island where one can hike, climb, camp, ride horseback, or canoe, as well as enjoy the usual water sports. There is city life and village life and lively cracker-barrel politics; there is art and history. There are even horse races. And just about all of it is accessible by plane, train, or good, uncrowded roads.

Because of the island's size, and the distance between its major resort centres, each town has developed its own character and attracted its own following. Port Antonio, on the east coast, is described by its devotees as a quiet, classier, and less developed village than the others. Negril, on the northwest coast, is also largely undeveloped, but has a more free-and-easy air about it: buff bathing, mushroom tea – that kind of thing. In between are the better-known tourist centres at Montego Bay, Runaway Bay, and Ocho Rios. The distances that isolate character as they separate these towns from one another, from the mountainous interior or from the cities of Kingston and Spanish Town in the south, are not large enough, however, to prevent a visitor based in one area from sampling one or more of the others.

What makes Jamaica especially attractive is the fact that most tastes and budgets can be met, and regardless of what one pays everyone can sample almost all of the island's pleasures (its many private beaches are an unhappy exception). We encountered Americans who had paid barely $300 for a week's stay, including air fare, and were using their no-frills hotels mostly as places to sleep. There were other visitors who had paid three or four times more than that for a week of pampered service, dress-up dinners and a place to read, undisturbed, by the sea.

After a few days it becomes apparent to a first-time visitor that there are also a few intangibles that contribute to the appeal of this country-size island. One of them is the innkeeping tradition, which goes back into the prejet days – in some places back to the 1920s and '30s, when the rich and titled and talented began to arrive from London and New York for 'the season.' Jamaica became the haunt of Noel Coward, Cole Porter, and Dorothy and Oscar Hammerstein II, among others. Those who did not have winter homes needed accommodations with the space and service required to entertain.

Now, Jamaica and those who come to it are very different, but an evening walk through the gentle grounds of the thirty-year-old Jamaica Inn in Ocho Rios, for example, rewards them with timeless vignettes: a waiter laying the table for a private dinner on a guest's book-strewn veranda, or the soft laughter of couples at cards. Years rather than yards separate the old Jamaica from the reggae discos up the road.

Jamaicans wrestle with their past. To many the grace and elegance of the old resorts are no more than reminders of a colonial age in which the Jamaican's lot was servility, not comfort. Others say they prefer the older brand of tourism, in which Europeans and Americans came and stayed and had a stake in Jamaica, to the newer variety of visitors who careen through their towns in tourist buses taking pictures of people trying to live their daily lives. In the 1970s suppressed resentments fuelled by the black power movement and a pro-Cuban, anti-American Government that encouraged independence of spirit and national identity, spilled into hostility and sometimes violence. As a result, the island's reputation plunged, and its tourist industry collapsed.

The descent, though swift, was short-lived, and visitors are returning to Jamaica, now under a new Government, at an increase of 20 per cent or more a year, and building seems to be going on around every resort centre. To someone new to the island, it is hard to imagine that this could ever have been considered a hostile and dangerous place, and many Jamaicans and foreigners alike say the fears that led people to sell homes and abandon holiday hotels were exaggerated. From one end of the island to another, my husband and I travelled without hotel reservations, making untouristy demands on overworked telephone operators and desk clerks, and encountered nothing but helpful, efficient people. 'We hope you'll come back' was the common farewell.

'I insist the best way to see Jamaica is by road,' an American living in Kingston told me when I suggested that it might be better to travel by air to cover as much as possible in just over a week on the island. It was good advice. We figured the rental car cost about $40 a day, including petrol, insurance and incidentals. For only a few dollars a day, we could have travelled by small local buses – we saw tourists doing that, at least along the coastal roads. On winding mountain roads, however, greenhorn riders would need strong nerves and stomachs to survive those lurching vans.

Most visitors land at Montego Bay and stay along the north coast, and fail to visit the much-maligned capital city of **Kingston**, where about a third of Jamaica's 2.5 million people live, many of them in poverty. But Jamaica's leaders have big plans for Kingston, the largest English-speaking city in the Caribbean and a tropical port that Prime Minister Edward P. G. Seaga would like to restore as Savannah, Georgia, has been restored. Mr. Seaga would also like to re-create, Williamsburg style, the old city of Port Royal, 'the wickedest city in Christendom' in the seventeenth century, which paid for its sins in a 1692 earthquake that dropped half of it into the sea from its perch on a spit of land.

Kingston's waterfront redevelopment area already has a large craft market and a National Gallery, with a collection spanning the history of Jamaican art. Among the works are sculptures of Edna Manley, the mother of former Prime Minister Michael Manley and a major figure in the development of art education in the country. Visiting collections of Caribbean and Latin American art are also exhibited. A display of objects and documents from the island's natural and political history can be seen at the Institute of Jamaica, also near the harbour. On the other side of town are Devon House, a nineteenth century mansion;

Hope Botanical Gardens and the Mona campus of the University of the West Indies, which has a well-stocked bookshop and a creative arts centre, both open to the public.

Twelve miles from Kingston is **Spanish Town**, the capital of Jamaica under Spanish occupation in the sixteenth century and under British rule until 1872. The Georgian town square, with its ethnographic and archaeological musuem, and the nearby cathedral (one of the oldest in the Caribbean) are worth seeing. A good road through hills, cultivated valleys, and a four-mile gorge called Fern Gully connects Kingston and Spanish Town with Ocho Rios in less than two hours.

West from Spanish Town, along another good highway, the visitor can drive in about the same time to **Mandeville**, a mountain town known for its sprawling Saturday market, its golf course, and its wildlife sanctuary at Marshall's Pen, with a 200-year-old Great House, the centre of plantation life. Mandeville has two hotels, neither of which are geared for holidaymakers. But one of them, the Hotel Astra, is fine for a lunch stop or overnight stay. In its Revival Pub, with paintings of revival cult rituals, visitors are reminded of another Jamaica, one where the hills are full of ghost stories. While the revival cults – mixtures of Christian and African beliefs and rituals – are said to be stronger in the cities, the sense of spiritual Jamaica strikes the visitor more clearly in its rural setting. In the mountains to the northwest of Mandeville, as well as in other rural areas, the Government's Memory Bank, an oral history project, is collecting tales along with traditional utensils, both of which link contemporary Jamaica to the African past.

The Government, past and present, has also been encouraging the production of traditional crafts for sale. Prime Minister Seaga says the best craftspeople are members of the Rastafarian movement, whose wood sculptures can be found for sale in the tourist centres along the north coast. To the inexpert eye, the wood carvers' stalls at Dunn's River Falls near Ocho Rios offered more interesting and imaginative pieces than those along the commercial strip running through the town centre. At Harmony Hall, also near Ocho Rios, a gingerbread-laced plantation house has been turned into a modest centre for the exhibition and sale of Jamaican paintings and crafts. For serious collectors, Kingston has a number of private galleries. Jamaican art does not reach the Haitian level, but it is developing, diversifing and drawing on a wide range of themes.

The north coast has its share of history as well as crafts and beaches. At St. Ann's Bay is the birthplace of Marcus Garvey, a Jamaican national hero who did much to foster black self-awareness in New York half a century ago. Nearby, at Nine Miles, is the grave of Bob

Marley, the reggae star who became a cultural figure of importance to a generation of Afro-Caribbeans. At Runaway Bay, slaves once escaped from plantation life. Seville Nueva was the first Spanish settlement on the island; Discovery Bay was where Christopher Columbus landed in 1494.

Many Jamaicans bemoan the development of the north coast, and send a stranger up there with intimations of Condado or Cancún. Happily, one discovers miles of open shorefront and a choice of places to stay outside the unattractive and crowded town of Ocho Rios or the city of Montego Bay, now Jamaica's second-largest population centre.

'So what was your favourite place?' people asked when we returned to Kingston from our hopscotch trip around Jamaica. 'Where will you go when you come back?'

The answer was easy: 'Negril.'

Negril is the kind of place where the people are so few and the beach so long (four or seven miles, depending on whether you count one part of it or more) that you can paddle around in your private sea for an hour or two without encountering anyone. With the exception of a walled-up development aptly called Hedonism II, Negril's hotels seem to attract people who like to manage on their own and who are from time to time marginally eccentric. A German gymnast limbered up on the beach in the morning. A cluster of Philadelphians discussed opera in the afternoon. One man brought his goggles and sun lotion to the beach every day in a leather attaché case.

In Negril a visitor doesn't feel cut off and fenced out from the rest of Jamaica; both residents and hotel guests stroll the beaches and swim in the long stretch of shallow sea. At day's end only fearless tropical fish come between you and the burst of the setting sun.

There are several attractive places to stay along the Negril beach front that are open all or most of the year. The Coconut Grove is all apartments, the Charela is a stylish ten-room inn. We chose the Sundowner, a twenty-six-room hotel presided over by a portly European who has achieved what we had begun to think was an impossible dream: the creation of a good kitchen in Jamaica. (Acquaintances report that the food is even better at the Charela.) Meals were expensive, as they seemed to be everywhere in the island's hotels and restaurants – a New York-style coffee-shop breakfast cost $8 each at the Sundowner. But meals there were on the whole very good.

One dinner ($18 fixed price) offered several imaginative entrées; we enjoyed a poached grouper with caper sauce and pork joint with a spicy gravy. The cold cucumber soup was exceptional.

Jamaican cuisine remains limited, with only a few of the touches that mark the regional cooking of the French islands (and Grenada). The pepper pot, a highly seasoned, thick calaloo soup, was good in most places, but goat or lamb curry was often tough and not well seasoned.

One of Jamaica's best-loved dishes is ackee and saltfish, a combination of cooked fruit – from a tree brought over from Africa in the eighteenth century – and salted cod, imported from northern waters. The blend of textures and flavours deserves the description 'unique'.

Fresh fruits abound and are sold at hundreds of small roadside stands. Along the south coast, fish vendors appeared at almost every turn of the road. For the visitor with kitchen facilities, it would be easy to gather materials for home cooking.

At the Hotel Astra in Mandeville, lunch (less than $10 for two) included a big helping of barbecued chicken and French fries and a couple of rounds of Red Stripe, a good local beer. It and a variety of rums are the island's main drinks.

In Kingston, a visitor has a choice of restaurants outside the hotels. A New Yorker living there suggested a few that had Jamaican settings. One was the Blue Mountain Inn, at the edge of town in the foothills of the island's best-known range (famous for its coffee). The menu was vaguely European, with meals costing up to $25 a person. The setting, however, is an old plantation house built along a riverbank.

In town the informal Hot Pot, near the major hotels and at the other end of the price range, offers local dishes for a few dollars a serving. Visitors also enjoy the terrace café at Devon House, where light drinks and refreshments are served in a setting of plants and white wicker.

For a taste of good Jamaican street food, ask for the best vendor of jerked pork or chicken: marinated, highly seasoned meat cooked over coals (traditionally in a pit with wood strips from the pimento tree for added flavour) and served with a hard-dough bread known as bammie. So popular are these dishes – usually cooked in the evening in an old metal drum turned on its side – that among the art on display at Harmony Hall is a sculpture of a drum-chicken vendor and his brightly painted wagon with its slogan: 'Season' right to de bone.'

SOME TIPS FOR THE TRAVELLER
Getting There
Air Jamaica, American, Pan American, Eastern, and Air Florida are among the airlines flying from New York or Miami to Jamaica's two international airports, at Kingston and Montego Bay. High-season economy round-trip fare is about $450 from New York to Montego Bay. Fares may be considerably lower at other times of year and are always lower when sold in combination with ground arrangements. Packages including air fare, hotel, and ground transportation start at about $389 and range as high as $2,000 for seven nights during the high season, lower from the end of April to December 15. Three-night and two-week packages are also offered by some hotels.

Where to Stay

Jamaica has nearly 150 hotels. In Ocho Rios they include the nineteen-room **Hibiscus Lodge,** Box 52, Ocho Rios (809 974 2676), with high-season rates of about $45 a night for one person and $57 for two in a room without meals. At the upper end of the scale is the spacious, secluded **Jamaica Inn**, Box 1, Ocho Rios (809 974 2514), with rates ranging from $170 for one to $360 for two with three meals. There are at least ten other hotels in the Ocho Rios area, including the **Turtle Beach Apartment Hotel**, Box 73, Ocho Rios (809 974 2801), near the centre of town. High-season rates there range from $80 to $100 a night without meals. East of Ocho Rios, near the harbour town of Port Maria, is the **Casa Maria**, Box 10, Port Maria St. Mary (809 994 2323), a quiet inn on a hill overlooking the sea but without a beach. Rooms without meals are $30 to $40; with meals, $45 to $70. In Runaway Bay, the **Silver Spray Resort**, Box 16, Runaway Bay (809 973 3413), a small seafront inn, appeals to readers and writers more than water-sports fans; the beach is tiny. Rooms range from $50 to $75 without meals, $75 to $125 with meals. The **Eaton Hall Great House**, Box 112, Runaway Bay (809 973 3404), is new despite its name, with rooms from $119 to $258 with meals.

Negril's hotels include the **Charela Inn**, Box 33, Negril (809 957 4277), with rooms from $100 for one to $150 for two with two meals a day. **Coconut Grove**, Box 12, Negril (809 957 4277), has attractive apartments overlooking the beach for $140 to $195, including two meals. **The Sundowner**, Box 5, Negril (809 957 4225), has rooms ranging from $85 for one to $145 for two with two meals. In Mandeville, **Hotel Astra**, 62 Ward Avenue (Box 60), Mandeville (809 962 3265; 809 962 3377), divides its rooms into ordinary, deluxe, and superior, with prices ranging from $40 to $85; no meals included.

In Kingston, the **Courtleigh**, 31 Trafalgar Road, Kingston 10 (809 926 8174), is quieter, smaller, and offers better service than the more over-worked Pegasus and other larger hotels. The Courtleigh's rates range from $70 for one to $90 for two. Rates are considerably lower – sometimes more than half the high-season rate – from late April to mid-December. All the above hotels offer private baths.

Currency and Documents

Visitors are required to pay hotel bills in foreign currency, but restaurant bills are usually paid in Jamaican currency. A recent devaluation has not significantly reduced prices, except for locally produced goods. Jamaican dollars may not be brought into or taken out of the country. Visitors from the United States and Canada do not need passports, but they must carry proof of citizenship or residency.

For more information on hotels, inns, and campsites, contact the Jamaica Tourist Board, 866 Second Avenue, New York, N.Y. 10017 (212 688 7650). For information on cottages and villas, contact the Jamaica Association of Villas and Apartments, 200 Park Avenue, Suite 229, New York, N.Y. 10166 (212 986 4317). Information is also available from Villas and Apartments Abroad, 19 East 49th Street, New York, N.Y. 10017 (212 759 1025).

SLOWING THE PACE IN BARBADOS

Flora Lewis

It's easy to understand why President and Mrs. Reagan picked Bellerive, the home of their old Hollywood friend Claudette Colbert, for their Barbados holiday several years ago. It is a cheerful, lovely house by the sea, not grandiose but informal and restful, and Miss Colbert is as beautiful, charming, and zestful at more than 80 as ever she was in her stardom.

The Reagans didn't actually stay with Miss Colbert. There are other houses on each side of Bellerive, separated only by hedges, and neither the narrow highway at the back nor the sea at the front can be blocked off to provide security. Instead, a house with a wall around it in the middle of the golf course was rented for the President and Mrs. Reagan but presumably they spent much of their time at the Colbert house.

I know there is a nice little beach below the garden and that the sea is calm and transparent because Barbados happens to be my favourite island, the place I go every year to get off the world. It really works. Somehow time slows down there. The biggest problems are about wangling fresh fish from a fisherman, about drains that have choked up again, or about which dinner guests will get along with the other guests. These concerns become all-absorbing and the world's problems seem too far away to be pressing.

The main question each morning is whether it's going to be another 'brochure day,' sparkling with golden sun dapples dancing on a sea of many colours: turquoise, lime, mauve, periwinkle, purple, but never flat blue. Sometimes it isn't. A storm far beyond the horizon may churn up the water and dull the sky, or the regular but brief and warm showers may turn into cloudbursts and last long enough to spoil outdoor plans, but those days are exceptions, surprising interruptions in the lolling, soporific cycle of days that pass so gently you forget their names.

Of course, that's the visitor's Barbados. People work there, and bustle about the streets of Bridgetown, the capital, and fret about their troubles. But it is hard to understand how they manage. It isn't an atmosphere for getting things done, and, in fact, a lot of things don't get done – or only very gradually. That doesn't matter. Impatience melts away and the pleasure of there being nothing to hurry about makes the pace an asset.

At one time, I was thinking far ahead of retirement and planning to spend most of the year in Barbados. Vegetating isn't so attractive as a full-time prospect. So I began to think how I could possibly get any work squeezed between the routine of swimming and tennis and gossip on the terrace and slow, friendly meals, and irresistible hours of just watching – chameleons courting on a branch, hummingbirds gorging the hibiscus, clouds scurrying off to the horizon. The sky is almost never empty and by looking to the east you can always tell whether it's going to rain in twenty minutes or whether a shower will soon stop. The trade winds that freshen what otherwise would be humid air bring all the weather from the Atlantic over the choppy green hilltops down to the Caribbean side of the island.

The solution I imagined to escaping these distractions would have involved building a special room. It would have unbroken walls above head level, with windows only under the roof to let in light but keep out the view. It would be air-conditioned, shut off from the balmy open warmth. It would be panelled with books and probably furnished darkly, leather or something tweedy. It would have to be a distinctly northern room that shut out ease and let worldly cares back in.

It was never built, so there's still no choice for me but dawdling in Barbados. I also used to think of lacing my visits with jaunts to other islands, by air or in the little boats that ply between them. I'm still curious to see more of the others, but it has never happened, because once I arrive in Barbados, I never want to leave until I simply have to.

Why this love affair? Let me count the ways. The west coast of Barbados which is the main tourist area – locally called the gold coast for its luxury – has been built up a lot in recent years, but it still isn't crowded and the hotels aren't too big, mostly two stories around a garden. The beaches are a series of little bays and inlets, cut off by rocks or coral reefs, so there is room for privacy; no Miami Beach scenes.

The island is small, 166 square miles in all, but deliciously varied. The roads are so narrow, winding between the cane fields or down the coast, that it takes a long time to go a few miles, and this turns almost any little journey into a major excursion. There are some big, empty beaches on the south and Atlantic coasts, fringed with palms and manchineals, where picknickers are almost sure to be alone.

Swimming is risky on the Atlantic side. Foaming breakers crash with the power to dash the unwary on the sharp reefs. But there is a wild, windy ocean aspect that makes a drastic change from the buoyant, sedate waters made for snorkelling or long swimming promenades along the Caribbean shore. There is something therapeutic in the west coast water. Accident victims and people with arthritis recover more quickly paddling in it, but the Atlantic side is bracing.

Most of the middle of the island is made up of cane fields climbing up and down the hills. Ramshackle villages dot the roadside, and from time to time there is a plantation house, surrounded by verandas and often filled with old mahogany and silver from England.

The foresight of the late Ronald Tree, who was largely responsible for developing the west coast for tourism, provided a jungly enclave of what Barbados must have looked like before the first settlers came in the seventeenth century. It's a national park called Welshman's Gully, a cool dark ramble through tropical plants, inhabited only by monkeys (brought in long ago by sailors) and birds who have their own touring transportation. Iris Bannocke's Andromeda is a different kind of tropical garden, with an immense variety of hot-climate plants and orchids. If it will grow in Barbados, Mrs. Bannocke grows it.

Mr. Tree was a loving developer – as concerned for the island as for its visitors, and that is the spirit in which museums, parks, festivals and pageants flourish. Bajans, the local elision of Barbadian, are proud of their homeland and their history and it makes them hospitable.

That is the most special part. Bajans are different from other West Indians. They seem more friendly, more self-respecting, less resentful, easier to mingle among. They are proud of that, too, and I've often asked them how they account for it. Everybody has a different answer, so I guess no one knows, but there are particularities.

When the first British settlers came, refugees from wars at home, there were Carib Indian relics but the island was uninhabited. It never changed hands, escaping the fighting and conquest to which almost all the other islands were subjected. Another explanation is that slavers, who brought Africans to the islands at different times, brought them from different West African tribes. Yet another is that, being the easternmost island, Barbados was the first stop for the slave ships and its planters picked the best human specimens.

At first, the island was settled only by small British farmers. Then some spies stole the secret of plantation sugarcane from the Portuguese in Brazil, and planters set out to make their fortunes. That is why they imported slaves, and every available inch of arable land was put to sugar. But unlike some other islands, the planters generally stayed to supervise their lands, and so they developed schools – at first for their own children, later for everybody.

As a result, Barbados today has near to complete literacy, a vigorous school system and strong churches, important to the social tone. One of its most attractive sights is the groups of children going to school in the morning and coming home along the roads in the afternoons. They are all in crisp, clean uniforms of assorted colours, healthy looking and obviously well cared for. Even in the poorest villages, one doesn't see a neglected child.

But maybe all this together doesn't explain why Bajans are Bajans. They simply are, not angels at all and perhaps no better than others, but generally agreeable.

For people who want to do things, there are all the usual water sports, horses to ride, polo matches to watch, golf, tennis, attractive restaurants (though with food no one can boast about), steel bands, nightclubs and so on. I suppose other islands offer the same. All I want to do there is nothing, and for me Barbados is the ideal place for it.

DOWN-TO-EARTH CREOLE COOKING

Craig Claiborne

In the last two decades there has been a gastronomic revolution in the Caribbean. When I first visited Martinique nearly two decades ago I wanted to taste the native cuisine, the unadulterated version of what I presumed to be Caribbean cooking, dishes made with conch (known locally as lambi), stuffed land crabs, cod fritters or beignets known as accra, fried or otherwise cooked oursins (sea urchins), and the powerful but delicious sauce known as sauce chien, which translates inelegantly as dog sauce and is made with oil, chopped onions, and peppers. When I asked for these things, the chefs said they were not for my palate, and I wound up with spurious versions of this food or, more often, simple platters of sautéed or grilled fish, steamed or grilled langouste (the clawless Caribbean version of lobster), or food that was generally bastard French.

When I arrived recently in Guadeloupe I discovered that there are now scores of chefs who proudly serve honest-to-their-roots cooking to the delight of visitors.

I find Creole cooking, as prepared in Caribbean kitchens, imaginative, appealing, and possessed of a unique character. It is not the Creole cooking of the American South but a blend of seasonings and flavours that are wholly of the region.

GUADELOUPE

One of the best examples of this cooking is the admirable preparations that emanate from the kitchen of a small, neat, and altogether charming establishment in the heart of Pointe-à-Pitre, a beguilingly but modestly decorated place known as **La Canne à Sucre.**

La Canne à Sucre (The Sugar Cane) at 17 rue Henri IV is a restaurant without artifice: a small room with eight or so tables, one wall covered with a large mirror, the other walls covered with engravings of native scenes. The tables are covered with linen, imported silver that resembles Christofle sterling and small flower arrangements.

The heart of the place is the kitchen, out of which came a heartening, appealing array of good things: a good-bodied fish soup with a tomato base, served with toasted croûtons; a fine sauce rouille, with its base of mayonnaise and garlic; and a small serving of accra, the tiny, airlike, crisp, crunchy fritters not made with salt cod but rather with malanga (a yamlike vegetable) and a giromon (a kind of pumpkin).

There were stuffed land crab (but served not in a crab shell as one might have hoped but in an individual ramekin), and an extraordinary, delicious dish of finely chopped andouillettes (not the sausage so famed in France but more like a very delicate version of the chitterlings of the American South). The andouillettes were inspired, but at the suggestion of my host we gave them added zest with a squeeze of lime and a gentle rubbing of a highly thermal yellow chilli pepper. The herring à la Creole made with chopped, smoked herring with lime and other seasonings was a masterful invention.

The main courses included a delectable dish of grilled lemon chicken smothered with onion rings and a brilliantly put-together dish of poached grouper with fresh mushroom sauce. The desserts were also inspired: a well-made coconut custard and a too-good-to-be-true sherbet of corrossol, little known at home; it translates as soursop, a dark green knobbly fruit with edible pulp. The meal was prefaced with a small glass of rum punch (native white rum, lime wedge, and sugar), and the wine of the meal was a Morgon, 1979.

All dishes at La Canne à Sucre are à la carte. The average price of a meal for one with wine is $25. Telephone: 82 10 19. La Canne à Sucre is closed Saturdays for lunch and all day Sunday. Visa and American Express cards accepted. Comfortably cool.

There is a woman in Guadeloupe who is referred to as the high priestess of Creole cooking. Her name is Violetta Chaville and her domain is a fairly large and festive restaurant called **La Créole,** situated on the edge of the town of Gosier en route to Ste. Anne. It has a sunny, friendly ambience with one of the walls studded with official documents that testify to Mme. Chaville's eminence.

Among her creations were an assortment of traditional appetizers including the ubiquitous fritters of salt cod, crisp and golden and known as *accras de morue*. There was also a well-made serving of stuffed land crab, called *crabes farcis*, and the classic blood sausage known both in France and the Caribbean as boudin, the difference being that in the island the sausage is a bit spicier (to my regret I find that most Creole boudins have had their spiciness toned down in deference to the average visitor's taste).

The most laudable offering from the Chaville kitchen was a casserole of court-bouillon, almost wholly different from the basic court-bouillon of the French kitchen where it is simply a herb-flavoured broth in which foods are cooked. In the Caribbean, it is a platter of fish simmered in a hearty, well-seasoned soup containing tomatoes, bay leaf, and other spices. The meal came with an abundance of rice. For dessert we had a dish of sliced pineapple and pistachio ice cream, undoubtedly an import. With the meal we had sipped a bottle of Muscadet. I found Chez Violetta almost the equal of but not superior to La Canne à Sucre.

All dishes at La Créole are à la carte. The average cost of a meal for one with wine is $18. Service included. Credit cards not accepted. The restaurant is open daily for lunch and dinner except Sunday and holidays. Telephone: 84 10 34.

On rare occasions I have tasted foods that have catapulted my taste buds into a state of ecstasy and my appetite into a feeling of gluttony. It happened in Guadeloupe in a fairly stylish establishment called **La Plantation**. The dish will undoubtedly seem odd to most Americans. It was a plate of preserved goose giblets, served luke-warm and sliced on salad greens with morsels of walnuts and cubes of toasted bread with a sauce made with hazelnut oil and raspberry vinegar combined by the chef-owner in such proportions as to border on wizardry. This is not a Creole creation but an audaciously good regional classic from France, where I had sampled it but never savoured it with such unbridled enthusiasm.

The dish appears on the menus of several French restaurants in the Caribbean, served as an appetizer. It engendered in me an enthusiasm such as to render anticlimactic any dish that might follow it. But the rest of the meal remained at a high level. A companion dined on a fine first course of tender, sliced smoked breast of goose (both the giblets and the goose breasts were French imports), which have the best qualities of an excellent prosciutto. Other dishes were good but less than ethereal: curried turtle soup, which lacked the morsels of turtle meat that could have given it authenticity, and an interesting but overly thickened coconut soup.

The main courses included excellent meaty jumbo crawfish in the shell, served in a tasty brown court-bouillon, and a scallop of veal, sautéed to a fine point and served with shrimp tails as a garnish. The dessert was a masterfully made parfait with a fine topping of chopped praline and chocolate sauce, which was a touch grainy. A good bottle of Riesling accompanied the meal.

La Plantation is in Gosier at the Bas-du-Fort Marina, which resembles an American shopping centre on the water. The restaurant is a bit understaffed and ill organized, but it has pleasant décor and decent piped-in music.

All dishes are à la carte. The average cost of a meal for one with wine is about $30. The restaurant is closed on Sunday and holidays. Most credit cards accepted. Service not included. Telephone 82 39 63.

A dinner at **La Chaubette** on the Route de la Riviera in Gosier, a ten-minute ride outside Pointe-à-Pitre, while not quite so inordinately good and served in less dignified surroundings, was, nonetheless, considerably appealing. The restaurant resembles a large, neat, but not too fancy roadhouse, with red print tablecloths and bamboo curtains. The service is polite but hesitant.

The name derives from a tiny clam that lives in Caribbean waters, and our meal began with an excellent clear soup made with these clams, a touch of cloves, sprigs of heart of celery, lemon juice, and strands of vermicelli. We feasted on an excellent serving of homemade *tête de porc maison* (hog's head cheese with a chopped onion vinaigrette), more stuffed crabs, served in the shell, and stuffed conch served in an oyster shell, all of it exceedingly tasty, although the crab and conch preparations seemed a bit overly breaded and lukewarm. We dined on tender grilled turtle steak, which is a good deal like beef in flavour and texture. It was served with lemon butter and parsley. We also sampled a first-rate ragout of octopus braised in a light tomato sauce. As a side dish we were served a purée of that fine Caribbean vegetable known as christophene (tropical squash). With the meal we had a bottle of Beaujolais-Villages. For dessert we had native bananas sugared and served hot, flaming with rum.

All dishes at La Chaubette are à la carte. The average cost of a meal for one with wine is about $20. Credit cards not accepted. Telephone: 84 14 29. Closed Sundays and in October. No air-conditioning.

IN MARTINIQUE:
CREOLE CUISINE WITH FLAIR

Craig Claiborne

I believe that the most celebrated Creole dish in the Caribbean is stuffed crab, and I also believe that one only rarely comes across a genuinely satisfying version of that dish. Most Caribbean cooks use too much breading and, for my taste, too little spice. In my travels about the Caribbean, I have kept account of the best dishes in any single category. I can therefore say without hesitation that not only the finest stuffed crab but also the finest avocado and langouste salad that I have sampled in those islands were served at the **Chateaubriand Restaurant** of the Hotel Bakoua Beach in Pointe du Bout, Martinique. The salad was prepared with a masterly blend of oil and lime with cubes of langouste and avocado, bits of the coral of the langouste, tomato, onion and parsley.

My main course was grilled carp with a refined version of the Caribbean sauce, known as sauce chien. Capers gave a distinctly French accent to the usual combination of oil, hot peppers, and lime juice. The fish was cooked to perfection – which is to say it was not overcooked. Grilled pork chops with a sauce charcutière, in this case a mustardy brown sauce with a touch of cream, were also exceedingly good. The meal ended with bananas flamed with rum. We sipped a white Macon-Villages with dinner.

The menu at Chateaubriand is extensive. Expect to pay about $17.50 for a meal for one with wine. Lunch at the Hotel Bakoua is served in the snack bar, where the menu is also a long one. Credit cards accepted. Telephone: 73 62 02.

I had another pair of stuffed crabs that almost fulfilled my expectations of the dish at a restaurant in Fort-de-France known as **La Grand' Voile**, which translates as the Big Sail. It is on the harbour and is often referred to as '*le restaurant le plus chic*,' the most stylish restaurant on the island. To me it certainly is. There is a handsome enclosed dining area as well as a terrace with views of windjammers, cruise ships, yachts, and single-masted and two-masted schooners. The service is uncommonly attentive and polite, and the food is excellent, a blend of Creole and French, with such items as foie gras, caviar, smoked salmon, langouste américaine, langouste thermidor, and various beef and veal dishes.

I had a light lunch there one day with a friend. One first course was the stuffed crabs – properly meaty, spicy, and served almost piping hot from the oven. The other, half an avocado garnished with large and small whole, tender shrimp, was a delight. We followed them up with a traditional French dish, veal scallops with a cream and morel sauce, and a Creole dish, grilled redfish with sauce piquante. The veal was good, but its sauce was thickened with a bit too much flour. With it we drank a Tavel rosé, 1979.

The desserts were a good coffee ice cream, served in a silver goblet with coffee poured over it and topped with whipped cream, and a first-rate lemon sherbet presented inside a frozen, hollowed-out lemon. All was delectable except the purported whipped cream, which tasted like it came from a spray can.

Two complete prix fixe menus of four or five courses each are available, priced from about $16 to $30, service included. Closed on Sunday. Telephone: 70 29 29.

The third-best stuffed crabs that I sampled on Martinique were at the curiously named **Le Matador**, a modestly designed, notably un-air-conditioned restaurant in Anse Matin, close to the Bakoua Hotel. Those crabs fell short of my idea of what the dish should be, but they were meatier and better seasoned than most. Another well-known Creole dish that appeared on the menu was a *blaff de poisson* – fish cooked in a light court-bouillon, with such seasonings as limes, onions, thyme, and hot chillies. At Le Matador the fish for an individual portion was half a small red snapper, and it was quite tasty, although the flavours were not assertive enough. A squeeze of lime helped. A third Creole dish, a colombo, or spicy stew of mutton including native vegetables such as christophene and pumpkin, was appealing.

A first course of fish soup with grated cheese and croûtons was a disappointment, for although it was edible it seemed insufficiently fresh. Similarly, the house white wine, a genuine *vin ordinaire*, was drinkable but thin and a bit acid.

A complete meal with wine for one will cost about $15. The restaurant is closed Tuesdays. Telephone: 66 05 36.

If physical surroundings were the principal criterion for a memorable dining experience, a fourth Martinique restaurant, **Le Tiffany**, in Fort-de-France, would get high marks. It is housed in a three-storey French colonial building and is reached by way of a winding highway. There is a lot of local art, both oils and watercolours, on the walls, and a single Tiffany lamp at the entrance. The menu is inviting, listing such specialities as asparagus in puff pastry, fillet of fish with chives, and sole with leeks.

My meal there began felicitously enough with a round, pillow-like appetizer of well-flavoured goat cheese floating in a light bath of hot cream. An order of thinly sliced fresh foie gras imported from France was doused with a touch of sweet sauternes (a fine sauternes is the ultimate beverage for foie gras), and it was good to the taste. But the main course, marinated fillet of pork Creole style, was disappointing. The pork had been held too long in its red-wine marinade and had become far too gamey.

The desserts, too, were a bit of a disappointment. A coconut custard was a trifle tough, and a chocolate pastry was ordinary. With the meal we drank a Brouilly.

A meal for one with wine averages $19. The restaurant, on the Croix de Bellevue, is open daily for dinner only. Credit cards accepted. Telephone: 71 33 82.

TWO ISLANDS À LA CARTE

Craig Claiborne

It has been a custom of mine to visit the Caribbean for the Christmas holidays for the last fifteen years and more. Over this period of time, I have sampled a great variety of restaurants, and have come to one unwavering conclusion about them: Almost all alter, sometimes drastically, from year to year. Changes of management are not uncommon, changes of staff are frequent, and chefs, in particular, move on to other establishments, or other islands, or back to France or the United States or wherever they originally came from. What follows is an account of dining experiences on two islands that I had known from earlier visits.

ST. MARTIN
In each of the last several years, I have looked forward to drinks and lunch on St. Martin at an establishment for the well-heeled known as **La Samanna.** The hours I have spent there have been consistently rewarding. There is a fine terrace overlooking a large pool, where you may sip your rum punch, Bloody Mary, Perrier, or what you will, while contemplating your choice of foods from an imaginative and impressively varied menu. There is no more conscientious kitchen to be found on the entire island.

My most recent lunchtime visit was nearly as felicitous as ever. The meal, in the company of three friends, was an almost total delight. It began with an excellent gazpacho, a very good vichyssoise and a laudable cold terrine of vegetables, layers of puréed artichokes and puréed carrots, surrounded by an impeccable light tomato sauce and made slightly peppery with fresh chillies. A bowl of minestrone – the soupe du jour – was innocuous, but seemed a curious item for a tropical menu.

La Samanna has a roofed-over but otherwise open dining room, surrounded by bougainvillaea and offering a spectacular view of the ocean. Among the main courses was a platter of grilled red snapper served with, according to the waiter, sauce Creole or sauce chien. One of the best foods we sampled was the meaty wild mushrooms known as cèpes, which were sautéed.

A dish of chicken salad was a palatal joy – although the guest to whom it was served found it a trifle oily. That oil, a hazelnut oil, was of the finest quality. I also admired the salad accompaniment, field-greens (known in French as mâche), and that fine Italian lettuce known as radicchio with its bright, red leaves, crunchy texture, and slightly bitter flavour. I was told by the kitchen that much of the fresh food is flown in from that bastion of fresh luxury ingredients, the Rungis market outside Paris. Thus the cèpes, radicchio and mâche.

The desserts were impressive, a vivid assortment of miniature tortes, glazed and topped with fresh fruits and berries. There was also a cake constructed of ladyfingers and filled with a slightly grainy chocolate mousse, as well as what may be the finest coconut sherbet imaginable. With the meal we drank a dry white Burgundy – a very good Meursault – priced at $30. Other wines at La Samanna are about $25 to $60.

I was left with one regret about that visit to La Samanna. Some of the choice items from the past, notably two salads, one of pigeon wings and another of sweetbreads, have been deleted from the menu.

La Samanna's menu is entirely à la carte. At lunch, the average cost for a meal for one is $25; at dinner, about $35 to $40. Credit cards accepted. Service charge not included. Closed in September and October. La Samanna is fairly close to the airport. Telephone: 87 51 22. Comfortably cool.

La Vie en Rose, a handsome upstairs establishment on the harbour in Marigot, the principal town on the French side of St. Martin, is one of the finest of the island's many fine French restaurants. The décor (mirrors, arches, ceiling fans, and candlelight) and views are impressive.

Although almost all the French restaurants on the island offer dishes built around puff pastry – that thousand-layered, buttery, lighter-than-air substance that can be baked in various shapes – the best we sampled was La Vie en Rose's pastry-enclosed fillets of red snapper on a bed of spinach. The meal began with a good onion soup au gratin. The main course was sliced, rare breast of duck – *magret du canard* – with herb butter. We drank an excellent Beaujolais, 1979; the food and wine service was attentive.

There were one or two flaws in the preparation of the meal. The sauce for the duck was too vinegary, the cheese on the onion soup too stringy. The coffee at the end of the meal was insipid.

La Vie en Rose is closed Sundays between Easter and Thanksgiving. After that it will be open for lunch and dinner seven days a week. The average cost of a meal for one at lunch is $17; at dinner, $35; wines from about $15 to $110. American Express card accepted. Telephone: 87 54 42. Comfortably cool.

L'Auberge Gourmande, also in Grand Case, may not have the most innovative menu outside France, but the dining room is comfortable and the kitchen is more than competent. Our party of four began a most agreeable meal with two excellent salads, a cream of carrot soup, and frogs' legs dijonnaise (in a light, hot, mustard, cream and herb sauce). The salads were substantial and dressed with a well-seasoned vinaigrette; one was made with grated carrots, sliced egg, tomato wedges and shrimp in the shells, the other with salad greens, walnuts, bits of cheese, and ham.

Among the main courses was cubed langouste – the clawless Caribbean version of lobster – in a baked, fish-shaped puff-pastry shell. We also had fillet of beef with the tasty wild mushrooms called morels and red snapper served two ways, with sliced toasted almonds and with blended seafood in a cream sauce.

Not a single main course was faultless; there were bits of bone in one serving of fish, the puff-pastry shell was a trifle burned, and the beef seemed a bit tenderized. We drank a chilled Chablis, one bottle of which was slightly madeirized (its somewhat brown aged flavour is something I have noted with many white wines in the Caribbean). A dessert of crêpes with crunchy apple slices and a dash or two of Calvados was capital.

All dishes at L'Auberge Gourmande are à la carte. The average cost of a meal for one is $16; wines from about $9 for a Côtes de Provence to $30 for a bottle of Beaune. The restaurant is closed Wednesdays until December 1, then open for dinner only, seven days a week. It also closes in August and September. To make a reservation you must stop by; there is no telephone. Credit cards not accepted. Service charge included. No air-conditioning.

ST. BARTHELEMY

For more than a decade my favourite island in the Caribbean has been St. Barthelemy, or St. Barts, and for several years my preferred restaurant has been **Castelets,** a fine retreat – with a few rooms and suites available – high atop a hill with a magnificent view. The quality of the kitchen may vary, but it is generally first rate, and the dining room delights with elegant silver, proper glassware, nice napery and good service. The restaurant and its adjacent hotel are owned by a New Yorker, Justin Colin, former president of the Ballet Theater Foundation and currently chairman of its executive committee, and the clientele has included Mikhail Baryshnikov and Gelsey Kirkland as well as Jessica Lange, Tennessee Williams, and Valéry Giscard d'Estaing.

My meal was shared with friends. It began with tender local clams served hot on the half shell with a garlic tartar sauce. We also had an excellent nouvelle-cuisine creation made of cubed langouste in a delicate mayonnaise with morsels of peach. Among the main courses was a local fish called cola. The menu also offered lamb and chicken dishes.

Desserts included a wedge of hot apple tart with freshly made vanilla ice cream, an excellent chocolate mousse made with bitter chocolate, and a lime sherbet. The sherbet tasted a bit artificial. With the meal we drank a nicely chilled bottle of Muscadet.

Castelets' menu is à la carte and changes with the season. A meal for one at lunch averages $12 to $20, at dinner, $30; wines from about $10 to $110. The restaurant is closed Tuesday and at lunch time on Wednesday. No credit cards accepted. Fifteen per cent service charge added. Telephone: 87 61 73. Windswept. Air-conditioning unnecessary.

One of the pleasantest and most casual places to dine on St. Barts is **Chez Francine** on St. Jean Beach next to the Eden Rock Hotel. It plays host to numerous celebrities each summer (recently among them were Raymond Oliver, former owner of the Grand Véfour restaurant in Paris, Sylvester Stallone, Lino Ventura, and Alain Delon, the actors, and Lee Radziwill).

The blackboard menu listed crudités, grilled chicken, black pudding, steamed lobsters, grilled steak, cheeses, ice creams, and a tarte maison. The food was exceptionally tasty. Among the crudités were grated carrots, grated cabbage (white and red), tomatoes and cucumbers, all with a fine-flavoured vinaigrette sauce. The lobsters, offered lukewarm or cold depending on how long they have been out of the kettle, were served with fresh mayonnaise and salad. With the meal I had a glass of Tavel rosé.

Prices range from about $8 for the grilled chicken to $12 for steak. The lobsters range from $12 to $24 depending on size. Wines are $7 a bottle for white, $8 for rosé, and $9 for red. Service not included. Credit cards not accepted. The restaurant, open for lunch only, is closed on Mondays and in June. Telephone: 87 60 49.

Each December over the years I have occupied a rented cottage at Village St. Jean in the area known as St. Jean. The cottage has an admirable view of the harbour and a reasonably spacious kitchen where I have prepared many a meal, including Christmas feasts. When I have felt like dining at home, principally at midday but without cooking, or when I have felt like taking a picnic to the beach, I usually go to the **Rotisserie** at rue La Fayette and rue Oskar II in the heart of Gustavia.

It is a small, whistle-neat place where the owners, a young couple, Pierre-Marie L'Hermite and his wife, Evelyne, turn out a variety of interesting foods cooked on the premises. There is pâté de campagne and pâté of liver (both about $5 a pound) and pâté of duck (about $8), as well as black puddings, onion tarts and other tarts, *pissaladières* (French pizzas), and first-rate roast chickens. The Rotisserie also offers an interesting assortment of salads. At Christmas-time they offer Brittany oysters flown in from France and fresh foie gras.

The Rotisserie is closed Saturday and Sunday afternoons and all day Monday. It is also closed each day from 12.30 to 4 pm. Telephone: 87 63 13. The bakery across the street has excellent French bread, croissants and pastries.

ISLAND HIDEAWAYS: A SAMPLER

Paul Grimes

To many people, 'Caribbean' is synonymous with 'escape.' To a select few, it isn't enough to escape to just any warm isle offering a reasonably comfortable hotel, edible food, a beach, water sports, golf and tennis. They also demand the ultimate in luxury and, often, maximum privacy, and are willing to pay $300 or more per person a day, including meals, to get what they want.

Most have favourite haunts and return there year after year. They are well known to their hosts, who cater to all their demands. But what about you? Suppose you want to join them but are unfamiliar with the Caribbean and don't know how to go about it? How do you find the luxury retreat that's ideal for you?

The question was put to a dozen experts on the Caribbean, people who know the resorts intimately: travel agents with a silk-stocking clientele, wholesalers who sell hotel packages (even at small hideaways) through travel agents and writers who specialize in Caribbean holidays.

Not every winter holidaymaker, famous or anonymous, craves the same degree of privacy; ask yourself how much you want when you begin to plan. Ian Keown, author of *Caribbean Hideaways*, says some resorts are so full of celebrities in midwinter that they could hardly be called retreats. 'Some people want to be recognized,' he said, 'although this doesn't necessarily mean that they want you to come over and say hello.'

Margaret Zellers, who wrote *Fielding's Caribbean* and *Caribbean the Inn Way*, says that for the VIP who doesn't want to be recognized – or anyone else who craves maximum privacy – she recommends renting a private home with full staff.

You can get details and make reservations before you leave the United States. All sorts of holiday properties, some barely large enough for a handful of guests, have representatives in the United States or can be booked through travel agents. If an agent does not know a property personally, he or she can get reasonably accurate information from the *Official Hotel and Resort Guide*, a three-volume looseleaf trade manual whose entries are updated periodically. Ownership and managements change occasionally, sometimes on short notice; it is wise to seek the advice of someone who has been there recently (a competent travel agent will know where to look).

OTHER QUESTIONS TO CONSIDER

What sort of luxury do you crave and how much are you prepared to pay for it? To some, luxury means a hedonistic world of whirlpool baths, water beds, fluffy towels, automatic coffeemakers and wet bars, colour television, stereo and a steak-and-eggs snack from room service at 3 am. If that is your dream, you won't find much of it anywhere in the Caribbean. But you are likely to find sumptuous comfort, spectacular vistas, and excellent service in the top resorts, if you don't mind occasional power cuts and shortages of drinking water, ice, and towels.

How important is gourmet cuisine? Before you decide on a resort or villa, ask about the meals there and at nearby restaurants. Luxurious lodgings do not necessarily mean that the meals will be at the same level, though sometimes you can strike it rich on local lobster. Many holidaymakers augment modest cuisine with steaks and the like brought from home. But be careful: If you plan to take prime steaks, packed frozen in dry ice by your neighbourhood butcher, be sure to keep them with you in carry-on baggage while travelling. A temporary loss could spoil the steak as well as the suitcase.

How do you get where you are going, and is it worth the trip? Some hideaways are accessible from New York only by two or three connecting flights, a bumpy taxi ride and sometimes a crossing by ferry or launch. Reaching your destination could take an entire day or longer and cost $500 or more.

I asked the experts to list the havens they would suggest to the uninitiated. My only condition was that all be available to the general public, though some require reservations far in advance. Besides Miss Zellers and Mr. Keown, they included Linda Gwinn, former travel editor of *Town and Country*; John H. Keller, president of Caribbean Holidays, a wholesaler who deals in hundreds of properties; and four New York travel agents: Lloyd Cole of Amsag Travel, who has long been active in Caribbean tourism; Mary Russell, president of Frederics-Helton; John Goodrich of Bellinger Davis; and Pat Quinard of MacPherson Travel.

Following are choices on which most agreed. The prices are minimums and usually do not include taxes and tips; many suites and cottages cost much more.

Petit St. Vincent Resort, Grenadines. An entire resort island with powdery beaches and twenty-two stone cottages built for privacy and view. Winter rates are about $250 a day for two, with all meals, and including service and tax (about $200 in the shoulder season). You fly nonstop from New York to Barbados, then fly to Union Island, and finally sail to the resort.

Cotton House, Mustique Island, St. Vincent, Grenadines. Restored or reproduced eighteenth century houses, plus an ultra-private beach cottage a quarter of a mile away. From $125 a person a day, including meals. For about $1,500 a week, including staff, you can rent Les Jolies Eaux, the house where Princess Margaret sometimes stays. Fly from New York via Martinique, St. Vincent, or Barbados.

Castelets, Saint Barthelemy, French West Indies. A ten-room mountaintop resort, away from the beach but with magnificent panoramic views. Tape decks in each room and elegant French cuisine. From $90 a day, including breakfast. (Miss Zellers, while commending Castelets, especially recommends the private villas on the island that can be rented through the Sibarth agency there for about $500 a week, including maid.) Fly from New York via St. Martin.

Guana Island Club, British Virgin Islands. An 850-acre private island off the coast of Tortola. A group of white cottages of native stone accommodate about twenty-five guests. From about $125 per day per person, including meals. Fly to San Juan, St. Thomas, or St. Croix, then take a short hop to Tortola where boatmen will meet you at the airport for a ten-minute cruise to Guana. Also reachable by launch from Tortola is the Peter Island Hotel and Yacht Harbour, where accommodations are distributed among A-framed chalets, a hilltop 'crow's nest' and a three-bedroom cottage on the beach. The atmosphere and cuisine, formerly Scandinavian, have been Americanized. From about $150 a day, including meals and use of most sports facilities.

Biras Creek, Virgin Gorda, British Virgin Islands. A remote Scandinavian-style cottage resort, with thirty suites on a beach and a main building – the principal gathering place – atop a hill. From about $150 a day, including meals. Fly to San Juan, change planes to Virgin Gorda, and take a taxi or car to Gun Creek Landing where, if you have telephoned from the island's airport, a launch will take you on the ten-minute sail to the resort.

Curtain Bluff Hotel, Antigua. A fifty-room beachside resort with a Swiss chef, fluffy towels (relatively rare in the Caribbean), and special appeal for aficionados of water skiing, sailing, snorkelling, scuba diving, tennis, and other outdoor sports. From about $140 a day, including breakfast and dinner. Fly nonstop to Antigua and take a taxi to the resort.

Coco Point Lodge, Barbuda. A string of houses and cottages along a spectacular beach, about twenty-seven miles northeast of

Antigua. From about $160 a day, including meals and drinks. Fly nonstop to Antigua and change planes for a short hop to Barbuda airport, a fifteen-minute drive from the lodge.

Half Moon Club, Montego Bay, Jamaica. The ambience and service have won accolades for this resort, which has 128 rooms and sixty-two apartments. From about $100 a person, including breakfast and dinner. (Miss Zellers also suggests the forty fully staffed luxury villas at the nearby Tryall Golf and Beach Club, available from about $1,400 a week.) Fly nonstop to Montego Bay and pick up a rental car or taxi.

Casa de Campo, La Romana, Dominican Republic. You won't get much privacy at this 300-unit, 3,000-acre resort near an old sugar town, but it has two golf courses, nine tennis courts, polo, deep-sea fishing, and more. Rates begin at about $85, without meals. It has an airport for private planes; otherwise fly to Santo Domingo and travel two hours by taxi.

Omitted from the list, though highly recommended by many, are the two Rockresorts established by the Rockefeller interests: Caneel Bay Plantation on St. John, U.S. Virgin Islands, and Little Dix Bay on Virgin Gorda, British Virgin Islands. No one questions their luxury, but many visitors feel they are not really hideaways.

A BOAT OF ONE'S OWN

William F. Buckley, Jr.

When, for the first time, our son would not be with us for Christmas we lost interest in spending it at home, and ever since then have gone to the Caribbean, though not to stay on islands. Our attachment to the Caribbean is to a way of visiting it; and for us this means by cruising sailboat.

Accordingly, although I have cruised the Caribbean more thoroughly than Christopher Columbus, I do not write this piece with any presumption of communicating the 'magic of the Caribbean,' as they call it in the coffee-table books when other words seem apologetic. But I am here to say that it is hard to have a happier time than cruising there.

In your own boat. Though, having said that, I confess I have not been aboard a commercial cruising boat during the conventional one or two weeks in the Caribbean. Probably there is much to be said for this way of seeing the islands, in preference to hotel life. But your very own boat is really the way to go, and one might as well quickly confront the proposition 'Isn't this out of the question for the average pocketbook?' The answer is: Yes. But so is a week aboard any of the more luxurious liners or a week at any of the fancier hotels. In round figures – if you include meals, drinks, tips, taxis – you are talking about something over $400 per couple a day, times seven comes to – well, close to $3,000 a week.

Last Christmas, we chartered a boat that cost $1,000 a day, including food, but not drinks, tips or taxis. Throw these in even profusely, and you are still short of $9,000 a week. But there are three couples sharing the boat, so that the cost, for each couple – less than $3,000 – is comparable to the hotels.

Until 1978, we holidayed in my own boat, a 60-foot schooner for which, when last I chartered it out, the price was $3,000 a week. In the six years since losing her, we experimented with several boats, discovering in due course a 71-foot ketch (it is a class called Ocean 71), my enthusiasm for which led me one spring to charter her from St. Thomas to the Mediterranean, whither she was in any case bound. I find it the (almost) perfect cruising boat (it is not air-conditioned). And in a piece that seeks to be persuasive about cruising in the Caribbean, it is worth telling you exactly what you get with a boat like *Sealestial*.

First the tangibles. There is a crew of four. A skipper (though I serve as my own), a first mate, a stewardess and a cook. There are three cabins, in descending order of luxury the owners' cabin, which has a dressing table, a huge stuffed chair for reading and working, a private bath including shower; a smaller but commodious cabin with hanging lockers and two bunks, sharing a shower and separate toilet with the third cabin – slightly smaller, but entirely comfortable.

The principal saloon, as sailors call it, is circular and would hold, comfortably seated, sixteen people. Eight can be seated around the coffee table that lifts and becomes the dinner table, opposite the bar, music quarry, and screen for films. The main cockpit you may choose to eat in, as you like; and the after cockpit fits snugly six people, if you wish to eat there, usually when under way. On deck there is more room that can be consumed by a dozen people who wish to lie and read, or to sun, whether or not the vessel is under sail. The rubber dinghy holds eight people, and there is diving equipment on board for four, with tanks that recharge in about half an hour. There is a radio that works, giving you almost instant contact with whomever you need to reach.

And the intangibles? You can rise in the morning, take stock of the wind and decide which island next to visit. You can decide when to set sail, after breakfast or after a tour of the island – after which, to be sure, you do not, not being John Gunther, come off as an expert on the subject of that island. You can, sailing along offshore by, say, a quarter of a mile (after you leave the Bahamas, the islands are nicely sheer), spot a beach and decide impulsively that you would like to swim off it. It happens to appeal – so you go no farther. There is no fixed itinerary, no deadlines. When there is such a thing – perhaps a couple of friends are flying in for a few days – you can make contingent arrangements. It is easy to book a little aeroplane to meet your boat at a convenient island.

It is most important to turn your watches to Buckley Watch Time. There are those who call this Daylight Time. But the two do not always correspond, because in certain circumstances Buckley Watch Time advances the conventional time by two hours. The practical meaning of it all, as I have elsewhere written, is that you can start the cocktail hour as the sun is setting, and eat dinner one hour later, at eight o'clock. Otherwise, you can find yourself drinking at six and eating dinner at seven. The former offends the Calvanist streak in a Yankee; the latter, the Mediterranean streak in a yacht owner. Dinner is protracted and leisurely, and after dinner, according to the inclinations of our companions, we gamble, or we watch a film, or we read; and, before retiring, we swim, and stare a little at the stars, and the moon, and listen to the little waves, from whose busty sisters we are, on the leeward side of the island, protected.

Last year, a week or two before the trip was to begin, I had a phone call from the yacht broker. A most unhappy development! Poor *Sealestial*! What outrageous people one finds in the world! And a brand-new motor at that! Unravelled, it gradually transpired that coming down after a summer in the Mediterranean, the yacht's brand-new engine gave trouble – somewhere off Casablanca, I think it was. The captain accepted a friendly offer of a few miles' tow, upon the completion of which the Good Samaritan put in a bill for the entire value of the boat, something on the order of three-quarters of a million dollars. They settled for less than that, but the negotiations would keep the boat from arriving in time for Christmas.

The resourceful broker was, however, armed for the contingency. She proposed that we accept one of *Sealestial*'s sister ships for one week, and that for the balance of our ten-day trip we ride, without extra charge, on a new vessel built by the owner of the *Sealestial*, a monstrous big sloop, yclept the *Concorde*, 88 feet, with room for twelve passengers, and a crew of six.

Boats that size move, for me, just on the other side of manageability; but the idea was seductive, and in any event there were no practical alternatives. The only nuisance lay in packing and repacking, the freedom from which is one of the splendid perquisites you inherit if you elect not to island hop from hotel to hotel.

And so we flew to St. Martin (a practical hint: endeavour to begin your cruise from an island to which you can fly without changing planes – and baggage).

The very first night out on a boat, away from a cold city, is an experience very difficult to compare with others, unless you get into the business of the day the gates opened and you left prison a free man. I suspect that many people cultivate, during the days and weeks before a holiday, a specially strenuous schedule, so that the contrary sensation of stepping into a boat and leaving forthwith for the privacy of a lagoon off somewhere becomes something like what the dope-afflicted call a rush.

St. Martin has two harbours, neither of them memorable, but both pleasant. We set sail for St. Barts, which is east, with its harbour so picturesque, always full of conventionally sleek but also idiosyncratic boats – the loners, who after transatlantic passages usually make land in Antigua, and almost all seem to have an appetite to see St. Barts, seventy-five miles northwest. But we had a secret destination. A few years ago we discovered a little cove on the west side of Anguilla, which is, I think, the only piece of property that has ever inclined me to imperialism. You will remember that before the Falklands, the last bellicose sally of the British fleet was an attack on Anguilla, which had declared its independence of the newly formed association of St. Kitts-Nevis-Anguilla, conscripting to that end something on the order of an eight-man constabulary. The Wilson Government sent a dreadnought, a few paratroopers, and twenty London policemen wearing winter woollies to put an end to this contumacy. I remember that the poor self-proclaimed president took a full-page ad in *The New York Times* asking for material assistance and that my secretary, taken by his poignant appeal, sent him $5 and received back a five-page handwritten note of devoted thanks. I was saying that I would like to become an imperialist, conquer Anguilla, and reward myself that little cove.

I don't really know what all goes on in Anguilla, and it is this ignorance about Caribbean life I do not pretend to conceal. All I know is that the word *anguila* in Spanish means 'eel,' and that the island, about eighteen miles along, slithers its way southwest to northeast rather as an eel, that a little bit south of our little anchorage and a couple of miles offshore is the quintessential little island, the kind you see drawn by cartoonists for the convenience of the caption makers. You know – a sand-oval not much bigger than a giant turtle, with one palm tree jutting up from the middle of it. It is visible from our little anchorage, a most awful tease, as though the man who does Macy's windows had sneaked in the night before to make fun of our perfection. Never mind, I say; never mind, Pat says; never mind, Dick and Shirley say, and Schuyler and Betty, and we raise our glasses to our perfect little anchorage, and pity the rest of the whole wide world.

I intended an overnight sail to the Virgins. I like one of these even when one cruises hedonistically. It has a way of reminding you that somebody has to grow the peaches, and whip the cream. It is really quite uncomfortable to wake at midnight and stand watch for four hours, but the idea was not more than a velleity, so that when the captain of the substitute boat, unaccustomed to my imperious ways, said he would rather sail during the day, I suffered him to do so, arriving just before dark at Road Town in Tortola, with its orderly, rounded quay, the yachts lined up European style, stern first, the museum reminding us of the bloody history of the Caribbean where for so many centuries the idea was that everyone should kill everyone else, while all the flag makers were kept busy changing prevailing standards, from Dutch, to French, Spanish, English, Danish.

But we had come to Tortola primarily to pick up two passengers, one of them our son, and we set out with great happiness the next morning, running over to Virgin Gorda for a dive, and then a long downwind sail to St. John and Caneel Bay, where we would yield our vessel and board the *Concorde*.

We spent Christmas night at a bay just north of Caneel, and that was wonderfully happy, with Pat's lights and trees and a great volume of gifts exchanged, some of them in the form of IOU's bearing pictures of gifts that lay in waiting for us back home but were too bulky to carry. (I was not about to bring to my son the collected works of the Beatles on discs to a vessel that does not have a disc player.) The music was splendid. Boats enjoy the advantage cars enjoy. Their shape makes for a natural baffle, so that indifferent cassette players give off a very full sound, and we had aboard not only the conventional Handel but some arrangements absolutely perfect of the Christmas carols (the Bach Choir, David Willcocks conducting) done with a special originality, designed to please those whose cup is very full.

Oh yes, the *Concorde*. It began to blow quite hard from the north, so that the question was where to go with it, and we ended by taking it on two or three twenty-mile triangular courses, as if racing. It is a most exquisitely designed boat, and the cuisine below cannot be matched in the best hotel in the Caribbean. But it is a little disheartening to see two girls wrestling with each of two coffee grinders needed to winch up and then swing in the tremendous sails. To sail it for an hour or two, returning to your point of origin, is on the order of what Virgil Thomson wrote about a composition by – was it Vaughan Williams? – that it was like boarding the *Queen Mary* in Manhatten in order to travel to Brooklyn.

But there is great pleasure to be got, if that is the kind of thing that appeals to you, in studying this boat at sea, driven by the hugest single sail I have ever seen. The silky-smooth-light-suntan-oil Caribbean we think of, and indeed often experience, can work its way up into quite a lather. When these things happen at sea, bound to far-off destinations, they can bring protracted discomfort. But when you cruise, the pain is going to go away sometime before sundown; and you are suddenly floating again, quite still, save for the little motion that reminds you you are on a vessel, quite alone if that is your mood, or socializing with good friends, if that is your mood; and that nothing is pressing, and tomorrow we will see what the wind is like and acknowledge that the Caribbean's weather, like its people, can be distinctive, different, pleasant, hospitable, alluring and also all those other things.

I despair of ever persuading great lots of people who spend the same money at hotels to try cruising. I experimented with every convention-al inducement when I owned a vessel for hire. I don't really know the reason for the general resistance, though, of course, seasickness figures in some cases. In others I suspect it is a slight fear. Of what? I don't really know, but again I suspect it is a fear that, on a boat, it is too easy to – act wrong. Well, it's true. It's easy to make a serious mistake if you're crewing for the America's Cup. But on the Caribbean, in a good boat, with competent crew, there isn't really anything you can do to disgrace yourself – I mean, that you couldn't as well do at the Paradise Beach Hotel. Do give it a try, but not on the *Sealestial* at Christmastime, because that's reserved until they lower me down.

THE RUMS OF THE ISLANDS

Frank J. Prial

Some people look at colour slides to help them recall their Caribbean trips. Others steal ashtrays and use them, like Proust's madeleine, to bring back island memories. Better than stealing towels, probably, but not much.

There is another way. Open a bottle of rum. In an instant, one conjures up the Caribbean. Nothing can evoke the dizzying perfume of bougainvillaea, the crystal-like air after a sudden shower, the empty whiteness of the beaches, and the vastness of a star-filled island night like rum.

Now it can't be just any rum. The spineless rums that are so popular these days – no colour, no taste, no bouquet – are not real rum. They're fine for singles' bars and bridge parties, but they bear about as much resemblance to real rum as a rhododendron does to a royal palm. Real rum is dark and robust and redolent of the cane fields. Or, it can be as smooth and elegant and complex as fine old cognac, and meant to be sipped on a veranda overlooking the sea.

Good rums are available in liquor stores, and there are still a few connoisseurs around to enjoy them. But, really, the place to get acquainted with rum is on its home ground, those islands in the Caribbean where sugarcane is grown.

Some people say rum was invented in the West Indies, but that's unlikely. Sugar wasn't, and rum comes solely from cane sugar. Most likely it came out of the Middle East or Africa with the first sugarcane. One story has Columbus bringing sugarcane from the Azores on his second voyage.

Certainly, though, the islands quickly made rum their own. And well they might. It's much cheaper – and more profitable – to ship rum than sugar. Just as it was cheaper for the American colonists to ship corn whisky back through the Cumberland Gap than corn itself.

One of the earliest written records of rum dates back to Barbados in the early 1600s, and it has been an integral part of island culture ever since. Today, Barbados continues to make some of the best rum in the world. Mount Gay, whose distillery can be visited year round, is a medium-bodied, amber-coloured rum with a mellow finish.

Rum ranges from pure white to mahogany in colour. The colour comes from tasteless caramel even if the rum has been aged in casks. Clear, light rum is usually made in a continuous-process still and, from juice to finished product, can be turned out in as little as a day. The heavier, more aromatic, richer rums are often made in old-fashioned pot stills and are fermented slowly, for up to twelve days. More body comes from the addition of dunder, the lees from previous distillations, to the fermentation process.

Rum's history has been as notorious as the islands that produce it. It fuelled the pirates of the Spanish Main and for 400 years the men of the British navy. It inspired Ernest Hemingway, who thought nothing of getting outside of six daiquiris each afternoon at La Florida, his favourite Havana bar, and it provided the noun root for a whole family of insults: rummy, rum-soaked, demon rum, and, of course, that infamous insult raised to the level of campaign rhetoric, 'rum, Romanism, and rebellion,' which helped to defeat James G. Blaine in the presidential campaign of 1884.

Rum was the currency of the slave trade: it came to New England as molasses, went to Africa as rum, and was exchanged for black men and women, who in turn were exchanged for molasses back in the islands. The French engaged in that business as well as the Americans, and they still bottle their rum in Bordeaux, one of the original ports of call in their own shameful triangle.

Rum was the working man's drink in the American colonies – until the frontiersmen settled down to cooking up corn likker. Rhum – with an 'h' – was the working man's drink in Paris until World War 1, when soldiers from Normandy introduced fiery Calvados into the trenches.

In the 1920s, rum-runners cluttered up deserted Florida beaches just as dope smugglers do today, and thirsty Easterners paid large sums for bad Cuban brew. During World War II, rum's shoddy reputation was further besmirched by merchants forcing throat-searing cases of it on customers with each bottle of black-market Scotch.

Rum has recovered nicely from those parlous times. At the moment, Bacardi is the leading brand in the United States, having sold almost nine million cases of rum to Americans in one recent year. But this is light stuff – for mixing. Most of it is made in Bacardi's enormous distillery just across the harbour from San Juan, Puerto Rico. A visit to Bacardi is as much a part of a Puerto Rican holiday as a visit to El Morro fort or the rain forest.

But Bacardi is the General Motors of rum and not everyone wants to drive a Buick. There are lots of other Puerto Rican rums, Ron Rico and Don Q among them.

Elsewhere among the islands, rum making is a bit less supercharged. The Appleton Plantation in Jamaica, Mount Gay in Barbados, Barbancourt in Haiti, and Clement and St. James in Martinique are much smaller distilleries, and their tours are somewhat lower keyed. Many small distilleries in the islands will let you wander around on your own so long as you promise to stay away from the cane crusher. You might fall in and ruin an entire day's work.

Most rum from the French islands is shipped to France – Bordeaux or Marseilles – in bulk. The steel tanks are cleaned, one hopes, and shipped back filled with inexpensive wine.

The rum business, like most businesses in the West Indies, can be most casual. Some years ago, while wasting time in a small Barbados hotel, I accompanied the innkeeper on a trip to his favourite distillery in the countryside. With us we carried three glass demijohns capable of holding five or six gallons each. The distillery turned out to be a corrugated tin shed, very rusty, run by two seedy old men. The jugs were filled and some money changed hands.

Back at the hotel every rum bottle behind the bar was topped off. The labels varied considerably but not the rum. Somehow it seemed appropriate. After all, isn't rum the stuff of highbinders and villains?

It should strike you then as altogether appropriate that you be outrageously overcharged for rum drinks in the islands. Bartenders, who may be lucky to make $50 a week, will soak you $10 for a sticky concoction in a coconut shell. Planters punch, a tall mixture of tropical fruit juices – usually from a can – and rum, can cost $5 or $6 or more.

No islander drinks these things, of course. In the French islands, a punch is a simple combination of rum, sugar and lime juice. Well, perhaps not so simple. There are probably fifty different kinds of punch, all made by steeping tropical fruits and spices in big glass jars filled with rum. The rum is ladled into small glasses, and the effect is delightful. The British and American islands, alas, offer only pale imitations of French punches.

On the other hand, the Jamaicans probably make the most elegant rums, the kind to be drunk neat, from snifters. When you are in Jamaica, try to search out some very old Lemon Hart, one of the best Jamaican rums. In Haiti, Barbancourt makes a fifteen-year-old Reserve du Domaine that is also in the top echelon. In Trinidad, Fernandes is a label to search out, as is Bermudez in the Dominican Republic.

Each island and most Central American countries have dozens of small distilleries that bottle for the local trade or for bulk shipments to Europe. It would be nice to be able to say that these rums are worth seeking out. Probably a few are. But most are raw and unpalatable. The bigger distilleries make the best rums, the ones worth bringing home.

Some distilleries make it easy to sample their wares. On Martinique, for example, the sixteen distilleries that make up Syndicat du Rhum de la Martinique offer tours and tastings from January through July. One Martinique company, Rhum St. James, has turned an old colonial mansion in the town of Sainte-Marie into a rum museum. On Guadeloupe, La Maison du Rhum in Bas du Fort, just outside Pointe-à-Pitre, offers tastings every day except Sunday.

COPING WITH LUXURY

Charlotte Curtis

The big thing about St. John Island is how small it is. Barely twenty square miles, and remote. A Virgin Islands national park mostly, with a couple of villages, the largest of which is Cruz Bay, a Caribbean backwater vaguely reminiscent of Pago Pago in the '50s but without the international shipping that gave that South Seas port its bawdy reputation. Bawdy, Cruz Bay is not. More a place to buy hot dogs or cold beer, a bedroom community and marina far outshone by Charlotte Amalie, the big, sprawling hill town on the island of St. Thomas miles across the bay. The only reason to mention Cruz Bay here is as the back door to Caneel Bay, the luxurious Rockefeller resort for the rich.

Arrive outside the hours that the Caneel Bay launch runs between Charlotte Amalie and the Caneel dock and you land at Cruz Bay among the porters, waiters and cleaning women whose daily labours guarantee the privileged their total leisure. Caneel is down the road, a brief taxi ride through a fragrant jungle to a guarded gate and into a lush, manicured enclave, 'enhanced,' the management contends, to preserve its natural beauty while serving 360 well-dispersed holiday-makers.

'You will notice our foliage-coloured vehicles, electric carts, unobtrusive signs, and other indications of a carefully planned program to reduce man's impact on this spectacular environment.' So reads the welcoming folder. Maybe that's why virtually none of the spacious rooms, whether upstairs or down, has an unobscured view of the water. It does not explain the roar and fumes of the ubiquitous tractors. Nor why the tractors are red. Perhaps they are painted to match the hibiscus.

All but invisible from the water and the sky, terraced one-room villas are strung out mostly along a series of private beaches, behind the seagrape. A few inland dwellings hug the tennis courts. No radios or television sets are provided. The New York newspapers do not arrive until after lunch. Caneel is not a place for romantically inclined singles, black-tie evenings, or golfers. There is no swimming pool. Room service is available but inefficient. So why go?

Snorkellers, including some of the least likely of the nation's celebrated chief executive officers, rave about the place, padding up out of
the clear waters in their flippers and Martian masks with tales of coral
fantasy worlds populated by stingrays, urchins, infinitesimal limpets,
enormous snails, and a rainbow of tropical plants and fish. Birdwatch-
ers, who in real life busy themselves with couture clothes and charity
balls, delight in the flocks of hummingbirds, warblers and water-fowl.
The ordinarily sedentary, temporarily detached from their European
cars, find biking or walking, rather than riding the jitney to one of three
very different dining spots, a rather special visual pleasure. Riders let
the horses take them into the highland forests for the views. Sailers sail
or sit back while a yacht tours them among the tiny cays. Readers
read. Fishermen fish, and tanners tan.

'The sun is so enervating,' a svelte Latin American explained one
night after yet another elaborate five-course dinner, and she may be
right.

Normally active, restless people who never get more than six hours
sleep in the pressurized North find themselves unable to keep their
eyes open after ten-thirty pm. The cocktail lounges, briefly crowded
before dinner, have few customers after ten. And there is a lot to be said
for the peace and tranquillity that edges in, disconnects the will, and
invisibly diminishes one's ability to act.

Decision-making is reduced to choosing pancakes or Cream of
Wheat with breakfast (though one may have both), when to swim and
at which beach, and how much to gorge oneself at dinner. Crises in the
Middle East and Central America begin to fade. Nobody mentions the
nation's budget deficit. Instead, you hear a lot about the beauty of the
place, the effectiveness of certain tanning lotions and insect repellents,
and whatever it is that keeps biting.

Debates concern how best to keep from tracking sand indoors,
where it ends up between the sheets, there to adhere to whatever lotion
was applied and grate against freshly sunned skin. The matter of
whether or not that's a booby or a pelican diving so masterfully after
fish is approached with caution. Some guests know the difference.

After two weeks of this sun, sand, water, sleep, food and a modicum
of sporting about, a neuroscientist of our acquaintance insisted that
the molecules of his brain were changed, and changed for the better.
Caneel, of course, claims no curative powers. But the absence of
telephones and the steady pounding of the surf help, and there is
exquisite drama in this natural world, some of it unavoidable.

Rain is inevitable in the tropics, and often more than something to
get in out of. Thankfully, Caneel Bay offers neither the monsoons and
killer floods of Louis Bromfield's India nor the relentless downpours
that drove everyone to drink in Somerset Maugham's account of Miss

Sadie Thompson's South Seas adventures. Still, an occasional deluge roars by, available in its entirety for observation.

Grey clouds appear, darkening the sky. Winds moan, whipping palms into a frenzy. Whitecaps appear where there were none. The temperature falls. The rain storms out of the east, hurling unsuspecting honey bees into the water. Minutes later, the sun returns. And the tides wash the bees onto the hot sand to wriggle helplessly and die.

Alfred Lord Tennyson found nature 'red in tooth and claw,' yet even in the dense, unimproved jungle Caneel adjoins, the only blood drawn is what the mosquitoes and their nipping confrères manage to extract from the visiting humans. Pelicans scoop up whole fish, pouching them in their expandable gullets for later consumption. Hawks cruise the breezes, their luck running to fish rather than small mammals. Mongooses scrap ferociously among themselves for bits of food but do no harm to one another. Groucho, a mostly white cat with a black moustache, slinks about, grateful for the tidbits left by strangers. Groucho is said to have mauled a rat, but that confrontation, if it ever took place, was held somewhere backstage.

Even though you don't have to spend much time in them, something should be said about the one-room villas. They are large and open on at least one side – sometimes more – giving one the sense of living outdoors. They are nicely underdecorated in earth colours, large enough to accommodate a seating area, and well lighted. All have ample cupboard space, showers, a terrace toward the water and sometimes a second, or inland, terrace. That the wooden louvres do not always work should be chalked up to the reality of the damp tropical climate.

Something should also be said about the dining centres, since they are most of the civilization one encounters. The biggest and most sociable, next to the offices and reception lounges on welcoming Caneel Bay itself, looks but does not quite see to Charlotte Amalie. It was there, after yet another glorious day, that a man employed to play the piano attempted a medley of what sounded like 'Ave Maria' (in a letter, he said it was Bach's Prelude No. 1), Mozart, 'Over the Rainbow,' 'The Man I Love,' 'Rhapsody in Blue,' 'Born Free,' and a spot or two of Scott Joplin.

Aside from the sour and missing notes, what was thrilling about his performance was the way in which he suddenly abandoned Mozart in midphrase and slid, some would say vaulted, into the exact point of 'Rainbow' where 'troubles melt like lemon drops' only to leap ever onward into the middle of the Gershwin, assuming, of course, that that really was a snatch of Gershwin he was playing.

Such are the excitements of the Caneel dining room. There is no escaping the crowds there, or the long drawn-out multicourse meals.

Though the periodic evening buffets are splendid, along with the homemade soups, the baked goods and the fresh fruits and vegetables, the chefs for the winter of 1984 indulged themselves in entirely too much oregano. And the dinner entrées routinely ran to something rubbery covered with an unfortunate variety of glups.

Handsome as it is, Caneel's big open-air pavilion smacks of Saturday night at the country club. It is no place for those who hope to escape the humdrum or their fellow man. Better to dine at the Sugar Mill, literally an old mill transformed into a small, informal dining terrace that specializes in charcoal-grilled chops, steaks, and a certain charm. The Sugar Mill is perhaps fifty steps above beach level, a dimly lighted climb ornamented with calla lilies, bougainvillaea, and invisible, squeaking frogs and, at the top, a view that reached beyond the anchorage of sailboats and yachts to the full expanse of the bays.

The dining is further enhanced by a delicious breeze, a band of steel drummers nostalgic for Jamaica or Tobago and a glimpse of Cassiopeia, the Pleiades, and all the other stars that roam the black night sky.

The third, medium-size, and quietest dining area sits among the flower-scented gardens and hedges on the heights to the west at Turtle Bay. Sometimes the jasmine is in bloom. At breakfast and dinner, the food is much the same as that served at Caneel, but it appears less slowly. Lunches are buffets. And Turtle Bay has a marvellously appointed terrace surveying a wild, islet-dotted Caribbean seascape. Only an occasional passing boat suggests the presence of man. At night, naturally enough, the view disappears, unless the moon is shining.

Caneel and Turtle bays have their own beaches – the former for extroverts who adore resort crowds, the latter for athletic types who don't mind a good hike down and back. Scott Beach is for dedicated tanners, daylong sun, and lots of space. Hawksnest, with its rocky, jungle outcroppings, its resident turtles, and its parade of distant islands, is virtually empty, mostly because the beach is narrow and the sun's angle shadows it before eleven am and after three pm. Other quiet, little-inhabited beaches are farther north.

In the end, of course, the rich, seasoned travellers who hit the Caribbean in winter don't come to see the Louvre, the Alps, the Great Wall, or each other. In winter, they are there to collapse and escape the frozen North. And the Caribbean is close compared to Acapulco, Baja California, Hawaii, or Tahiti. That they return again and again to Caneel Bay is not surprising. They rarely stay more than two or three weeks. They're spared the few chores, such as they are, of running a rented house. And depending where you look, St. John has the blue hills and forests of Jamaica, the serene grandeur of Barbados, and some of the world's best beaches.

IF YOU GO
Planning
Caneel Bay feels as if it's at the end of the world, and it isn't. The problem is finding an agent who understands the intricacies of Virgin Islands travel and the necessity for booking flights that land in St. Thomas without intermediate stops. The point of the exercise is to get to St. Thomas without having to change planes somewhere in the Caribbean, thereby risking the possibility of delayed or missing luggage. And arrival time in St. Thomas should be planned to fall within the hours that the Caneel Bay ferry service is running. Otherwise, you end up having to fend for yourself, which is all right for old hands but not for anyone making his or her first trip.

Reservations
If you book a year in advance, you can probably have a room on the beach of your choice. But don't count on it. Rock resorts, operator of Caneel Bay, says it gives 'all consideration' to requests for a specific location or room, but makes no promises. Downstairs rooms tend to be warmer, noisier, sandier, and faster to the beach. Upstairs rooms are cooler, more private, and the view, what there is of it, is wider. Deluxe rooms are not significantly different from Superior.

Rates until April 14: $255 a day for two in a garden terrace room, $320 for two in a Superior room, $350 for two in a Deluxe room, $370 a day for two in a room at Scott Beach. Lower rates (called shoulder season) prevail between April 15 and May 14 and November 1 and December 19 (the range: $195 to $275), and still lower summer rates are in effect from May 15 to October 31 ($170 to $250). All rates include three meals a day in any of the resort's three dining areas and free use of tennis courts, small sailboats, beach, and snorkelling equipment and bicycles.

Travellers who have trouble walking should reserve a downstairs room, and if the trouble is serious enough to require a wheelchair you may want to reconsider. If you're pretty good with a cane, go ahead, but know that there is lots of walking. Comfortable shoes are a necessity. Do not take more luggage than you can handle yourself. The day of porters is numbered, and while the Caneel staff is obliging, you'll find yourself carrying bags somewhere coming or going.

Caneel Bay should be told your time of arrival in order to meet you. Once your plane has landed and you have you luggage, take a taxi or jitney to the National Park dock at Red Hook Landing, where you will meet the ferry ($9 a person one way) that will whisk you across the open water to the Caneel dock on St. John Island. That trip can be cool and/or very wet and often requires a raincoat, a scarf for women, and some sort of hat for men. If you think of it, and you should, pick up a green *Caribbean Nature Guide* on the dock in St. Thomas before you embark. It is the only good account of the local fish.

Musts
Take any medications you'll require. The resort has a small shop selling

suntan lotions, clothing, sweets and some paperbacks. But the nearest chemist and shopping centre are miles away and a dreadful inconvenience. Since the choice and availability of reading material is limited, bring your own.

Though the resort supplies snorkelling equipment, dedicated snorkellers will want to bring their own. If you care about birds, bring binoculars.

If you can't help following the news of the world, bring a short-wave radio capable of getting the BBC as well as local stations. Diehards may want to consider packing a small, desktop television set, since it actually pulls in the network news programmes. If you want a daily newspaper, sign up immediately at the Caneel shop and they'll save one for you.

If you're interested in an excursion into the British Virgin Islands, you must have proof of citizenship, such as a passport, a birth certificate or a voter's registration card.

Dress Code

Shorts, dry bathing suits with shirts or beach wraps and tennis attire are acceptable in public areas throughout the day. Shoes or sandals required. After seven pm, men are expected to wear jackets, with or without ties, except on nights specifically designated as informal. Bermuda-length shorts are considered appropriate for men if worn with knee socks.

By day women wear shorts, skirts or pants with shirts or blouses, or well-covered bathing suits. At night, Caneel's 'gracious informality' suggests 'either cocktail dress, appropriate pantsuit or long skirts.' Evening dresses are few and far between, though long skirts are popular. 'Cocktail dress' is widely interpreted to include almost any late-day silk or linen suitable for New York streets in summer. Sweaters are invaluable, since there's a nip in the air.

Caneel specifically frowns on T-shirts, tank tops, and flat sandals after dark. It is not a formal place in the sense of big evenings in the Hamptons, but you can't be too informal either.

Activities Desk

Independent, seasoned travellers often figure they can skip all those exercise classes, planned garden walks, cocktail cruises, hikes, slide shows and movies. But even the most introverted should stop by the activities desk now and then to check the various bulletin boards just in case. For example, an island cruise combined with swimming, snorkelling and a beach barbecue is offered at $15 a person, and if you simply cannot function without shopping, there's a daylong cruise over to Charlotte Amalie ($18 round trip).

A REDISCOVERY OF ISLANDS

Derek Walcott

On a short visit home to the island of St. Lucia last summer we were put in a hotel that was actually a series of ascending bungalows with spacious verandas with its own cable car, overlooking a marina. You crossed the cove from the landing on the opposite side to reach this hotel, in a small boat with an open cabin. From the boat the angle of the cable-car track looked almost vertical and the highest bungalow inaccessible without the cablecar.

The marina was only a part of the huge, dark green cave that is Marigot bay. There is no local village on the rim of the bay, perhaps because there's no beach to speak of, or perhaps because the hills around it are so steep. But there were canoes now and then, and villagers fishing or swimming. The villagers worked in the hotel, and you saw their two different lives: the one lived working in the hotel and the other in the wooden houses along the steep road down to the cove, which was as sinuous as the cable-car rails were straight. The hills were thick and green around the cove and they made the expensive yachts whiter, and the hill with its white cottages was full of flowering trees, as carefully landscaped as a bouquet, bougainvillaea, and allamanda. The place was new to me. Not just the hotel and the marina, but the cove itself. It had always seemed too dark and deep. It had a disturbing peace. It was too complete. Perfection can disturb, and it was a perfect place.

It had also been given a colourful name, or so whoever rechristens these perfect places in the archipelago believed. Hurricane Hole. I didn't know if Hurricane Hole meant a place where hurricanes hid, which meant a destruction more disturbing than its peace, or a place where hurricanes originated, which is illogical. But I suppose the name is another bar name, a fortifying name for courageous yachts-men, the sort of name that they give to complicated drinks.

I hated the name because it made me feel worldwise and heroic. Foreign, in other words. All around our islands, especially where there are luxury hotels, these unanimous rechristenings are given to places, as if they were lounges or suites, so that the tourist can feel at home while the natives feel translated. So it remains Marigot, for me, without all that windy nonsense of pirates and buccaneers, naval battles and smugglers. Yachtsmen like to look piratical and foreigners like history. Tourists are voracious about maps, and they keep their heads down so steadily, and are so careful about where they are exactly, that if they move from one marina to another, from one hurricane hole to the next, it's hard for them to know which island they're on, and with homely names given to their lounges and restaurants and to whole harbours now, it isn't their fault that these places blur their features, and that they can't tell St. Vincent from St. John's, and simply call our immense archipelago, 'the islands.'

Tourist-knocking is easy. It's mainly done by other tourists, the most sincere of whom feel they have an intimacy with the place that the paler arrivistes will never have, a knowledge deeper than a tan. But unless one lives where one is, all of us are tourists.

The hotel at Hurricane Hole looked exclusive, and that was something to get over as soon as possible, so at its dining tables, just as the other tourists do, one listened for accents and measured the cost in sacrifice of its guests by class. This is a shocking truth that has not been revealed before. But we, whose backgrounds were not posh, look for others of similar and especially of inferior origins, so that we may send them a swift glare of merciful contempt. Hurricane Hole indeed. Tax shelter, you mean. You mean adding up the bill surreptitiously. You mean seeing the shadow of the front-desk cashier fall on the candlelit dinner table. You mean the horror of feeling the tan fade, the glow diminish from your heat-waxed skin like the dinner candle. Unless one of those dream yachts in the cove is yours, or even one of those cabin cruisers that are parked like cars at a drive-in watching the moon over Marigot. This nastiness is envy, you can understand that, can't you?

My hostility to the privilege of the place dissolved pretty quickly once arrangements were made and I knew I could afford it, because I was on assignment for a magazine, so that someone else was paying the bill. After a diffident languor, that easy snobbery of those used to comforts was easy, in addition to which I spoke the language like a native since I was one, to the waitresses, to the waiters to show that nothing had changed me and I was still one of the boys, and I could size up the day visitors who couldn't afford the place behind a real tan, with an affable sneer and nod at their pink legs and loud towels, and their pitiful air of abashment at the whiteness of the cottages, the cabin cruisers and the cable-car tracks that went past the bougainvillaea and the allamanda with the serene assurance of a saint ascending, or an executive's lift.

This has economics and politics in it, not to mention race, class, and history, but we may be on a break here. I had my own macho fantasies.

I may still have them. I used to wish that our forests were jungles, that our rivers had crocodiles, that I could bluster, sun-cracked and grizzled, through all the channels of the archipelago, and put in at places called Hurricane Hole with other sailors and make heartbreaking wisecracks to the blonde behind the bar, and be well loved by the natives until somebody told me I was one. I wasn't going to be anybody's sidekick, the faithful and all-wise guy who gets killed at about two-thirds of the way into the movie, so that the hero and the blonde at the bar could have a mutal heartbreak that would draw them closer. Not over my dead body. But whether you liked it or not, what happened at Hurricane Hole was inevitable. Hating the place, I knew I would come to at least like it. I knew it would happen because the hills and the dark green cove didn't care whether they were liked or not, whereas one felt that the cable car was terribly concerned and steeply eager to please.

And I knew it would happen after one night in the place. In the morning, before sunrise. When I got up. Regardless of what time I fell asleep. And I had better be prepared for it, braced with a cup of coffee, when I would step out onto the cool floorboards of the veranda, and feel, not see, the wetness of the flowers and the cool, even cold, dark green width of Marigot Bay, very dark green in the middle, and, O! annihilation of the complaining self, the first wind with light in it! Look, this can happen to anybody. It does. And if there's no coffee or a cigarette with it, you would go crazy and rage at the complacency of the harbour and the colouring sky. But, on the other hand, if you accept it as sacramental, requiring like any rite its smoke and icons, its communion in cafeine, it makes you not an addict to what will probably kill you, but the servant of the morning, watching its benediction down the aisle of the islands. Blue mountains, towns, country roads, closed shacks, empty wharves, unawakened harbours, even on the cold iron tracks of the cable car, benediction.

All the mornings of my life that I have rediscovered in different islands of the archipelago have been particular and without anonymity or repetition. Getting up in a house in the Virgin Islands before actual light, or in Tobago or Jamaica is very different and particular. Not even coffee (instant, with milk, disgustingly over-sugared) makes all those mornings the same. Not even the fact that then is when you begin to work, not always before a view. But best (not the work, the happiness, however brief), close to the sea. There's as much sugar in my body as there's salt, as much cane as surf, because they're where I'm from.

So of course it happened. That the next morning I was out on the veranda early, watching a long, black-hulled yacht move out to the mouth of the cove with barely a line of wake behind it, and a man in the skiff it was serenely towing, leaving even more space and more stillness and, what else is there to call it but a beauty so assured, a calm so inviolable, a newness so old that in a little while it began to hurt.

And it really is like looking at another when you are falling in love, but it is even more frightening in wonder if you have fallen in love with someone whose beauty is from this place. The hairs on her wrist like the far wisps of trees. And they weren't simperers who have compared the beloved's forehead to the sun rising. Yet, what's remarkable is that thirty years later, watching the cove take colour and the sea deepen in the sun, you needn't remember your first love, or how it was when you were young and you were going to sail the roughest channels of the islands, but that your fifty-year-old body could still be filled with a gratitude that brings tears. But then, everything else is just as wet. The cable car's iron tracks. The roofs. The grass. How many such mornings one is thankful for.

It's something like going to mass I suppose. The Catholic church is smart to have its five o'clock morning masses, and in the islands, where the morning stillness can reverberate like the rings of a bell, like the rings made by a fish that leaps out of the cold sea, or even the silent rings made by the bell-like allamanda that falls in full bloom on the wet grass between the shuttered bungalows.

I have seen so many bays of this kind. So many morning valleys. So many blue hills change into ordinary day, and so many quiet roofs, but nothing written can get near them. You can only pray that you get the wind in, and the light, and there's nothing wrong in spending all the mornings of your life trying to do it, because it is tougher than steering boats through hurricanes. From the Virgins to Tobago, down the whole arc. I used to count on my fingers when I was younger the different islands I knew. There were ones I was determined to hate, like the resort with its white yachts and cabin cruisers, like the Virgin Islands. Too American, I imagined. Too brash. Too many yelping tourists. Too many tough, barefooted yachtsmen having tough drinks in Hurricane Holes.

But, you see, I didn't know about the water. How clear it gets the farther north you go. I didn't know I would like even the buildings in the early morning around the airport. I mean the cold wire fences and the old tyres under the morning sea almonds. And one thing I certainly did not know was the small harbour of St. John's. That it could be so perfect and yet so right that it was I, the watcher, who felt inexact.

There are other places. All their daybreaks different. There are places that remain astonishing even with the noise of the restaurant, the noise of power boats, and planes landing and taking off. And there's one place in the Virgin Islands, the only thing that I'll tell you about it is that it's on St. Thomas, that remains the best from morning to noon to night. But I won't. Not because I'm selfish, though that too, but because no one must subject it, for one second, to that hostile, guarded look I gave the hotel at Marigot, because it is like someone you love, when you are falling in love, that you don't want judged for a single flaw, because to see its smallest flaw is an insult.

AROUND THE CARIBBEAN: VACATION PREVIEW OF THIRTY-FOUR ISLANDS

Stanley Carr

Golden beaches, gentle seas, constant sunshine and dining under the stars are the shared attractions of all the Caribbean islands, but the differences among the islands can be striking. Some are mere dots on the ocean, literally large enough to contain only one resort. Others are island nations with distinct heritages and a broad range of attractions for the visitor. Large or small, they all brace in the autumn for what they hope will prove to be a heavy migration of 'snowbirds' during the winter.

The following review of major Caribbean islands and the Bahamas includes a selective list of accommodations and restaurants. Accommodations range from quiet guesthouses and smaller hotels of quality to large hotels complete with casinos and nightclubs. The restaurants listed vary, too, ranging from those with European chefs and tables that must be reserved in advance to plainer establishments that have good reputations and are among the best on the smaller islands. (The price given after each restaurant is the approximate price, per person, of a full meal with a glass of wine.) Some islands, of course, have many more hotels, inns, and restaurants than others, but a short selection has been made for each island.

The words *moderate* (up to $100 a night for two people, without meals), *expensive* ($100 to $200), and *luxurious* (over $200) are used to indicate rates at the accommodations; MAP (modified American plan) signifies that the rate includes breakfast and dinner. The rates are for the high or winter season, which in most of the Caribbean begins on December 15 and normally continues through April 15. (Off-season rates can be as much as 40 per cent lower.) All prices are in United States dollars.

Apart from the telephone numbers of the official tourist boards, the telephone numbers in this compendium are local ones. The area code for most of the Caribbean is 809, but for some islands, including the French West Indies, international dialling codes are used, and these are given in the notes headed **The Island**.

ANGUILLA
Caribbean Tourism Association, 20 East 46th Street, New York, N.Y. 10017 (212 682 0435).
The Island
Improvements to the surface of the little airport on Anguilla in 1983 have made for smoother landings. The thirty-five-square-mile, virtually flat island, a short hop by small plane (or water taxi to Blowing Point) from St. Martin, is the kind of place for holidaymakers who want little more than a book and a beach. Several housekeeping units are available. Tourism development has been slow, the way the islanders prefer. Hotel tax: 5 per cent; service charge: 10 per cent; departure tax: $3.
Hotels
Rendezvous Bay (moderate, MAP), twenty rooms, seven cottages on the beach. Tennis court, restaurant, snorkelling and fishing gear available. Big display of bougainvillaea.

Cul de Sac (moderate), six studios near beach at Blowing Point. Family atmosphere, with cooking in your own units or eating in the restaurant (see below).

The Mariners (moderate), in Sandy Ground, opened in September 1983 next to the restaurant of the same name; West Indian-style cottages, with kitchens, and balconies overlooking the sea; maid service.
Apartments
Rainbow Reef (moderate), four two-bedroom units near the beach.

Seahorse Apartments at Sea Feathers Bay (moderate), four one-bedroom units at Blowing Point.
Restaurants
Cul de Sac (telephone 2815) is said to be the best on the island. French dishes; about $20–$25 a person for dinner. Open for lunch.

The Mariners (telephone 2671), at Sandy Ground, lobster and chicken in local style; about $15–$25.

The Riviera (telephone 2833), at Sandy Ground. A South of France atmosphere; specialities: fish soup Provençale, crayfish, conch Creole, homemade desserts. About $20.
Transportation
From New York on American or Pan Am to St. Maarten (Dutch side), then on Winair. From Miami on Eastern. From San Juan and St. Thomas with Crown Air. Daily boat service from Marigot, St. Martin.
ANTIGUA
Antigua Department of Tourism, 610 Fifth Avenue, New York, N.Y. 10020 (212 541 4117).

The Island

Lord Nelson's restored dockyard at English Harbour is a major attraction, but the island's focal point is St. John's, home of a market (Saturday mornings are best) and St. John's Cathedral. A good choice of smallish hotels – there are, with one exception, no big tour-group places – and many of them have tennis courts. Hotel room tax: 6 per cent; most hotels and restaurants add a 10 per cent service charge; departure tax: $3.50.

Hotels

Halcyon Cove Beach Resort and Casino (expensive), 154 rooms, on the sea at Dickenson Bay, tennis, water sports, pool, restaurant over the water called the Warri, and a nightclub named Chips.

Hawksbill Beach Hotel (expensive, MAP), seventy-two rooms, some in cottages, on west side of island ten minutes from St. John's. Has four beaches, pool, tennis.

Half Moon Bay Hotel (expensive, MAP), ninety-nine rooms on a good beach on the Atlantic side; its several courts represent one of the best tennis facilities in the Caribbean. Pool.

Long Island (luxurious, with three meals), a 300-acre private island resort with two beaches that opened in December 1983. Most of the twelve cottage rooms have a separate sitting room; dinner is served in an old estate house; tennis, hiking trails, archaeological digs, and trips to Antigua. Rates also include some water sports, afternoon tea – and laundry. Additional accommodations at the resort were scheduled to be completed by the end of 1984.

Restaurants

Le Bistro (telephone 23881) at Hodge's Bay is widely thought of as the best restaurant on the island. Elegant atmosphere, serving local variations of French cuisine and a variety of wines. Reservations recommended. About $50.

Dubarry's (telephone 21055) in the Barrymore Hotel near St. John's. Continental cuisine; $22–$30.

Victory (telephone 24317), old ship's décor, situated in a shopping area built in renovated warehouses at Redcliff Quay, near the U.S. Embassy in St. John's. Lobster and other seafood dishes. About $30.

Transportation

From New York on Pan Am, BWIA, and American; from Miami on Eastern and Pan Am.

ARUBA

Aruba Tourist Bureau, 1270 Avenue of the Americas, New York, N.Y. 10019 (212 246 3030).

The Island

Hundreds of modern hotel rooms, the rattle of slot machines in casinos, and considerable night life centred on the five largest hotels along Palm Beach help make the island lively. The landscape is more dramatic than pretty, but shoppers are charmed by the many imported goods sold at low-duty prices. The annual Aruba Carnival starts in late January or early February and continues for a month. International dialling code: 011 599 8. Room tax: 5 per cent; most hotels add a service charge of 10 to 15 per cent; departure tax: $5.75.

Hotels

Concorde Hotel and Casino (expensive), 500 rooms, five restaurants, nightclub, beach, pool, water sports on premises, tennis, casino, entertainment, dancing. Big and glamorous on the hotel strip.

Divi Divi Beach Hotel (expensive), 152 rooms, two restaurants, beach, pool, tennis, entertainment, dancing. Barefoot casual, friendly and isolated.

Holiday Inn Aruba Beach Resort (expensive), 390 rooms, four restaurants, nightclub, beach, pool, water sports, tennis, casino, entertainment, dancing. Big-resort style.

Talk of the Town (moderate), sixty-four rooms, three restaurants, nightclub/disco, beach, pool, entertainment, dancing. In town but on the ocean and quieter.

Bushiri Beach Hotel (moderate), fifty rooms, two restaurants, beach, pool, entertainment, dancing. Government-owned and linked with trainee programme, but the students are not used as staff. Good restaurant. Between the hotel strip and Oranjestad.

Restaurants

La Dolce Vita Ristorante (telephone 25675), in an old Aruban home, Italian cuisine, including chicken Vesuvio, lobster fra diablo, and vittelo alla Chef Bartolucci (he's from Connecticut). Antipasto bar. Often crowded. About $20.

Heidelberg (telephone 26888), full German cuisine, prepared personally by the owner, Manfred Hein. Goulash soup, spiced veal, stuffed rainbow trout, young duck with dried fruits. About $15.

Papagayo (telephone 24140), big and new, dining amid profusion of tropical plants, a fish pond, and exotic, caged tropical birds. Chops, steaks, and seafood. About $20.

Chefette (telephone 23270), in the country in Bubali, small and cozy, indoor or outdoor dining to catch the breezes. Aruban and Creole food, also steaks and chops. About $15.

Among the many snack bars, a good one is **Yvonne's** (telephone 27208) in Palm Beach near many of the hotels. It makes deliveries; one speciality: homemade pisca tempera, a cold fish dish with spices.

Transportation

From New York on American. From Miami on Eastern or A.L.M. Antillean Airlines.

THE BAHAMAS

Bahamas Tourist Office, 10 Columbus Circle, New York, N.Y. 10019 (212 757 1611).

The Islands

There's more than Nassau, the capital, on New Providence, and Freeport on Grand Bahama, the places that attract the most tourists. The Bahamas, which start fifty miles from Florida, can be counted in their hundreds, but only a few are inhabited, and of these, the Family Islands, as they're known – Eleuthera and the Exumas among them – attract many unostentatious but nonetheless affluent visitors. (The Family Islands used to be called the Out Islands; the Bahamian Government changed the name because it felt the old one made the islands sound inaccessible.) The smaller islands offer considerable tennis and scuba and skin diving; the main islands have those attractions, too, as well as many urban resort comforts. Hotel room tax: 6 per cent; some restaurants add a 15 per cent service charge; departure tax: $5.

Hotels

Ambassador Beach Hotel (expensive), Nassau, on Cable Beach, with 383 rooms. Extensive renovations were completed in 1984. Golf course across the street. Only two tennis courts. Four restaurants; more being added.

Cable Beach Manor (moderate), Nassau, studios and one- and two-bedroom units, all with housekeeping facilities, on Cable Beach. Private beach and pool. Shopping nearby.

The Ocean Club (expensive), Paradise Island, built by Huntingford Hartford; seventy rooms and suites. Quiet, with courtyard terrace for dining. Villas with private Jacuzzis. Nine lighted tennis courts, pool.

Lucayan Bay Hotel (moderate), Freeport, Grand Bahama Island, home of the International Underwater Explorers Society; 168 rooms, two restaurants, pool, boat docking, diving. Entertainment every night.

Peace and Plenty (moderate), Exuma, thirty-two rooms near private beach and grouped around pool. Informal atmosphere and local social centre. Restaurant and bar.

Coral Sands Hotel (moderate), Harbour Island, Eleuthera, on a long private beach, with garden and thirty-three rooms. Restaurant, tennis court.

Restaurants

Del Prado (telephone 5 0324), West Bay Street, Nassau. Wide selection of Continental dishes, including grouper flambé, escallope of veal, and lobster flavoured with brandy. About $30.

Pilot House (telephone 2 8431), East Bay Street, Nassau. Bahamian and Continental dishes served in casual outdoor atmosphere; near Yacht Haven and favoured by yachting set. About $30.

The Terrace (telephone 2 22836), Parliament Street, Nassau. Alfresco dining with salad bar and hot and cold buffet; $8–$15.

Lucaya Country Club (telephone 373 1066) in Freeport, overlooks golf course. French cuisine; $25–$30.

Transportation

From New York on Pan Am, Delta, Air Florida, and Eastern. From Miami on Air Florida, Bahamas Air, and Eastern. Chalk's International operates regular seaplane service between Miami and Paradise Island, Bimini, and Cat Cay.

BARBADOS

Barbados Board of Tourism, 800 Second Avenue, New York, N.Y. 10017 (212 986 6516).

The Island

Britishness survives – although Barbados has been independent since 1966 – in such things as military-style brass bands, a passion for cricket, orderliness, conservative clothes, and afternoon tea (in some hotels, too). This is a place well equipped for tourism, offering everything from quiet coves to sprawling resorts. Flights around the Monday and Tuesday before Ash Wednesday are busy because they are the days of the Trinidad Carnival, and most planes bound for Trinidad stop in Barbados. Be firm with beach vendors. Hotel room tax: 8 per cent; hotels add a 10 per cent service charge; departure tax: $6.

Hotels

Cobblers Cove (expensive), a quiet haven in a horseshoe-shape setting on the beach at St. Peter, eleven miles from town. The thirty-eight suites each have balcony or terrace, walk-in kitchen, and living room as well as bedroom. Pool.

Coconut Creek (expensive, MAP), in well-planted grounds and on beach at St. James, six miles from Bridgetown; forty-nine rooms, some suites, and housekeeping apartments; English-style pub, pool.

Coral Reef Club (expensive to luxurious), also at St. James, eight miles from town; elegant layout of cottages in gardens and on beach, seventy-five rooms, pool.

Sandy Lane (luxurious, MAP), with 115 rooms, a Trusthouse Forte hotel built in Georgian style, the most luxurious hotel on the island, in St. James. A rather dressy crowd drops in for afternoon tea, drinks, or Sunday brunch. Pool, tennis, and its own golf course.

Ragged Point (moderate, MAP) one of several good guesthouses; in St. Philip, ten rooms, not air-conditioned, pool.

Restaurants
Bagatelle Great House (telephone 50666), an old governor's mansion in St. Thomas that presents an experience, if not haute cuisine. Dining by candlelight, with a long menu; beef Wellington a speciality. About $20.

Brown Sugar (telephone 67684), at Aquatic Gap, St. Michael, within walking distance of some Bridgetown hotels. Well-prepared Barbadian dishes such as pepper pot soup and flying fish. Reservations advised. About $15.

Pisces (telephone 86558), an attractive fish restaurant on the water at St. Lawrence Gap, Christ Church. Specializes in seafood; dining by candlelight among tropical plants. About $15.

Transportation
From New York daily and nonstop on American, BWIA, and Pan Am. From Miami on Eastern and BWIA daily; also on Pan Am but less frequently.

BONAIRE

Bonaire Tourist Information Office, 1466 Broadway, Suite 903, New York, N.Y. 10036 (212 869 2004).

The Island
Travellers arriving at the modern airport building find that the trade winds constantly blowing across this Dutch island provide the air-conditioning. Tourism has been growing steadily, thanks to good diving, bird watching (including flamingos) in a huge game preserve, grottoes carved by the sea, and the islanders' reputation for extending a warm welcome in a place that's almost always sunny. International dialling code: 011 599 7. Hotel room tax: 5 per cent; restaurants add a service charge of 10 to 15 per cent.

Hotels
Flamingo Beach Hotel (moderate), 110 rooms, with balconies or patios over the sea, two restaurants, beach, pool, diving centre; attracts the younger set.

Hotel Bonaire (moderate), the biggest hotel on the island (145 rooms) and the only one with a casino; cosmopolitan and rather sedate. Beach and pool.

Habitat (moderate), nine two-bedroom cottages with kitchens on the compound of a well-known diving specialist and instructor, Don Stewart. For divers: rustic but adequate, friendly, with restaurant and ocean frontage.

Restaurants
Chibi Chibi (telephone 8285), alfresco dining under a thatched roof and overlooking the sea, which is illuminated at night for fish feeding. Fresh seafood a speciality. About $15.

Den Laman (telephone 8955), with an entire wall occupied by an aquarium; serves lobster and Creole fish dishes. About $17.

Transportation

From New York on American via Curaçao, connecting with A.L.M. Antillean Airlines to Bonaire. From Miami on A.L.M. (on weekends, nonstop) and on Eastern to Curaçao with Bonaire connection on A.L.M.

CAYMAN ISLANDS

Cayman Islands Tourist Board, 420 Lexington Avenue, New York, N.Y. 10017 (212 682 5582).

The Islands

Investors have pumped a lot of money into Grand Cayman since it became an offshore banking centre, a development that has helped lead to a growth in condominium building. The other two members of this trio of British outcroppings, Cayman Brac and Little Cayman, are clinging to their isolation. The Caymans' major attractions for the active are diving and fishing. Grand Cayman, being mostly flat, is good for bicycles and mopeds (for rent). A 15 per cent service charge is added to restaurant bills; departure tax: $5.

Hotels

Holiday Inn (expensive), 215 rooms, the largest hotel in the islands, on the beach on Grand Cayman's west coast. Restaurant, pool, beach bar, shopping, and water sports.

Royal Palms of Cayman (moderate), also on Grand Cayman; sixty-two rooms; with a restaurant, shops, pool, and beach bar.

Tiara Beach Hotel (moderate), on Cayman Brac; twenty-eight rooms, pool, restaurant, and access to diving and other water sports.

Restaurants

Grand Old House (telephone 92020), in the Petra Plantation House built in 1900; specializes in seafood and European dishes, with selection of twenty main courses. Dinner is served on the Victorian veranda. Good wine list; reservations essential. About $50.

Cayman Arms (telephone 92661), overlooking Georgetown harbour, has a British pub atmosphere and serves daily lunch and dinner specials as well as regular seafood dishes. About $30.

Transportation

From Miami, daily jet service on Republic Airlines and Cayman Airways. Cayman also has three or four flights a week from Houston to Grand Cayman and two a week from Miami to Cayman Brac.

CURAÇAO

Curaçao Tourist Board, 400 Madison Avenue, Suite 311, New York, N.Y. 10017 (212 751 8266).

The Island

Opinions differ on whether Willemstad, the capital built and well laid out by the Dutch in the style of their homeland, retains much charm now that duty-free shops and night spots stand next to the old gingerbread buildings. But the city's sights (including the old Mikve Israel-Emanuel Synagogue) are still the main attractions here. The best way to see the rest of this mostly flat, sandy island is on horseback, in early morning or late afternoon. International dialling code: 011 599 9. Hotel room tax: 5 per cent; most hotels add a service charge of 10 to 15 per cent; departure tax: $3.50.

Hotels

Curaçao Concorde Hotel-Casino (expensive), 199 rooms, a South American high-rise atmosphere; three restaurants, nightclub, beach, water sports, pool, tennis, dancing, entertainment. Formerly the Hilton.

Las Palmas Hotel and Vacation Village (moderate), 100 rooms, also has 94 villas for four to six, all at a flat charge of $130 a day. The grounds and immaculate lawns are more elegant than the rooms; nightclub, short walk to beach, pool, tennis, dancing.

Curaçao Plaza Hotel (expensive), 254 rooms, in Willemstad, no beach but great view over the harbour. Three restaurants, casino, nightclub, pool, entertainment.

Restaurants

Tavern Restaurant Wine Cellar (telephone 70669), on the outskirts of the capital in a roomy nineteenth century Dutch landhaus. Continental and American cuisine. About $20.

La Bistroelle (telephone 76929), known for its melon à la mode (melon with smoked salmon and asparagus) and moules in a light whisky sauce as well as prime U.S. meats and Curaçao dishes. About $18.

Golden Star (telephone 54795) offers Keshi Llena (a cheese entrée cooked with several meats) and funchi (local breads) among its Dutch Antillean specialities. About $10.

Transportation

From New York on American; from Miami on A.L.M. and Eastern.

DOMINICA

Caribbean Tourism Association, 20 East 46th Street, New York, N.Y. 10017 (212 682 0435).

The Island

Canefield, a five-minute drive from Roseau, the capital of this once-British colony, is the better airport for most visitors, although it takes only nineteen-seater planes. The taxi ride to Roseau (where most hotels are) from the other airport, Melville Hall, takes nearly two

hours, includes rough roads, and costs about $16. (The largest planes
there are forty-nine-seaters.) Bird watchers, botanists, canoeists, and
hikers who like mountainous jungle areas find plenty of rewards. The
island's allure is its wildness, and there are no duty-free shops and little
night life. Hotel room tax: 10 per cent; most hotels add a 10 per cent
service charge; departure tax: $3.

Hotels
Sisserou (moderate, MAP), twenty rooms with sea view about half
a mile south of Roseau; restaurant, pool, hot mineral baths. The hotel
will arrange safari tours.

Castaways (moderate, MAP), the only beach hotel in Dominica;
with snorkelling, boating, deep-sea fishing, and windsurfing; twenty-
seven rooms, restaurant; twenty-five minutes from Roseau. The
American owners have lived on the island for twenty years.

Kent Anthony's Guesthouse (moderate), in the centre of Roseau;
eighteen rooms, restaurant. Rebuilt after damage by Hurricane Daisy
in 1979.

Restaurants
Guiyave (telephone 2930), in Roseau, serving lunch only. A meal of
local dishes will cost about $6; with dishes like steak, lobster, and
mountain chicken, about $12. Closed Sunday.

Orchid (telephone 3051), a new restaurant in a garden setting in
Roseau. Lunch or dinner of local dishes, $6; à la carte special orders,
$12. Closed Sunday.

Transportation
From Antigua and Barbados on L.I.A.T.; from Martinique on Air
Martinique; from Guadeloupe on Air Guadeloupe; from St. Lucia on
Winlink.

DOMINICAN REPUBLIC
Dominican Republic Tourist Information Centre, 485 Madison
Avenue, New York, N.Y. 10022 (212 826 0750).

The Island
On this eastern two-thirds of the island of Hispaniola, which the
republic shares with Haiti, the style is strictly Latin. Siestas close
stores and museums, dinner is at nine – or later – and if you stray from
the major tourist haunts there's a need for at least some Spanish.
Peaks, valleys, and sugar plantations mark the rugged terrain between
the capital, Santo Domingo, and the deluxe resorts that have sprung
up on the north and south coasts. (Your out-of-town hotel may be a
long way from the airport.) Note the capital's cluster of restored
sixteenth century buildings and, in the southeast of the country, Altos
de Chavon, an artists' village built in sixteenth century Spanish
style. The value of the peso against the dollar has been fluctuating a

great deal. Hotel room tax: $5; most hotels add a 10 per cent service charge, and some add an energy charge; departure tax: $4.

Hotels

Hotel Santo Domingo (expensive), in Santo Domingo, 385 rooms, pool, tennis, sauna, masseur, bars.

Santo Domingo Sheraton (expensive), 260 rooms, all with view of the Caribbean. Casino, pool, sauna, gym, two tennis courts, evening activities including piano bar and disco.

Hotel San Geronimo (moderate), in heart of Santo Domingo and within walking distance of downtown. Pool, view of the Caribbean. For the economy-minded.

Concord Dominicano (moderate), in Santo Domingo, 316 rooms, piano bar, disco, sauna, casino, eight tennis courts.

Restaurants

Café St. Michel (telephone 567 0570, 567 7922), Santo Domingo, French cuisine. Relaxed ambience. About $15.

Mesón de la Cava (telephone 532 2615, 533 2818), Santo Domingo, a cave fifty feet below ground. Steep staircase. Italian and Continental cuisine, good service. About $12.

Restaurant Lina (telephone 689 5185), Santo Domingo, a varied wine selection. Continental cuisine, Spanish specialities. About $15.

Lago Enriquillo Restaurant (telephone 533 7444), Santo Domingo, Chinese restaurant overlooking man-made lake. Serves American Indian cassava bread with garlic butter. About $12.

Transportation

From New York on American, Dominicana de Aviacion, Eastern. From Miami on Eastern, Dominicana de Aviacion, Air Florida.

GRENADA

Grenada Tourist Board, 141 East 44th Street, New York, N.Y. 10017 (212 687 9554).

The Island

The State Department, in an announcement dated November 18, 1983, following the invasion, advised Americans wishing to travel to Grenada that 'it is now considered safe to do so.' Pearls Airport was open to commercial traffic, the announcement said, and telephone, telegraph, and telex services were 'nearly back to normal.' Very few holidaymakers went to Grenada that winter, but the island's tourist industry hoped for a substantial increase in the number of visitors during the 1984–1985 season. They also expected that the Point Salines Airport, designed to take jet aircraft, would become operational, if not completed, late in 1984 and that perhaps one of the major airlines would start a weekly service from the United States. As for hotel rooms, there was, with one or two exceptions, no shortage. A spokesman for the tourist board in New York said the much admired Ross' Point Inn would continue to serve as the U.S. Embassy until either October 1984 or March 1985, and it was expected that the Grenada Beach Hotel, the island's largest hotel, would continue to accommodate American military personnel until April 1985. Hotel tax: 7½ per cent; most hotels add a 10 per cent service charge; departure tax: $2.

Hotels

Spice Island Inn (expensive, MAP), on Grand Anse Beach, offers twenty beach suites and ten others each with its own private pool. Quiet atmosphere; restaurant.

The Flamboyant (moderate), one- and two-bedroom cottages with kitchens and with views of the Caribbean and St. George's harbour; within walking distance of Grand Anse Beach. Maids and cooks available.

Cinnamon Hill and Beach Club (expensive), the island's first condominium hotel, on a hill above Grand Anse Beach, with views of St. George's. Pool, restaurant.

Blue Horizons Cottage Hotel (moderate), is a seven-minute walk from Grand Anse Beach and consists of cottages and efficiencies, all with kitchenette. Pool, tropical garden, La Belle Creole Restaurant.

Restaurants

Mama's, on Old Lagoon Road, St. George's, is renowned for its eighteen-course meals, from crab and callaloo soup to sea-moss ice cream, served to groups of eight or more at about $10 a person. Smaller groups are welcome but they get fewer courses. Reservations necessary (call Mama's daughter, Cleo, at 2299).

The Nutmeg (telephone 2539), in St. George's, on second floor, with views of the port; a variety of local dishes. About $10.

Transportation

From Barbados or Trinidad on L.I.A.T.

GUADELOUPE

French West Indies Tourist Board, 610 Fifth Avenue, New York, N.Y. 10020 (212 757 1125).

The Island

On this overseas region of France the language is French and the currency is the franc. Guadeloupe is really two islands, flat Grande-Terre and mountainous Basse-Terre, connected by a drawbridge, and resembling a butterfly in shape. Most hotels are on Grand-Terre, which includes the capital, Pointe-à-Pitre. Tourism is highly developed here and includes night life strongly addicted to dancing the beguine and the calypso. International dialling code: 011 596. Restaurants usually add a service charge of 10 to 15 per cent. (Travellers wishing to obtain information in person should go to the French Government Tourist Office, 628 Fifth Avenue.)

Hotels

Auberge de la Vieille Tour (moderate), eighty-two rooms near centre of Gosier, a sea-orientated hotel with two restaurants, two bars, private beach, pool, tennis, free use of sailing equipment.

Meridien Hotel (expensive), 272 rooms, in St. François; with three restaurants, windboarding, private beach, tennis (four courts), pool, big-game fishing. Near casino and golf course. A forty-five-minute drive from the Pointe-à-Pitre airport.

Relais du Moulin (moderate), near Ste. Anne, twenty rooms in bungalows, near sea with private beach. Pool, tennis court, archery, horseback riding. A forty minute drive from airport.

Hotel du Bois Joli (moderate), at Terre-de-Haut on Iles des Saintes, south of the main island. The hotel is at one end of the small island, isolated from the main town but near two beaches. Transport to and from the town is regularly scheduled by car or boat (ten minutes). Of the twenty-one rooms, thirteen are air-conditioned.

Restaurants

La Plantation (telephone 82 39 63), at Bas-du-Fort Marina; specialities include goose giblet salad and freshwater crayfish. Good wine selection and Cuban cigars. About $30.

Le Bistrot (telephone 84 13 82), Petit-Havre, with hilltop setting on Grand Bay. Specializes in seafood (ray, shark, snapfish) and Creole cooking. About $20.

La Canne à Sucre (telephone 82 10 19), in Pointe-à-Pitre, serves Creole cuisine, stuffed crabs, crayfish dishes. About $25.

Transportation

From New York on American and Pan Am. From Miami on Air France and Eastern.

HAITI

Haiti National Office of Tourism, 1270 Avenue of the Americas, Suite 508, New York, N.Y. 10020 (212 757 3517).

The Island

The republic's reputation for repression and poverty has long inhibited tourism. The number of visitors dropped precipitously after the summer of 1982 when Haitians were identified as a 'risk group' for the disorder known as Acquired Immune Deficiency Syndrome (AIDS) – along with homosexual men, intravenous drug users, and haemophiliacs – by the U.S. Centers for Disease Control in Atlanta, Georgia. The disorder is still mysterious, but physicians believe that it is probably transmitted by sexual contact, injections or transfusions from AIDS victims. The Centers for Disease Control have now dropped the words *risk group* from their references to AIDS. Travellers who do visit the island – there were few tourists in the 1983–1984 season – praise its dramatic landscapes, a culture that blends French and African, comfortable resorts, and artwork. Hotels in Port-au-Prince are close to sightseeing, but those in the hills are cooler and more relaxed. International dialling code: 011 509 1. Hotel room tax: 5 per cent; most hotels add a 10 per cent service charge; departure tax: $10.

Hotels

Hotel Splendid (moderate, with light breakfast), Port-au-Prince, in residential district five minutes from downtown; forty rooms, air-conditioned, pool, restaurant featuring nightly piano; viola music in restored turn-of-the-century mansion.

El Rancho (moderate, with mountain-view suites more expensive), Pétionville, twenty minutes from downtown Port-au-Prince. Known as perhaps Haiti's most luxurious hotel, 105 rooms. Meal plan available. Casino, two restaurants, new nightclub. Two pools, whirlpool, sauna, tennis court.

Mont Joli (moderate), in Cap Haitien, the second largest city. View includes the historic Citadel of King Henri Christophe. Forty rooms, air-conditioned, pool in tropical mountain setting.

Restaurants

Le Select (telephone 5 3285), rue Jean-Claude Duvalier, Port-au-Prince, in residential area ten minutes from downtown. Haitian cuisine, well prepared, served on terrace or in garden of gingerbread turn-of-the-century house. Speciality: guinea hen with special Haitian rice and beans and fried plantain, $4.50. Average dinner, $10, not including wine.

Le Rond Point (telephone 2 0621), Port-au-Prince, a traditional meeting place, offering luncheon special on weekdays at $4.25. Specialities: steak au poivre flambé, $7.75; shrimps in shell steamed with spices, $3.75. Average dinner, $12.

La Glacière (telephone 6 0666), in Cayes, Haiti's third-largest city, is a three-hour ride from Port-au-Prince on a paved highway. A converted ice factory opened recently as a spacious ten-table restaurant. Poisson gros sel (Haitian fish), about $3.50; goat ragout, $4.50. Highest price on à la carte menu, about $6. Excellent service.

Transportation

From New York on American; from Miami on Eastern or Air Florida.

JAMAICA

Jamaica Tourist Board, 866 Second Avenue, New York, N.Y. 10017 (212 688 7650).

The Island

The major resort areas – Montego Bay, Ocho Rios, Negril, Runaway Bay and Port Antonio – are in the north and west and separated from the capital, Kingston, in the south, by a range of mountains. The island offers plenty of sightseeing and side trips for holidaymakers who need a change from its beaches and sea. There's plenty of tennis and golf, too. Hotel room tax: $10 (but subject to change); some hotels add 10 per cent service charge; restaurants add a service charge of 10 to 15 per cent; departure tax: $6.

Hotels

Tryall Golf and Beach Club (expensive, MAP) is on 2,200 acres on the north coast twelve miles from Montego Bay. Its hub is the forty-four-room great house; there are also forty villas, each with private pool, rented by the week (luxurious, no meals). Own golf course, six tennis courts, horseback riding, pool with swim-up bar, and water sports.

Trident Villas and Hotel (expensive, MAP), Port Antonio, villas amid walled gardens and waterfalls in a tranquil setting of fourteen acres. The beach is small but a free boat takes guests to Frenchman's Cove. Pool, tennis; restaurant in 'château' with turrets.

Half Moon Club (expensive), a sprawling, comfortable complex on the sea at Montego Bay; 190 units ranging from rooms to cottages and suites, some with private or semiprivate pool. Golf, thirteen tennis courts, squash, sauna.

Sandals Resort Beach Club (luxurious: all inclusive weekly tariff for two, with all meals), on eastern side of Montego Bay, is for adult couples only and attracts mostly young people. It's on thirteen acres, with a long beach and 173 rooms, all with ocean views. Water sports and health club, restaurant and bars.

Restaurants

Almond Tree (telephone 974 2676), in the Hibiscus Lodge at Ocho Rios, alfresco and overlooking the sea; seafood and Jamaican dishes. About $25–$50.

Richmond Hill Inn (telephone 952 3859), on a hill overlooking Montego Bay; steaks and lobster. About $25–$30.

Transportation

From New York on Air Jamaica, American, and Pan Am. From Miami on Air Jamaica, Air Florida, Eastern.

MARTINIQUE

French West Indies Tourist Board, 610 Fifth Avenue, New York, N.Y. 10020 (212 757 1125).

The Island

Pointe du Bout on the east coast, where many new hotels have been built around a marina, is, for visitors at least, the liveliest part of this overseas region of France. Those preferring quieter surroundings should head for the inns in the north, an area of rain forests and mountains, and south. Fort-de-France, the capital, is a twenty-minute ferry ride from Pointe du Bout. Shoppers will like the French goods, including perfume and Limoges china, but the island has a strong Creole tradition of crafts – appliquéd hangings, dolls, baskets, and jewellery. French and Creole cuisine, French and Creole language. (Note: Travellers wishing to obtain information in person should go to the French Government Tourist Office, 628 Fifth Avenue.) International dialling code: 011 596. A service charge of 10 to 15 per cent is usually added to restaurant bills.

Hotels
Bakoua Beach Hotel (expensive), at Pointe du Bout, one of the best on the island; ninety-eight rooms, all with balcony or patio, most with sea views, but some with only a shower. Pool, two tennis courts, sailboats, water sports. Its restaurant, Chateaubriand, is a fine one.

Leyritz Plantation (moderate), tucked away in a mountain setting at Basse-Pointe in the north, and different in that it is a restored eighteenth century house in a garden setting and not on the ocean. Views of the sea from most of the twenty-five rooms. A starting point for hiking.

Meridien Martinique (expensive), at Pointe du Bout, looking across the bay to Fort-de-France, seven stories and 303 rooms, all with balconies. About 150 rooms face the bay, the others the marina. Water sports, two tennis courts.

Restaurants
La Grand' Voile (telephone 70 29 29), highly regarded French restaurant created by a couple from Lyons, on the second floor of the Yacht Club in Fort-de-France. About $20.

Le Colibri (telephone 75 32 19), in a private home at Morne des Esses; sea urchin tarts and stuffed pigeon are among the specialities. About $15.

Le Tiffany (telephone 71 33 82), a pink-and-white gingerbread house in Fort-de-France, serving classic French and nouvelle cuisine in an elegant atmosphere. Reservations recommended. About $20.

Transportation
From New York on American and Pan Am. From Miami on Eastern and Air France.

MONTSERRAT
Caribbean Tourism Association, 20 East 46th Street, New York, N.Y. 10017 (212 682 0435).

The Island

From the middle of December to New Year's Day this tiny British colony – a fifteen-minute flight from Antigua – takes an enthusiastic approach to the holidays with parades and parties, singing and steel bands. Among the celebrants visitors may notice some red-haired islanders speaking a brogue that sounds Irish. The reason: Early settlers included a contingent from Ireland. After your taxi ride (about $10) from airport to hotel, you'll need a rental car to get around the island, much of which is mountainous and forested. No big hotels. Hotel room tax: 7 per cent; most hotels add a 10 per cent service charge; departure tax: $5.

Hotels

Vue Pointe (expensive, MAP), twelve hotel rooms and twenty-eight cottages overlooking Isles Bay, a fifteen-minute drive from Plymouth. Two minutes' walk from beach, freshwater pool, tennis, restaurant. Its bar attracts sailors who tie up at a nearby dock.

Coconut Hill (moderate, MAP) is a converted plantation house, with nine rooms, set in gardens on the outskirts of Plymouth and overlooking the sea. It has a small bar and restaurant – the local dishes include mountain chicken.

Restaurants

Benham Valley (telephone 5553), in a former private home on a hillside, within walking distance of the Vue Pointe. Continental dishes. About $16.

Transportation

From Antigua on L.I.A.T.

NEVIS

Eastern Caribbean Tourist Association, 220 East 42nd Street, New York, N.Y. 10017 (212 986 9370).

The Island

In the little port of Charlestown a small crowd gathers every morning at ten to watch the major event of the day: the unloading of the ferry from the sister island of St. Kitts. The pace is slow and high life nonexistent, and the unpretentious inns constitute the major attraction. The one main road circles the island; the minor roads wind off to the hotels and beauty spots. Power failures are not uncommon. Hotel room tax: 5 per cent; departure tax: $4.

Hotels

Rest Haven Inn (expensive, MAP), thirty-five rooms, some with kitchens, on the beach in Charlestown, with pool and restaurant.

Pinney's Beach Hotel (expensive), thirty-six simply furnished rooms on the beach in Charlestown, with pool, restaurant, and facilities for fishing.

Nisbett Plantation Inn (expensive, MAP), twenty rooms, set in coconut plantation beside Newcastle Beach. Tennis, fishing, horseback riding; restaurant in plantation house.

Transportation

From St. Kitts on L.I.A.T. and daily ferries (except Thursday and Sunday).

PUERTO RICO

Commonwealth of Puerto Rico Tourism Company, 1290 Avenue of the Americas, Suite 3704, New York, N.Y. 10104 (212 541 6630).

The Island

Beyond the busy capital of San Juan, with its enormous hotels, casinos and night life, lies an island that offers the kind of quiet hideaways, relaxed atmosphere and good tennis and golf facilities that many travellers seek on other islands farther away. Ponce and Fajardo are among the towns offering a less bustling but more Spanish alternative to the big city. The 700-mile coastline has many beaches, although the better ones may take some finding, and the interior is dominated by mountain ranges. In San Juan, drivers should steer clear of rush hours: The traffic jams can rival those of Manhattan, particularly for visitors going to or from the airport. Hotel room tax: $6.

Hotels

Condado Holiday Inn (moderate), the liveliest hotel in San Juan, 587 rooms; discothèque and nightclub on the lobby floor; a supper club with a Las Vegas-type revue, nightclub, casino and an Italian and Mexican restaurant on the mezzanine; and two restaurants, one French, the other Chinese, in its Laguna wing.

Palace Hotel (moderate to expensive), in the Isla Verde hotel area near the airport; supper club presents a revue on ice.

Palmas del Mar (expensive), resort, near Humacao, built like a series of Mediterranean villages on a 3½-mile stretch of beach on the south coast; 102 rooms, eighteen-hole golf course, twenty tennis courts, and four pools.

Eight small inns and hotels, all moderately priced, are operated under the government's paradores programme. They range from the tiny eight-room Parador Martorell, off the beach in Luquillo, where the rates include breakfast, to the fifty-room Hotel La Parguera. The forty-eight-room Baños de Coamo, high in the hills outside the town of Coamo, has thermal baths.

Restaurants

Au Cheval Blanc (telephone 721 1000), French restaurant in the Condado Holiday Inn. About $35.

Fontana di Roma (telephone 724 6161), Italian restaurant in the Dupont Plaza Hotel. About $30.

La Casona (telephone 727 2717), at 609 San Jorge Street, in Santurce, a ten-minute drive from the Condado hotel district. Spanish-Continental cuisine. About $30.

El Callejón de la Capilla (telephone 725 8529), 317 Fortaleza Street, serves Puerto Rican dishes such as plantain-based dishes or asapoas, which are rice dishes. About $15.

La Familia Restaurant (telephone 883 2640), Route 690, Kilometre 7.1, near the Dorado Beach Hotel, serves fresh seafood and steaks in a family atmosphere. About $10.

Transportation
From New York, Miami, and other East Coast cities on Eastern, American, Capitol, and Arrow.

SABA

St Maarten–Saba–St. Eustatius Tourist Information Office, 25 West 39th Street, New York, N.Y. 10018 (212 840 6655).

The Island
What attracts people to this tiny mountainous island with one switchback road and no beaches are the beauty of its landscapes and seascapes and the charm of its miniature scale. Everything is small: houses clinging to the hillsides, churches, streets, gardens, and, of course, the inns and guesthouses. Furthermore, only twenty-seater planes serve the island, and seats can be hard to get. International dialling code: 011 599 4. Hotel tax: 5 per cent; hotels and restaurants add a service charge of 10 to 15 per cent.

Hotels
Captain's Quarters (moderate), a guesthouse in white clapboard buildings in Windwardside; ten rooms, pool.

Cranston's Antique Inn (moderate), six rooms in The Bottom.

Scout's Place (moderate), in Windwardside; five rooms, open-air dining terrace.

Restaurants
Captain's Quarters (telephone 2201), American and European fare mixed with local fish and vegetables. About $11.

Scout's Place (telephone 2205), about $11.

Transportation
From St. Maarten on Winair; from St. Kitts via St Eustatius on Winair.

ST. BARTHELEMY

French West Indies Tourist Board, 610 Fifth Avenue, New York, N.Y. 10020 (212 757 1125).

The Island

On eight-square-mile St. Barts, a rental car is needed almost anywhere the visitor stays – to explore the hills and coral-sand coves and to get into the capital, Gustavia. It's a pretty town but stay out of it when the cruise ships call. Hotels are small and the restaurants are busy enough for reservations to be essential. (Travellers wishing to obtain information in person should go to the French Government Tourist Office, 628 Fifth Avenue.) International dialling code: 011 596. Some hotels add 10 or 15 per cent tax and service charge.

Hotels

El Sereno (expensive), the former Sereno Beach Hotel at Grand Cul-de-Sac, has been refurbished by new owner; twenty rooms, La Toque Lyonnaise Restaurant, pool.

Filao Beach Hotel (expensive), on the main beach at St. Jean Bay where most water sports are concentrated; thirty rooms, each named for a French château, in two-room beach bungalows, pool.

The Village Saint Jean (moderate), on a hill above St. Jean Bay; twenty-five units include rooms, villas, and apartments; pool.

Tom Beach (moderate), on St. Jean Beach, next to the Chez Francine Restaurant, is a new addition, consisting of twelve rooms, each with kitchenette.

Restaurants

Au Port (telephone 87 62 36), on second floor overlooking the harbour. Some thirty dishes include foie gras flown in weekly from France, and there are fifteen desserts. Evenings only. About $25.

Castelets (telephone 87 61 73), at Morne Lurin on one of the island's highest points and decorated with French provincial antiques. Cold cubed langouste with mayonnaise and diced peaches, fish mousse on a bed of spinach. Closed Tuesday for lunch and dinner and Wednesday for lunch. Reservations. About $35, not including wine.

Chez Francine (telephone 87 60 49), overlooking St. Jean Bay; open only for lunch and closed Monday. Fresh langouste and kebab and homemade pies. Casual atmosphere. No reservations. Main courses, about $8–$24.

Transportation

From St. Maarten on Winair and from St. Martin by Air Guadeloupe; from St. Thomas on Virgin Air; from Guadeloupe on Air Guadeloupe and Air St. Barts. Catamarans sail daily from St. Maarten, about an hour's crossing.

ST. CROIX

U.S. Virgin Islands Division of Tourism, 1270 Avenue of the Americas, New York, N.Y. 10020 (212 582 4520).

The Island

The largest of the U.S. Virgin Islands (eighty square miles), St. Croix is less mountainous than the other two. It has two towns, Christiansted, a harbour protected by reefs, and Frederiksted, a deep-water port that is a ten-minute drive from Alexander Hamilton Airport. Christiansted's boutiques offer low-duty buys and some local handicrafts, but there are fewer shops than in St. Thomas. (Items made in the U.S. Virgin Islands are not subject to duty.) Off the coast is the only national park that is partially under water. Hotel tax: 5 per cent; most hotels add a service charge of 10 to 15 per cent.

Hotels

Grapetree Beach (expensive), eighty-six rooms with patios overlooking the Caribbean, on easternmost part of the island, six miles from Christiansted. Tennis, pool, water sports, restaurant.

Caravelle (moderate), forty-six rooms (with refrigerators), old, established hotel in town of Christiansted and close to shops. Pool, beach nearby, restaurant.

Restaurants

Barbara McConnell's (telephone 772 3309), in Frederiksted, serves mostly in its garden behind an old townhouse; roast lamb in ginger and burgundy, salmon mousse, ham with drunken beans, homemade pastries and bread. Lunch, about $12; dinner, about $20. Reservations required. Closed Sunday.

Comanche (telephone 773 2665), in Christiansted, greenery and rattan in a harbourside pavilion with ceiling fans; curried seafood, curried chicken, lobster, and 108 wines listed. Lunch, about $9; dinner, about $19.

Transportation

From New York on American (direct); via San Juan on American, Eastern, and Capitol. From San Juan on Coral Air, Crown Air, Ocean Air, and Air V.I.

ST. EUSTATIUS

St. Maarten–Saba–St. Eustatius Tourist Information Office, 25 West 39th Street, New York, N.Y. 10018 (212 840 6655).

The Island

Burros and guides may be hired to visit the Quill, an extinct volcano that shelters a tropical rain forest in its crater. The trip is one of the few structured outings on an island, known as Statia, whose relaxed style has been little affected by tourism. Just a few inns to choose from. International dialling code: 011 599 3. Room tax: 5 per cent; hotels and restaurants add a service charge of 10 to 15 per cent.

Hotels

Old Gin House (expensive), six rooms on the beach in a reconstruction of an eighteenth century building that once housed a cotton gin, and fourteen rooms across the street beside a pool surrounded by tropical gardens. The dining room, the Mooshay Bay Publick House, attracts many visitors.

Golden Rock Resort (moderate), at Zeelandia on a two-mile stretch of beach, with ten rooms, pool, La Maison sur la Plage restaurant with open-air terrace.

Restaurants

Stone Oven (telephone 2272) decorated with sculptures and paintings and offering a range of West Indian and Continental fare. Curried turtle, stuffed land crab. About $20.

Talk of the Town Bar and Restaurant (telephone 2236), local dishes, $7.

Transportation

From St. Maarten or Saba on Winair.

ST. JOHN

U.S. Virgin Islands Division of Tourism, 1270 Avenue of the Americas, New York, N.Y. 10020 (212 582 4520).

The Island

Two-thirds of the island is preserved in the Virgin Islands National Park, making it the right spot for nature lovers and campers. The one town, Cruz Bay, is tiny, but there are a few boutiques and small restaurants. To find out anything, check the bulletin board at the dock, which is also the place to find a tour driver who'll show you the lookout points and the park. The park rangers are well informed about the island's birds and vegetation. Hotel tax: 5 per cent; most hotels add a service charge of 10 to 15 per cent.

Hotels

Caneel Bay (luxurious), the renowned Rockresort, elegant and understated, with 168 rooms, and all facilities, including sailing. Three restaurants. Guests are transported free to the hotel on Caneel's ferry from Red Hook, St. Thomas.

Carla's Cottages (expensive), at Cruz Bay, only four rooms, but deluxe and secluded, with tropical gardens and great views. With restaurants and spa and near beach.

Campgrounds

Cinnamon Bay (cottages, tents, bare sites; rates are higher than many other campgrounds but certainly moderate when compared with hotel costs), first class, run by the National Park Service, which conducts activities and has equipment for rent. Restaurant.

Maho Bay Camps (tent-style canvas cottages), first class, in the National Park but privately operated. Activities centred on the ecology. Restaurant.

Transportation
The major route is the ferry ($2) from Red Hook, St. Thomas. Limited air service on Virgin Islands Seaplane Shuttle Service from St. Thomas and St. Croix.

ST. KITTS
Eastern Caribbean Tourist Association, 220 East 42nd Street, New York, N.Y. 10017 (212 986 9370).

The Island
Basseterre, the capital, has undergone some changes with the addition of a deep-water port and pier, but it still has some fine examples of West Indian architecture, including the Circus with Big Ben, a green stone clocktower at its centre, and the black-and-white Treasury building on the waterfront. The island is made for quiet touring, and new nonstop flights make it easier to reach. Hotel room tax: 7 per cent; hotels add a service charge of 10 to 15 per cent.

Hotels
Royal St. Kitts (expensive, MAP), 138 rooms, at Frigate Bay; casino, eighteen-hole golf course, tennis, pool.

Ocean Terrace Inn (expensive, MAP), overlooking Basseterre at the western end of the city; thirty-nine rooms, pool, outdoor dining, and a marina. Scuba diving and other water sports.

Fair View Inn (expensive), a renovated plantation great house with cottages in rear in the mountain region of the island about three miles west of Basseterre; thirty rooms. Dining room, pool. Must drive to beach.

Restaurants
Bistro Creole (telephone 4138), in Basseterre, Creole cuisine. About $8.

Transportation
From New York on Pan Am and BWIA. From Miami on Pan Am. From Barbados on L.I.A.T. or BWIA.

ST. LUCIA
St. Lucia Tourist Board, 41 East 42nd Street, New York, N.Y. 10017 (212 867 2950).

The Island
St. Lucia has some of the finest shoreline in the Caribbean; Marigot Bay, one of the prettiest coves in the world; inland jungle; and two forested mountains, the Pitons. It also has a docile volcano, Mount Soufrière, where visitors may wander among the mudholes and sulphur pits of its crater. Aside from its natural beauty, the island has plenty of historical sites. Accommodations range from luxury resorts

to guesthouses. Hotel room tax: 7 per cent; most hotels add a service charge of 10 per cent; departure tax: $5.

Hotels

Cunard La Toq (expensive), 150 rooms and 60 villas on 100 acres with gardens overlooking the ocean south of Castries. Tennis, nine-hole golf course, pool, entertainment, restaurant.

Steigenberger Cariblue (moderate), 102 rooms on Cap Estate on the island's northern tip and overlooking the ocean. Restaurant, hiking trails, pool, horseback riding nearby.

Dasheene (expensive), twenty-two villas and apartments on a hilltop in the Piton area and overlooking the Piton mountains; pool, bus service to beach provided. Maid service available. Restaurant.

Anse Chastanet (moderate), twenty bungalows near the community of Soufrière, own beach, snorkelling and scuba programme, restaurant.

Restaurants

Green Parrot (telephone 23 399), outside Castries and commanding panoramic view; pumpkin and callaloo soups, flying fish dishes; Creole and French cuisine. About $22.

Pat's Pub (telephone 28 314), overlooking harbour at Rodney Bay; Creole dishes, steaks, and seafood. About $22.

Rain (telephone 23 022), in Castries, run by an American expatriate and named for the W. Somerset Maugham story, with appropriate wicker chairs, ceiling fans, and drinks with Polynesian names. Varied menu. About $15.

Transportation

From New York on Pan Am and BWIA; from Miami on Eastern and BWIA.

ST. MAARTEN

St. Maarten–Saba–St. Eustatius Tourist Information Office, 25 West 39th Street, New York, N.Y. 10018 (212 840 6655).

The Island

St. Maarten, the Dutch side of the island it shares with the French dependency named St. Martin, is American in style and the visitor hears only an occasional word of Dutch. This is a populous island offering everything most winter holidaymakers seek: good beaches, golf, tennis, sea excursions and a wide variety of hotels. The area around the central square of Philipsburg, the capital, is often crowded with traffic and shoppers. International dialling code: 011 599 5. Hotel room tax: 5 per cent; most accommodations add a service charge of 10 to 15 per cent, some add an energy surcharge, departure tax: $5.

Hotels

Cupecoy Beach Resort (expensive), 235 deluxe units, some with ocean view, others facing garden. Freshwater pool, restaurant, nightly entertainment.

Maho Reef and Beach Resort (expensive), on beach at Maho Bay, 140 rooms, casino, nightclub, terrace restaurant overlooking the sea. Pool, four tennis courts.

Sint Maarten Beach Club, Hotel and Casino (expensive), on Great Bay Beach in Philipsburg and close to shopping. Water sports, restaurant; some rooms are across the road from the beach, and all have kitchenettes.

Summit Hotel (moderate), on bluff overlooking Simpson Bay Lagoon, sixty-eight suites with balconies. Glass-bottom boat and other water sports facilities, tennis court, short walk to beach, restaurant.

Restaurants
Café Royal (telephone 3443), garden seating in Royal Palm Plaza, international cuisine. Reservations advised. About $20.

Chesterfield's (telephone 3484), Great Marina Bay; steaks, seafood, duck, lobster, with quiches at lunchtime. Lunch, about $13; dinner, about $20.

Callaloo (no phone), on Front Street, Philipsburg, an indoor and outdoor gathering place serving pizza, hamburgers, and Creole dishes; $5-$8.

Transportation
From New York on American and Pan Am, from Miami on Eastern; from Dallas/Fort Worth on American.

ST. MARTIN
French West Indies Tourist Board, 610 Fifth Avenue, New York, N.Y. 10020 (212 757 1125).

The Island
The French side of the island shared with Dutch St. Maarten is quieter than its neighbour. Its capital, Marigot, is smaller and less crowded, has a small harbour and two main shopping streets lined with restaurants, galleries and boutiques. Restaurant fanciers should also visit Grand Case where about eighteen restaurants are concentrated on one street, most of them French but some serving Indonesian or Italian dishes. There are fewer hotel rooms than on the Dutch side and reservations should be made early. (Travellers wishing to obtain information in person should go to the French Government Tourist Office, 628 Fifth Avenue.) International dialling code: 011 596. Some hotels add a service charge of 10 to 15 per cent; departure tax (from Dutch side): $5.

Hotels
Grand St. Martin Beach Resort (expensive) was opened in

December 1983 on the site of the former Grand St. Martin Hotel; eighty-three condominium-style studios and one- and two-bedroom suites. Restaurant, nightly entertainment, pool, water sports.

Grand Case Beach Club (expensive), forty-eight apartments at edge of Grand Case Village, five minutes north of Marigot. New apartments being added. Restaurant, called Waves; tennis court lighted for night play; water sports centre.

Hévéa (expensive), a five-room guesthouse in Grand Case. Recently added a French dining room.

Restaurants

La Rhumerie (no phone), in Colombier; perhaps the best Creole food on the island, including herbed conch and curried goat, as well as French dishes, including snails. About $25.

Chez Lolotte (telephone 87 53 38), Marigot; French and Creole cooking – stuffed land crabs and turtle steak, for example – in an enclosed tropical garden. About $30.

Le Nadaillac (telephone 87 53 77), rustic tables by the sea in Marigot, with preserved goose and giblet salad among the specialities. Dinner only. About $40.

Le Vie en Rose (telephone 87 54 42), opposite Marigot's wharf, offers various seafoods baked in a mould and French specialities. On second floor; ask for balcony table. About $35.

Transportation

From New York on American and Pan Am; from Miami on Eastern. All these airlines fly into the Queen Juliana Airport on the Dutch side of the island.

ST. THOMAS

U.S. Virgin Islands Division of Tourism, 1270 Avenue of the Americas, New York, N.Y. 10020 (212 582 4520).

The Island

Charlotte Amalie's role as premier cruise port in the Caribbean and duty-free shopping centre means that its downtown streets are busy with shoppers whenever cruise ships call. Tourist officials hope that the port's new dock, the Crown Bay Project, which will accommodate the largest ships including *Queen Elizabeth 2* and the *Norway*, and the extension of Harry S. Truman Airport to take big jets and make landings easier – and safer – will be completed in 1985. Outside the town, the island has hills rising to 1,500 feet and sloping down to bays on the southern coast and to long beaches on the northern coast, especially at Magens Bay. Hotel tax: 5 per cent; most hotels add a service charge of 10 to 15 per cent.

Hotels

Bluebeard's Castle (expensive), eighty-four rooms on a hill overlooking the harbour and a ten-minute walk from Charlotte Amalie, but not on a beach. Saltwater pool, tennis, two restaurants, free bus and admission to Magens Beach.

Lime Tree Beach Hotel (expensive), on Frenchman's Cove, with eighty-four rooms; sea-orientated with free scuba and snorkelling lessons, two tennis courts, pool, restaurant.

Virgin Isle Hotel (expensive), 210 rooms, most with balconies; on a hill overlooking the harbour and about ten minutes' drive from Charlotte Amalie. Not on the water but with free bus to beach club. Pool, tennis and discothèque.

Bolongo Bay Beach (expensive), a secluded setting on Bolongo Bay, but with lively entertainment; thirty-seven rooms; several tennis courts, pool, restaurant.

Restaurants
Bartolino (telephone 774 8554), in Frenchtown; some tables on open-air terrace; emphasis on Italian dishes. About $18-$25.

L'Escargot (telephone 774 7077 on Creque's Alley in the city; 774 6565 in the old Sub Base area), French cuisine, with a variety of seafood. About $22.

Danny's Fisherman's Wharf (telephone 774 6669), on the water, with deck, in the Sub Base section, with a rustic décor; seafood, including Alaska crab, sole, and rainbow trout. About $20-$25.

Transportation
From New York on American nonstop, and via San Juan on Eastern, Capitol, and American. From San Juan on Prinair, Air V.I., Crown Air, and Ocean Air. From Miami on Eastern.

ST. VINCENT AND THE GRENADINES
Caribbean Tourism Association, 20 East 46th Street, New York, N.Y. 10017 (212 682 0435).

The Islands
A steady stream of sailboat people as well as land travellers, who fly in from Barbados and the surrounding islands, are attracted by the opportunities to explore St. Vincent's volcanic beaches and the mountains, as well as the capital, Kingstown, a busy centre for inter-island traffic. Sights: the Botanic Garden in Kingstown, established in 1763, and Indian Bay, the best beach. The open-air buses are good for getting around.

Of the little Grenadines (with St. Vincent they constitute an independent nation within the British Commonwealth) the chief islands are Young, Bequia, Mustique, Palm, Union, Mayreau, Cannouan and Petit St. Vincent. These are real hideaways, with few hotels, for those who like privacy. Hotel room tax: 5 per cent; 10 per cent service charge added to hotel bills; departure tax: $5.

Hotels

Grand View Beach Hotel (moderate, MAP), St. Vincent, twelve rooms, five minutes from the airport and ten minutes from Kingstown. Set in eight acres of landscaped tropical gardens with view of the Grenadines. Pool.

Mariner's Inn (moderate, MAP), St. Vincent, a colonial hotel in a garden setting with seventeen rooms on Villa Beach on the southern coast, two miles from the airport and four miles from Kingstown. Restaurant.

Sunset Shores Hotel (moderate to expensive, MAP), nineteen rooms, on the white-sand Indian Bay Beach, two miles from the airport. Restaurant speciality: local West Indian food. There's also a poolside barbecue.

Sunny Caribbee (moderate), on the beach on Bequia, overlooking Admiralty Bay, and accessible by motor schooner from St. Vincent. Has seventeen cabanas and eight rooms in old colonial style and a restaurant. Tennis, pool.

Palm Island Beach Club (expensive, MAP), on Palm Island, twenty-four bungalows; scuba diving and other water sports. The open-air restaurant has views of other islands in the chain. Reached from Union Island on hotel boat.

Cotton House (luxurious, MAP), on Mustique, with nineteen rooms by the sea; tennis, sailing, fishing, and scuba diving.

Restaurants

The Wheelhouse (telephone 61618), St. Vincent, specializes in local dishes made from local produce. Fish and chicken dishes: about $8; steak, $10; lobster, $12.

Caribbean Sailing Yacht Club Restaurant and Bar (telephone 84031) at Rapho Mill on the windward side of St. Vincent. Local cuisine, approximately $12 (lobster dinner is $16).

Indian Bay Restaurant and Bar (telephone 84001), outside Kingstown, St. Vincent, on Indian Bay Beach, with views of Young Island. Serves local dishes, lobster, fish, sweet potatoes. Lunch, $8; dinner $10.

Sunny Grenadine Restaurant (telephone 88327), in Clifton, on Union Island, overlooking the sea, and serving lobster and local dishes. About $12.

Frangipani (telephone 83255), on the beach in Port Elizabeth, Bequia; beef and local vegetables, kingfish and rice, pumpkin pie. About $12.

Cotton House (telephone 84621), on Mustique, casually elegant, offering fish and other island specialities. The restaurant serves what Craig Claiborne calls 'some of the best French-Caribbean food' he has eaten. Non-guests can make reservations and dinner costs about $25.

Transportation

From Barbados to St. Vincent on L.I.A.T., or St. Vincent and the Grenadines Air Services to St. Vincent, then by boat or small plane. From Martinique or St. Lucia on Air Martinque to St. Vincent. From St. Lucia on Winlink to St. Vincent. From Barbados to Mustique on Air Mustique.

TOBAGO

Trinidad and Tobago Tourist Board, 400 Madison Avenue, New York, N.Y. 10017 (212 838 7750).

The Island

Tobago compensates for the lack of cosmopolitanism evident on its larger partner, Trinidad, twenty-two miles away, with a tranquil atmosphere. (The two islands became independent of Britain in 1962.) It's a place of small communities set around a central forest reserve, and it is mostly mountainous, except in the west, with coconut palms lining the beaches. It would be difficult for anyone to keep busy here. Hotel room tax: 3 per cent, most hotels add a 10 per cent service charge.

Hotels

Crown Reef Hotel (expensive, MAP), a five-minute drive from the airport and within walking distance of Store Bay; 115 rooms. Restaurant; lawn tennis courts nearby.

Sandy Point Beach Club (moderate), at Crown Point, forty-two rooms, ten minutes from airport; restaurant, tennis.

Arnos Vale Hotel (expensive, MAP) on the western side of the island, in Plymouth, about thirty minutes from the airport; twenty-eight rooms.

Restaurants

Old Donkey Cart House (telephone 3551), in a Victorian cottage on Bacolet Street, Scarborough; seafood, salads, quiches, cheeses, German wines, noon to 2 am. About $15.

Kariwak Village (telephone 8545), in Store Bay, local dishes by owner-chef and noted for sugarless fresh-fruit drinks. About $15.

Transportation

From Trinidad on the Trinidad Tobago Air Service, a shuttle that runs hourly, takes fifteen minutes and costs about $15. The ferry from Port of Spain to Scarborough takes more than five hours and costs about $6.

TORTOLA

British Virgin Islands Tourist Board, 370 Lexington Avenue, New York, N.Y. 10017 (212 696 0400).

The Island

Most activity centres on Road Town, a haven favoured by sailors and a main anchorage for boat charters. Smuggler's Cove, with its snorkelling reefs, Cane Garden Bay, and Long Bay are among the best-equipped beaches (restaurants and changing rooms), but the swimming is just as good on many other stretches. U.S. currency is used here even though it's a British territory. Most hotels are small and run by married couples. Neighbouring Peter Island, with its one resort, is reached on a twenty-minute ferry ride. Hotel tax: 5 per cent; most hotels add a 10 per cent service charge; departure tax: $5 by air, $3 by sea.

Hotels

Prospect Reef (moderate), an extensive resort in Road Town with 130 rooms, its own harbour and marina and sports facilities reached along pathways bordered by tropical vegetation. Six pools, six floodlit tennis courts, restaurant.

Treasure Isle Hotel (moderate), forty rooms with balconies overlooking Road Bay, the island's largest harbour; bar; restaurant; powerboat trips to other islands; pool. Water sports with instruction, beach club at Coopers Island.

Long Bay Hotel (moderate) is about twenty-five minutes from Road Town; thiry-seven rooms, with beach (and lively surf), beach bar, restaurant, pool, tennis, nine-hole pitch-and-putt golf.

Restaurants

Upstairs, Downstairs (telephone 42136) at the Village Cay Marina in Road Town has a semiformal dining room upstairs with British fare (roast beef and Yorkshire pudding) and Continental dishes, and a buffet luncheon. About $20 for dinner. Snacks and sandwiches downstairs.

Fort Burt Hotel (telephone 42587), on a hill with views over Road Town, varied menu ranges from lobster, conch, and scallops to beef Wellington. About $22.

Transportation

From New York on Eastern, American, Capitol, or Arrow Air to San Juan; then with Air B.V.I. or Crown Air to Tortola. From St. Thomas there is a daily ferry that takes forty-five minutes for about $12 one way, half price for children.

TRINIDAD

Trinidad and Tobago Tourist Board, 400 Madison Avenue, New York, N.Y. 10017 (212 838 7750).

The Island

Port of Spain, the capital of Trinidad and Tobago, is a port and cosmopolitan city of a quarter of a million people that offers a great deal of sightseeing but no beaches. For sand and sea you must drive over the mountains to Maracas Bay or go by boat to the islands off the northwest coast. Hotels are difficult to categorize because they vary tremendously, reflecting the island's different races and cultures. Waterfalls, Victorian buildings and remote villages as well as the Asa Wright Nature Centre and the Caroni Bird Sanctuary are on the sightseeing agenda. Carnival is on the Monday and Tuesday before Ash Wednesday. Hotel room tax: $3; most hotels add a 10 per cent service charge; departure tax: $8.50.

Hotels

Hilton International (expensive), the largest hotel in the country, in uptown Port of Spain, with 431 rooms, two restaurants, two bars, resident band, swimming, tennis, shopping.

Holiday Inn (expensive), in downtown Port of Spain, 235 rooms, pool, shops and La Ronde and Grill Room restaurants. Two resident bands; cultural shows on Sunday and Thursday.

Normandie (moderate), in uptown Port of Spain, a quiet residential area at back of the prime minister's house, forty-four rooms, some with views of the northern range. The hotel has pool, disco, and restaurant.

Restaurants

Café Savanna (telephone 62 26441 4), on ground floor of the Kapok Hotel and owned by the people who run the Tikki Village restaurant on the top floor. Price range for entrées is about $9 for baked bluepoint oysters to more than $25 for lobster tails in cream sauce flamed with brandy.

Captain Cook (telephone 62 24512), 12 Western Main Raod, St. James, just outside the capital; local dishes. About $25.

Chaconia Inn Restaurant (telephone 629 2101), 106 Saddle Road, Maraval; with pigeon pea soup, steaks, chops, fried chicken, baked leg of lamb, salads. About $20.

Golden Dragon Restaurant (telephone 62 52373), Philip and Fraser streets, Port of Spain; Creole and Chinese dishes. From $10.

Transportation

From New York on Pan Am, BWIA, and American. From Miami on Eastern and BWIA, stopping in Barbados.

TURKS AND CAICOS

Turks and Caicos Tourist Board, P.O. Box 592617, Miami, Fla. 33159 (305 871 4207).

The Islands

Fugitives who really mean to get away from it all head for this British chain of islands and cays – if they've heard of them. Most of the inhabitants of these virtually secret places live on Grand Turk, South

Caicos and North Caicos, and most visitors who join them go for the miles of untrodden beaches and the surrounding rings of live coral, the diving and fishing. Accommodations are limited.

Hotels

Third Turtle Inn (expensive), fifteen rooms on Providenciales Island (known as Provo), on a hill overlooking the harbour. Tennis, windsurfing; also scuba diving available to guests who are certified divers. Restaurant.

Hotel Kittina (moderate), twenty-six rooms on Grand Turk, with a restaurant and dining outside on the patio.

Erebus Inn (moderate), twelve rooms at Turtle Cove on Providenciales Island. Scuba is available for certified divers. Restaurant.

Restaurants

Henry's Roadrunner Restaurant (telephone 4238), Blue Hill, Providenciales. Native cooking, mostly seafood, and Continental as well. Approximately $10.

Transportation

Air Florida or Cayman Air from Miami to Grand Turk. T.C.N.A. (Turks and Caicos National Airlines) connects with other islands. Bahamas Air, flies from Nassau to South Caicos. T.C.N.A. connects with other islands.

VIRGIN GORDA

British Virgin Islands Tourist Board, 370 Lexington Avenue, New York, N.Y. 10017 (212 696 0400).

The Island

The second largest island of the B.V.I. chain offers resort accommodations from simple to elegant. It attracts many sailing people, who wander around Spanish Town and sometimes fan out to the mountains in the north and the beaches on the southern shore. Most people eat in the hotels, since there isn't much of an alternative. The main sightseeing spot is the Baths, where huge rocks have shaped themselves into entrances to pools and grottoes. Hotel room tax: 5 per cent; some hotels add a 10 per cent service charge; departure tax: $5 by air, $3 by sea.

Hotels

Little Dix Bay (luxurious, with all meals), a 500-acre resort, now with eighty-two rooms, built by Laurance S. Rockefeller in 1966. Secluded cottages among palms, with restaurant and bar and all facilities from tennis to boat taxi.

Biras Creek Hotel (luxurious, with all meals), thirty rooms on 150 acres in an isolated position on North Sound and reached by hotel launch. The full facilities include restaurant, marina, tennis, and boats to nearby beaches.

Olde Yard Inn (expensive), eleven rooms, not on a beach and without a pool, but with a good restaurant and a lively bar. Well situated for getting around.

Transportation

From St. Thomas or San Juan on Air B.V.I. or Crown Air. From Tortola by Air B.V.I. or Speedy's Fantasy Ferry (thirty-minute ride, $10).

THE MAGICAL REEF
ABOVE AND BELOW

Robert Reinhold

An eerie blackness descends over the Great Barrier Reef on a moonless December night. On a tiny coral cay called Heron Island, it is nearing midnight. All is silent, save for the soft lapping of high tide sending foamy tongues of water washing up the dunes. And then slowly, like a scene from a science-fiction film, great dark hulking forms begin to rise from the Coral Sea. Soon there are dozens of them creeping out of the warm water, and they grow larger as they head for the dunes.

The forms are giant sea turtles, weighing as much as 300 pounds, and they are about to perform a primordial ritual of procreation that has gone on at high tide every summer night for hundreds of millions of years. A group of human visitors watches in awe as the instinct-driven creatures struggle awkwardly over the dunes and begin to fling clouds of sand as they dig holes to lay their eggs.

Suddenly, another form materializes out of the darkness. It is Phil Reed, a young marine biologist with the Queensland National Parks and Wildlife Service, who heads the turtle research station on the island. Politely but firmly, he asks the tourists to douse their flashlights, which frighten the turtles away. 'The turtles are very timid when they come out of the water,' he says. 'As you can imagine, they spend most of their lives at sea and are very insecure on land.'

He finds a turtle deep in a sand hollow. He bends over and gently scoops away some sand from her rear, revealing a clutch of dozens of white eggs the size of Ping-Pong balls. In about nine weeks, he explains, the hatchlings will emerge and make a mad nocturnal dash for the sea. Fifty years later, he adds, the sexually mature females will return to some rookery like this to start the process again.

For the traveller who delights in witnessing the wonders of nature, there is perhaps no more attractive destination than the Great Barrier Reef. A chain of 2,500 individual coral reefs and islands, it stretches 1,600 miles along the Queensland coast of northeast Australia. Together they form an ecosystem of incredible richness – and present a beauty that seems to resist adequate description in words.

One has only to don a snorkel mask and swim a few hundred yards off Heron Island to enter a shimmering world of colours that for once seem to equal the tourist brochures: brilliant purple parrot fish, striped angelfish, spotted red coral trout, sweetlips, moray eels, and giant manta rays. More than four hundred species of fish alone, not to mention an almost infinite variety of sea cucumbers and other marine invertebrates. The island itself is a veritable aviary. Crammed onto a cay that is only one mile around are more than 17,000 noddy terns, nesting on every available tree branch. There are muttonbirds, reef herons, white-breasted sea eagles.

Most visitors to the region probably never see the actual reef, for it lies from thirty-five to a hundred miles offshore and is difficult to reach. Accommodations are mostly in coastal towns and on close-in islands that are distant from the teeming outer edge of the reef, and many tourists see only the close-in 'fringe reefs,' which, while nice enough, are not the real thing.

To drink deeply in the true reef experience one should stay on a true coral cay – formed by the accumulation of sand and vegetation on top of coral. But only three of these cays have tourist accommodations: **Green Island**, near Cairns at the northern end of the reef, and **Heron** and **Lady Elliot islands** toward the southern end near Gladstone. Heron lies forty-five miles off the coast, exactly on the Tropic of Capricorn, and can be reached only by helicopter from Gladstone. The ride is expensive, but it's worth it to stay right on the reef, even if the accommodations leave something to be desired.

Although the Barrier Reef first made its presence known in 1770 when it made splinters out of Captain James Cook's ship the *Endeavour*, the Australian Government, surprisingly, has only recently moved forcefully to protect it from overuse and abuse. It has created a vast Great Barrier Reef Marine Park, over some opposition from the Queensland state government. By 1982, only one tiny section – the 4,500 square miles surrounding Heron Island – had been officially established. The entire reef covers about 133,000 square miles.

Plans to expand beyond that ran into opposition from the politically conservative Queensland government, attempting to preserve its rights to explore for oil in the coastal area behind the reef. At issue was how close to the shore the park should begin. And since the Queensland park people administer the park, there were fears the state would undermine the Canberra Government's plans. 'They can do what they like or they can say what they like and it's not going to make any difference,' Queensland's Premier, Johannes Bjelke-Peteron, said at one point. 'What do you think they can do? Can they hang us? Can they jail us?' The *Melbourne Age* newspaper observed: 'Cynics might think it was a cruel God who could create such a wonder as the Reef and then put it in Queensland.'

Nonetheless, by late 1983 the issue had been largely resolved and about 99 per cent of the reef region declared within the park's protection. Added in 1983 were a vast section along the Cairns coast and an Inshore Southern Section. Oil drilling has been forbidden in all designated areas.

The average visitor will know little of this bickering as he boards the helicopter for the thirty-minute hop to Heron from the grimy industrial town of Gladstone. The helicopter skims the turquoise waters and soon one can see the first of the sand-ringed reef islands. Below, giant turtles bob in choppy waters and sharks make large arcs in search of prey. The helicopter puts down on the beach near the wreck of an old warship, and newcomers are greeted by a sign warning that all flora and fauna – above and below water – are protected. Guests are led on foot into the resort, where cabins and suites are scattered among the trees. While the management makes some gesture at providing 'resort' amenities, this is not the place to come to sip daiquiris in air-conditioned rooms, widen a potbelly on gourmet foods, or dance till dawn. The older rooms, separate little cabins called lodges, are rather worn, and the sanitary conditions of the communal toilet and shower facilities suggest a lax management.

The food, served in a pleasant open-air dining room, is plentiful and tasty, but unremarkable. There is a bar and occasional evening entertainment. But the real entertainment is natural, which is why Heron is a major international destination for scuba divers. But you don't have to know how to put on a tank to enjoy it. Even those unable or unwilling to venture into the water can get a good taste of nature during low-tide reef and island walks, conducted free by the island staff.

But every effort should be made to see the reef from the water. Twice each day a flat-bottom boat takes scuba divers and snorkellers out to different spots on the massive, luxuriant reef. One of the most spectacular coral formations is the Bommie, a few hundred yards from the harbour, and a swim over it for thirty minutes is alone worth the fare from the United States. One recent afternoon a flock of snorkellers jumped in over the Bommie and instantly found themselves surrounded by an impenetrable cloud of baitfish, tiny silvery slivers that were so thick, visibility was reduced to zero. When the school passed, the snorkellers found themselves amid a convoy of six-foot whaler sharks devouring the baitfish.

A minor panic broke out among the swimmers, who beat a splashy retreat to the boat. The boatman assured everybody that there had been no shark attacks here in thirty-two years because the sharks were so well fed on fish. Of course, he was in the boat. But it is true that shark attacks, which are frequently a threat elsewhere in Australia, are almost unknown on the reef.

Heron was not always a tourist attraction. It was first occupied in 1923 as a turtle-soup factory, and any turtle unlucky enough to wander up to lay eggs was promptly canned. Fortunately for modern-day visitors, the business went broke. The resort was created by an air pilot, Captain Christian Poulson, whose family sold it to the present proprietors, P & O Australia, Ltd., a shipping line.

And today what makes the island all the more attractive to serious nature buffs is that it is the site of a special reef research station affiliated with the University of Queensland. The director, Ian Lawn, welcomes visitors, who can look in on various experiments on marine algae, coral, fish, plants, birds and other denizens of the complex biological web that is the reef. One problem: the destruction of coral by crown-of-thorns starfish.

The visitor fortunate enough to arrive during the turtle nesting season, from November until February, can tag along with Mr. Reed, the turtle expert. He and his staff of four occupy two tiny trailers down the beach from the resort. Nightly they roam the beach, tagging turtles, counting and measuring eggs – all in an effort to improve their understanding of the turtle life cycle so as to manage the creatures better. Except for aboriginal peoples on reservations, no one may kill sea turtles in Australia. As a result they are abundant here.

The Heron rookery serves about 700 green turtles and thirty of the rarer loggerheads. Each female will venture onto the beach six or eight times during the season, laying about 120 eggs each time. Mr. Reed and his assistants are eager to talk to tourists, seeing it as an opportunity to educate them about protecting the animals. He advises people to keep a good distance from the turtle while she crawls up the beach and digs her hole, but that once she starts laying eggs she seems to lose her timidity.

In a chat one evening as he awaited the high tide, Mr. Reed said that the biggest threat to turtles was not tourists but the electric lights that have come with the rapid development of the tropical Queensland coast. This is because the tiny hatchlings, emerging at night, use the light differential between sky and sea as their directional cue. Artificial lights confuse them, and they usually die if they do not reach the life-sustaining sea by the time the scorching sun rises.

Mr. Reed recalled a woman, unable to understand English, who became irate when she saw him digging up eggs to measure them. Thinking she was protecting the turtles, she walked down the beach every night covering over their tracks in the sand so that Mr. Reed could not find the turtles. 'She thought we were eating the eggs,' he said.

Getting to Heron

The Great Barrier Reef, which is mostly in the tropics, is a year-round destination. To witness the turtle show on Heron Island, it is best to go during the Austral spring and summer, roughly from November through February. The island is accessible either by helicopter, for about $180 round trip, or, for those willing to risk a queasy stomach to save $100, by launch for about $80. Both leave from Gladstone, a short hop from Brisbane. (These and all following prices are given in U.S. dollars, calculated at the exchange rate of 96 U.S. cents to the Australian dollar; this rate has been fluctuating widely in recent years, however, so prices should be regarded only as approximate.)

Accommodations

There is only one place to stay on the island, the **Heron Island Resort**. It has twenty-two 'lodges,' really cabins without private baths, as well as fifty-seven more modern motel-like 'suites,' mostly with private baths, and a large 'beach house' for two. Rates, which include all meals, are about $65 per person per night sharing at the lodges, from about $100 to $115 sharing for the suites, and about $240 total for two persons in the beach house. There is a small surcharge during holiday periods. (A diving shop offers everything needed by snorkellers and scuba divers at standard rates.) Package deals offer substantial discounts over these room rates, but can be obtained only in Australia.

There are only two other true coral cays with overnight accommodations. Green Island, to the north, is open to day trips by boat from Hayles Wharf in Cairns and therefore receives more tourists than Heron. Accommodations there are much more modest, and less expensive, than at Heron. The other, Lady Elliot Island, near Heron, is also for the budget-minded. It has only camping and tents for rent. Day trips can also be made to Lady Elliot from Brisbane and Surfer's Paradise on the Gold Coast for about $180, including lunch and glass-bottom boat.

Reservations

Travel agents and most international carriers will make bookings for the reef resorts at the full rates. But the thrifty traveller willing to take a chance can save substantially by waiting until arrival in Australia. Discount deals are offered by Ansett and Trans-Australia Airlines from Sydney and other major cities. Inquiries can also be addressed directly to the Heron resort at P.O. Box 72, Hamilton, Queensland 4007. Or you can book through the Queensland Government Tourist Bureau, Adelaide and Edwards streets, Brisbane, Queensland 4000. It also has offices in Sydney and other major Australian cities. The bureau not only provides information but serves as a ticketing and booking agent for all destinations in Queensland, including all three reef islands. Its personnel were particularly helpful on a recent visit when airline delays caused havoc with reservations on Heron.

Further information is available from the Australian Tourist Commission, 636 Fifth Avenue (Suite 467), New York, N.Y. 10111, or 3550 Wilshire Boulevard (Suite 467), Los Angeles, Calif. 90010, or from the Queensland Government Tourist Bureau at the same LA address.

NOTES ON THE CONTRIBUTORS

R. W. APPLE, Jr., is chief of *The New York Times*'s London bureau.

MARGARET ATWOOD's most recent books are *The Dancing Girls and Other Stories*, *Bodily Harm*, a novel, and *Second Words*, a collection of essays. She lives in Toronto.

PETER BENCHLEY is the author of *Jaws*. His most recent novel is *The Girl of the Sea of Cortez*.

NELSON BRYANT writes the Outdoor column for the Sports section of *The New York Times*.

WILLIAM F. BUCKLEY, Jr. is the editor of *National Review*. His most recent book is *The Story of Henri Tod*.

HORTENSE CALISHER is a novelist and critic whose works include *False Entry*, *Journal from Ellipsia*, and *The New Yorkers*. Her most recent book is *Mysteries of Motion*.

JOHN CANADAY was formerly art critic for *The New York Times*. His latest book is *What Is Art?*

STANLEY CARR is an editor on the staff of *The New York Times* Travel section.

CRAIG CLAIBORNE is the food editor of *The New York Times*.

FRANK CONROY is the author of *Stop-Time*.

HARRY CREWS has written a number of novels as well as *Blood and Grits*, a collection of essays.

BARBARA CROSSETTE is chief of the Bangkok bureau of *The New York Times*.

CHARLOTTE CURTIS is associate editor of *The New York Times*.

HERBERT GOLD, who lives in San Francisco, has written a dozen novels; most recently, *True Love*.

PAUL GRIMES is the principal writer of the Practical Traveler column of *The New York Times*.

ALJEAN HARMETZ, the Hollywood correspondent for *The New York Times*, is the author of *The Making of the Wizard of Oz*, a book about the movie industry in the 1930s and 1940s.

DAVID HARRIS is a writer who lives in San Francisco. His latest book is *Dreams Die Hard: Three Men's Journey Through the Sixties*.

DONAL HENAHAN is the chief music critic of *The New York Times*.

WARREN HOGE, foreign editor of *The New York Times*, was formerly chief of its bureau in Rio de Janeiro.

MAUREEN HOWARD'S most recent novel is *Grace Abounding*. Her memoir, *Facts of Life*, won a National Book Critics Circle award in 1978.

FLORA LEWIS is foreign affairs columnist for *The New York Times*.

ROBERT LINDSEY is chief of the Los Angeles bureau of *The New York Times*.

ALISON LURIE, a novelist and critic, is also the author of *The Language of Clothes*.

PETER MAAS is the author of *Serpico*, *The Valachi Papers*, and most recently, *Marie: A True Story*.

MALACHI MARTIN'S books include *The Final Conclave*, *King of Kings*, a recreation of the life of David, *The Decline and Fall of the Roman Church*, and *There Is Still Love*.

CLIFFORD D. MAY is chief of the Abidjan, Ivory Coast, bureau of *The New York Times*.

COLLEEN MCCULLOUGH, the Australian author of *The Thorn Birds* and *An Indecent Obsession*, lives on Norfolk Island, 930 miles from Sydney in the South Pacific.

EDWIN MCDOWELL is the publishing correspondent for *The New York Times*.

RICHARD J. MEISLIN, former Caribbean correspondent of *The New York Times*, is Mexico City bureau chief.

GORDON MOTT is a writer who lives in Mexico City.

ENID NEMY is a reporter and columnist for *The New York Times*.

ADAM NICOLSON is the author, with Charlie Waite, of *The National Trust Book of Long Walks in England, Scotland, and Wales* and *Long Walks in France*.

JOYCE CAROL OATES is the author of *The Profane Art: Essays and Reviews*. Her most recent novel is *Mysteries of Winterthurn*.

EUGENE C. PATTERSON is the editor of the *St. Petersburg Times*.

ROGER TORY PETERSON is the editor of The Peterson Field Guide Series.

FRANK J. PRIAL is a reporter and wine columnist for *The New York Times*.

V. S. PRITCHETT, the author and critic, lived in London. His last book was *More Collected Stories*.

ROY REED, a former *Times* correspondent, is a writer who teaches journalism at the University of Arkansas.

ROBERT REINHOLD is a national correspondent of *The New York Times*.

MORDECAI RICHLER is a Canadian novelist and screenwriter. His most recent work is *The Best of Modern Humor*.

ALAN RIDING, chief of the Rio de Janeiro bureau of *The New York Times*, was formerly chief of its Mexico City bureau.

JAMES ROSENQUIST is a painter.

JAMES SALTER is a novelist and author of the screenplay for the movie *Downhill Racer*. His latest book is *Solo Faces*.

WILLIAM E. SCHMIDT, chief of the Atlanta bureau of *The New York Times*, was formerly chief of the Denver bureau.

HAROLD C. SCHONBERG is the cultural correspondent and former senior music critic of *The New York Times*.

BUDD SCHULBERG's works include *What Makes Sammy Run, Writers in America: The Four Seasons of Success*, and the screenplay for *On the Waterfront*.

DAVID SHRIBMAN, a native New Englander, is a former correspondent in the Washington bureau of *The New York Times*.

MARLISE SIMONS, a *Times* correspondent based in Rio de Janeiro, was formerly based in Mexico City.

MARK SOSIN is the author of *Practical Light Tackle Fishing*, and co-author of *Practical Fishing Knots* and *Practical Black Bass Fishing*.

MURIEL SPARK, the British novelist and poet, was born in Edinburgh but has lived in Italy for seventeen years. She is the author of more than twenty books, among them *The Prime of Miss Jean Brodie, Territorial Rights*, which was set in Venice, and *Loitering With Intent*. Her latest novel is *The Only Problem*.

JOHN UPDIKE is the author of *Hugging the Shore: Essays in Criticism*. His most recent novel is *The Witches of Eastwick*.

PETER VIERTEL, a novelist and screenwriter, lives part of the year in Switzerland. His most recent novel is *American Skin*.

DEREK WALCOTT is a poet and playwright who divides his time primarily between Trinidad and the United States. His latest collection of poetry is *Midsummer*.

ELIE WIESEL is an author and Andrew Mellon Professor of the Humanities at Boston University.

JOHN NOBLE WILFORD is science reporter for *The New York Times*.

JOSÉ YGLESIAS is a novelist and critic. Among his works are *The Franco Years* and *In the Fist of the Revolution*.

ABOUT THE EDITORS

A. M. ROSENTHAL is the executive editor of *The New York Times* and has been in charge of its news operations for the past fifteen years. He is the recipient of a Pulitzer Prize for his work as a foreign correspondent for *The New York Times*. Mr. Rosenthal is the author of *38 Witnesses* and co-author with Arthur Gelb of *One More Victim*.

ARTHUR GELB is deputy managing editor of *The New York Times* and supervisory editor of the new Sophisticated Traveller magazine. He was formerly chief cultural correspondent of *The Times*. He is co-author with his wife, Barbara, of the Eugene O'Neill biography, *O'Neill*.

MICHAEL J. LEAHY is the editor of *The New York Times* Travel section. He has been a *Times* editor since attending Columbia University's Graduate School of Journalism, where he won a Pulitzer Travelling Fellowship that took him around the world. NORA KERR, deputy editor of the Travel section, was formerly an assistant metropolitan editor of *The Times*.

INDEX

Abercrombie and Kent International, Inc., safari tours, 234

Aberdares, Kenya, 229

Abetone, Aspen, 127

Abominable SnowMansion, Taos Ski Valley, 109

Academy of Sciences, San Francisco, 68

Acosta, Iquitos, 222

Abode Inn, Carmel, 168

Akakura, Japan, 125

Albert Hall, London, 23

Alex and Walter's Gymnasium, Los Angeles, 184

Algarve, Portugal, 223–227

Alice Springs, Australia, 236

All Hallows-by-the-Tower, London, 43

Almond Tree, Ocho Rios, 314

Alpenglow Lodge, Alta, 103

Alps, Switzerland, 118–123

Alta, Utah, 100

Amazonas, Iquitos, 222

Amazonas Hotel, Manaus, 221

Amazon Basin, 215

Ambassador Beach Hotel, Nassau, 304

Amelio's, San Francisco, 65

Anaconda Hotel, Leticia, 221

Anahuacalli Museum, Mexico City, 199

Anglican Cathedral of the Holy Trinity, Quebec, 74

Anguilla, West Indies, 282, 301

Anse Chastanet, St. Lucia, 323

Antigua, West Indies, 301

Antlers Room, Vail, 125

Antonio's, Rio, 213

Apple Tree Restaurant, Taos, 109

Aquatic Park, San Francisco, 66

Arnos Vale Hotel, Tobago, 328

Aruba, West Indies, 302

Asa Branca, Rio, 214

Asia Gardens, San Francisco, 65

Aspen, Colorado, 124

Athenaeum, London, 22

Attitash, Bartlett, 94

Attitash Mountain Village, Bartlett, 94

Auberge de la Vieille Tour, Guadeloupe, 312

Au Cheval Blanc, San Juan, 317

Augustus, Belém, 221

Au Port, St. Barthélemy, 319

Aux Anciens Canadiens, Quebec, 71, 75

Aventine walls, Rome, 57

Baal-Hazor, Israel, 39

Bagatelle Great House, Barbados, 306

Bahamas, British West Indies, 304

Bakoua Beach Hotel, Martinique, 315

Balclutha, San Francisco, 69

Balsams/Wilderness Grand Resort Hotel, Dixville Notch, 94

Baños de Coamo, Coamo, 317

Barbados, West Indies, 259–262, 305

Barbancourt, Haiti, 287

Barbara McConnell's, St Croix, 320

Barbuda, West Indies, 277

Bartolino, St. Thomas, 326

Basilica of Notre-Dame, Quebec, 74

Bayou Petit Caillou, Florida, 155

Bayou Teche, Florida, 156

Bayreuth, West Germany, 31

Beaudoin House, Quebec, 74

Beaver Club, Montreal, 58

Bel-Air Hotel, Beverly Hills, 169, 184

Belém, Brazil, 220

Bellerive, Barbados, 259

Benham Valley, Montserrat, 316
Ben's, Montreal, 59, 62
Bentley's, London, 24
Bermudez, Dominican Republic, 287
Bethel, Israel, 39
Bethlehem, Israel, 40
Beverly Hillcrest, Beverly Hills, 174
Beverly Hills, California, 169–176
Beverly Hills Hotel, 169
Beverly Hilton, Beverly Hills, 169
Beverly House, Beverly Hills, 169
Beverly Rodeo, Beverly Hills, 175
Beverly Wilshire, Beverly Hills, 169, 184
Big Sur, California, 65, 244
Big Yellow House, Santa Barbara, 166
Bikram Choudhury's Yoga College of India, Los Angeles, 184
Biltmore, Santa Barbara, 166
Biras Creek Hotel, Virgin Gorda, 277, 331
Bistro Creole, St. Kitts, 322
Bistro Gardens, Los Angeles, 184
Black Mountain, Jackson, 93
Bluebeard's Castle, St. Thomas, 325
Blue Goose, Eunice, 159
Blue Horizons Cottage Hotel, Grenada, 311
Blue Mountain Inn, Kingston, 257
Boca Raton, Florida, 139
Boca Raton Hotel, 140
Bolongo Bay Beach, St. Thomas, 326
Bonaire, West Indies, 306
Borda Gardens, Cuernavaca, 189
Boudin King, Jennings, 158
Bow Wine Vaults, London, 45
Breakers Hotel, Palm Beach, 141
Bretton Woods, New Hampshire, 92
Brompton Oratory, London, 23
Brown Sugar, Barbados, 306
Bruce Safari Limited, Kenya Safaris, 234
Bugaboo Lodge, Canadian Rockies, 128
Bushiri Beach Hotel, Aruba, 303
Butcher Shop, Carmel, 168

Cable Beach Manor, Nassau, 304

Caesar Park, Rio, 213
Café Bonaparte, Quebec, 71, 75
Café de Paris, Montreal, 59
Café la Siesta, Quebec, 71
Café le Rétro, Quebec, 71
Café L'Europe, near Sarasota, 144
Café Royal, St. Maarten, 324
Café St. Michel, Dominican Republic, 310
Café Savanna, Trinidad, 330
Café Sport, San Francisco, 65
Caicos, West Indies, 330
Callaloo, St. Maarten, 324
Canaveral, Florida, 145
Canecao Hall, Rio, 212
Caneco 70, Rio, 212
Caneel Bay, St. John, 278, 289
Caneel Bay (hotel), St. John, 289, 321
Cannon Mountain, New Hampshire, 93
Cape Sable, Florida, 134
Captain Cook, Trinidad, 330
Captain's Quarters (hotel), Saba, 318
Captain's Quarters (restaurant), Saba, 318
Caravelle, St. Croix, 320
Caribbean Islands, 300–337
Caribbean Sailing Yacht Club Restaurant and Bar, St. Vincent, 327
Carla's Cottages, St. John, 321
Carmel, California, 165, 247–251
Carmel Art Association, 251
Casablanca, San Francisco, 67
Casa Che, Snowmass, 126
Casa Cordova, 109
Casa de Campo, La Romana, 278
Casa Maria, 258
Casanova, Carmel, 168, 251
Castaways, Dominica, 309
Castelets, St. Barthélemy, 272, 277, 319
Cavalier Inn, 167
Cayman Arms, Cayman Islands, 307
Cayman Islands, West Indies, 307
Centaur, Montreal, 61
Century Plaza, Beverly Hills, 169

Certified Travel Consultants/Safari and Tours, Kenya Safaris, 234

Chaconia Inn Restaurant, Trinidad, 330

Chamisal Vineyard, San Luis Obispo, 164

Chapultepec Castle, Mexico City, 199

Chapultepec Park, Mexico City, 199

Charela Inn, Negril, 256, 258

Charlotte Amalie, St. Thomas, 325

Charmer's Market, Santa Monica, 184

Chart House, Santa Barbara, 166

Chasen's, Los Angeles, 185

Chateaubriand Restaurant, Pointe de Bout, 267

Château Champlain, Montreal, 58, 62

Château Frontenac, Quebec, 75

Chefette, Aruba, 303

Chesa Grishuna, Klosters, 120

Cheshire Cheese, London, 48

Chesterfield's, St. Maarten, 324

Chez Francine, St. Barthélemy, 273, 319

Chez Grandmère, Aspen, 124

Chez la Mère Michel, Montreal, 59

Chez Lolotte, St. Martin, 325

Chibi Chibi, Bonaire, 306

Chico's Bar, Rio, 212

Cholula, Mexico, 187

Chuck's Steak House, Santa Barbara, 166

Church of the Nativity, Bethlehem, 41

Ciatur, Belém, 221

Cinnamon Bay, St. John, 321

Cinnamon Hill and Beach Club, Grenada, 311

Circular Militar, Belém, 221

Circus Maximus, Rome, 54

Citadel, Quebec, 70

Clube do Samba, Rio, 212

Clube Gourmet, Rio, 213

Club XIX, Carmel, 168

Cobblers Cove, Barbados, 305

Coconut Creek, Barbados, 305

Coconut Grove, Negril, 256

Coconut Hill, Montserrat, 316

Coco Point Lodge, Barbuda, 277

Colisée, Quebec, 71

Colonia Guerrero, Mexico City, 201

Colony, 144

Comanche, St. Croix, 320

Concord, Dominicano, Dominican Republic, 310

Concorde Hotel and Casino, Aruba, 303

Condado Holiday Inn, San Juan, 317

Coober Pedy, Australia, 237

Cook Shack, Vail, 89

Copacabana Palace Hotel, Rio, 213

Coral Reef Club, Barbados, 305

Coral Sands Hotel, Harbour Island, 304

Cotton House (hotel), Grenadines, 277, 327

Cotton House (restaurant), Grenadines, 327

County Courthouse, Santa Barbara, 162

Courtleigh, Kingston, 258

Coyoacan, Mexico City, 201

Cranmore Mountain Lodge, Kearsarge, 94

Cranston's Antique Inn, Saba, 318

Cross Country Cookery, Snowmass, 127

Cross Creek, Florida, 147

Cross Creek Lodge, Cross Creek, 148

Crown Reef Hotel, Tobago, 328

Cruz Bay, St. John, 289

Crystal Palace, Aspen, 126

Cuernavaca, Mexico, 188

Cul de Sac (hotel), Anguilla, 301

Cul de Sac (restaurant), Anguilla, 301

Cunard La Toq, St. Lucia, 323

Cupecoy Beach Resort, St. Maarten, 323

Curaçao, West Indies, 307

Curaçao Concorde Hotel-Casino, 308

Curaçao Plaza Hotel, 308

Curtain Bluff Hotel, Antigua, 277

Cuvilliestheatre, Munich, 33

Cyrano's II, Vail, 89

Da Giggetto, Rome, 55

Dali Museum, St. Petersburg, 144

Dana Place Inn, Jackson, 94

Danny's Fisherman's Wharf, St.
    Thomas, 326
Dansk, Carmel, 251
Dasheene, St. Lucia, 323
Davos, Switzerland, 119
Del Monte Forest, California, 166
Del Prado, Nassau, 304
Den Laman, Bonaire, 306
Devon House, Kingston, 257
De Young Museum, San Francisco, 68
Divi Divi Beach Hotel, Aruba, 303
Dome of the Rock, Jerusalem, 39
Dominica, West Indies, 308
Dominican Republic, West Indies, 309
Don Cesar Beach Resort, St.
    Petersburg, 143
Don Giovanni, Iquitos, 222
Dothan, Israel, 38
Double Hook/Le Crochet Double,
    Montreal, 60

Eaton Hall Great House, Runaway
    Bay, 258
El Callejón de la Capilla, Puerto Rico,
    318
El Camino Real, California, 161
El Rancho, Haiti, 313
El Sereno, St. Barthélemy, 319
El Toula, Rome, 56
Emilio Goeldi Museum, Belém, 217
Enrico's, San Francisco, 65
Erebus Inn, Providenciales Island, 331
Eunice, Louisiana, 158
Everglades, Florida, 134
Everglades National Park, Florida,
    134–136
Excelsior Grao Para, Belém, 220
Ex-Hacienda del Cortes, Cuernavaca,
    193

Factors Walk, Savannah, 151
Fair View Inn, St. Kitts, 322
Far Horizons, 144
Filao Beach Hotel, St. Barthélemy, 319
Finnochio's, San Francisco, 65
Fior D'Italia, San Francisco, 64
Fiorentino, Rio, 213
Flamboyant, Grenada, 311

Flamingo Beach Hotel, Bonaire, 306
Fontana di Roma, Puerto Rico, 318
Fort Burt Hotel, Tortola, 329
Fort Mason, San Francisco, 67
Fort Point, San Francisco, 68
Fortt's, London, 24
Four Winds Travel, Inc., Kenya
    Safaris, 234
Frangipani, Grenadines, 327
Fred's Lounge, Manou, 159

Garrick Club, London, 22
Gasthaus Eggerwirt, Kitzbühel, 83
Gasthof Gramshammer (Pepi's), Vail,
    125
Ghirardelli Square, San Francisco, 67
Giolitti's, Rome, 54
Glacier Express, Switzerland, 121
Golden Dragon Restaurant, Trinidad,
    330
Goldener Greif, Kitzbühel, 84
Golden Gate Bridge, San Francisco, 68
Golden Gate National Recreation
    Area, California, 68
Golden Gate Park, San Francisco, 68
Golden Rock Resort, St. Eustatius, 321
Golden Room, Rio, 214
Golden Star, Curaçao, 308
Grand Case, St. Martin, 325
Grand Case Beach Club, St. Martin,
    325
Grand Old House, Cayman Islands,
    307
Grand St. Martin Beach Resort, St.
    Martin, 324
Grand View Beach Hotel, St. Vincent,
    327
Grapetree Beach, St. Croix, 320
Great Barrier Reef, 235, 333
Green Island, Great Barrier Reef, 334
Green Parrot, St. Lucia, 323
Greens, San Francisco, 67
Greenwich Observatory, London, 25
Grenada, West Indies, 310
Grenadines, West Indies, 326
Grensejakobselv, Norway, 98
Grotto of the Nativity, Bethlehem, 41
Gstaad, Switzerland, 122

Guadeloupe, French West Indies, 263, 311
Guana Island Club, Tortola, 277
Guimas, Rio, 214
Guiyave, Dominica, 309

Habitat, Bonaire, 306
Hacienda del Cocoyoc, 191
Hacienda Galindo, 191
Hacienda San Miguel Regla, 194, 196
Hahnenhof, Kitzbühel, 83
Haight Street, San Francisco, 69
Haiti, West Indies, 312
Halcyon Cove Beach Resort and Casino, Antigua, 302
Half Moon Bay Hotel, Antigua, 302
Half Moon Club, Montego Bay, 278, 314
Ham House, London, 23
Hannes Schneider Ski School, Mount Cranmore, 91
Hard Rock Café, Los Angeles, 185
Harrod's London, 24
Hawksbill Beach Hotel, Antigua, 302
Hearst Castle, San Simeon, 165, 168
Heidelberg, Aruba, 303
Hemphill/Harris Travel Corporation, Kenya Safaris, 234
Henry's Roadrunner Restaurant, Provideciales Island, 331
Heritage Inn, San Luis Obispo, 167
Heron Island, Great Barrier Reef, 334
Heron Island Resort, Great Barrier Reef, 337
Hévéa, St. Martin, 325
Hibiscus Lodge, Ocho Rios, 258
Highlands Inn, Carmel, 251
Hilton International, Trinidad, 330
Hippopotamus, Rio, 210
Hoffman Mountain Ranch Vineyard, Paso Robles, 164
Holiday Inn, Cayman Islands, 307
Holiday Inn, Trinidad, 330
Holiday Inn Aruba Beach Resort, 303
Holiday Inns, Beverly Hills, 169
Hollywood, California, 177–185
Hotel Astra, Mandeville, 258
Hotel Bonaire, 306

Hotel Colonial, Leticia, 221
Hotel de Turistas, Iquitos, 222
Hotel du Bois Joli, Guadeloupe, 312
Hotel Garni, Saanen, 127
Hotel Golf and Sport, Saanen-Moser, 127
Hotel Jerome, Aspen, 128
Hotel Kittina, Grand Turk, 331
Hotel la Parguera, Puerto Rico, 317
Hotel Meridien, Rio, 213
Hotel Nacional, Rio, 213
Hotel Regente, Belém, 220
Hotel St. Bernard, Taos, 109
Hotel San Geronimo, Dominican Republic, 310
Hotel Santo Domingo, Dominican Republic, 310
Hotel Solimoes, Tabatinga, 221
Hotel Splendid, Haiti, 313
Hotel Tropical, Manaus, 221
Hotel Tropical, Santarem, 221
Hot Pot, Kingston, 257
Houma, Louisiana, 155
Huejotzingo, Mexico, 187
Hurricane Hole, St. Lucia, 295
Hyde Street Cable Car, San Francisco, 66

Il Buco, Rome, 55
Indian Bay, Florida, 144
Indian Bay Restaurant and Bar, St. Vincent, 327
Indulgence, New Orleans, 154
Inns of Waterville Valley, 94
Interconnect Adventure, Wasatch Range, 100
Inter-Continental, Rio, 213
Ipanema beach, Rio, 212
Iquitos, Peru, 222
Isle of Dogs, London, 25
Ivalo, Finland, 96

Jamaica, West Indies, 252–258, 313
Jamaica Inn, Ocho Rios, 258
Jennings, Louisiana, 158
Jerusalem, Israel, 40
Jezreel, Israel, 37
J. N. 'Ding' Darling Wildlife Refuge, Sanibel, 138

Jungle Gardens and Bird Sanctuary, Florida, 156

Kariwak Village, Tobago, 328
Kent Anthony's Guesthouse, Dominica, 309
Ker & Downey, Kenya Safaris, 234
Key West, Florida, 133
Kiandra Lodge, Vail, 88
King Charles, St. Petersburg, 143
King's Road, London, 22
Kingston, Jamaica, 254
Kirkenes, Norway, 97
Kitzbühel, Austria, 80
Klausner, Kitzbühel, 83
Klosters, Switzerland, 120

La Bella Fontana, Los Angeles, 173
La Bistroelle, Curaçao, 308
La Bohème, Carmel, 251
La Canne à Sucre, Guadeloupe, 263, 312
La Casona, Santurce, 318
La Cave, Kitzbühel, 84
La Chaubette, Guadeloupe, 266
La Créole, Guadeloupe, 264
La Dolce Vita Ristorante, Aruba, 303
Lady Elliot Island, Great Barrier Reef, 334
La Em Casa, Belém, 221
La Espada, Puebla, 188
La Familia Restaurant, Puerto Rico, 318
La Glacière, Haiti, 313
Lago Enriquillo Restaurant, Santo Domingo, 310
La Grand' Voile, Fort-de-France, 267, 315
La Lagunilla Flea Market, Mexico City, 201
La Maison du Rhum, Guadeloupe, 288
La Mansion, 191
La Plantation, Guadeloupe, 265, 312
La Playa Hotel, Carmel, 251
La Rhumerie, St. Martin, 325
La Samanna, St. Martin, 270
Las Mananitas, Cuernavaca, 189

Las Palmas Hotel and Vacation Village, Curaçao, 308
La Terraza de Marti, Key West, 134
Latin Quarter, Montreal, 59
La Toque, Los Angeles, 178
La Tour, Vail, 89
La Trouvaille, Houma, 155
L'Auberge du Bon Vivant, near Sarasota, 144
L'Auberge Gourmande, St. Martin, 272
L'Auberge St.-Tropez, Montreal, 59, 62
Lauderdale, Florida, 137
La Vie en Rose, St. Martin, 271, 325
Le Bercail, Montreal, 59, 62
Le Bistro, Antigua, 302
Le Bistrot, Guadeloupe, 312
Le Café de la Place, Montreal, 61
Le Cerf, Rougemont, 125
Le Colibri, Martinique, 315
Le Continental, Quebec, 71, 75
Le Dome, Los Angeles, 185
Left Bank, Vail, 89
L'Eglise de Notre Dame, Montreal, 60
Le Matador, Anse Matin, 268
Le Nadaillac, S. Martin, 325
Le Poulbot, London, 45
L'Ermitage, Beverly Hills, 169
Le Rond Point, Haiti, 313
L'Escargot, Carmel, 251
L'Escargot, St. Thomas, 326
L'Escoffier, Los Angeles, 172
Le Select, Haiti, 313
Les Enfants du Pirée, Montreal, 59
Les Jolies Eaux, Grenadines, 277
Le St.-Amable, Montreal, 59, 62
Le Théâtre de Quat' Sous, Montreal, 61
Le Théâtre du Nouveau Monde, Montreal, 61
Leticia, Colombia, 221
Le Tiffany, Fort-de-France, 268, 315
Leyritz Plantation, Martinique, 315
Liberty's, London, 22
Lime Tree Beach Hotel, St. Thomas, 326

Lindblad Travel, Inc., Kenya Safaris, 234
Little Dix Bay, Virgin Gorda, 278, 331
Little Nell's, Aspen, 127
Lobo Lodge, Carmel, 251
Lodge at Pebble Beach, Carmel, 168
Lodge at Vail, 88
London, England, 19–25, 42–51
Long Bay Hotel, Tortola, 329
Long Island, Antigua, 302
Loon Mountain, New Hampshire, 94
Lower Town, Quebec, 73
Lucaya Country Club, Freeport, 305
Lucayan Bay Hotel, Freeport, 304
Luciano's Antiques, Carmel, 165, 251
Lyme Inn, Lyme, 94

Mackey Travel, Kenya Safaris, 234
Madonna Inn, San Luis Obispo, 167
Maho Bay Camps, St. John, 321
Maho Reef and Beach Resort, St. Maarten, 324
Maison Chevalier, Quebec, 74
Ma Maison, Los Angeles, 184
Mama's, Grenada, 311
Mammoth Hot Springs Hotel, Mammoth Hot Springs, 116
Mamou, Louisiana, 159
Manaus, Brazil, 221
Mandeville, Jamaica, 252
Mansion House, London, 45
Margrave, Bayreuth, 33
Marigot Bay (Hurricane Hole), St. Lucia, 295
Mariners (hotel), Anguilla, 301
Mariner's (restaurant) Anguilla, 301
Mariner's Inn, St. Vincent, 327
Maritime Museum, San Francisco, 66
Marks and Spencers, London, 24
Marriott's Mark Resort, Vail, 88
Martinique, French West Indies, 314
Masai Mara Game Reserve, Kenya, 228
Maspero's, New Orleans, 155
Maxwell's Plum, San Francisco, 67
Megiddo, Israel, 37
Meridien Hotel, Guadaloupe, 312
Meridien Martinique, Martinique, 315

Meson de la Cava, Dominican Republic, 310
Mexico City, 198–202
Miami, Florida, 136
Middle Temple Lane, London, 22
Mission Ranch, Carmel, 251
Mission San Luis Obispo de Tolosa, San Luis Obispo, 164
Mission Santa Barbara, Santa Barbara, 163
Mission Santa Ynez, 164
Mission Street, San Francisco, 68
Modesto Lanzone's, San Francisco, 67
Monaco, Manaus, 221
Montego Bay, Jamaica, 253
Monterey Peninsula, California, 166, 247
Monterey Vineyards, Gonzales, 164
Mont Joli, Haiti, 313
Montreal, Canada, 58–62
Montserrat, West Indies, 315
Monument, London, 44
Mortons, Los Angeles, 185
Mount Cranmore, New Hampshire, 93
Mount Gilboa, Israel, 38
Mount Washington, New Hampshire, 90
Mount Washington Hotel, Bretton Woods, 92
Mozarteum, Salzburg, 33
Munich, West Germany, 33
Muni Pier, San Francisco, 66
Museum of Anthropology, Mexico City, 199
Museum of Modern Art, Mexico City, 199
Museum of Natural History and Gladwin Planetarium, Santa Barbara, 163

Nablus-Shechem, Israel, 38
Nain, Israel, 37
National Museum of Interventions, Mexico City, 199
National Theatre, Prague, 32
National Viceroy's Museum, Tepotzotlan, 190

Nazareth, Israel, 36
Negril, Jamaica, 256
Nepenthe, Big Sur, 167
Nevis, West Indies, 316
New England Inn, Intervale, 94
New Hampshire ski country, 90–93
New Orleans, Louisiana, 154–160
Nisbett Plantation Inn, Nevis, 316
Njambi Tours, Kenya Safaris, 234
Nobel Jones, London, 21
Normandie, Trinidad, 330
Normandy Inn, Carmel, 167, 251
North Beach, San Francisco, 64
North Beach Restaurant, San
     Francisco, 65
Notre-Dame-de-Bonsecours,
     Montreal, 60
Notre-Dame-des-Victoires, Quebec,
     74
Nutmeg, Grenada, 311

Oaxaca, Mexico, 206
Oaxtepec, Mexico, 189, 192
Ocean Club, Paradise Island, 304
Ocean Terrace Inn, St. Kitts, 322
Ocho Rios, Jamaica, 255
Old Donkey Cart House, Tobago, 328
Olde Yard Inn, Virgin Gorda, 332
Old Gin House, St. Eustatius, 320
Oratoire de St.-Joseph, Montreal, 60
Orchid, Dominica, 309
Our Lady of the Remedies, Cholula,
     188
Outremont, Montreal, 61
Oz, Rome, 55

Pacific Heights, San Francisco, 68
Palace Hotel, Puerto Rico, 317
Palazzo Venezia, Rome, 54
Palenque, Mexico, 206
Pall Mall, London, 22
Palmas del Mar, near Humacao, 317
Palm Beach, Florida, 140
Palm Island Beach Club, Grenadines,
     327
Pantheon, Rome, 53
Papagayo, Aruba, 303
Parador Martorell, Luquillo, 317

Parador Ticuna, Leticia, 221
Parc du Mont Ste.-Anne, Quebec, 75
Park City, Utah, 102
Passetto, Rome, 55
Patout's Restaurant, New Iberia, 156
Pat's, Henderson, 158
Pat's Pub, St. Lucia, 323
Patzcuaro, Mexico, 207
Peace and Plenty, Exuma, 304
Pea Soup Andersen's, Buellton, 167
Perilli, Rome, 53
Peter Island Hotel and Yacht
     Harbour, Tortola, 277
Petit St. Vincent, Grenadines, 276
Piazza di Spagna, Rome, 53
Pickle Family Circus, San Francisco,
     64
Pier 39, San Francisco, 66
Pilot House, Nassau, 304
Pine Inn, Carmel, 167, 251
Pink's, Los Angeles, 184
Pinney's Beach Hotel, Nevis, 316
Pisces, Barbados, 306
Pizzeria da Ivo, Rome, 54
Plaza de Garibaldi, Mexico City, 201
Polk Street, San Francisco, 67
Polo Lounge, Beverly Hills, 184
Port Antonio, Jamaica, 253
Port Royal, Jamaica, 254
Pousada do Infante, Sagres, 224
Prague, Czechoslovakia, 32
Prospect Reef, Tortola, 329
Puebla, Mexico, 187
Puerto Rico, West Indies, 317

Quebec, Canada, 70–75
Queen Elizabeth, Montreal, 59
Queretaro, Mexico, 191
Quill, St. Eustatius, 320

Ragged Point, Barbados, 305
Rain, St. Lucia, 323
Rainbow Reef, Anguilla, 301
Ramada Inns, Beverly Hills, 169
Ramat Rachel, Israel, 40
Ramon's, Cocoa Beach, 146
Red Jacket Mountain View Motor
     Inn, Bartlett, 94

Relais de Moulin, Guadeloupe, 312

Rendezvous Bay, Anguilla, 301

Restaurant Lina, Dominican
    Republic, 310

Rest Haven Inn, Nevis, 316

Revival Pub, Mandeville, 255

Richmond Hill Inn, Montego Bay, 314

Rio de Janeiro, Brazil, 208–214

Rio Palace, Rio, 213

Ritz Café, Montreal, 59

Ritz Carlton Hotel, Montreal, 59, 61

Riviera, Anguilla, 301

Road Town, Tortola, 329

Robert Talbott Company, Carmel, 251

Rocky Point, Big Sur, 167

Rod and Gun Lodge, Everglades City,
    135

Rodeo Drive, Los Angeles, 181

Rome, Italy, 52–57

Rotisserie, St. Barthélemy, 273

Royale, Quebec, 73

Royal Opera, Stockholm, 33

Royal Palms of Cayman, Cayman
    Islands, 307

Royal Poinciana Playhouse, Palm
    Beach, 141

Royal St. Kitts, St. Kitts, 322

Rufino Tamayo Museum, Mexico
    City, 199

Runaway Bay, Jamaica, 253

Saba, West Indies, 318

Sagres, Portugal, 224

Saidye Bronfman Centre, Montreal, 61

St. Alban, London, 50

St. Andrew-by-the-Wardrobe,
    London, 48

St. Andrew Holborn, London, 48

St. Anne and St. Agnes, London, 48

St. Anton, Austria, 80

St. Augustine and St. Faith, London,
    50

St. Barthélemy, French West Indies,
    318

St. Bartholomew the Great, London,
    46

St. Benet's Welsh Church, London, 48

St. Bride, London, 48

St. Clement Eastcheap, London, 49

St. Croix, U.S. Virgin Islands, 319

St. Dunstan-in-the-East, London, 44,
    51

St. Edmund the King and Martyr,
    London, 49

St. Eustatius, West Indies, 320

St. James Garlickhythe, London, 49

St. John, U.S. Virgin Islands, 289, 321

St. Kitts, West Indies, 322

St. Lawrence Jewry, London, 49

St. Lucia, West Indies, 322

St. Maarten, West Indies, 323

St. Magnus the Martyr, London, 44,
    49

St. Margaret Lothbury, London, 49

St. Margaret Pattens, London, 49

St. Mark's Church, Venice, 28, 55

St. Martin, French West Indies, 281,
    324

St. Martin Ludgate, London, 49

St. Martinville, Florida, 157

St. Mary Abchurch, London, 44, 49

St. Mary Aldermary, London, 49

St. Mary-at-Hill, London, 44, 50

St. Mary-le-Bow, London, 45, 50

St. Mary Somerset, London, 51

St. Mary Woolnoth, London, 45

St. Michael Paternoster Royal,
    London, 50

St. Moritz, Switzerland, 122

St. Nicholas Cole Abbey, London, 50

St. Olave Jewry, London, 51

St. Paul's Cathedral, London, 42, 46

St. Petersburg, Florida, 143

St. Peter Upon Cornhill, London, 50

St. Sepulchre, London, 46, 50

St. Stephen Walbrook, London, 45, 50

St. Thomas, U.S. Virgin Islands, 325

St. Vedast, London, 50

St. Vincent, British West Indies, 326

Salzburg, Austria, 33

San Angel, Mexico City, 201

San Antonio, Texas, 203

Sandals Resort Beach Club, Montego
    Bay, 314

Sandy Lane, Barbados, 305

Sandy Point Beach Club, Tobago, 328
San Francisco, California, 63
San Francisco Mime Troup, San Francisco, 64
Sanibel Island, Florida, 138
San Juan del Rio, Mexico, 192
San Martin Texmelucan, Mexico, 187
San Simeon, 165
Santa Barbara, California, 162
Santa Maria Aventina, Rome, 56
Sant'Allessio, Rome, 56
Sant'Anselmo Hotel, Rome, 56
Santarem, Brazil, 221
Santa Sabina, Rome, 56
Sant'Eustachio, Rome, 54
Santo Domingo Sheraton, Dominican Republic, 310
San Ysidro Ranch, Santa Barbara, 166
São Conrado beach, Rio, 209
Savannah, Georgia, 149–153
Schloss Lebenberg, Kitzbühel, 83
Schweben Kapelle, Kitzbühel, 84
Scott Beach, St. John, 293
Scout's Place (hotel), Saba, 318
Scout's Place (restaurant), Saba, 318
Seahorse Apartments, Anguilla, 301
17 Hundred 90 Inn, Savannah, 151
Shabu-Shabu, Carmel, 251
Shaft, Aspen, 126
Shiloh, Israel, 39
Shomron-Sebaste, Israel, 38
Silver Spray Resort, Runaway Bay, 258
Silves, Portugal, 224
Simpson's-in-the-Strand, London, 24
Sint Maarten Beach Club, Hotel and Casino, St. Maarten, 324
Sir John Soane's Museum, London, 22
Sir Loin, Rio, 212, 213
Sisserou, Dominica, 309
Sistine Chapel, Rome, 53
Smetana Museum, Prague, 33
Smoked Fish, St. Petersburg, 144
Snow Lodge, 116
So Delicias, Belém, 221
Soho, London, 22
Solvang, California, 163
South Molton Street, London, 22

Spago, Los Angeles, 185
Spanish Town, Jamaica, 255
Spice Island Inn, Grenada, 311
Stauffenberg, Taos, 105
Steigenberger Cariblue, St. Lucia, 323
Stephan's Studio, Los Angeles, 184
Stockton Street, San Francisco, 65
Stone Oven, St. Eustatius, 320
Sugar Mill, Caneel Bay, 292
Summit Hotel, St. Maarten, 324
Sundial Lodge, Carmel, 251
Sundowner, Negril, 258
Sunny Caribbee, Grenadines, 327
Sunny Grenadine Restaurant, Grenadines, 327
Sunset Plaza, Los Angeles, 181
Sunset Shores Hotel, St. Vincent, 327
Sun Valley, Idaho, 126
Suore Comaldolesi Convent, Rome, 56
Suttons, London, 23
Swann's Oyster Bar, San Francisco, 67
Sweet Basil, Vail, 89
Sydney, Australia, 235
Symposium, Montreal, 59
Syndicat du Rhum de la Martinique, Martinique, 288

Talk of the Town, Aruba, 303
Talk of the Town Bar and Restaurant, St. Eustatius, 321
Taos Ski Valley, New Mexico, 105
Taruma, Manaus, 221
Tasmania, Australia, 237
Tavern Restaurant Wine Cellar, Curaçao, 308
Taxco, Mexico, 192
Tearoom Alpenrose, Vail, 125
Teatro Amazonas, Manaus, 218
Teatro da Paz, Belém, 217
Teatro La Fenice, Venice, 33
Telfair Mansion, Savannah, 152
Teotihuacan, Mexico City, 189
Tepito, Mexico City, 201
Tepotzotlan, Mexico, 190
Tepoztlan, Mexico, 189
Tequisquiapan, Mexico, 194
Terrace, Nassau, 305
Théâtre 'Cadien, Lafayette, 157

Third Turtle Inn, Providenciales Island, 331

Thunderbird Chalets, Taos Ski Valley, 107

Thursday Island, Australia, 236

Tiara Beach Hotel, Cayman Islands, 307

Tiffany Green, Snowmass, 127

Timber Mill, Snowmass, 126

Tlayacapan, Mexico, 189

Tobago, West Indies, 328

Tom Beach, St. Barthélemy, 319

Torcello, Venice, 29

Tortola, British West Indies, 282, 328

Tosca's, San Francisco, 65

Trader Vic's, Los Angeles, 172

Treasure Isle Hotel, Tortola, 329

Trident Villas and Hotel, Port Antonio, 314

Trinidad, West Indies, 329

TriPyramid Town Houses, Waterville Valley, 94

Tryall Golf and Beach Club, Montego Bay, 314

Tula, Mexico, 189

Turismo Bradesco, Belém, 221

Turks, British West Indies, 330

Turtle Bay, St. John, 292

Turtle Beach Apartment Hotel, Ocho Rios, 258

Tyl Theatre, Prague, 33

Tyrol, Austria, 80

Tyrol, Kitzbühel, 83

Unterbergstuben, Kitzbühel, 84

Upper Town, Quebec, 74

Upstairs, Downstairs, Tortola, 329

U.S. Café, San Francisco, 65

U.S. 101, California, 162

Ute City Banque, Aspen, 126

Vagabond House Inn, Carmel, 167, 251

Vail, Colorado, 85–89

Venice, Italy, 26–30

Ventana, Big Sur, 243

Via Marmorata, Rome, 53

Victoria Bakery, San Francisco, 65

Victory, Antigua, 302

Village of Loon Mountain, 94

Village Saint Jean, St. Barthélemy, 319

Villa Medici, Rome, 55

Villa of the Knights of Malta, Rome 56

Villa Wahnfried, Bayreuth, 31

Virgin Gorda, British West Indies, 282, 331

Virgin Islands (*see also specific islands*), 319–332

Virgin Islands National Park, 321

Virgin Isle Hotel, St. Thomas, 326

Vue Pointe, Montserrat, 316

Wagner Museum, Bayreuth, 31

Warsaw, Poland, 33

Wasatch Range, Utah, 100

Washington Square, San Francisco, 64

Washington Square Bar and Grill, San Francisco, 64

Washington Square Inn, San Francisco, 64

Waterville Valley, New Hampshire, 94

Welshman's Gully, Barbados, 261

Westin Hotel, Vail, 88

Westminster Abbey, London, 25

Westmount, Montreal, 60

Westwood Marquis, Beverly Hills, 175

Wheelhouse, St. Vincent, 327

Whitewater Bay, Florida, 134

Whitney's Village Inn, Jackson, 94

Wildcat, Pinkham Notch, N.H., 94

Wildcat Inn and Tavern, Pinkham Notch, 94

World Travel Consultants, Inc., Kenya Safaris, 234

Worth Avenue, Palm Beach, 141

Xochicalco, Mexico, 192

Ybor City, Florida, 142

Yellowstone National Park, 113

Yvonnes's, Aruba, 303

Zelazowa Wola Museum, Poland, 33

Zermatt, Switzerland, 84

Zocalo, Mexico City, 200

Zona Rosa, Mexico City, 200

Zürich, Switzerland, 122

Zur Tenne, Kitzbühel, 83